Exclusions from Patentability

Exclusio… … of
exclusions … tion
since its fi… ion.
The analy… as
UPOV, th… ech
Directive … ons.
Particular … ost
contentiou… nts,
life forms … ost
influential … ave
been interp… of
the exclusi… ent
interpretati…

SIGRID ST… d at
the Vrije U…

JULIAN CO… tent
attorney an… and
trade mark … his
and not tho…

Cambridge Intellectual Property and Information Law

As its economic potential has rapidly expanded, intellectual property has become a subject of front-rank legal importance. *Cambridge Intellectual Property and Information Law* is a series of monograph studies of major current issues in intellectual property. Each volume contains a mix of international, European, comparative and national law, making this a highly significant series for practitioners, judges and academic researchers in many countries.

A list of books in the series can be found at the end of this volume.

Exclusions from Patentability

How Far Has the European Patent Office Eroded Boundaries?

Sigrid Sterckx

and

Julian Cockbain

CAMBRIDGE
UNIVERSITY PRESS

CAMBRIDGE
UNIVERSITY PRESS

University Printing House, Cambridge CB2 8BS, United Kingdom

Cambridge University Press is part of the University of Cambridge.

It furthers the University's mission by disseminating knowledge in the pursuit of education, learning and research at the highest international levels of excellence.

www.cambridge.org
Information on this title: www.cambridge.org/9781107542624

First published 2012
First paperback edition 2015

A catalogue record for this publication is available from the British Library

Library of Congress Cataloguing in Publication data
Sterckx, Sigrid, author.
Exclusions from patentability : how far has the European Patent Office eroded boundaries? / Sigrid Sterckx and Julian Cockbain.
pages cm. – (Cambridge intellectual property and information law)
Includes bibliographical references and index.
ISBN 978-1-107-00694-2 (hardback)
1. Patent laws and legislation–Europe. 2. European Patent Convention (1973) 3. European Patent Office. I. Cockbain, Julian. II. Title.
KJC2725.S77 2012
346.2404'86–dc23
2012015929

ISBN 978-1-107-00694-2 Hardback
ISBN 978-1-107-54262-4 Paperback

To Peter Messerli

Chairman of the Enlarged Board of Appeal of the European Patent Office, 1996–2011

Aside from the globalisation and harmonisation of patent law, the patent universe has been growing in another manner: the scope of what is regarded as patentable subject-matter has quietly expanded. This expansion has occurred in two ways. First, the scope of patentable subject-matter has been given an inclusive interpretation. Secondly, the restrictions on patentability have been narrowly interpreted … Patent offices can, through their decisions, include more things in the scope of patentability or narrow the operation of restrictions on patentability. Moreover, if they are supranational entities, as in the case of the EPO, they can exercise a profound harmonising influence on national systems. English courts, for example, have pointed out that it is of the 'utmost importance' that the exclusions in section 1 of the UK Patents Act 1977 should have the same interpretation as the EPO gives to the exclusions contained in Article 52 of the EPC. The EPO has been singularly successful in giving a narrow reading to the limits on invention and patentability contained in Articles 52 and 53 of the EPC. In interpreting the historical text that surrounds the creation of the EPC, … the EPO has suggested that the widest possible conception of patentability was a predominant conception. This conclusion has led to another … exceptions to patentability have to be narrowly construed … The effect of the assumption is to make the restrictions on patentability function weakly, if at all … A crucial aspect to the expansion of [the concept of patentability] has been the development of juridical arguments and theories that have enabled [patent applicants] to overcome existing bars. One of the interesting things is that, while these arguments are often analytically weak, they have been readily accepted by the patent community in the name of adapting the patent system to changing circumstances of technology and innovation. There is nothing wrong in adapting systems of law to changing circumstances. The crucial thing is that such adaptations must be governed by the public purposes that are embedded in patent law and the broader public ethic rather than private purposes. In the case of the adaptation of the patent system it is not at all clear that this has been the case.

(Drahos 1999: 442–3, footnotes omitted)

Contents

Acknowledgements

We would like to thank various people who have played an important role in the creation of this book. Sigrid would especially like to thank her parents, Marie-Louise and Wilfried, for the immense moral support they give her for all the projects she undertakes and for being the most loving parents anyone could wish for.

Julian is very grateful to his children Ben, Ella and Bea for their encouragement towards this book project. He also wishes to acknowledge the inventors he has worked with over the last thirty-five years. Their creativity and dedication and the countless exciting exchanges he has had with them, working out where inventions lie, are a major reason why he continues to be so passionate about working in the field of patents.

We also thank, from the bottom of our hearts, Tressilian, who is not only our 'Limo Services and General Happiness Provider', but who has also encouraged us non-stop on the long road towards this book and helped us immensely with various correction and lay-out tasks.

While this book was being written, Sigrid's god-daughter, Marie Djara, was born and the joy and happiness she brought provided a constant source of energy.

Colleagues and friends An, Farah, Annelies, Freddy, Gilles, Lieven, Bob, Lotte, Sandra and Didier, Etienne and Josiane, Els, Heather, Tanja, Lucienne, Noortje, Rani, Shala and Stephanie – many thanks to all of you for your moral support!

A heartfelt thank you also to Sigrid's doctoral students Jo, Kasper, Kristof, Pieter and Wouter, as well as to her teaching assistant Kjell, for their warm encouragement and for understanding that, with pain in her heart, she had to neglect them for far too long to make sure this book would get finished.

Sigrid would like to express special gratitude to Bart Claes, who, just when she was about to give up her first research project on patents because it was so complicated, helped her understand a great deal, and thanks to whom she realised that the patent system is the most fascinating topic any researcher could dream of investigating. Bart, I expect you will disagree with a lot of the views expressed in this book, but, well, you are to some extent morally complicit in its making because you opened my eyes to the magic of patents!

A special word of thanks also to Peter Drahos, Rainer Moufang and Daniel Alexander, who for a long time have been and continue to be a wonderful source of intellectual inspiration for Sigrid. Thanks also to Wolfgang Roepstorff of the EPO for his help in finding missing details from the EPO records.

Last but not least, we wish to say a few words about Peter Messerli, to whom this book is dedicated. We do not know him personally, but we dedicate our book to him because, in our view, all but the very first of the decisions of the EPO Enlarged Board of Appeal taken under his chairmanship show that it is thanks to his remarkably sharp mind, combined with integrity and genuine concern, that the law is taken seriously – not at all in an uncritical, purely 'law-abiding' spirit, but rather the contrary, with clear awareness of the crucial role of patents in society – that the erosion of the EPC exclusions from patentability, which had been occurring to an alarming extent, has been partially undone in recent years. We find it truly encouraging to see how some of the boundaries are being rebuilt, and we can only hope that the successor of Peter Messerli – who, sadly, retired at the end of November 2011 – will ensure that the 'rebuilding' work that remains to be done will continue in the spirit of Peter Messerli.

Table of cases

EPO cases

All EPO Board of Appeal decisions may be accessed from the EPO website, www.epo.org/law-practice/case-law-appeals/basic-search.html by following the instructions provided there (last accessed 6 December 2011).

Enlarged Board of Appeal decisions:

Technical Board of Appeal decisions:

Other cases:

These are set out in the form ‘Country code-Short title or first party’, ‘date of publication or of decision’, ‘Short title or parties to the case’, ‘Court’, ‘publication details’.

DE-Sprachanalyseeinrichtung (2002), 'Sprachanalyseeinrichtung' (Speech analysis apparatus)(DE-BGH), [2002] *IIC* 33(3), 343–8 83
EU-Brüstle (2011), *Oliver Brüstle* v. *Greenpeace* (EU-CJEU), C-34/10 Decision of the Court of Justice of the European Union, 18 October 2011 304–5
EU-Netherlands (2001), *Kingdom of the Netherlands* v. *European Parliament and Council of the European Union* (EU-ECJ), Case 277/98, Decision of the European Court of Justice, 9 October 2001 292
NL-Taste of Nature (2012), *Taste of Nature Holding BV* v. *Cresco Produktie Maatschappij BV and Cresco Handels BV* (NL-Court of The Hague) 191
UK-Aerotel (2006), *Aerotel Ltd* v. *Telco Holdings & Ors* (UK-CA), [2006] *EWCA* Civ 1371 67, 91, 113, 321
UK-CFPH (2005), *In the matter of Patent Applications GB 0226884.3 and 0419317.3 by CFPH L.L.C.* (UK-PCt), [2005] *EWHC* 1589 (Pat) 129
UK-Genentech (1987), *Genentech Inc.'s Patent* (UK-PCt), [1987] *RPC* 553–98 117
UK-Genentech (1989), *Genentech Inc.'s Patent* (UK-CA), [1989] *RPC* 147–288 117
UK-Wyeth (1986), 'Second medical use/WYETH and SCHERING' (UK-PCt), [1986] *OJ EPO* 175–92 167
US-AMP (2010), *Association for Molecular Pathology, et al.* v. *U.S. Patent and Trademark Office, et al.*, (US-DC, S.D.N.Y.), No. 09 Civ. 4515, 94 *United States Patents Quarterly* 2d, 1683 130–1, 133, 290
US-Diamond (1980), *Diamond* v. *Chakrabarty* (US-SC),447 U.S. 403 130, 132
US-Funk (1948), *Funk Bros. Seed Co.* v. *Kalo Inoculant Co.* (US-SC),333 U.S. 127 130, 132
US-Mayo (2012), *Mayo Collaborative Services, et al.* v. *Prometheus Laboratories, Inc.* (US-SC), 566 130
US-Morton (1862), *Morton* v. *New York Eye Infirmary,* (US-DC, S.D.N.Y.), 17 *F. Cas.* 879 114, 320

Table of international conventions and regulations

CFREU 2000, Charter of Fundamental Rights of the European Union, *OJ* C364, 18.12.2000, pp. 1–22

CEPL 1965, Convention relating to a European Patent Law, final unsigned draft of 22 January 1965 (see Document 2335/IV/65-E, Section 1)

CPC 1975, Convention for the European Patent for the Common Market (Community Patent Convention)

CEPC 1961, European Convention for facilitating the filing of applications for patents in respect of the same invention in several States and the examination thereof, November 1961 (referred to in Document EXP/Brev (61) 8)

CPVRR 1994, Council Regulation (EC) No. 2100/94 of 27 July 1994 on Community plant variety rights, *OJ* L227, 1.9.94, p. 1

EBD 1988, Directive 98/44/EC of the European Parliament and of the Council of 6 July 1998 on the legal protection of biotechnological inventions (European Biotech Directive), *OJ* L 213, 30.7.1998, pp. 13–21

EPC 1973, Convention on the Grant of European Patents (European Patent Convention) of 5 October 1973 (published as EPO 2006)

EPC 2000, Convention on the Grant of European Patents (European Patent Convention) of 5 October 1973 as revised by the Act revising Article 63 EPC of 17 December 1991 and the Act revising the EPC of 29 November 2000 (published as EPO 2010a)

OC 1997, Convention for the Protection of Human Rights and the Dignity of the Human Being with regard to the Application of Biology and Medicine: Convention on Human Rights and Biomedicine, Council of Europe, Oviedo, 4 April 1997

PC 1979, Paris Convention for the Protection of Industrial Property of March 20, 1883, as revised at Brussels on December 14, 1900, at Washington on June 2, 1911, at The Hague on November 6, 1925, at London on June 2, 1934, at Lisbon on October 31, 1958, and at Stockholm on July 14, 1967, and as amended on October 2, 1979, Geneva: World Intellectual Property Organization, 1991

PCT 1970, Patent Cooperation Treaty (PCT) Done at Washington on June 19, 1970 and Regulations under the Patent Cooperation Treaty (published in WIPO 1970: 11–161)

SPC 1963, Convention on the Unification of Certain Points of Substantive Law on Patents for Invention, Strasbourg, 27.XI.1963, European Treaty Series – No. 47, Strasbourg: Council of Europe

TRIPS 1994, Trade-Related Aspects of Intellectual Property Rights, Annex 1C of the Marrakesh Agreement Establishing the World Trade Organization, signed in Marrakesh, Morocco on 15 April 1994

UDHR 1948, Universal Declaration of Human Rights, United Nations, Geneva, 10 December 1948

UPOV 1961, International Convention for the Protection of New Varieties of Plants adopted by the Diplomatic Conference on December 2, 1961

UPOV 1991, International Convention for the Protection of New Varieties of Plants of December 2, 1961, as revised at Geneva on November 10, 1972, on October 23, 1973, and on March 19, 1991

VC 1969, Vienna Convention on the Law of Treaties 1969: Done at Vienna on 23 May 1969, Treaty Series 331

Table of official documents

Explanation of document numbering

(1) References to UPOV *travaux préparatoires* have fabricated numbers to allow them to be listed in this section. Thus UPOV (nn) X is the Xth document for year 19nn. All are to be found in UPOV (1974) at the page numbers given.
(2) Documents BR/xx/yy and M/zzz are the *travaux préparatoires* for EPC 1973.
(3) Documents EXP/Brev xxx are the *travaux préparatoires* for the SPC.
(4) Documents IV/nnn/yy and nnn/IV/yy are *travaux préparatoires* for the CEPL.
(5) Documents CA/xxx and MR/xxx are *travaux préparatoires* for the revision of EPC 1973 to produce EPC 2000.
(6) Documents, from 1962, numbered nnnn/IV/yy are from the EEC's PWP for the year 19yy (e.g. 1962), where successive texts are denoted by an increment in the number yy, i.e. 1, 2, 3, etc. These texts follow from the earlier numbering system of IV/nnnn/yy.

MR/DCD 1/00 (2000), *Revision of the European Patent Convention*, Drafting Committee, 27 November 2000 64

MR/2/00 (2000), *Basic proposal for the revision of the European Patent Convention*, EPO Administrative Council, 13 October 2000 93

MR/3/00 (2000), *Draft Revision Act*, EPO Administrative Council, 30 October 2000 63

MR/3/00 Rev. 1 (2000), *Draft Revision Act*, Secretariat, 29 November 2000 63

MR/8/00 (2000), *Article 14 etc.*, French Delegation, 17 November 2000 63

MR/15/00 (2000), *Proposed amendments to Articles 52(2)(c) and 105(a) to (c)*, Danish Delegation, 20 November 2000 63

MR/18/00 (2000), *Basic Proposal – Explanatory notes – Article 54(4) and Article 54(5)*, Swiss Delegation, 21 November 2000 64

MR/24/00 (2003), *Conference of the Contracting States to revise the 1973 European Patent Convention: Munich, 20 to 29 November 2000 – Conference Proceedings*, 15 July 2003 64–5, 170

PCT/DC/5 (1969), *Regulations under the Patent Cooperation Treaty (Draft)*, BIRPI, 11 July 1969 (referred to in WIPO 1970: 177) 39, 104

PCT/I/3 (1967), *Patent Cooperation Treaty (Draft)*, BIRPI, 31 May 1967 (referred to in WIPO 1970: 741–2) 39

PCT/III/5 (1968), *Patent Cooperation Treaty (Draft)*, BIRPI, 15 July 1968 (referred to in WIPO 1970: 742) 39

Res (49) 27 (1949), *European Patents Office*, Council of Europe, 4 November 1949 21

Res (52) 51 (1952), *Plan of future work of the Committee of Experts on Patents*, Council of Europe, 12 September 1952 21

UPOV (57) 1 (1974), *Lettre circulaire d'invitation adressée par le Ministère des Affaires étrangères de la République française aux ambassadeurs de France accrédités dans les états invités*, France, 14 February 1957, in UPOV (1974: 13–14) 25

UPOV (57) 3 (1974), *Aide-mémoire concernant les questions soulevées par la protection des obtentions végétales (annexé aux lettres circulaires d'invitation)*, France, 14 February 1957, in UPOV (1974: 16–17) 25

UPOV (57) 5 (1974), *Délibérations de la Conférence: Allocutions d'ouverture de la Conférence, Allocution prononcée par M. Darras, représentant le Secrétaire d'état à l'industrie et au commerce*, UPOV, 7 May 1957, in UPOV (1974: 22) 26

UPOV (57) 6 (1974), *Procès-verbal résumé des délibérations de la première session de la Conférence établi par le Secrétaire de la Conférence, M. Laclavière*, UPOV, 7–11 May 1957, in UPOV (1974: 23–6) 26

Abbreviations

AIPPI	Association Internationale pour la Protection de la Propriété Intellectuelle
ASSINSEL	Association internationale des sélectionneurs professionnels
BGH	Bundesgerichtshof, Federal Supreme Court, Germany
BIRPI	Bureaux Internationaux Réunis pour la Protection de la Propriété Intellectuelle (United International Bureau for the Protection of Intellectual Property)
CA	Court of Appeal
CEPC	European Convention for facilitating the filing of applications for patents in respect of the same invention in several States and the examination thereof
CEPL	Convention relating to European Patent Law
CFREU	Charter of Fundamental Rights of the European Union
CIOPORA	Communauté Internationale des Obtenteurs de Plantes Ornamentales de Réproduction Asexuée
CJEU	Court of Justice of the European Union
CoE	Council of Europe
CM	Committee of Ministers, Council of Europe
CPC	Convention for the European Patent for the Common Market (Community Patent Convention)
CPL	Committee on Patent Law
CPVRR	Council Regulation (EC) No. 2100/94 of 27 July 1994 on Community plant variety rights
EBD	Directive 98/44/EC of the European Parliament and of the Council of 6 July 1998 on the legal protection of biotechnological inventions (European Biotech Directive)
EBoA	Enlarged Board of Appeal, European Patent Office

ECHR	European Convention on Human Rights
ECJ	European Court of Justice, European Union
EEC	European Economic Community
EPC	European Patent Convention
epi	Institute of Professional Representatives before the European Patent Office
EPO	European Patent Office
EPOR	*European Patent Office Reports*
EU	European Union
FIS	Federation Internationale du Commerce des Semences
GATT	General Agreement on Tariffs and Trade
IGC	Intergovernmental Conference
IP	intellectual property
NAFTA	North American Free Trade Agreement
OC	Convention for the Protection of Human Rights and the Dignity of Human Being with regard to the Application of Biology and Medicine: Convention on Human Rights and Biomedicine (Oviedo Convention)
OECD	Organisation for Economic Co-operation and Development
OEEC	Organisation for European Economic Co-operation
OJ	*Official Journal of the European Union*
OJEPO	*Official Journal of the European Patent Office*
PC	Paris Convention for the Protection of Industrial Property
PCt	Patents Court, United Kingdom
PCT	Patent Co-operation Treaty
PWP	Patents Working Party
RPC	*Reports of Patent, Design and Trade Mark Cases*
SACEPO	Standing Advisory Committee before the EPO
SPC	Convention on the Unification of Certain Points of Substantive Law on Patents for Invention (Strasbourg Patent Convention)
TBoA	Technical Board of Appeal, European Patent Office
TRIPS	Agreement on Trade-Related Aspects of Intellectual Property Rights 1994
UDHR	Universal Declaration of Human Rights
UNFAO	United Nations Food and Agriculture Organisation
UNICE	Union des Industries des pays de la Communauté européenne

UPOV	International Convention for the Protection of New Varieties of Plants
VC	Vienna Convention on the Law of Treaties
WIPO	World Intellectual Property Organization
WP-I	Working Party I
WTO	World Trade Organization

1 Introduction

> I do not wish to make a secret of the fact that I see the best solution for the future in a total repeal of the exclusionary provisions currently in force in the European Patent Convention and in national patent legislation.
>
> (Straus 1987: 737)

> [The point is not] that intellectual property is undeserving of protection, but rather that such protection as it gets ought to reflect its unique susceptibility to conceptual imprecision and to infinite replication ... [T]he field of intellectual property [begins] to resemble a game of conceptual Pac Man in which everything in sight is being gobbled up.
>
> (Lange 1981: 147, 156)

1.1 The most basic of the safeguards

The basic requirements for patentability under modern international patent law are that there be an invention and that it be new, non-obvious and useful. Those requirements alone, however, leave certain subject-matter capable of being patented that may nonetheless be inappropriate for patenting. As a result we have both statutory exclusions from patentability and, where the words of the statute are insufficient, judicially derived exclusions. The subject of this book is the statutory exclusions under the European Patent Convention.

Exceptions to patentability, as well as restrictions on patent holders' ability to enforce their patents, have long provided important safeguards to society, nascent industries, academics, farmers, members of the medical professions and the public at large. Such safeguards include: exclusions to what may be patented; requirements to be met before a patent may be granted; limitations to the duration of the patent; requirements to be met for the maintenance of the patent; limitations on the actions a patent holder may ask the courts to restrain; restrictions on the ability of patent holders to collaborate to exclude others from the market;

restrictions on the ability of a patent holder to prevent resale of products he has put on the market; and the possibility to challenge the validity of the patent. Of these safeguards, the most basic are the exclusions to what may be patented, for, if no patent can be granted, the remaining safeguards are unnecessary.

In this introductory chapter the importance of the existence of limitations to patenting will be highlighted from an ethical perspective, focusing on various arguments that have been invoked to justify patents while at the same time paying attention to some important historical and economic developments.[1]

1.2 The 'New Wealth of Nations'

The economic importance of intellectual property rights has increased enormously, especially in the last three decades, to the extent that some commentators refer to intellectual property as the 'New Wealth of Nations'.[2] This has to do with diverse factors, for example the continuing increase of the commercial value of scientific and technological information in various domains. The idea that the true wealth of a country lies in its inventions and innovations began to prevail after the Second World War, for example in the writings of the well-known economist Jacob Schmookler (Schmookler 1965).

Another trend that has boosted the economic importance of intellectual property rights is the fact that global economic competition is not only increasing, but is also increasingly centred on technological leadership. Technological innovation becomes ever more important in export policies. As noted by Keith Maskus, an eminent specialist on the economics of intellectual property: 'goods that rely extensively on [intellectual property rights] protection tend to be among the fastest-growing items in international trade and also are distinctive in terms of international comparative advantage' (Maskus 2000: 73).

The debate on the desirability of (particular aspects of) the patent system has a very long and turbulent history. The entry into force of the TRIPS Agreement (the Agreement on Trade-Related Aspects of Intellectual Property Rights 1994) – a component of the agreement establishing the World Trade Organization that has resulted in a globalisation of strong protection and enforcement standards for intellectual property rights, including patents – has by no means silenced this

[1] In the interest of brevity and in view of the focus of this book, these comments will not be in depth. The relevant issues are discussed in more detail in Sterckx (2005).

[2] See for example Shulman (1999: 13) and Warshofsky (1994: 1).

debate but rather reinvigorated it. As noted by Maskus and Reichman in the preface to an influential analysis of the ways in which the current global intellectual property regime is affecting the provision of public goods and technology transfer:

> There has emerged, at an unprecedented level, both a globalized regime of private rights in information and new foundations for a basic international system of innovation. This new system will have profound implications for the nature of such processes as innovation, technology transfer, market competition, and economic development. It also raises essential and sometimes disturbing questions about potential impacts on the ability of governments to provide critical public goods, both within and across countries. Such goods include public health, nutrition, education, environmental protection, cultural identity, and other elements of social importance that must rely increasingly on the exercise of private rights over technical inputs. (Maskus and Reichman 2005a: xiii)

Attempts to justify the patent system or, put differently, to identify the 'fundamental nature' of the patent system,[3] can be based on three foundations: natural rights; distributive justice; and utilitarian arguments. As we will briefly explain in the following three sections, each of these justificatory attempts involves several problems.

1.3 Natural rights as the foundation for patents?

A natural rights justification would imply that man has a natural right to his ideas and that society is obliged to recognise and enforce that right. From this perspective, the use of ideas without the authorisation of their 'owner' must be regarded as theft. A 'natural' property right is to be considered as a moral imperative, that is, this property right takes precedence over social institutions and should be respected whatever the consequences.

Debates on the natural rights argument for patents frequently refer to John Locke's highly influential 'labour theory of property', which he formulated in Chapter V of his *Second Treatise on Government* (1690) (Locke 1988: 285–302).

[3] We borrow the use of the words 'fundamental nature' in this context from Edith Penrose, a noted commentator on the economic aspects of the patent system: 'Only in the first of the international conferences that led to the [1883 Paris Convention – see Chapter 2] did the delegates try to lay down the basic justification for patents ... [T]hey were unable to agree which of the various theories were the "true" ones. They therefore in subsequent conferences refrained from stating explicitly just what should be considered the fundamental nature of the patent law. They ... wisely left each delegate free to adhere in good conscience to any theory of the patent system that pleased him' (Penrose 1951: 20).

Locke wanted to ground his general theory of government in natural law, and one of the things he sought to 'prove' in the context of this project was that property rights could be explained in accordance with natural law. In his *Essay Concerning Human Understanding* (1690), Locke had already explained that God was a 'maker' and that, by virtue of the analogy between God and man, both being 'makers', anything true of one will be true of the other (Tully 1980: 37–8). The act of creating, he argued, gives rise to a right to the creation, and this includes the right to *use* the creation in certain ways. More specifically, the right created is a *property right*. God has a property right over man and man, made by God in his image, has a property right over his own creations.

According to Locke, property is conditional upon convention and agreement of the members of society: 'by *positive agreement*, [they] *settled a Property* amongst themselves, in distinct Parts and parcels of the Earth' (Second Treatise, Chapter V, section 45) (Locke 1988, emphasis in original). This needs to be emphasised since Locke's property theory is commonly interpreted as a justification of private property through proof that private property is natural, whereas in fact he drew attention to the conventional (as opposed to natural) character of private property.

Locke used two basic propositions as a starting point to establish how men might come to have a property right to things which God had given to mankind in common. His first proposition was that the preservation of mankind is a fundamental law of nature. It is God's will. From this, Locke inferred that man has a natural obligation to ensure his preservation. This then was said to imply that man has *a natural right* to his preservation and to the *means* necessary for his preservation (e.g. meat and drink) (Second Treatise, Chapter V, section 25) (Locke 1988).

The second basic proposition was that God had given the earth to mankind in common. However, for the 'fruits' of the earth to be of any use or benefit to any particular man, there necessarily had to be a way to *appropriate* these 'fruits' so that others could no longer claim them (Second Treatise, Chapter V, section 26) (Locke 1988).

Locke also asserted that everyone has a property right over his own person[4] and thus also over the labour of his body and the work of his hands (Second Treatise, Chapter V, section 27) (Locke 1988). This brought him to his famous explanation of the origin of property: the appropriation of a thing occurs by man applying his *labour* to it, by *mixing* the thing with his labour. By means of his labour, he adds something

[4] The reader should note that many commentators, e.g. in debates on organ sales, mistakenly claim that Locke argued for property in the *body* rather than the *person*.

of his own to the thing and thereby excludes others from having a right to it. For such acquisition of property, the consent of the other 'Commoners' is *not* required according to Locke (Second Treatise, Chapter V, section 28) (Locke 1988). Appropriation can never amount to robbery of others because everybody has the right to his share and no more. 'His share' means what he can use, so there can be no violation of the rights or liberties of others (Second Treatise, Chapter V, sections 36 and 46) (Locke 1988).

However, Locke stipulated two conditions ('provisos') that must be met in order for the appropriation to be justifiable. First, there must be 'enough, and as good left in common for others' (Second Treatise, Chapter V, section 27) (Locke 1988). Thus, the appropriation of things is only permitted if, afterwards, a sufficient number of the same or similar things remain. The second proviso is that there should be no waste. Man is not allowed to appropriate more than he can use (*even* if he made the things in question himself) (Second Treatise, Chapter V, section 31, 37 and 38) (Locke 1988).

For the purposes of our discussion, the key question is of course whether Locke's arguments regarding property are applicable to *intellectual* property. Some commentators clearly think they are (see, for example, Baird 1983 and Spector 1989). We will come back to this. However, Robert Nozick, the libertarian philosopher who elaborated a so-called 'entitlement theory' of property (Nozick 1974), which is partly based on Locke's theory, has raised the following pertinent question:

> Why does mixing one's labor with something make one the owner of it? Perhaps because one owns one's labor, and so one comes to own a previously unowned thing that becomes permeated with what one owns. Ownership seeps over into the rest. *But why isn't mixing what I own with what I don't own a way of losing what I own rather than a way of gaining what I don't?* ... If I own a can of tomato juice and spill it in the sea so that its molecules (made radioactive, so I can check this) mingle evenly throughout the sea, do I thereby come to own the sea, or have I foolishly dissipated my tomato juice? (Nozick 1974: 174–5, emphasis added)

Furthermore, if mixing labour with something would give rise to a property right, a further question arises as to the *boundaries* of that property right: what exactly has become the property of the person who performed the labour and how should this be determined? This question can also be formulated in terms of the *value* of the result. A difference exists between the value attributed to the object of the labour and the value attributed to the labour itself (or the *added* value). Determining the proportionality of each of these values in respect of the total value of the object to which labour has been applied can be very difficult, which poses a problem for the justificatory strength of the labour theory of property.

Moreover, 'intellectual objects' do not suddenly appear out of the blue, but usually stem from ideas of predecessors. The labour of these predecessors also contributes to the total value of the final result. This has important ramifications for the question as to who is entitled to the value of the final result. As Hettinger rightly notes:

> A person who relies on human intellectual history and makes a small modification to produce something of great value should no more receive what the market will bear than should the last person needed to lift a car receive full credit for lifting it. If laboring gives the laborer the right to receive the market value of the resulting product, this market value should be shared by all those whose ideas contributed to the origin of the product. The fact that most of these contributors are no longer present to receive their fair share is not a reason to give the entire market value to the last contributor. (Hettinger 1989: 38)

Again, it may be hard, and sometimes virtually impossible, to determine the relative share of each of the different components in the final result.

Let us now briefly examine whether Locke's two provisos (the 'enough and as good' condition and the 'non-waste' condition) are only relevant in the context of physical or tangible things, or whether they are also applicable to intellectual or intangible objects.

As for the second 'proviso' – man is only allowed to appropriate what he can use – the question arises, for example, whether ideas can ever be wasted. It seems improbable that an idea as such can be 'wasted', but surely the possibilities offered by an idea can be. If a person acquires an intellectual property right to something and does nothing with it, the 'non-waste' provision would be violated. If something were left unused by the appropriator, *while others needed it*, the waste would be all the greater.

One aspect of the patent system that can certainly generate waste is the fact that the patent system in its present form does not oblige patent holders to 'work' (exploit) their invention. The history of the patent system shows that this has not always been the case. Naturally, such 'working requirements' have always been defended on utilitarian grounds (see below), that is on the basis of a positive balance of societal benefits over disadvantages. For in a patent system grounded in natural law, the essence of the patent right would imply that the patent holder decides what happens with the object of the patent, that is he could not be forced to use the object of the patent.

Moreover, even if a patent *is* exploited, waste may still occur. After all, the result of granting a patent is that the patentee can put restrictions on the use of the invention. Since an important feature of the subjects of patents is what economists call their 'non-excludability', that is the fact that they can be used by many people *simultaneously*, artificially limiting their use can indeed amount to waste. The extent of the waste will depend on the utility of the invention for those who, because of the patent, are forbidden from using the invention.

So far we have considered the second proviso. As far as Locke's first proviso is concerned – 'enough and as good left in common for others' – many commentators perceive no problems with respect to intellectual property. Hughes, for example, states that:

> [A] growing set of central ideas are never permitted to become private property and are held in a *permanent common*. By preventing private control of these particular ideas, intellectual property law resolves a major inequity often present in physical property systems. Even in a vast wilderness, an individual should not be permitted to claim certain physical goods as property because their extraction from the common will not leave 'as good and as many' for the remaining individuals. (Hughes 1988: 319, emphasis in original)

However, the set of things that are not under consideration for privatisation is growing smaller, instead of growing bigger as Hughes claims, and it is precisely the set of things on which intellectual property rights can be claimed that is growing (see, for example, Shulman 1999 and Boyle 2003).

Nozick has applied Locke's 'enough and as good' proviso to the rights conferred by a patent. He correctly observes that, when an object becomes somebody's property, the situation of all the others *changes* since the object can be used by others only if the owner allows this. According to Nozick: 'The crucial point is whether appropriation of an unowned object worsens the situation of others' (Nozick 1974: 175). He believes this is not necessarily the case, and provides the following illustration:

> If I appropriate a grain of sand from Coney Island, no one else may now do as they will with *that* grain of sand. But there are plenty of other grains of sand left for them to do the same with. Or if not grains of sand, then other things. Alternatively, the things I do with the grain of sand I appropriate might improve the position of others, counterbalancing their loss of the liberty to use that grain. (Nozick 1974: 175, emphasis in original)

However, when applied in the context of patents, Nozick's arguments do not seem convincing. As to his statement that, if not enough samples of a specific object remain for others to use, sufficient samples of *another* object will be available to them, it can be argued that this is immaterial if that particular object is exactly the one they need (e.g. a specific drug). The fact that they are excluded from using that object as a result of the grant of a patent *does* imply that they are worse off than they might be.

As to Nozick's argument that the situation of others can be *improved* as a consequence of what the owner does with the object, and that this can compensate for the fact that others are not allowed to use the object, we need to point out once more that, certainly in the post-TRIPS world we find ourselves in, patentees are under no obligation to do anything with their invention.

Nozick further argues that the existence of a patent does not deprive others of anything since, were it not for the inventor, the subject-matter of the patent would not exist (Nozick 1974: 181). However, we may assume that at some point in time another person would have independently discovered it, and this could be a reason for putting a time limit on patent rights. Everybody who is aware of the enormous number of patent disputes regarding priority is familiar with the phenomenon of simultaneous independent inventing. Nozick himself acknowledges that a patent deprives independent inventors and argues that independent inventors should have the right to use their invention (Nozick 1974: 182).

The natural rights argument for patents became very popular in the nineteenth century, albeit mostly in continental Europe (Dutton 1984: 18; MacLeod 1988: 197, 199). It has been called a 'tired old ghost' (Schiff 1971: 73), but in fact the natural rights justification is frequently used in current debates on patenting. Sixty years ago Edith Penrose made an important observation that remains valid today:

> [T]he loose use of the word 'stealing' remains in most patent discussions to remind us of the natural property right conception of patents. Stealing ... is used in a [wide] and [vague] sense to include the use by another of a man's ideas even though they are not in fact patented or patentable under the law applying to him who uses them. Upon this concept all charges of 'piracy' are based when they are leveled against nations who permit their nationals to use freely inventions patented elsewhere but which are not patentable under their own laws. (Penrose 1951: 24–5)

Referring to natural law as justification for the patent system, both as we know it today and as it has existed in the past, is problematic for several reasons, inter alia: the fact that certain categories are excluded from patentability; the fact that the validity of patents is limited in time and space;[5] the fact that an independent inventor cannot use her own

[5] Patents granted under a system based on natural rights could be expected to be perpetually valid (or at least valid until the death of the patent holder) and to be globally enforceable.

invention if someone else already has a patent on it;[6] the fact that patents are only granted if certain requirements (novelty, inventive step, applicability and sufficiency of disclosure) are met; and the fact that patents can be declared void.

1.4 Distributive justice as the foundation for patents?

Let us now take a look at the second type of justification for the patent system. According to the distributive justice argument, it is only *fair* that society rewards inventors since they do society a service. The establishment of a patent system is justified because it would be unfair to allow people a 'free ride' at the expense of others who apply themselves to the act of inventing. Free-riders, by definition, have not invested time or money in the development of an invention, thus it would be unacceptable to allow them to compete with the inventor under normal market conditions.

Several problems arise when evaluating the patent system from a distributive justice perspective. We will only mention a few here, without elaborating. First, there are two possible grounds for reward: the *extent of the effort* and the *value of the result achieved*. Which of these two criteria should determine whether or not a person deserves a reward? The value of the result is often influenced by factors on which the person can have no impact (e.g. luck). As rightly noted by Hettinger, giving a greater reward to 'workers' whose products have greater social value might be justified if this is needed as an incentive, but this has nothing to do with giving a person what she *deserves* (Hettinger 1989: 42). The extent to which someone has made an effort is obviously more difficult to determine than the value of the result of her efforts, but pragmatic arguments such as this are not decisive in a framework of distributive justice.

It seems that the patent system does not give proper consideration to the extent to which an applicant has tried, although the patentability requirement of non-obviousness might create the impression that it does. First of all, inventors who have tried very hard, but ultimately produce nothing that works, are not rewarded under the patent system. If we accept the justice-based principle that efforts must be rewarded, then

[6] This could be justified on utilitarian grounds (see below), by referring to the incentive effect of the patent system, which would be eroded if independent inventors were also allowed to lay claim to the invention. But a justification of the exclusion of independent inventors on the basis of natural rights is clearly problematic, since from this perspective independent inventors have the same natural property right to their invention as the inventor who was the first to knock at the door of the patent office.

unsuccessful inventors who have made efforts also deserve a reward. Moreover, findings in fields that are excluded from patentability (e.g. mathematical formulae) can also involve huge efforts and/or represent a great service to society. Does fairness not require that people who work in these fields also be rewarded with patents?

Obviously, patents represent only one of the possible reward mechanisms. Hettinger has rightly observed that the argument that an inventor deserves to be rewarded does *not* imply that inventors deserve an exclusive right of ownership on their invention: 'The mistake is to conflate the created object which makes a person deserving of a reward with what that reward should be. Property rights in the created object are not the only possible reward. Alternatives include fees, awards, acknowledgements, gratitude, praise, security, power, status, and public financial support' (Hettinger 1989: 41).

What about the proportionality of the reward? Adam Smith considered the patent system to be the fairest mechanism for rewarding inventors:

> For if the legislature should appoint pecuniary rewards for the inventors of new machines, etc., they would hardly ever be so precisely proportioned to the merit of the invention as this [the patent grant] is. For here, if the invention be good and such as is profitable to mankind, he will probably make a fortune by it; but if it be of no value he will also reap no benefit. (Meek *et al.* 1978: 83)

Indeed, under a system based on distributive justice every inventor would be rewarded according to his merit. However, in its current form the patent system offers no guarantee as to the proportionality of the effort/service provided by the inventor and the reward received. For there is no link at all between the social usefulness of an invention on the one hand and the scope and duration of protection of the patent on the other hand. Admittedly, the patentability requirement of 'sufficiency of disclosure' should (at least theoretically) guarantee some 'correspondence' between the actual *contribution* the invention represents and the specific *scope* of the legal protection awarded to the patentee, but this bears no relevance to the *social merit* of inventions. All patents may be kept in force for twenty years, irrespective of the social usefulness of the invention in question and irrespective of the effort invested in developing the invention. However, it is not easy to remedy this rigidity, for it would be very difficult to fairly determine the proper level of reward on a case-by-case basis.

Finally, yet another problem concerns the unequal access to inventions that results from the granting of patents. Is this not unfair too? From a utilitarian perspective (see below) the unequal access to inventions is defended by referring to the incentive it generates – if people expect to have control over the use of the inventions they produce, more inventions will be produced and society will benefit. This kind of argument, however, cannot be decisive within a framework of distributive justice; what matters here is whether or not granting patents is fair. Is it fair to allow inventors to decide who may use the inventions? Should we not also apply the perspective of distributive justice to the (in)equality of access to inventions between rich and poor countries? Due to the globalisation of high levels of patent protection and enforcement since the 1990s, access to certain technologies is becoming increasingly difficult and increasingly expensive for poor countries. We will come back to this in the next section.

1.5 Utilitarianism as the foundation for patents?

The utilitarian[7] argument for patents was formulated very simply by the founding father of utilitarianism, Jeremy Bentham: 'he who has no hope that he shall reap will not take the trouble to sow' (Bentham 1785: 71). More specifically, the utilitarian justification entails two arguments. According to the first argument, without the prospect of an exclusive right to use the invention (and a chance of recouping the investment made in developing it), there would not be enough investment in research and development and thus too few inventions and innovations. Proponents of this argument claim that the patent system represents an indispensable incentive to invent and innovate.[8] The second part of the utilitarian justification holds that the patent system encourages inventors to disclose their inventions instead of keeping them secret. Thus the patent system is said to promote the dissemination of technological information, which encourages technological progress, which in turn enables economic growth.[9]

[7] Utilitarianism is an ethical theory according to which, put simply, an act (or a policy) is morally right if it results in a positive balance of good over bad consequences.

[8] Invention has to do with ideas as such, whereas innovation concerns the application and the marketing of inventions. As Fritz Machlup put it in an authoritative study of the economic aspects of the patent system: '*inventive* activity must precede the patent, whereas *innovating* activity may follow it' (Machlup 1958: 56, emphasis in original).

[9] We will not go into the 'incentive-to-disclose' argument here, but merely wish to make two remarks. First, that the validity of this argument relies on a serious application of the patentability requirement that the invention must be disclosed in sufficient detail in the patent application. See, for example, Art. 83 EPC. In other words, it relies on patent offices not granting patents with unduly broad claims, a duty that they do not always take seriously. Second, proponents of the 'incentive-to-disclose' argument often describe the patent system as a kind of 'social contract': society grants the inventor a temporary monopoly in return for which the inventor discloses his secrets.

The utilitarian justification is considered by most commentators as the most convincing foundation for the patent system. This type of argumentation was also frequently used in the context of attempts to convince developing countries to sign up to the TRIPS Agreement – although, in reality, (threats of) trade sanctions proved much more effective (Sell 2003).

In order for the utilitarian justification of the patent system to be convincing, three things need to be shown: that the patent system encourages inventions and innovations; that no better system exists or can be established to achieve this purpose; and that the encouragement of inventions and innovations is itself justifiable on utilitarian grounds. Moreover, if the patent system turns out to be the most suitable mechanism to encourage inventions and innovations, it should be investigated whether the advantages of this system outweigh the costs.

As to the latter, Jeremy Bentham may have claimed about the patent system that 'it produces an infinite effect and costs nothing' (Bentham 1785: 71), but in reality the costs are huge, due to various factors. To mention only three examples: the costs of simply keeping the patent system going (thousands of highly qualified patent examiners, armies of administrative personnel, translation costs, and so on); the fact that, even though some inventions are only made possible by the availability of patents, the public must pay a monopoly price for all patented inventions; and the enormous costs related to the ever increasing number of patent litigation cases (which obviously have an impact on the real costs of the introduction of innovations and which have the perverse effect that more resources that would normally be spent on research are now diverted to pay lawyers and legal costs).

As mentioned earlier, the proponents of the 'incentive to invent and innovate' argument point out that, if competitors were to be allowed to 'free-ride', the incentive to invent and innovate would be eroded. Thus a special incentive is needed to ensure that enough people are prepared to invest in research and development. This has to do with the fact that knowledge possesses the characteristics of a so-called 'public good'. According to the utilitarian argument for patents, the government must intervene in the 'production' of knowledge because the market does not offer an efficient solution for the production of 'public goods'.

Without patents, they argue, technological information would be kept secret or disseminated much later. However, in many cases the 'secrets' behind an invention can easily be uncovered once an invention is brought onto the market. Thus some scepticism seems to be necessary with regard to the assertion that patents are an 'altruistic alternative' to trade secrets.

The key characteristics of 'public goods' are 'non-rivalry' in consumption and 'non-excludability' in use. Knowledge shares these characteristics. First, it 'can be used again and again without exhausting it' (David 1993: 25). Second, the *production* of knowledge requires enormous resources, but as soon as it is produced, knowledge costs comparatively little to *reproduce*. It is difficult, and sometimes even impossible, to prevent others from appropriating the advantages of knowledge – thus it is at least partially non-excludable. In view of these 'public good' characteristics, it is impossible to bring about an optimal allocation of means for the production of knowledge (inventions) via the market, and hence government intervention is necessary, as Nobel laureate Kenneth Arrow explained in the 1960s in his classic analysis (Arrow 1962: 609–10).

The failure of the market as regards the production of 'public goods' can be solved in three ways: the granting of subsidies (in the case of knowledge production examples include systems of prizes and of research grants); direct production by the government (e.g. by laboratories or agricultural research stations run by the state); and the grant of monopolies (e.g. patents).[10] These mechanisms are frequently used simultaneously. The third model, that is granting patent monopolies, is not necessarily the best, for patents may severely limit the dissemination and use of inventions.

Most proponents of the 'incentive-to-invent-and-innovate' argument for patents would probably agree that, ideally, inventions should be spread as widely as possible and used as early and as intensively as possible, in order to allow society to enjoy the full benefits of new inventions. Patents, however, have the opposite effect: the use of a patented invention is limited and its price can be kept artificially high. Defenders of the 'incentive' argument note, however, that for inventions to be at all usable, they need to be developed first – that is, enough people have to be found willing to invest in the development of inventions. Thus, they argue, only by limiting the use of inventions can society ensure that enough inventions come about.

The availability of patents clearly results in more inventions. As far as we are aware, nobody questions this. However, this does not necessarily imply that the patent system induces technological progress, as claimed by the advocates of the utilitarian justification. The 'sixty-four million dollar question' is thus: which of the two trends (the incentive effect or the limitation-of-dissemination effect) is the strongest? Clearly, such a

[10] For an interesting discussion of the benefits and shortcomings of each of these three mechanisms in the case of production of knowledge, see David (1993: 32–6).

question cannot be answered merely on the basis of theoretical reasoning. Empirical research is just as necessary.

Until recently, little empirical research was available on the economic effects of the patent system, and the available research findings raised serious questions regarding the validity of the utilitarian justification of the patent system, except as far as the pharmaceutical and, to a lesser extent, the chemical sector were concerned (Scherer *et al.* 1959; Taylor and Silberston 1973; Mansfield 1986; Levin *et al.* 1987; Cohen *et al.* 2000). These studies were hardly taken into account by policymakers, even though some of them were government-funded.

Since 2000 a number of in-depth analyses have been published regarding the global economic effects of the recent worldwide strengthening of intellectual property rights, especially patents (see, for example, Maskus 2000; Maskus and Reichman 2005a). Again, there appears to be little sign that policymakers are taking these important empirical studies seriously, although they contain various relevant messages. Maskus and Reichman, for example, two of the most prominent US commentators on intellectual property, observe:

> We find it ironic that, as tariffs, quotas, and other formal barriers to trade are dismantled, there has been a strong push to re-regulate world technology markets ... Indeed, the progressive re-regulation of world markets for knowledge goods is not driven by a broad consensus of economic agents [even] in the developed world. Rather, pressures to elevate IP [intellectual property] norms are exerted by powerful private interests whose lobbying activities hold sway in legislative and regulatory initiatives in rich countries and international forums. ... These efforts are largely detached from the traditional goal of domestic IP systems to strike a balance between commercial profitability and public-interest concerns. (Maskus and Reichman 2005b: 6–7)

> Drawing the lines between knowledge goods accessible to all and those subject to private property rights has always been a delicate, controversial, and economically uncertain task in even the most developed economies. Periods of relatively weak and relatively strong levels of protection have alternated over time ... with little consensus in law or economics about the cumulative lessons to be learned. How to ensure that the social benefits of maximizing investment in current innovation are not offset by the social costs of deterring future innovation and impeding current competition is no clearer today than it was 50 years ago. (Maskus and Reichman 2005b: 16)

Some of the issues that keep resurfacing when one looks at the historical and economic literature on the patent system are: should patents be thought of as rights or as privileges, and – a related question – should the essence of the patent system lie in the promotion of private interests of inventors and investors or in the promotion of the public interest? Since the 1990s we have witnessed an extension of the concept of patentability which poses various problems and which has come about with little or no public debate. Today we increasingly find that, for things that previously belonged to the public domain, private patent rights are being issued, even though according to a serious and non-industry-biased interpretation of the law this should be impossible. Was not patent law supposed to prevent the public domain – sometimes referred to in US legal judgements as 'the public storehouse of knowledge' – from shrinking?

This trend of the extension of the concept of patentability raises many questions: for example, what are the implications for society at large and for particular groups within society (such as consumers, patients, farmers, etc.), and to what extent are patent offices and patent owners answerable to the public? In this book we focus on how one particular patent office, the European Patent Office (EPO), has contributed to this trend. In view of the fact that more and more national courts in Europe bring their case law into line with that of the Technical Boards of Appeal and the Enlarged Board of Appeal of the EPO, the EPO's case law has become overwhelmingly important for the patent community throughout Europe. Moreover, it is observed with great interest by other patent jurisdictions such as the USA, Japan and China.

As is clear from our discussion of the traditional justifications for the patent system, the view that inventors have a natural (i.e. inherent) right to patents is unconvincing. As noted a long time ago by a certain Reverend Rogers, Professor of Political Economy at Oxford: 'Nor do vague and angry declarations that invention is property, and the lavish use of the expressions "pirate" and "pilfer", and "stealing the fruit of other men's minds and labour", prove more than that certain persons gain an advantage rightly or wrongly, which they wish to keep' (Rogers 1863: 128). Instead, patents ought to be seen as privileges granted to inventors by or on behalf of the state to further the public interest. We will elaborate on this in Chapter 8. Accordingly, it is perfectly reasonable for the legislator to make the grant of patents subject to various conditions and safeguards. The most basic of these is the stipulation of the categories of subject-matter for which patents are not to be granted. It is important that these boundaries to the patent-eligible are not eroded by patent offices overstepping their mandate. The topic of this book is a study of those boundaries within the European Patent Convention and, more specifically, the extent to which boundary erosion has occurred and the extent to which the boundaries are being rebuilt.

In the following chapters we will first look at the history of how the exclusions from patentability laid down in the European Patent Convention came about (Chapter 2). In Chapters 3 to 8, we investigate the ways in which the exclusions from patentability of computer programs, discoveries, methods of medical treatment and diagnosis, essentially biological processes for the production of plants and animals, plant and animal varieties, and inventions the commercial exploitation of which would contravene 'ordre public' or morality, have been (re)interpreted by the Technical Boards of Appeal and the Enlarged Board of Appeal of the EPO. Each of these chapters describes the relevant case law and subsequently provides critical comments on the (re)interpretations of the exclusions by the EPO, focusing on the extent to which each of these boundaries to patentability has been subject to erosion. Finally, before concluding in Chapter 10, we make some suggestions as to how the exclusions can be interpreted in a coherent way (Chapter 9).

2 The historical development and current scope of the European Patent Convention

> [B]ack in 1960 ... we first met in Brussels ... as representatives of [the six EEC] ... countries ... [W]e had been shaped by our experiences in World War II and we approached with enthusiasm and determination the task of promoting European Integration, thus helping to create a situation in which war between our countries could never again be either possible or conceivable. The group included my four German friends: Kurt Haertel,[1] Albrecht Krieger,[2] Romuald Singer,[3] and Klaus Pfanner[4] ... These four friends did more than merely work with me towards a common goal. As a Dutchman who had spent some difficult years as a student in the Dutch resistance against the occupying troops, I had emerged from the war with a hostile attitude to the Germans. My friends were able to show me a different Germany, and different, democratic and spiritually open-minded Germans who had outgrown nationalism.
>
> (van Benthem[5] 1993)

2.1 Introduction

The European Patent Convention (EPC)[6] is a multinational treaty, in operation since July 1978, which established a system under which patent applications could be filed, examined for patentability under a common standard, granted by a single body, the European Patent Office (EPO), and then brought into force as patents equivalent to those granted by the national patent offices in the Contracting States[7]

[1] Dr Kurt Haertel (°1910–+2001), to our minds the father of the EPC.
[2] Dr Albrecht Krieger, later chairman of the Administrative Council of the EPO.
[3] Dr Romuald Singer, later the first chairman of the EBoA.
[4] Dr Klaus Pfanner, later the Deputy Director General of WIPO (World Intellectual Property Organization).
[5] Dr Johannes Bob van Benthem, the first president of the EPO.
[6] References to the EPC throughout this book are to the current version, EPC 2000, rather than the original version, EPC 1973, unless the Article or Rule in question is otherwise identified.
[7] As of 6 December 2011: *Albania*, Austria, Belgium, Bulgaria, *Croatia*, Cyprus, Czech Republic, Denmark, Estonia, Finland, France, Germany, Greece, Hungary, *Iceland*,

and the Extension States,[8] a set of countries that now encompasses most of Europe and all of the European Union (EU) countries. The EPC's common standard for patentability has, de facto, become the 'European' common standard.

As with most patent laws, the EPC contains provisions that exclude certain subject-matter from patentability. Exclusions from patentability can be expected to derive from an understanding that an invention may be one to which the state does not wish to grant its imprimatur, for example the morality-based exclusions. They can also be expected to derive from an understanding that certain things are part of our common heritage, free to all, monopolisable by no one. Further, it can be expected that certain activities should not be constrained by fear of patent infringement, or indeed cannot practically be constrained (e.g. mental acts). Finally, some activities are protected by other laws, for example properly belonging to the field of the creative arts, that is artistic activities rather than industrial ones. These are perceived as being more correctly protected by copyright rather than patents since their originality lies in their form rather than in the underlying concepts.

2.2 The international harmonisation of patent law

While patent law is now extraordinarily uniform globally, this has not always been the case. At different stages in the relatively recent past, many countries have been without patent laws (e.g. The Netherlands and Switzerland – see Schiff 1971), have had patent laws from which many categories of inventions (for example medical treatments, pharmaceuticals, foodstuffs and life forms) have been excluded from patentability (e.g. the USA, UK and Germany, among many others), or which have favoured local inventors (e.g. the USA and UK).

The Convention on the Grant of European Patents (European Patent Convention), the EPC, with which we are concerned here, represents only *one* facet of the international harmonisation of patent laws that has been under way since the late nineteenth century. The stages of patent law harmonisation may be summarised as follows:

- the adoption of local or national patent laws, generally accepted as having begun in Venice in 1474 (Prager 1944, Mandich 1948);

Ireland, Italy, Latvia, *Liechtenstein*, Lithuania, Luxembourg, *Former Yugoslav Republic of Macedonia*, Malta, *Monaco*, the Netherlands, *Norway*, Poland, Portugal, Romania, *San Marino*, *Serbia*, Slovakia, Slovenia, Spain, Sweden, *Switzerland*, *Turkey* and the United Kingdom. Countries in italics are not European Union Member States.

[8] As of 6 December 2011: Bosnia and Herzegovina, and Montenegro.

- the adoption in 1883 of an international agreement as to certain basic reciprocities, the Paris Convention for the Protection of Industrial Property 1883 (PC 1883);
- the efforts by the Council of Europe (CoE) to harmonise first formalities relating to patent applications and then substantive requirements for patentability, in the latter case leading to the adoption in 1963 of the Strasbourg Patent Convention (SPC 1963);
- the negotiations beginning in 1957 which led in 1961 to the adoption of the Convention Internationale pour la Protection des Obtentions Végétales (International Convention for the Protection of New Varieties of Plants) (UPOV 1961);
- a temporary attempt in 1961 by the CoE to produce a Convention allowing for a single examination and the grant of a 'European Patent', perhaps the true precursor of the EPC, namely the Draft European Convention for facilitating the filing of applications for patents in respect of the same invention in several States and the examination thereof, which, for want of a better name, we will refer to as the Council of Europe Patent Convention (CEPC 1961);
- the stalled attempt in 1965 by the European Economic Community (EEC – then a group of six European nations – the Federal Republic of Germany (West Germany), France, Italy, The Netherlands, Belgium, and Luxembourg) to set up a system for the granting of European Patents, the Convention relating to European Patent Law (CEPL 1965);
- the creation in 1970, following the suggestion of the USA, of an international system for patent applications, the Patent Cooperation Treaty (PCT 1970);
- the creation in 1973 of a common system for the examination and grant of patents in Europe, that is the European Patent Convention (EPC 1973);
- the stalled attempt to create a patent system for the EU, which led to the signing in 1975 of the Community Patent Convention (CPC 1975);
- the negotiation, from 1986 to 1994, of global minimum requirements for patentability in the Uruguay round of the negotiations on the Global Agreement on Tariffs and Trade, resulting in the World Trade Organization (WTO) and the Agreement on Trade-Related Aspects of Intellectual Property Rights (TRIPS 1994);
- the debates, starting in 1988, which led in 1998 to the modification of the EU's requirements for patentability of biotechnology as set out in Directive 98/44/EU (the European Biotech Directive – EBD 1998)

and to the introduction in September 1999 into the Implementing Regulations of the EPC of corresponding Rules; and
- the modification in 2000 of the EPC, inter alia to achieve greater compliance with TRIPS, the amended law having entered into force in 2007 (EPC 2000).

This harmonisation process is not complete, not even at the EU level – as of June 2012 the CPC is not in force after thirty-seven years. Global harmonisation continues and revision of TRIPS continues to be discussed.

The first stage of *global* harmonisation was the Paris Convention of 1883 (Penrose 1951, Bodenhausen 1969), which gave rise to the priority right and to national treatment,[9] but included no provisions as to what would constitute patent infringement or what was patentable.

For harmonisation regarding what is patentable, we must look elsewhere and identify where, when, how and why the exclusions from patentability currently present in the EPC appeared. The legislative history of the exclusions from patentability in Europe can be seen to relate to three sets of exclusions:

- those of Art. 53(a) and (b) EPC, which were essentially agreed in the drafting of the SPC;
- those of Art. 52(2) and (3) EPC, which began life in the drafting of the CEPL, were transferred to the drafting of the EPC and were modified to some extent by the adoption of PCT Rule 39.1; and
- that of Art. 53(c) EPC, which began with the CEPL, was first placed with the precursor of the Art. 52(2) EPC exclusions to avoid conflict with the SPC, was transferred to Art. 52(4) EPC 1973 under the legal fiction of non-susceptibility to industrial application, and in the revision to produce EPC 2000 was transferred to Art. 53(c) EPC.

The development of these exclusions was not straightforward and has involved an interplay between the development of several different international intellectual property laws and treaties as well as political and economic developments spanning more than half a century.

[9] That is the right to claim the filing date of the first patent application covering an invention in corresponding patent applications filed in other countries party to the Paris Convention, and the right to have one's patent application in a Paris Convention country examined in the same way as an application filed by a national of the country would be.

2.3 The early history

Before the Second World War, the German chemical industry had an almost overwhelmingly dominant position globally, backed up by its national and foreign patents (Jeffreys 2008, Dutfield 2009). During that war, as with the First World War, German-owned patents were of course seized by Allied governments as enemy property (Wadlow 2010). In April 1945 American forces also seized the papers of the German Patent Office, which had been hidden, for safe-keeping, in a mine near Heringen in Hessen (Haddon 2008, Walker 1946). Those papers, tons in all, were eventually transferred to the US Department of Commerce. The German Patent Office did not start receiving patent applications again until 1948, and when the first post-war patent was issued, it was numbered 800001 to reflect the missing files.

Following proposals by, among others, Winston Churchill, the CoE was set up in 1949. In August 1949 the Committee of Ministers of the CoE placed the creation of a European Patent Office on their agenda, and in November 1949 they instructed their Secretary-General to collect all useful material regarding the creation of a European Patent Office, to prepare a report on the best way of handling it, and if necessary to call on the services of experts appointed by their governments (Document Res (49) 27-E). A Committee of Experts was formed in 1950 and presciently reported in 1952 that the recommendation could not be carried out immediately. The Committee of Experts was instructed to proceed (Document Res (52) 51-E).

In January 1953 the Committee of Experts sent a questionnaire to Member States asking what was excluded from patentability in those countries, in particular in relation to: '(1) Substances, especially chemical substances[;] (2) Foodstuffs, including tobacco and other luxuries[;] (3) Medicines and medical appliances [; and] (4) Further exceptions, including inventions contrary to law and morality' (Document EXP/Brev (53) 3: 2).

The Committee of Experts drafted two Conventions, the first dealing with patent application formalities (signed in December 1953) and the second dealing with classification (signed in December 1954). Then they turned to unification of substantive laws. A first draft of a European convention on patents had in fact been prepared by Dr Eduard Reimer in 1953 (see Document EXP/Brev (53) 19, and Wadlow 2008: 369–70), but, as Wadlow comments, the proposals: 'were too far ahead of their time to be adopted.' A study on substantive points of patentability was presented for the Committee of Experts by Roger Gajac in November 1955. This 'Gajac study' sought to set out the common features of possible exclusions from patentability, and needs to be quoted at length (authors' translation from French), for it provides the foundation, as well as a rationale, for most of the exclusions set out in Art. 52 and Art. 53 EPC:

1. Invention and discovery:

As a general rule, a patent can only protect an invention (a creation) and not a discovery, that is the mere becoming aware of a pre-existing reality. A natural product or a natural phenomenon could no more be the object of patent protection than the revelation of a law of nature, even though a patentable technical indication may be based on a discovery, and the scientific expression of an empirically known causality may, for example, provide an industrial activity with a precise and constant character and therefore yield a patentable application, if it takes the form of a concrete technical instruction addressed at industry.

2. Industry and agriculture:

The word 'industry', understood as a defined field of economic activity, can be interpreted – in France – in a narrow sense (as opposed to agriculture) or in a broad sense, as all human activity that is oriented towards practical goals. It appears that, even in France, both meanings in turn have prevailed in judicial interpretation …

These uncertainties are reflected in the diversity of national practices.

(a) It is nevertheless admitted without restriction that agricultural inventions, in view of their purpose or the origin of the products they relate to, although industrial through their implementation, fall under the scope of application of the law. The same holds for inventions relating to the manufacturing of tools.

(b) The divergences arise with regard to purely agricultural activities, without 'industrial' implementation, that is methods for or products of cultivation or breeding. The patentability of both currently seems totally excluded in countries such as the United Kingdom, Ireland, Luxemburg or The Netherlands. The other countries – the majority – (France, Germany, Italy, the Scandinavian countries, Switzerland) acknowledge, more or less firmly, the patentability of methods (such as methods for treating seeds enabling a uniform germination). However, the patentability of the products themselves, that is the new types[10] of plants (or possibly animals) is admitted in only a few countries (Germany, France, Italy), where the question moreover is not definitively resolved, either in legal doctrine or in practice. The exclusion from patentability of agricultural products, it is true, has to do with other criteria than the criterion of belonging to the domain of 'industry' (the possibility of a sufficient description or a repetition, the scope of the monopoly guaranteed by the patent) since, from this

[10] In the original 'espèces', which according to the Collins–Robert French–English Dictionary (Atkins *et al.* 1987: 272) translates as: 'species; … sort, kind, type.'

strict point of view, there is no more reason to exclude the product than the process.

3. Systems, methods and so on:

If the patentability of inventions relating to agricultural techniques remains subject to divergent responses, this is not the case for inventions in the field, not of 'industrial' techniques, but of financial, accounting, commercial, publicity, educational, military, tourist, medical, and so on techniques. All national practices agree on excluding monetary, insurance, accounting, calculation, education, publicity, and so on systems, as well as rules of games or methods of medical treatment, from the scope of application of the law.

On the other hand, the manufacturing of products or appliances, of which the non-industrial techniques make use, obviously falls within the boundaries of industry. In this respect, the field of industrial techniques is broader for 'products' than for methods, since a product, even applicable to other techniques, is necessarily industrial through its manufacture, whereas a method can only have an industrial character if it makes use of natural resources and not merely of the faculties of the human mind. That is how, unlike 'abstract' curative methods, medical products or instruments would be patentable everywhere without consideration of public interest or societal ethics.

4. Scientific principles and theories:

All the countries' practices are also in agreement that purely scientific doctrines, principles or theories are excluded from the scope of the application of the law, whereas their industrial applications are not ...

5. Creations of form:

It is obviously a general rule that creations of form fall outside patent protection and fall within the scope of the special protection of designs and industrial models. Likewise, ways of typographical presentation of printed material would only fall under the remit of the laws relating to artistic property ...

Ordre public, morality:

In all countries' practices (if not in their laws – the Belgian law remains silent in this respect), one finds a prohibition on patenting inventions that are contrary to 'ordre public' or morality ...

The applications of this rule, which are always extremely rare, seem to address similar considerations. The refusal or invalidation of a patent may stem from either the fundamentally illicit nature of the invention (the application of which would in itself be criminal), or from it being prohibited by specific legal or regulatory provisions. The possibility of a partially licit application is always sufficient to ensure patentability. Sometimes it is required, in such a case, that the illicit application be subject to a formal disclaimer. (Document EXP/Brev (53) 18 rev: 4–7 and 22, references omitted)

In October 1956 Eduard Reimer,[11] on behalf of the German experts, put forward a more concrete proposal (the 'Reimer proposal') as to what should not be eligible for patents:

No invention shall be patentable when it is simply a question of:

(a) scientific principles and theories,
(b) instructions to the human brain, such as accounting systems and rules of games,
(c) the creation of aesthetic forms,
(d) the bringing to light of a pre-existing fact (discovery). (Document EXP/Brev (56) 8: 8)

This was said to list, on the basis of the Gajac study, 'cases where the question of patentable invention does not arise' (Document EXP/Brev (56) 8: 3). The experts considered that the Gajac study was 'of a restrictive nature' and that it could be supplemented. The Reimer proposal also suggested that European patents should be granted in respect of inventions that were 'capable of industrial application', deeming that this term should: 'be taken in the widest sense as applying not only to industry and agriculture as such but also to the extraction of mineral resources, the working of the earth, action exercised on the *development* of plants and animals and the *utilization* of natural produce such as flowers, fruits, seeds, tobacco leaves, mineral water, wine, beer and flour' (Document EXP/Brev (56) 8: 8, emphasis added). It will be seen that these extended examples relate to processes rather than to products as such, that is they give no suggestion that plants, animals or natural materials should themselves be patentable. Indeed, in the body of the text it was stated that the German experts considered that: 'there are no unresolvable differences between the patent laws of the different European countries – with the possible exception of the question of extending patentability to cover *methods of breeding* plants and animals' (Document EXP/Brev (56) 8: 2, emphasis added).

In March 1957 the Treaty of Rome was signed, coming into force in January 1958 and creating the EEC, the forerunner of the current EU, uniting six European countries (France, the Federal Republic of Germany, Belgium, Luxembourg, The Netherlands and Italy). One may suspect that getting the EEC up and running distracted attention from the project for a European Patent Office and a common European patent law. Indeed, between October 1955 and June 1960 things had not progressed enough in the patent field to hold a full meeting of the

[11] President of the German Patent Office. Unfortunately, Dr Reimer's involvement in the European patent law project was cut short by his death in 1957.

CoE Committee of Experts. Nonetheless, a meeting of the Bureau of the Committee of Experts in May 1960 asked the Committee's rapporteurs to complete their reports.

2.4 Plant variety protection – the negotiations leading to UPOV 1961

Although the issue of some form of intellectual property protection for plant breeders was discussed at the AIPPI (Association Internationale pour la Protection de la Propriété Intellectuelle) Congress in Vienna in 1952, there was no agreement as to the form such protection might take. Plant breeders had hoped for protection by way of a patent or equivalent right. At the request of the plant breeders' association ASSINSEL (Association internationale des sélectionneurs professionnels) following their June 1956 congress, in February 1957 the French government invited the governments of twelve other European countries to a diplomatic conference to discuss the possibility of drafting an international convention to provide protection to new breeds of plant. The term actually used was '*nouvelles obtentions végétales*' (Document UPOV (57) 1: 14). The accompanying *aide-mémoire*, intended to serve as the starting position for the discussions, also used the terms new plant variety (*nouvelle variété de plante*), plant novelty (*nouveauté végétale*) and race (*race*) (Document UPOV (57) 3: 16). The first Diplomatic Conference took place in May 1957 and was attended by delegates from Austria, Belgium, Denmark, France, Italy, The Netherlands, Norway, Spain, Sweden, Switzerland and the Federal Republic of Germany. The German delegation included Dr Klaus Pfanner and the French delegation included Guillaume Finniss, the director of the French Patent Office and a member of the CoE's Committee of Experts on Patents. Three organisations were also represented: BIRPI (Bureaux Internationaux Réunis pour la Protection de la Propriété Intellectuelle (United International Bureau for the Protection of Intellectual Property) – the predecessor of WIPO (the World Intellectual Property Organization)); OEEC (the Organisation for European Economic Co-operation – the predecessor of the OECD (the Organization for Economic Co-operation and Development)); and UNFAO (the United Nations Food and Agriculture Organisation).

In his introductory address at the conference, Mr Darras, representing the French Secretary of State for Industry and Commerce, commented that some countries excluded food materials from patentability and that others had special legal instruments for protecting plants. More interestingly, he mentioned that: 'It must be understood that plants, unlike industrial products, can reproduce themselves and that this ability raises serious problems, on the one hand in proving infringement, and on the other in regulating the use of her harvest by the purchaser of the propagating material, for example seeds, tubers, and so on' (Document UPOV (57) 5: 22, authors' translation from French). The different government delegations explained whether and how new types of plant could be protected in their countries. In Germany patent protection was possible. In Austria no one had applied for a patent on a plant since 1940, and any such application would be rejected. The Belgian Patent Office had granted about twenty patents for plants, but Belgian patent applications underwent no substantive examination and so 'it was difficult to comment on their value'. Similarly such patents were granted in France but without 'any guarantee as to their value'. In Italy patents had been granted for plants, while in Switzerland the Federal Courts had revoked patents granted for plants (Document UPOV (57) 6: 23–4, authors' translation from French).

The delegations agreed to use the broad term plant novelties (*nouveautés végétales*) to cover the subject-matter for which protection might be sought and described the requirements the plant 'variety' (*variété*) would have to meet – distinctiveness, sufficient homogeneity, and stability from generation to generation on reproduction or whatever form of multiplication. The variety could thus be, for example, a pure line, a clone or possibly an F1 hybrid.

The *breeders' right* was agreed at this first conference, that is the clause providing that other plant breeders could use a protected variety as the starting material for generating new varieties. This immediately put the new form of protection outside the field of patents and the distinction between patents and plant variety protection was explicitly acknowledged (Document UPOV (57) 6: 25–6).

The delegates agreed to appoint a Committee of Experts to draft the UPOV Convention. They met for the first time in April 1958 and appointed Jean Bustarret (later the director of the renowned French Institut National de la Recherche Agronomique) as president. The experts were drawn from Austria, Belgium, Germany (including Klaus Pfanner), Spain, Norway, Denmark, Italy, Sweden, Switzerland, The Netherlands, France, the UK, BIRPI and UNFAO.

Our emphasis on the wording used for the subject-matter of plant variety protection is to demonstrate that the term 'plant variety' did not have a precise meaning but meant no more than 'type of plant' or 'kind of plant'. The Committee of Experts indeed felt that the term 'variety' was unsatisfactory and that the word 'cultivar' should be used instead

(Document UPOV (58) 1: 33). Nonetheless, in the Annex to the minutes of the Committee's meeting, the term plant novelty (*nouveauté végétale*) was used and explained as 'a new variety or cultivar' (*variété ou cultivar nouveau*) (Document UPOV (58) 1: 34).

The Committee of Experts met again in September 1958 with the French delegation including Roger Gajac of the CoE Committee of Experts on patents. The experts could not agree on a satisfactory response as to what categories of plants should be protected. However, they agreed that, in principle, protection could extend to all members of the plant kingdom. It was agreed that the Drafting Committee should meet at the turn of the year. Rough drafts of the types of Article the Convention should contain were appended to the minutes of the meeting. In these Annexes, the terms 'plant novelty' and 'new variety' were used (Document UPOV (58) 2: 38–9).

The Drafting Committee met in January and April 1959 and produced a first preliminary draft (*avant-projet*) of the UPOV Convention (Document UPOV (59) 1). Art. 1(1) referred to the proposed subject-matter as 'plant novelty' (*nouveauté végétale*). Art. 4(1) qualified this to refer to 'plant novelty – new species, variety or cultivar' (*nouveauté végétale – espèce, variété ou cultivar nouveau*). Art. 4(1)(a) required that the novelty must result from a labour of genetic improvement and not merely from the use of a pre-existing plant material. Art. 4(1) also set out the properties required for a variety to be protectable, namely distinguishing characteristics capable of being described (optionally being physiological rather than morphological characteristics), sufficient homogeneity, and stability following successive reproductions or multiplications. Art. 13(1) confirmed that the Convention applied to all kinds and species of plant (*genres et espèces de végétaux*), subject to any relevant exclusions being made. Art. 3 provided the breeders' right mentioned above.

With this draft before them, the Committee of Experts had its third meeting in June/July 1959. The German delegation included Dr Kurt Haertel as well as Klaus Pfanner. The Committee agreed that the (genetic) improvement required by Art. 4(1)(a) of the draft corresponded to 'breeding' or *Züchtung* (Document UPOV (59) 2).

In January 1960 the Group of Legal Experts, including Pfanner, Bustarret, Finniss and Gajac, met to discuss the relationship between the proposed UPOV Convention and the existing Paris Convention. At this meeting the question of a ban on double protection was discussed. The legal experts finally agreed that 'for a same species or group of species, there can be only one form of protection', that is, depending on the choice of the contracting state, a plant variety falling within a particular species could not be protected both as a plant variety and by a patent (Document UPOV (60) 1: 51, authors' translation from French).

The Drafting Committee met again in January 1960 and produced a revised preliminary draft of the UPOV Convention (Document UPOV (60) 2). Following this, Art. 1(1) contained an even longer list of the synonyms for 'plant variety' ('plant novelty – new species, variety, cultivar, line, clone'), Art. 3(2) had a clause confirming that 'variety' was used in this and subsequent Articles 'to designate a defined plant type', and yet the text continued to refer to plant novelties. No exclusion of double protection was yet present.

In February 1960 the Committee of Experts had their fourth and last meeting. They identified certain questions relating to the relationship between plant breeders' rights and patents that needed to be addressed:

> [W]ill it be possible for certain countries to protect plant novelties via patents ... [and] can one allow the co-existence of a patent with the new plant breeders' right? ... The Legal Experts have arrived at the following conclusions ... Against the objections of some amongst them, they have not rejected the possibility of countries which absolutely desire to do so to continue to protect plants via patents while adhering at the same time to the new Convention ... The majority of the experts were of the opinion that for a particular species only one form of protection should be available. (Document UPOV (60) 3: 57, authors' translation from French)

The Committee of Experts also decided that the Drafting Committee should define the word 'variety' in Art. 1.

A final revised draft (the '*projet*') was produced in April 1960 (Document UPOV (60) 4). Art. 1(1) referred to a new plant variety (*variété végétale nouvelle*). In Art. 1(2) it was stated that: 'the word variety in the sense of the present Convention applies to any cultivar, clone, line, stock, hybrid susceptible of being cultivated and meeting the conditions of Article 6(1)(c) and (d)' (Document UPOV (60) 4: 61, authors' translation from French). Art. 4(1) confirmed that the Convention was applicable to all botanical kinds and species of plant (*genres et espèces botaniques de végétaux*). The draft was still silent as to double protection.

In September 1960 the president of the Committee gave his final report (Document UPOV (60) 5). The Committee, considering that the new Convention should leave Member States free to adopt the mode of protection they considered most suitable, had refrained from adopting any provision that would *forbid* the Member States that wished to protect new plants via patents from doing so. The majority of the experts, however, had made it clear that, for varieties of any single botanical species, only one mode of protection should be available in each Member State. The desire to see a ban on double protection had thus been clearly stated during the UPOV negotiations well before the first drafts of the SPC and CEPL were produced for discussion.

The different governments made observations (Document UPOV (61) 1) on the draft and in July 1961 the French government invited them to the second and final Diplomatic Conference, which was to take place from 21 November to 2 December 1961. The Diplomatic Conference was attended by Germany, France, Austria, Denmark, Belgium, The Netherlands, the UK, Italy, Finland, Spain, Sweden and Switzerland, as well as by delegates from the EEC, OECD, UNFAO, BIRPI, AIPPI, ASSINSEL, FIS (the Federation Internationale du Commerce des Semences) and CIOPORA (the Communauté Internationale des Obtenteurs de Plantes Ornamentales de Réproduction Asexuée). After the first plenary session, work proceeded in committee and the minutes of the committees show that the General Committee put four questions to the Legal Committee, which may be rendered as: (1) can the UPOV Convention coexist with the Paris Convention; (2) can the UPOV Convention coexist with other national intellectual property laws, in particular patent laws; (3) where more than one system for intellectual property protection can coexist, can the plant breeder acquire protection under more than one such system or must she select just one to benefit from; and (4) what relationship is the UPOV Convention to have with BIRPI (Document UPOV (61) 9: 119).

The Legal Committee was not of one mind on the first question, with Italy being notably out of line. The majority decision, however, was that the UPOV Convention could coexist with the Paris Convention. The UK delegation felt that it was necessary to establish a separate Convention (UPOV), and the Dutch delegation agreed, 'considering it impossible to protect plant novelties under the legislation relating to patents of invention' (Document UPOV (61) 9: 119, authors' translation from French). The Legal Committee's answer to the second and third questions deserves to be quoted in full:

> According to the French delegation, countries that wish to allow two laws to coexist must be permitted to do so when the scope is not the same. This opinion is, in its mind, *even more important as the domain of patent law has a tendency to spread.* The representative of BIRPI believed that if this coexistence were permitted and if the choice were to be left to the plant breeder, the two laws would conflict. In conclusion, the Committee considered that it was necessary to allow the national legislatures the choice of the system of protection, *but that for one and the same species there could be no cumulative protection.* (Document UPOV (61) 9: 119, authors' translation from French, emphasis added)

At the final plenary session of the Diplomatic Conference on 2 December 1961, the text proposed by the General Committee was adopted with minor modifications and signed. The ban on double protection and the definition of plant variety appeared in Art. 2 UPOV 1961 as follows:

(1) Each member State of the Union may recognise the right of the breeder provided for in this Convention by the grant either of a special title of protection or of a patent. Nevertheless, a member State of the Union whose national law admits of protection under both these forms may provide only one of them for one and the same botanical genus or species.
(2) For the purposes of this Convention, the word 'variety' applies to any cultivar, clone, line, stock or hybrid which is capable of cultivation and which satisfies the provisions of subparagraphs (1)*(c)* and *(d)* of Article 6.

When UPOV was amended in 1978 (UPOV-1978), the definition of variety was deleted. When it was amended again in 1991 (UPOV-1991), a new definition was introduced, the prohibition on double protection was removed, and a farmer's privilege was added – providing that Member States might restrict the breeder's rights in order to permit farmers to use, for propagating purposes and on their own holdings, the product of the harvest that they had obtained by planting the protected variety on their own holdings.

2.5 The parallel drafting of the SPC and the CEPL (with UPOV 1961 in the background)

The preparation of a preliminary draft SPC was agreed by the CoE Committee of Experts at its meeting in November–December 1960. At that meeting the Committee was advised that a working party of the heads of various examining patent offices had met several times in the previous five years to draft a convention to facilitate the making of patent applications in different countries for the same invention. In January 1961 that working party adopted a resolution expressing the wish that the convention on which they had been working, the CEPC, be concluded within the framework of the CoE and that the working party should become a sub-committee of the Committee of Experts (Document EXP/Brev (61) 2 rev: 2).

At their November 1960 meeting the Co-ordinating Committee of the Patents Working Party (PWP) of the EEC had 'concluded that the concept of patentability in the European patent law must be as wide as possible' and 'that European patents should not be granted for inventions relating to new plant varieties' (Document IV/2071/61-E, Section 14: 5–6). Should individual countries wish to grant patents for new plant varieties, that could of course be done via national law but not via the Convention relating to European Patent Law (CEPL). In December 1960 the preparation of a draft of the CEPL was agreed by this Co-ordinating Committee. From this stage until the signature of the SPC in November 1963, the work on the SPC and the CEPL would proceed side by side with several individuals being deeply involved in both.

For the CoE's Committee of Experts' November–December 1960 meeting, a report on the unification of the legislation had been prepared by Guillaume Finniss of the French Patent Office (and of the UPOV Committee of Experts). The Finniss report proposed the exclusion of new varieties of plants:

> It would be inexpedient to try to impose a common solution for the highly controversial question of the patentability of new plant varieties ... It is known, moreover, that the legal protection of new plant varieties is at present under study in another context, following the French Government's initiative in calling a conference in 1957 ... with the object of drafting a convention on the subject. (Document EXP/Brev (60) 7 (1960))

At the November 1960 meeting Finniss also explained in detail the problems of achieving harmonisation in respect of purely agricultural inventions (Document EXP/Brev (60) 7, quoted in Pila 2009: 448 and referred to in Moufang 1991: 13).

A draft of the SPC was produced in March 1961 containing, in Arts. 1 and 2, the precursors to the 'morality' and 'agriculture' exclusions of Art. 53(a) and (b) EPC:

> Inventions, the exploitation of which would be contrary to the public interest (ordre public ou bonnes moeurs), shall not be patentable ...
>
> Nevertheless, the contracting States shall not be bound to provide for the grant of patents, in respect of new plant or animal species [or of processes directly employed to obtain such species]. (Document EXP/Brev B (61) 3: 6)

A first preliminary draft of the CEPL and comments on that draft were presented in March 1961 before the first meeting of the EEC's Patents Working Party (PWP) in April 1961. Art. 12 [Art. 53 EPC][12] read:

> European patents shall not be granted in respect of:
>
> 1. Inventions the exploitation of which [either in the territory of all Contracting States or in the territory of individual Contracting States] would be contrary to morality or 'ordre public'.

[12] Where appropriate, the number of the corresponding Article of the EPC will be included in square brackets.

2. Inventions relating to the production of or a process for producing a new plant variety or a new animal species. This provision shall not apply to processes of a technical nature.
3. [Inventions which must be kept secret for reasons relating to the defence of one of the Contracting States.][13] (Document IV/2071/61-E Section 13: 3)

The accompanying comments confirmed that the tentative draft of Art. 11 [Art. 52 EPC] was based on the 'Reimer proposal', and copies of the Reimer proposal, the Gajac study and a report by Dr Kurt Haertel (the chairman of the PWP) dated July 1960 (Document Haertel, the 'Haertel Study') were considered. Referring to the Haertel Study, it was noted that mention of technical progress might be problematical but that it was: 'apparent from the comments in ... the Reimer Proposal that it is unnecessary to incorporate the concept of "technical progress" in a European patent law since it is self-evident that an invention contributes to technical knowledge and must therefore constitute technical progress' (Document IV/2071/61-E, Section 14: 4).

Regarding the proposed exclusion of 'new plant variety or a new animal species', it was commented that:

> Even if protection of new plant varieties and processes for producing new plants is excluded under European patent law, European patents will still have to be granted for processes which, while being applicable to plants, are of a technical nature, e.g. processes for producing new plants by irradiation of the plants themselves or the seed with isotopes. (Document IV/2071/61-E, Section 14: 5–6)

It was confirmed that these comments applied also to new animal species.

On the definition of industrial applicability, the warning was sounded that: 'it should be noted that the concept of "industrial application" is apparently interpreted differently in the individual countries of the Common Market and that, in particular, purely agricultural processes are not regarded as patentable in all countries' (Document IV/2071/61-E, Section 14: 7).

The EEC's PWP, under the chairmanship of Haertel, met for the first time in April 1961 and also considered the draft SPC produced in the previous month. At this first meeting the Reimer Proposal was considered by Haertel not to give a clear and precise definition. The PWP agreed not to include any exceptions, that is not to include more than the equivalent of Art. 52(1) EPC in Art. 11. They also agreed not to include a definition of technical progress. On Art. 12 [Art. 53 EPC

[13] The square brackets in draft laws under discussion imply that the bracketed text is tentative. Paragraph 3 was later deleted.

1973], the Co-ordinating Committee had given instructions that only inventions contrary to morality or 'ordre public' should be excluded. However, Haertel proposed that 'inventions relating to new plant or animal varieties be excluded as well'. After some discussion the PWP agreed to set 'ordre public' aside and consider: whether it was necessary to provide such exceptions; what the definition of morality should be; whether there was a European definition of morality; whether national definitions of morality should be applied; and whether something should be treated as unpatentable if it was contrary to morality in only one state (Document IV/2767/61-E: 6).

The following day, the PWP agreed that inventions that were contrary to morality should be unpatentable. Nonetheless:

> The Working Party recognised that there was no European definition of morality. The German delegation and the Chairman preferred to refer to national concepts. But the majority felt that if such a stance were taken, it would give too great a prominence to national concepts in the European Convention. The Working Party unanimously thought that interpretation of the concept of morality should be a matter for the European institutions. It was therefore enough to mention the concept of morality in Article 12, paragraph 1, without giving further details.
>
> The Chairman made two reservations. First he pointed out that the European Office was liable to interpret the concept of morality in a manner at variance with a national concept, a point on which the States were particularly sensitive. Secondly, the Chairman felt that when examining the problem of revocation, the problem of revocation of a European patent in one State on the grounds that the patent was contrary to morality there would have to be examined in greater depth ... As regards 'ordre public', the Working Party investigated in what States that concept existed and how it was interpreted. It found that in the Netherlands the concept was particularly wide and the exclusion applied to an invention which merely contravened a single law. In all other States, apart from Germany, the 'ordre public' requirement existed but had no practical significance ... Two solutions were put forward:
>
> (1) making no mention of 'ordre public' in the European Convention, or
> (2) mentioning 'ordre public' but qualifying it with a rider that the mere fact that an invention was contrary to a national law was not sufficient for 'ordre public' to be invoked. (Document IV/2767/61-E: 7–8)

The exclusion of '[i]nventions relating to the production of or a process for producing a new plant variety or a new animal species' was approved unanimously. However, the exclusion of 'processes of a technical nature for producing new vegetable or animal species' was delayed to allow further discussion. One delegate, Klaus Pfanner, 'stated however that a distinction had to be drawn between production by biological means and production involving external technical factors' (Document

IV/2767/61-E: 8). As discussed above, Pfanner had been a representative for Germany during the UPOV negotiations.

As a result of this first meeting of the PWP, the wording of Art. 12 [Art. 53 EPC 1973] was revised to:

> European patents shall not be granted in respect of:
>
> 1. *1st variant:*
>   inventions the exploitation of which would be contrary to morality;
>   *2nd variant:*
>   inventions the exploitation of which would be contrary: (a) to morality, (b) [to the fundamental principles of] 'ordre public': the mere fact that a legal provision prohibits the exploitation of an invention shall not be decisive for the application of this Article.
> 2. new plant varieties or new animal species and purely biological processes for producing them. (Document IV/2498/1/61-E: 3)

The CoE Committee of Experts then met in May 1961, considered the draft SPC text proposed in March 1961 and the comments of the EEC's PWP from April 1961, and agreed some changes to the 'morality' and 'agriculture' exclusion clauses, which then came to read:

> There shall be no obligation to grant patents for inventions, the exploitation of which would be contrary to 'ordre public' or morality …
>
> Nevertheless, the Contracting States shall not be bound to provide for the grant of patents, in respect of new plant or animal species or of purely biological, horticultural or agricultural (agronomic) processes. (Document EXP/Brev (61) 2 rev: 26)

Regarding the words 'ordre public', the CoE Committee of Experts commented that: 'For the English text, [it had] decided to insert the French words "ordre public", those words to be taken in a narrow sense' (Document EXP/Brev (61) 2 rev: 10). More interestingly, it was stated in relation to Art. 1 of the draft SPC, which provided that 'patents shall be granted for any new inventions susceptible of industrial application', that the notion of 'invention' itself served to exclude certain subject-matter: 'It was understood that scientific laws and theories, instructions to the human brain (such as accounting systems or rules of games), creations of form and the mere disclosure of a pre-existing fact (discovery) do not fall under the notion of "invention"' (Document EXP/Brev (61) 2 rev: 10).

Art. 2 of the draft SPC from March 1961 was revised: 'The last phrase of the second paragraph ("purely biological, horticultural or agricultural processes") [being] added to meet the observations of certain experts' (Document EXP/Brev (61) 2 rev: 10–11).

In November 1961 the sub-committee of the CoE Committee of Experts proposed a draft of the CEPC (Document EXP/Brev II (61) 5).

However, later that month at the meeting of the Committee of Experts itself, Haertel:

> speaking as Chairman of the Common Market Working Party rather than as a German expert, said that the Convention under consideration by that Working Party [i.e. the CEPL] would be open to accession by other States [i.e. it would not be restricted to members of the EEC]; it had the same objectives as the draft [CEPC] before the Committee of Experts, but was much more comprehensive. (Document EXP/Brev (61) 8: 12)

Some of the experts wanted to press ahead with the CEPC; others felt that in view of the CEPL it was better to postpone any consideration of the CEPC. The latter group won out and the CEPC disappears from our story.

At this same November 1961 meeting the wording of Arts. 1 and 2 of the draft SPC was again revised. As concerns the exclusions from patentability, the 'morality' clause in Art. 1 was essentially unchanged. However, despite the suggestion from the Scandinavian delegations that the second part of Art. 2, or at least the final part referring to biological processes, be deleted (Document EXP/Brev (61) 5, referred to by Moufang 1991: 16), the 'agriculture' clause of Art. 2 was instead amended to become Art. 2(2) and to read: 'Nevertheless, the Contracting States shall not be bound to provide for the grant of patents in respect of plant or animal varieties or of essentially biological processes for the production of plants or animals' (Document EXP/Brev (61) 8: 16).

Thus, while commenting that the 'allusion to "plant or animal varieties" remains much as it was' (Document EXP/Brev (61) 8: 4), the Committee had nonetheless settled on this term 'plant or animal varieties', presumably to avoid confusion by reflecting the language of the UPOV Convention settled that month. However, as Crespi (1992: 169–70) points out, even those working on plant breeders' rights 'especially in the context of UPOV, have not found it necessary in the past to fix upon a rigid definition of the term'.

On the question of 'processes for the production of plants or animals', the narrow term 'purely' was replaced by the broader term 'essentially', with the Committee commenting that:

> The processes for 'the production of plants or animals' referred to in the new text include those which may produce *known* varieties as well as those which may produce *new* ones, it being understood that only new varieties can eventually qualify for protection *in themselves*. Selection or hybridisation of existing varieties may be mentioned as examples of such processes (in the vegetable kingdom). The new text specifies that the processes which may be ineligible for patents are *essentially* (and no longer *purely*) biological. It was evident that the exclusion should be extended to cover processes which were fundamentally of

this type even if, as a *secondary* feature, 'technical' devices were involved (use of a particular type of instrument in a grafting process, or of a special greenhouse in growing a plant), it being understood that such technical devices may perfectly well be patented themselves, but not the biological process in which they are used. (Document EXP/Brev (61) 8: 5, emphasis in original)

This clearly demonstrates that the exclusion of 'essentially biological processes' in Art. 53(b) EPC relates to processes for the production of known types of plants and animals as well as of new types, and was confirmed in the CoE Council of Ministers report in August 1962 in essentially the same terms (Document CM (62) 160: 4).

In Spring 1962 AIPPI submitted comments on the draft SPC, asking for clarification on the question of the patentability of microbiological processes (Document EXP/Brev (62) 1, referred to in Moufang 1991: 17). This was supported by the British, Swedish and Swiss delegations.

At the fifth meeting of the EEC's PWP in April 1962, the PWP decided to endeavour, for Arts. 11 and 12, to follow closely the wording of the draft Arts. 1 and 2 SPC. For Art. 12(2) it was decided to adopt the wording of draft Art. 2(2) SPC. However, following a proposal from the French delegation, a reference to publication was inserted into Art. 12(2) [Art. 53(a) EPC] (Document 3076/IV/62, Section 4: 137). This amendment was later challenged unsuccessfully by the Swiss delegation, but was removed some thirty-eight years later in the revision of the EPC that produced EPC 2000.

The draft CEPL was in a form ready for publication in May 1962. Art. 12 [Art. 53 EPC 1973] had become Art. 10 and had been brought into line with the draft of Art. 2 SPC to read:

European patents shall not be granted in respect of:

(a) inventions the publication or exploitation of which would be contrary to morality *or* to the fundamental principles of 'ordre public', *provided that this Article shall not apply merely because the exploitation of the invention is prohibited*;
(b) plant or animal varieties or *essentially* biological processes for the production of *plants or animals.* (Document 4488/IV/62-E, emphasis in original)

Meanwhile, Art. 9 [Art. 52(1) EPC] contained no list of exclusions and read: 'European patents shall be granted for any inventions which are susceptible of industrial application, which are new and which involve an inventive step' (Document 4488/IV/62-E).

At the sixth meeting of the EEC's PWP in June 1962, the question of putting an exemption for microorganisms into the exclusion of

Art. 10(b) (i.e. Art. 53(b) EPC) was discussed, but was not acted on (Document 6551/IV/62-E: 7–8).

The CoE Committee of Experts met in July 1962, considering what was, with minor unsubstantial differences, the final text of the exclusion of Art. 2 SPC. Following AIPPI's comments, Art. 2(b) included an exemption for microbiological processes and their products, and, bringing the text into line with the draft CEPL, Art. 2(a) now referred to 'publication' as well as 'exploitation':

> The Contracting States shall not be bound to provide for the grant of patents in respect of
>
> (a) inventions the publication or exploitation of which would be contrary to 'ordre public' or morality, the mere prohibition of the exploitation of the invention not making it so contrary.
> (b) plant or animal varieties or essentially biological processes for the production of plants or animals; this provision does not apply to micro-biological processes or the products thereof. (Document CM (62) 160: 11)

At the tenth meeting of the EEC's PWP in September 1963, the majority agreed to leave Art. 9 [Art. 52(1) EPC] specifying just the requirements of novelty, inventive step and industrial application: 'Mr *Pfanner* made the point that it would be inappropriate to change this article which had influenced the formulation of the Strasbourg draft at a time when the latter draft was soon to be signed.' The wording was to be brought into line with the SPC draft and a proposal to introduce the microorganism exemption into Art. 10(b) [Art. 53(b) EPC] was agreed (Document 9081/IV/63-E-Final, Section 11: 64–5, emphasis in original).

The SPC was considered by the meeting of the Ministers' Deputies in October 1963 and signed in November 1963.

Work on the CEPL continued. At the fourteenth meeting of the EEC's PWP in June 1964, the chairman noted that: '[the German and Dutch] delegations had been asked to draw up a note clarifying Article 9 of the Convention with a list of what would not be considered inventions. It would specify, in particular, that methods of medical treatment were excluded from patentability.' Although not directly pertinent to exclusions from patentability, an exclusion from infringement was discussed and:

> the Working Party decided to provide that prescriptions prepared by a pharmacist on a doctor's instructions would not constitute infringement if the pharmacist's preparation was the same as a medicament protected by a patent. … The Working Party thought that such a provision could be included in the

Convention. It felt that while its practical scope was quite small, its psychological impact was considerable. Such a provision recognised the principle of freedom to exercise the medical profession. (Document 6498/IV/64-E, Section 3: 13)

The question of providing patent protection for 'second indications', that is inventions relating to the second or further medical use of a material already known to have a medical use, was discussed with no outcome (Document 6498/IV/64-E-Final, Section 3: 14–15).

In October 1964, for the fifteenth meeting of the PWP, the German and Dutch delegations had submitted their proposal (Document 9663/IV/64) for a list of subject-matter that should not be considered eligible for patenting. This was essentially an extended version of the Reimer proposal. The PWP had to consider whether to insert the listing into Art. 9 [Art. 52 EPC] or Art. 10 [Art. 53 EPC]. The listing included methods of therapy and it was considered that although their inclusion would have the same effect irrespective of which Article was used as the vehicle, Art. 9 should be used since Art. 10 corresponded exactly to Art. 2 SPC. The inclusion of diagnostic methods was also agreed (Document 11821/IV/64-E, Section 8: 3–4).

In January 1965 the final revised draft of the CEPL was produced with Art. 9 and Art. 10 [Art. 52 and 53 EPC 1973] as follows:

Article 9

(1) European patents shall be granted for inventions which are new, which involve an inventive step and which are susceptible of industrial application.
(2) The following in particular shall not be regarded as inventions within the meaning of paragraph 1:
    (a) scientific knowledge and theories as such;
    (b) mere discovery of substances occurring in nature;
    (c) purely aesthetic creations;
    (d) financial or accounting systems, rules for playing games or other systems, insofar as they are of a purely abstract nature;
    (e) methods of therapy, including diagnostic methods.

Article 10

European patents shall not be granted in respect of:

(a) inventions the publication or exploitation of which would be contrary to 'ordre public' or morality, provided that the exploitation shall not be deemed to be so contrary merely because it is prohibited by laws or regulations in some or all of the Contracting States;
(b) plant or animal varieties or essentially biological processes for the production of plants or animals; this provision does not apply to microbiological processes or the products thereof. (Document 2335/IV/65-E)

There the question of a unified European law on the grant of patents rested until 1969.

2.6 The 1960s pause and the arrival of the PCT

The UK had applied to join the EEC in 1961 and was rebuffed by France in 1963. Negotiations continued, but France's President Charles de Gaulle again indicated that he would veto the UK's entry in November 1967. De Gaulle resigned in April 1969. A limitation on the national ability to define what was or was not patentable, when a major European competitor was not so limited, would clearly have been contrary to the national interests of Germany and France (especially given Germany's history of manipulating patent law to its advantage – see Dutfield 2009), and it is accordingly of little surprise that further progress on harmonisation in the European Community stalled.

With development of a unified European patent law on hold, the forum for international harmonisation shifted in 1966 to BIRPI.[14] The US delegation made a proposal to the International (Paris) Union for the Protection of Industrial Property and in September 1966 the Executive Committee of that Union recommended BIRPI (now WIPO) to study possible solutions for reducing duplication of effort by applicants and national patent offices. A draft Patent Cooperation Treaty was produced in May 1967 (Document PCT/I/3) and a revised draft was produced in July 1968 (Document PCT/III/5).

The PCT was and is a system whereby a single patent application may potentially become a national or regional patent application in any of the Contracting States. The first substantive step in the handling of a PCT application is an 'International Search' conducted by one of many national or regional patent offices. At the time the PCT was signed, and indeed at the time it came into force, the relevant patent offices did not all have experience in searching inventions in all technological fields.

Thus, importantly, draft Rule 39.1 PCT set out the subject-matter that the international searching authorities would not have to search. This 1969 draft, which was adopted with little change, listed most of the exclusions from Arts. 9 and 10 CEPL, but also included 'mere presentations of information' and 'computer programs to the extent that the International Searching Authority is not equipped to search prior art concerning such programs' (Document PCT/DC/5).

[14] In 1893 the secretariats of the Paris Union and the Bern Union were joined in BIRPI. In April 1970 WIPO incorporated BIRPI and its functions.

2.7 The process restarts

From May 1969 to June 1972 a series of Intergovernmental Conferences (IGCs) were arranged by European countries to work towards a common system for the grant of patents (the 'Luxembourg Conferences'). At the first IGC a memorandum was submitted confirming that the six Member States of the EEC had studied the possibility of setting up such a system and concluded that two conventions were required, one open to all European countries and the other covering the EEC, that is the EPC and the CPC (Document BR/2/69). The CEPL, the SPC and the 1968 draft of the PCT were considered.

The drafting of the substantive parts of the EPC was to be the work of Working Party I (WP-I), which held its inaugural meeting in May 1969 chaired by Haertel. WP-I began with a version of Art. 9(2) [Art. 52(2) EPC 1973], which read:

(2) Inventions within the meaning of paragraph 1 shall in particular exclude:
- (a) scientific deductions and theories as such;
- (b) the mere discovery of materials occurring in nature;
- (c) purely aesthetic creations;
- (d) methods of financing and book-keeping, the rules of games and other systems, in so far as they are of a purely intellectual nature;
- (e) methods of treatments, including methods of diagnosis.

At the first meeting of WP-I in July 1969, the UK and Swedish delegations suggested that the list of subject-matter that should not be deemed to be inventions should be placed in the EPC Rules rather than in Art. 9 [Art. 52 EPC 1973]. WP-I disagreed, arguing that the list 'was a substantial provision fixing the conditions for the grant of patents'. Regarding the contents of the list, WP-I incorrectly commented that it was based on draft PCT Rule 39. This was incorrect since, to a large extent, the list corresponded to Art. 9(2) CEPL 1965. The exclusion of presentations of information and computer programs had not been suggested at this stage. The draft of Art. 10 [Art. 53 EPC 1973] was based on Art. 2 SPC (Document BR/7/69: 9–10).

Following the first meeting of WP-I, Art. 9(2) [Art. 52(2) EPC 1973] was amended to include methods of surgery and to make minor amendments to sub-paragraphs (a) and (d):

- (a) scientific and mathematical theories as such; ...
- (d) commercial, financial or book-keeping methods, the rules of playing games and other systems, in so far as they are of a purely intellectual nature;
- (e) therapeutic or surgical methods for treatment of the human or animal body, and diagnostic methods. (Document BR/6/69)

Although the July 1969 text of Rule 39.1 PCT included computer programs and presentations of information, the text of Art. 9(2) [Art. 52(2) EPC 1973] remained essentially unchanged until January 1971, that is well after the PCT rule was proposed and indeed after the PCT had been finalised in June 1970.

The second IGC in January 1970 considered the case of computer programs, which had been made unpatentable in the revised French patent law of 1968, but considered that 'the present state of developments did not allow it to be determined whether computer programmes could be the subject of a patent' (Document BR/26/70: 7).

WP-I returned to the list of exclusions in Art. 9(2) [Art. 52(2) EPC 1973] in its seventh meeting in January 1971, and generally followed the German delegation's suggestion to align the text with the PCT rule (e.g. deleting 'as such' from sub-paragraph (a)), but decided to leave the treatment of animals, computer programs and presentations of information for further discussion (Document BR/94/71: 10). By the end of January 1971 the exclusions in Art. 9(2) [Art. 52(2) EPC 1973] thus came to read:

(a) scientific and mathematical theories;
(b) the mere discovery of materials occurring in nature;
(c) purely aesthetic creations;
(d) schemes, rules or methods of doing business, performing purely mental acts or playing games;
(e) methods for treatment of the human [or animal] body by surgery or therapy, as well as diagnostic methods;
(f) [mere presentations of information;]
(g) [computer programmes.] (Document BR/88/71)

At the fourth IGC in April 1971 it was agreed that WP-I should re-examine Art. 9(2), in particular the bracketed provisions, in view of the comments made by interested parties. It was also asked to consider whether Art. 10(b) [Art. 53(b) EPC] was compatible with the nature of plant and animal varieties as non-inventions (Document BR/125/71).

WP-I addressed these points at its ninth meeting in October 1971, agreeing to the Swiss proposal to change 'mathematical theories' to 'mathematical methods', to the deletion of the brackets around 'animals' in sub-paragraph (e), and to the deletion of the brackets around sub-paragraphs (f) and (g). It rejected proposals to exempt from sub-paragraph (b) 'materials isolated and defined for the first time', to exempt from sub-paragraph (e) new therapeutic applications of known substances and processes and laboratory equipment used for diagnosis, and to delete 'animals' from sub-paragraph (e). The first of these rejections is notable in view of the Rules introduced into the EPC September 1999 following the adoption of the EBD. Regarding processes and laboratory equipment, it was considered that processes would be excluded insofar as they were used by doctors and that the equipment was in any event not excluded. On the subject of computer programs, the UK delegation had argued that they should not be patentable and that a computer program 'was merely the mathematical application of a logical series of steps in a process which was no different from a mathematical method excluded under [sub-paragraph] (a). However some form of protection might be desirable for computer programmes but this, which might be considered by WIPO, called for some new form and not under existing patent laws'. The UK's definition was not adopted, the decision being to leave this to the EPO and the national courts. It was considered that some protection might be given to computer programs, but *not* patent protection (Document BR/135/71: 47–50).

Yet again the UK's proposal to delete Art. 9(2) [Art. 52(2) and (4) EPC 1973] and to place the exclusions in the Rules (where they could be altered on the basis of a simple majority in the EPO's Administrative Council) was rejected on the basis that 'amendments to the rules [*sic*] on patentability were of such importance that it was undesirable to allow the provisions to be amended by the [EPO's] Administrative Council. The development of patent law should be left to the courts and *the question of amendment should be left to revision by a Diplomatic Conference*' (Document BR/135/71: 51, emphasis added). This should later have given the Boards of Appeal clear guidance that the EPC Rules should not be used to construe the exclusions narrowly and that judicial sleight of hand should not be used to emasculate the exclusions.

On the question whether Art. 10(b) [Art. 53(b) EPC] was incompatible with UPOV, it was agreed that it was not. Moreover, the UK delegation's suggestion to delete 'essentially biological processes' from this exclusion was rejected.

As a result, Art. 10 was left unchanged and sub-paragraphs (a) and (d) to (g) of Art. 9(2) [Art. 52(2) and (4) EPC 1973] were revised to read:

(a) scientific theories and mathematical methods; ...
(d) schemes, rules or methods of doing business, performing purely mental acts or playing games;
(e) methods for treatment of the human or animal body by surgery or therapy, as well as diagnostic methods;
(f) mere presentations of information;
(g) computer programmes. (Document BR/139/71)

The exclusions were considered again by the fifth IGC in January/February 1972, where yet again it was necessary to reject proposals to delete the exclusions of Art. 9(2) [Art. 52(2) and (4) EPC 1973] or to shift them into the Rules. The IGC rejected these proposals 'since it considered it necessary, from the entry into force of the system, to create the greatest possible legal certainty in this field' (Document BR/168/72: 9). Likewise it stated that '[s]ubject to final drafting, paragraph 2 will thus remain in the Convention, and it may only be amended by means of a revision of the Convention'. Certain of the delegations had thought it '*was inappropriate to insert a fundamental subject such as that of patentability in the Implementing Regulations which were subordinate to the Convention*' (Document BR/168/72: 12, emphasis added). As we noted earlier, one would have thought that such comments would have made it clear to the EPO Examiners and Appeal Boards that they should not ignore or interpret away the exclusions set down in the Articles of the EPC and to the members of the Administrative Council that they should not amend the EPC Rules so as to restrict the scope of the exclusions. Sadly, this was not sufficiently clear, as will be explained in this book.

The IGC also rejected a suggestion to make the list of exclusions in Art. 9(2) exhaustive 'so as to retain the flexibility necessary to the system' (Document BR/168/72: 9). The wording of Art. 9(2), however, was not fully to the IGC's satisfaction and WP-I was instructed to review several points: the Yugoslav delegation had asked that scientific discoveries be added to the exclusions of sub-paragraph (a); the possibility of combining sub-paragraphs (a), (d), (f) and (g) was to be evaluated; the retention of 'animals' in sub-paragraph (e) was to be pondered over; the manner of protecting new medical indications for drugs was to be investigated; the exclusion of only 'physical' methods of therapy was of concern; and just what might be an excluded method of diagnosis came to the surface. This last issue is of interest since the act of diagnosis, unless performed by a computer, is a mental act, and the wording of an exclusion of methods of diagnosis might readily allow it to be side-stepped. The exclusions of presentations of information and of computer programs were generally accepted but it would be inaccurate to say that the exclusion of computer programs was trouble-free and unanimously approved.

In their eleventh meeting, in February/March 1972, WP-I addressed these issues, agreeing to revise sub-paragraph (a) to exclude scientific discoveries 'as such' (a Swiss proposal) and to delete sub-paragraph (b). Here it must be remembered that the words 'as such' have immense importance to the exclusions of Art. 52(2) EPC. The relocation of the exclusion of computer programs to sub-paragraph (d) was considered, with the UK delegation being concerned that this might allow such programs to 'be able to obtain patent protection by indirect means and that, broadly speaking, the free development of precedents – which is of paramount importance in this still very uncertain field – would be hindered'. Most of WP-I agreed with the relocation as the inclusion would 'make for the exclusion of computer programs as such, while allowing precedents to be used to assess the patentability of any related inventions'. The majority were concerned that a sub-paragraph devoted *only* to computer programs might be interpreted as excluding inventions *related to* a program. WP-I agreed to add 'the use of computers' to the exclusions of sub-paragraph (d). Despite the assertion that this would change little, happily the proposal was not followed (Document BR/177/72).

On the question of the new therapeutic use of a known substance, there were concerns as to how this could be covered: 'It was recalled that, at least in practice, it was not open to the proprietor of such a patent to institute legal proceedings against a person infringing the patent, namely a doctor or possibly a pharmacist'. Patent protection via purpose-limited product claims was considered by WP-I to be the more satisfactory route and sub-paragraph (e) was amended following proposals by the French delegation. The applicability of the medical treatments exclusion to animals was confirmed, and the French proposal to restrict the excluded diagnostic methods to those 'applied to the human or animal body' was accepted. WP-I agreed that the medical treatments exclusion did not cover psychological procedures or autopsies, and that diagnostic apparatus would in principle be patentable. The Dutch delegation had suggested that surgery for destructive purposes (e.g. sterilisation of insects) should explicitly not be excluded. WP-I agreed that such treatments should not be excluded but thought that no amendment was needed (Document BR/177/72: 4–6).

As of May 1972, the list of non-inventions read as follows:

(a) scientific theories, discoveries and mathematical methods as such;
(b) purely aesthetic creations;
(c) schemes, rules and methods for performing purely mental acts, playing games or doing business, and programs for computers;
(d) methods for treatment of the human [or animal] body by surgery or therapy and diagnostic methods practised on the human [or animal] body; this provision shall not apply to inventions having as their subject-matter substances or compounds, whether or not known, which are used for the first time for the purposes of practising such methods;
(e) mere presentations of information. (Document BR/199/72: 56)

At this stage, the 'as such' qualification of the exclusions, which occurs in Art. 52(3) EPC, began to be a topic of concern. At the third meeting of the Co-ordinating Committee in June 1972, the Swiss delegation argued that any mathematical methods and their use should be considered as 'intellectual activities and therefore excluded from patentability'. The Committee agreed and considered that the words 'as such' in sub-paragraph (a) should apply to discoveries only (Document BR/218/72: 4).

The sixth and last IGC took place later in June 1972. The endgame would lie in the Munich Diplomatic Conference of September/October 1973. The Swiss had been concerned that 'as such' in sub-paragraph (a) should apply only to discoveries, and the importance of this term was coming to centre stage. The IGC agreed. The Swiss felt that prophylactic treatments should be mentioned explicitly – the IGC disagreed. The Dutch and Austrian delegations were concerned about the wording of the exclusion as applied to the treatment of animals. The IGC disagreed, holding that 'the intention behind this text was merely to exclude from patentability all therapeutic treatments practiced on animals, the aim of this provision being to exclude from patentability treatments falling within the meaning of treatments intended to cure or alleviate the suffering of animals' (Document BR/219/72: 8–11).

The question of patent cover for compounds found to have a use as a drug or another such use was becoming more pressing. The IGC:

> noted that extending the scope of [the first medical use provision in Art. 54 EPC] beyond instances of use for the first time in an absolute sense comprised a modification of the compromise proposal ... [and indeed] it did not appear justified to exonerate for the purposes of patentability use for the first time of a substance or composition whether or not known, from the conditions of patentability referred to in [Art. 52(1) EPC]. (Document BR/219/72: 11)

Patent cover for known substances found to have (different) medical uses was therefore not yet settled.

2.8 The home straight – the Munich Diplomatic Conference of September/October 1973

In December 1972 the draft of the EPC that would be considered at the Munich Conference was ready. The exclusions, now in Arts. 50 and 51 [Arts. 52 and 53 EPC 1973] were listed as:

(a) discoveries as such, scientific theories and mathematical methods;
(b) purely aesthetic creations;
(c) schemes, rules and methods for performing purely mental acts, playing games or doing business, and programs for computers;

(d) methods for treatment of the human or animal body by surgery or therapy and diagnostic methods practised on the human or animal body;
(e) mere presentations of information.

...

(a) inventions the publication or exploitation of which would be contrary to 'ordre public' or morality, provided that the exploitation shall not be deemed to be so contrary merely because it is prohibited by law or regulation in some or all of the Contracting States;
(b) plant or animal varieties or essentially biological processes for the production of plants or animals; this provision does not apply to microbiological processes or the products thereof. (Document M/1)

The 'as such' provision of Art. 52(3) EPC had yet to appear, and the patent-eligibility of substances found for the *first* time to have medical utility was now provided for by a special exemption to the definition of novelty in Art. 52(5) [Art. 54(5) EPC 1973].

In the months before the conference, delegations made further submissions and suggestions for amendment. In March 1973 the UK delegation wished it understood that 'therapy' was 'concerned with the treatment of illness or disease and does not extend, in the case of animals, to treatments effected with a view e.g. to increasing the quantity or quality of the ultimate product' and generally expressed concern with the introduction of purpose-limited product claims (Document M/10: 42–43). Under UK patent practice, a purpose limitation for a product had simply been interpreted as meaning that the product was *suitable for* the specified purpose and not as meaning it required an intention that it be used for that purpose, that is requiring the state of mind of a potential infringer to be relevant to the question of whether infringement had occurred.

The German delegation, also in March 1973, made particularly crucial proposals to limit the effect of the exclusion of things not considered to be inventions, by the inclusion of a separate paragraph applying the 'as such' qualification to *all* such exclusions and to remove medical methods into a separate paragraph *not* qualified by the 'as such' provision. Since the very first proposal that medical methods should be excluded, it had been appreciated that their placement in a clause of their own or with the exclusions of Art. 53 EPC 1973 had been considered to be equivalent. Qualifying words such as 'purely', 'merely' and 'as such' had *never* been used in relation to the medical methods exclusion. Indeed, twenty-seven years later the medical methods exclusion would eventually find its way into Art. 53(c) EPC.

In 1973, however, the legal fiction that medical methods were not susceptible of industrial application was the German delegation's preferred route: 'Pursuant to paragraph 2(a), discoveries – as such – are not regarded as inventions within the meaning of paragraph 1. A similar limitation is also contained in (e) (mere presentations of information). This could lead to the erroneous conclusion that a broad interpretation should be given to items not limited in this way in paragraph 2' (Document M/11: 64).

This was not a recommendation that the exclusions be construed narrowly. It was simply a suggestion that an unnecessarily broad construction of an exclusion without the qualification might be the unintended result. The German delegation continued with their recommendation:

> The limitation should therefore be set forth in a general manner in a separate paragraph. In addition it might be considered illogical to include (d) [i.e. the medical methods] in the list since it [(d)] deals with inventions proper, according to the normal use of the term, which are traditionally excluded from patentability because they are not susceptible of industrial application. The items covered in paragraph 2(d) should therefore be the subject of a separate provision in a separate paragraph. (Document M/11: 64)

In June 1973 the Dutch delegation indicated that the reassurance that substances and compositions are not excluded from patentability, simply because medical methods using them were, should extend to apparatus too. It also sought clarification that the exemption in the definition of novelty, permitting purpose-limited product protection, should be limited to the first medical use. This was reiterated in September 1973 (Documents M/32 and M/52/I/II/III).

The Conference took place in September and October 1973, with the final text of EPC 1973 being agreed after much deliberation. In Main Committee I the chairman (Haertel) commented on the exclusion of programs for computers saying that, at the sixth IGC in June 1972, the attempt to define programs had been in vain and that '[t]he European Patent Office would simply have to be relied upon subsequently to interpret this expression unequivocally' (Document M/PR/I: 28).

Regarding the medical methods exclusion, Main Committee I 'endorsed the United Kingdom delegation's interpretation of the text (see M/10 ...) whereby "treatment of the animal body by therapy" means the treatment of illness or disease and not, for example, treatment effected with a view to increasing the quality or quantity of the production of an animal product' (Document M/PR/I: 28). The German delegation had suggested that the medical methods be placed in a separate exclusion as actual inventions for which only the industrial application was lacking. Main Committee I agreed to put this to the Drafting Committee (Document M/PR/I: 28). The

Dutch delegation wanted it to be made clear that medical instruments should not be excluded – Main Committee I agreed to put this to the Drafting Committee, but the German delegation thought it unnecessary (Document M/PR/I: 28).

Various parties, in particular the UK and Ireland, yet again proposed putting the Art. 50(2) [Art. 52(2) and (4) EPC 1973] exclusions into the EPC Rules. The German delegation '*thought it was inadmissible, as a matter of principle, for the question of the patentability of such subject-matter or activities to be left to the Administrative Council to decide*'. This position was supported by Yugoslavia, Sweden and Portugal. The French delegation pointed out that 'Article 50 [Art. 52 EPC] was a fundamental Article of the Convention. The provisions governing patentability should not be left to the Administrative Council; the latter *ought not to be able, irrespective of the legal and technical means employed, to amend the individual provisions on its own responsibility*.' The Swiss delegation agreed that the provisions should not be moved and the UK delegation renounced the idea (Document M/PR/I: 28, emphasis added).

On a proposal from the German delegation (Document M/11: 64), Main Committee I agreed to specify in paragraph 3 that 'the patentability of the subject-matter and activities listed in paragraph 2 was excluded only to the extent to which an application or patent related to the subject-matter or activities as such' (Document M/PR/I: 29).

Regarding the Swiss suggestion (Document M/54/I/II/III: 7) that in Art. 51(a) [Art. 53(a) EPC 1973] the reference to 'publication' be deleted, the chairman appeared to be clearly unhappy and the Swiss delegation backed down (Document M/PR/I: 29). The suggestion was later revived and followed in the 2000 revision of the EPC.

On the special provision for purpose-limited product claims for substances found for the first time to have medical use, the Dutch delegation wanted the wording improved. 'It said that on no account did it wish, with its proposal [Document M/32], to break away from the principle that only the first application in respect of the use of a known substance or composition in a method for treatment of a human or animal body by surgery or therapy is patentable, and not the second and subsequent applications'. Main Committee I referred this to the Drafting Committee (Document M/PR/I: 29). The Yugoslav delegation thought the wording unclear and the chairman clarified that:

> [T]he aim … was to make clear that a known substance (or a known composition) which, since it formed part of the state of the art, was no longer patentable, nevertheless could be patented for the first use in a method for treatment of the human or animal body by surgery or therapy; however, a further patent

could not be granted if a second possible use were found for the same substance, irrespective of whether the human or animal body was to be treated with it ... The Chairman noted that his views were shared by the Governmental delegations. (Document M/PR/I: 29)

UNICE (Union des Industries des pays de la Communauté européenne) suggested that a first human use would not prevent a first animal use and vice versa, but the chairman (Haertel) pointed out that Main Committee I did not want to endorse that position (Document M/PR/I: 29). Rapporteur Paul Braendli (later the second president of the EPO) reported that Main Committee I confirmed that the Art. 50(2) [Art. 52(2) EPC] exclusions were basic principles of the Convention and that only the *first* medical use was patentable by virtue of Art. 52(5) [Art. 54(5) EPC 1973] (Document M/Annex I: 184).

The exemption to the provisions relating to novelty that allowed the purpose-limited product protection of substances found for the first time to have a medical use was contained in Art. 54(5) EPC 1973.

In parallel with the EPC, work had continued on a patent convention covering the European Union. This, the CPC, was signed in 1975 and applies the same criteria for patentability as the EPC. However, as of December 2011 the CPC has yet to come into force.

The EPC and the PCT came into effect in July 1978 and the national laws of the EPC Contracting States were brought substantially into line with the EPC.

2.9 Discontent sets in

In the early years of the operation of the EPO, there were numerous amendments to the EPC Rules but none to the Articles. However, even in those early years it became clear that certain of the exclusions to patentability were hindering the possibilities for patenting subject-matter in certain industries, in particular computing, pharmaceuticals and agrochemicals.

From February 1980 to June 1985 attempts were made, unsuccessfully, to strengthen patent protection globally by amendment of the Paris Convention, which, like the PCT, is administered by WIPO (Sell 1998: 107–40). In October 1983 the European Commission indicated that the legal situation within the EU concerning biotechnology suffered from deficiencies and discrepancies in statute law and a general shortage of case law, and recommended that it should work out proposals for a European approach to intellectual property rights in this field (Document COM(83) 672 final/2: Annex). In June 1985 the European

Commission announced its intention of proposing measures concerning patent protection of biotechnological inventions (Document COM(85) 310: 37).

In March 1986 the 'Intellectual Property Committee' was founded by Pfizer, IBM and eleven others: Merck, General Electric, DuPont, Warner Communications, Hewlett-Packard, Bristol-Myers, FMC, General Motors, Johnson and Johnson, Monsanto and Rockwell International. This organisation was to play a key role in the negotiation of TRIPS in the context of the Uruguay round of the General Agreement on Tariffs and Trade (GATT), which began in September 1986 and which, from the outset, was intended to address the question of intellectual property rights. In June 1988 the basic framework for agreement between Japan, the USA and the European Union on intellectual property rights had become clear.

In October 1988 the European Commission put forward its proposal for the EBD (Document COM(88) 496 final SYN 159). In the document accompanying this first draft, it was stated that:

> The provisions of the Directive systematically *adapt* existing patent law principles to the field of biotechnology with the aim of securing the application of patent laws in this important area as effective [*sic*] as possible … [T]his Directive should allow inventors and investors in the Member States to benefit from patent protection as effective as that in the competitive markets of Japan and the United States of America. (Document COM(88) 496 final SYN 159: 6, emphasis added)

The Commission acknowledged the existence of the EPC and the EPO, but indicated that the position with the EPC was unsatisfactory:

> Although the solutions provided for in the Examination Guidelines of the EPO offer valuable guidance for the examining organs of the EPO, … they are handicapped by the fact that they are neither binding on the Board of Appeals of the EPO … nor on national courts … There is no mechanism in the EPC, such as by Examination Guidelines, to provide for *mandatory* guidance on the questions arising in respect of patenting biotechnological inventions … As regards the scope of protection of biotechnological inventions and the interrelation between the effects of patents and plant breeders' rights, the EPC does not regulate these issues and thus no competence of the European Patent Office exists. (Document COM(88) 496 final SYN 159: 17, emphasis added)

Paying lip service to the fact that the EPC is not an EU instrument and thus that the EU has no power to impose its own interpretation of the provisions of the EPC, the Commission commented that: 'The proposed Directive is intended to coexist, and not to interfere with, the existing international legal network in which the EPC, the UPOV

Convention and the Budapest Treaty are the cornerstones. It is therefore indispensible that any proposal must be compatible with the provisions of these conventions' (Document COM(88) 496 final SYN 159: 22). Thus the Commission argued that the proposed Directive 'respects the limitations existing under the pertinent provisions of the EPC' and that it was therefore primarily based on four assumptions concerning the EPC's exclusions. However, two of the assumptions that were listed were clearly incorrect: 'plant and animal varieties *as such* ... are excluded from patent protection' and 'methods for treatment of the animal body by surgery or therapy and diagnostic methods practised on the animal body are not regarded as inventions which are susceptible of industrial application *if practised for a therapeutic purpose*' (Document COM(88) 496 final SYN 159: 23, emphasis added). Moreover, the Commission considered that it was 'clear that the proposed Directive will not interfere with the EPC, nor will it establish any interdependence in a legal sense between the two bodies of law' (Document COM(88) 496 final SYN 159: 25).

Almost in the same breath, the Commission demonstrated that the intention was *not* to maintain compatibility or avoid interference with the EPC: 'It is clear that the framework of the current rules on the patenting of living matter now reflects incorrect assumptions ... [T]he Directive provides for principles which will ensure that such rules remain strictly limited to their original aim' (Document COM(88) 496 final SYN 159: 24). Likewise, it commented that '*on the whole* the proposed Directive corresponds to the EPC' (Document COM(88) 496 final SYN 159: 24, emphasis added). The EBD *was* intended to coerce the judgments of the EPO: 'where provisions of the Directive clarify questions not yet answered in the Examination Guidelines of the EPO, they do so with the necessary legislative authority ... [T]he Directive will offer the EPO firm grounds on which to develop further its patent granting practice according to the latest needs of industry and science in biotechnology' (Document COM(88) 496 final SYN 159: 25).

Art. 3 of the first draft EBD read as follows:

1. Micro-organisms, biological classifications other than plant or animal varieties as well as parts of plant and animal varieties other than propagating material thereof of the kind protectable under plant variety protection law shall be considered patentable subject matter ...
2. Notwithstanding the provisions of paragraph 1, plants and plant material shall be considered patentable subject matter unless such material is produced by the non-patentable use of a previously known biotechnological process. (Document COM(88) 496 final SYN 159: 75)

Draft Art. 3(1) would have overridden Art. 53(b) EPC by categorically stating that only plant and animal varieties in integral form, that is as such, and any plant propagating material protectable by plant variety protection should be excluded from patentability. Draft Art. 3(2) overrode Art. 3(1) and went even further – the only plants and plant materials that could be excluded were those produced by the non-patentable use of a known *biotechnological* process.

In the commentary on the draft, the Commission pulled out of thin air the *ratio legis* for Art. 53(b) EPC as being that the excluded subject-matter lacked industrial applicability. Likewise it confirmed that its intention with Art. 3(1) was that: 'it is not plants and animals in general which are excluded from patentability but only plant and animal varieties *as such*, i.e. in the genetically fixed and stable form of a variety. Thus, Article 3 first sentence will establish the principle that patent protection is available for plant and animal material which is not a variety' (Document COM(88) 496 final SYN 159: 34–5). The reader will recall that the 'as such' qualification of Art. 52(3) EPC applies to the exclusions of Art. 52(2) EPC and *not* to those of Art. 53 EPC.

Art. 4 of the first draft of the EBD read as follows: 'Uses of plant or animal varieties and processes for the production thereof shall be considered patentable subject matter' (Document COM(88) 496 final SYN 159: 75). This of course is contrary to the 'essentially biological processes' exclusion of Art. 53(b) EPC.

Art. 6 of the first draft of the EBD provided that: 'A process consisting of a succession of steps shall be regarded a microbiological process, if the essence of the invention is incorporated in one or more microbiological steps of the process' (Document COM(88) 496 final SYN 159: 75). This clearly would have placed a constraint on the interpretation of the word 'essentially' in Art. 53(b) EPC. That this was intended is clear from the commentary: 'The Article will make it necessary for the principle to be adopted that a multi-step process in which the essence of the invention is incorporated into a microbiological step is not deprived of its microbiological character simply because the process contains other, non-microbiological, steps' (Document COM(88) 496 final SYN 159: 40). This of course would make the question of whether a multi-step process is 'essentially biological' one of presentation and of comparison with the prior art.

The meaning of 'essentially biological processes' was returned to in Art. 7 of the draft EBD, which stated: 'A process in which human intervention consists in more than selecting an available biological material and letting it perform an inherent biological function under natural conditions shall be considered patentable subject matter' (Document

COM(88) 496 final SYN 159: 76). This in effect is a redefining of 'essentially' as 'purely'. This is confirmed in the accompanying commentary:

> [I]t is necessary to lay down a principle of patent laws which establishes the extent to which human intervention is required in order to ensure that an invention will be considered patentable subject matter. In this connection, it is important to distinguish between traditional breeding activities and other forms of human intervention in biological matter ... Article 7 of the Directive ... is intended to exclude only traditional biological breeding activities based upon selection and as such may be regarded as slightly more liberal than the Guidelines [for Examination in the European Patent Office]. ... Any human intervention aside from selection ... would remove the process from the field of 'essentially biological' processes. (Document COM(88) 496 final SYN 159: 40–1)

The EBD was intended to satisfy the interests of industries besides the agro-industry. The exclusion of 'discoveries' in Art. 52(2) EPC, of concern to the biotech industry in general and to the pharmaceutical industry, was addressed in the drafts of Arts. 8 and 9 EBD:

> A subject matter of an invention, including a mixture, which formed an unseparated part of a pre-existing material, shall not be considered unpatentable for the reason only that it formed part of said natural material ...
>
> A subject matter of an invention, including a mixture, which formed an unseparated part of a pre-existing material, shall not be considered as an unpatentable discovery or as lacking novelty for the reason only that it formed part of said natural material. (Document COM(88) 496 final SYN 159: 76)

This is saying that a natural product, when isolated or purified, shall be patentable as a product per se, and that it is not only its novel and inventive *use* that may be patented. The accompanying commentary considered that: 'Where a substance is claimed in a form which results from human intervention in the material world, it is more than a mere discovery, irrespective of whether the intervention is simple or complex. Article 9 is necessary to ensure that this distinction is correctly applied in patent law' (Document COM(88) 496 final SYN 159: 43).

In March and May 1990 the EU and the USA submitted their draft proposals for TRIPS, which would form part of the Uruguay round of negotiations on GATT. A first draft of TRIPS was ready by December 1990, and a 'final' draft was issued by Director General Dunkel in December 1991. In 1993 the North American Free Trade Agreement (NAFTA) was signed, including TRIPS-like provisions on intellectual property rights. TRIPS was eventually signed in April 1994 and came into effect in January 1995 (see e.g. Drahos and Braithwaite 2002, Sell

2003, Matthews 2002). Art. 27 TRIPS mandated minimal requirements for patent protection of inventions:

1. Subject to the provisions of paragraphs 2 and 3, patents shall be available for any inventions ... in all fields of technology, provided that they are new, involve an inventive step and are capable of industrial application ...
2. Members may exclude from patentability inventions, the prevention within their territory of the commercial exploitation of which is necessary to protect *ordre public* or morality, including to protect human, animal or plant life or health or to avoid serious prejudice to the environment, provided that such exclusion is not made merely because the exploitation is prohibited by their law.
3. Members may also exclude from patentability:
   (a) diagnostic, therapeutic and surgical methods for the treatment of humans or animals;
   (b) plants and animals other than micro-organisms, and essentially biological processes for the production of plants and animals other than non-biological and microbiological processes.

While it will be clear to the reader that the list of potentially unpatentable inventions permitted by TRIPS closely follows the exclusions in the EPC, as otherwise the signing of TRIPS would have required extensive and time-consuming EPC modification, some modification of the EPC would nevertheless become required.

After passing though many stages, the amended proposals for the EBD were considered by the European Parliament in May 1994. The Parliament's proposed amendments were, to some extent, adopted (Document COM(94) 245 final) and by January 1995 a compromise text was put forward. By this stage biotechnology had become a sore topic in Europe and in March 1995 the European Parliament rejected the draft EBD. A revised text was produced in December 1995 (Document COM(95) 661 final). Art. 2(3) of the 1995 draft stated that, for the purposes of the EBD: '"essentially biological process for the production of plants or animals" means any process which, taken as a whole, exists in nature or is not more than a natural plant-breeding or animal-breeding process' (Document COM(95) 661 final: 30).

Art. 3(2) of the draft EBD stated that 'the subject of an invention capable of industrial application which relates to an element isolated from the human body or otherwise produced by means of a technical process shall be patentable, even if the structure of that element is identical to that of a natural element' (Document COM(95) 661 final: 30). Art. 8 provided that biological materials should not be considered to be discoveries simply because they existed in the natural world. In effect, this was intended to assert that *things* could not be discoveries, just ideas, phenomena and processes.

In line with T-19/90 Onco-mouse/HARVARD (see Chapter 8), Art. 9(2)(b) of the draft EBD declared unpatentable: 'processes for modifying the genetic identity of animals which are likely to cause them suffering or physical handicaps without any substantial benefit to man or animal, and also animals resulting from such processes, whenever the suffering or physical handicaps inflicted on the animals concerned are disproportionate to the objective pursued' (Document COM(95) 661 final: 31).

In July 1997 the European Parliament approved the draft EBD, subject to certain amendments being made. The amended text was produced in August 1997 and approved by the European Parliament in May 1998. The EBD was published in July 1998, on the same day that the Technical Board of Appeal of the European Patent Office (TBoA) 3.3.04 issued its written decision in T-1054/96 (I) Transgenic plant/NOVARTIS, referring questions on the patentability of plant varieties to the Enlarged Board of Appeal of the European Patent Office (EBoA).

The final form of the EBD contained many passages that sought to impose particular meanings on the exclusions of the EPC. Perhaps the most egregious is the definition of 'essentially' in Art. 53(b) EPC as meaning 'entirely'. Thus Art. 2(2) EBD reads: 'A process for the production of plants or animals is essentially biological if it consists entirely of natural phenomena such as crossing or selection.' This left open the question as to what else would be 'natural phenomena' if the crossing and selection techniques used by breeders were considered to be natural.

This emasculation of the Art. 53(b) EPC exclusion of 'essentially biological processes' was reinforced by Art. 4(3) EBD, which provided that the acknowledgement in Art. 4(1)(b) EBD that essentially biological processes were unpatentable should 'be without prejudice to the patentability of inventions which concern a microbiological or other technical process'. In other words, involvement of a *single* step in a multi-step process that is 'technical' or 'microbiological' would be sufficient for the exclusion to be evaded.

In Art. 2(3) EBD a definition was given for 'plant variety': 'The concept of "plant variety" is defined by Article 5 [CPVRR].'

Acknowledging that 'plant and animal varieties' were not patentable, Art. 4(2) EBD proceeds to allow plants and animals to be patented if claimed at a *higher taxonomic level* than 'variety': 'Inventions which concern plants or animals shall be patentable if the technical feasibility of the invention is not confined to a particular plant or animal variety.' However, this wording does permit the alternative interpretation that it is the patentability of *processes* performed on or with plants or animals that is being recognised. Nevertheless, the EPO currently follows the first interpretation when applying the exclusion of plant and animal varieties.

One addition to the exclusions of the EPC that was included in the EBD was that of '[t]he human body, at the various stages of its formation and development' (Art. 5(1) EBD). This, however, we suspect, was already excluded by the contrary to morality or 'ordre public' provisions of Art. 53(a) EPC. Indeed, it seems instead to be a back-door way of relaxing the Art. 52(2) EPC exclusion of discoveries, since Art. 5(2) EBD goes on to state that: 'An element isolated from the human body or otherwise produced by means of a technical process, including the sequence or partial sequence of a gene, may constitute a patentable invention, even if the structure of that element is identical to that of a natural element.'

Art. 6(1) EBD anticipated the elimination of 'publication' and the qualification of 'exploitation' by 'commercial' in the wording of Art. 53(a) EPC (changes which occurred in the 2000 revision of the EPC). Art. 6(2) EBD then went on to list examples of subject-matter that should be unpatentable under Art. 53(a) EPC. Many of these seem likely to have been excluded by Art. 53(a) EPC without need of clarification from the EBD.

In September 1999 the EPC Rules were amended to introduce provisions closely mirroring the terms of the EBD and shortly thereafter, in December 1999, the EBoA issued its decision G-1/98 Transgenic plant/NOVARTIS II, which generally followed the EBD. From then, it was not until G-2/07 Broccoli/PLANT BIOSCIENCE, in December 2010, that the EBoA was prepared to acknowledge that there was a conflict between what was deemed patentable for EU countries according to the EBD and what was deemed unpatentable under the EPC.

2.10 The 2000 revision of the EPC

In 1997, that is after TRIPS but before the EBD had been agreed, the then president of the EPO (Ingo Kober) had come to believe that revision of the EPC was desirable. However, in January 1998 the European Commission's representative at the sixth meeting of the EPO's Committee on Patent Law (CPL) commented that the proposed

EBD 'was compatible with the EPC, and therefore, no revision of the EPC would be needed' (Document CA/PL PV6: 22).

At the seventh meeting of the CPL in May 1998, the EPO took up the question of deleting computer programs from the exclusions of Art. 52(2) EPC. It should be noted that TBoA 3.5.01's landmark decision T-1173/97 Computer program product/IBM, deciding that computer programs were patentable, was issued in written form in March 1999. At the meeting: 'the EPO emphasised the importance of protecting software-related inventions. Deleting Article 52(2) would send an important psychological signal ... In revising Article 52(2), discussions would not be confined to computer programs, but would extend to all the Article's exceptions' (Document CA/PL PV7: 9). In reply: 'The Portuguese delegation opined that the fathers of the EPC did not consider that computer programs constituted inventions, and that this view should be taken into account' (Document CA/PL PV7: 9). The Belgian delegation doubted that the time was ripe for deleting the exclusion (as a European Directive[15] on the patentability of computer-implemented inventions was then under consideration which has since fallen by the wayside): 'and the EPO confirmed it was preferable to wait for the developments in Brussels' (Document CA/PL PV7: 10).

In November 1998, at the eighth meeting of the CPL, after the EBD had been agreed and published, and before G-1/98 Transgenic plant/NOVARTIS II had been issued, the EPO commented on the need to adapt the EPC to comply with the EBD: 'Regarding the adaptation of the EPC to confirm with [the EBD] ... the Office emphasised that the [EBD] merely reflected the existing practice of the EPO and the boards of appeal. For the time being, it would be sufficient to amend the Implementing Regulations; the Administrative Council would have to authorise the Committee to study the necessary modifications' (Document CA/PL PV8: 1).

On the question of immoral inventions, as covered by Art. 53(a) EPC 1973, at that meeting the attendees were told that 'The EPO took the view that inventions relating to anti-personnel mines *per se* should be excluded from patentability as contrary to "ordre public" and morality; administrative measures to this effect had already been taken' (Document CA/PL PV8: 5). The reader should note that in September 1977 the United Nations had produced the UN Convention on the Prohibition of the Use, Stockpiling, Production and Transfer of

[15] Document COM(2002) 92 final. Interestingly, this did not suggest that computer programs *themselves* might be patentable, just programmed apparatus and processes carried out on such apparatus through the execution of software.

Anti-Personnel Mines and on their Destruction, a convention to which all EPC Member States are signatories.

Computer programs would not go away. The CPL was advised in January 1999 of the discussions of the Standing Advisory Committee before the EPO (SACEPO)[16] in September 1998, which gave unanimous support for the deletion of computer programs from Art. 52(2) EPC and '[s]upport for clarification to the effect that genetically modified plants and animals may be patented and appropriate steps to be taken to align the EPC to the EU biotechnology directive' (Document CA/PL 2/99: 1–2).

Following the SACEPO meeting, in March 1999 the president of the EPO (Ingo Kober) addressed the question of drawing the teeth of the exclusions from patentability found in the EPC. On the medical methods exclusion of Art. 52(4) EPC 1973, the president commented:

> The exclusion of medical methods from patenting is based on the assumption that, for ethical and social reasons related to ensuring provision of medical services for the public, the exercise of medical skills should not be restricted or hindered by patents as a matter of principle. A doctor is not in 'industry' [van Empel 1975: 63]. The Enlarged Board of Appeal has noted in this regard that the intention of this provision is to free from constraint non-commercial and non-industrial medical and veterinary activities (G 5/83 [Second medical indication/EISAI]). (Document CA/PL 7/99: 1)

The president continued:

> As part of the deliberations on the revision of the EPC, it is necessary to examine whether it is still justifiable to exclude all medical methods from patentability ... and whether the real intention of the provision to exempt medical practitioners and veterinary surgeons from patent rights when treating individual patients directly should not be achieved in other more appropriate ways. In this regard it is necessary to examine whether it is justifiable to exclude entirely from patentability useful inventions for maintaining or restoring health of humans and animals and thereby run the risk of failing to use or impeding the role of patent protection in promoting innovation in this technical field of public interest. (Document CA/PL 7/99: 2)

In the same month the president suggested various revisions to the EPC, in particular the insertion into Art. 52(1) EPC of the words 'in all fields of technology' (in order to make the EPC TRIPS-compliant) *and the deletion of Art. 52(2) EPC in its entirety* (Document CA/PL 6/99). Even the first of these proposals was not as innocent as it might seem. It was an attempt to set in stone the 'technical character' approach set

[16] An organisation set up by the first president of the EPO, van Benthem, and containing representatives from industry, the patent professions and academia.

out the week before by TBoA 3.5.01 in T-1173/97 Computer program product/IBM:

All attempts to establish a suitable definition of the term 'invention' which would meet with the approval at European or even international level have so far failed. It has, however, been part of the European legal tradition since the early days of the patent system that patent protection should be reserved for creations in the technical field. The subject-matter of a patentable invention must therefore have a 'technical character' or – to be more precise – involve a 'technical teaching', i.e. an instruction addressed to a person skilled in the art as to how to solve a particular technical problem using particular technical means ... The non-inventions listed by way of example in Article 52(2) EPC confirm that only a technical invention understood in this way can and should be patentable. The subject-matter and activities in Article 52(2) either contain no technical teaching at all, such as discoveries and scientific theories, or cannot be deemed part of the realm of technology, such as rules and methods for performing mental acts or doing business, even though all these things may well be susceptible of industrial application. Rules [42 and 43] EPC also give a clear indication that patentable inventions must have a technical character. (Document CA/PL 6/99: 1)

The president also attempted to minimise the extent to which the exclusions in the EPC should be considered to have been well thought through:

The list of non-patentable subject-matter in Article 52(2) EPC was the subject of lively discussion both in the lead-up to and at the Munich Diplomatic Conference in 1973. There is no such list in the Strasbourg Convention of 1963 ... It was enshrined in European patent law in close adherence to the PCT (Rules 39.1 and 67.1 PCT), which had been drawn up shortly before, and partly based on national provisions. It was proposed at the time of the Munich Conference that part or all of the list be transferred to the Implementing Regulations in order to be able to take better account of scientific and technical developments. But there was no support for these proposals because the list was considered to cover fundamental rules of substantive patent law, and it was felt that their amendment could not be left to the Administrative Council. (Document CA/PL 6/99: 2)

Turning to the exclusion of computer programs, the one 'dealt with' by the '*technical character*' approach, the president commented:

As regards the exception provided for in Article 52(2)(c) and (3) EPC, which excludes 'programs for computers' as such from being regarded as inventions, the Office and the boards of appeal have always interpreted and applied the EPC in such a way that this exception in no way excludes appropriate protection for software-related inventions, that is inventions whose subject-matter consists of or includes a computer program. This practice can be summarised as follows: an invention which when viewed as a whole makes a technical contribution to the prior art, e.g. by means of a particular technical effect, is patentable even if a computer program is involved in its implementation. (Document CA/PL 6/99: 3)

This of course justifies patent protection for computer-implemented inventions rather than for computer programs per se. Mentioning that there had been pressure for reform on computer programs and business and mathematical methods, the president continued:

Nor is the argument convincing that computer programs are always of a technical character. This is not the case merely because they are intended for use in the operation of computers. A computer program may or may not involve a technical teaching. On the other hand, the current wording of Article 52 EPC does not completely exclude the possibility of a computer program being deemed not to be patentable even if it is of technical character ... There now appears to be broad consensus that Article 52 should be amended, at least as far as this point is concerned. (Document CA/PL 6/99: 4–5)

On the question of simply deleting Art. 52(2) EPC, as repeatedly proposed by the UK during the negotiations leading up to the adoption of the EPC in 1973, the president went on to say:

It is further proposed that paragraphs 2 and 3 of Article 52 EPC be deleted, as they are no longer necessary or desirable. If Article 52(1) EPC were to be amended as proposed, thus making it clear that only technical inventions are patentable, there would no longer be any need for the exceptions in paragraph 2 ... The deletion of Article 52(2) and (3) EPC would get round the problems associated with the application and interpretation of any exception to patentability (what is a computer program as such?), but would not mean that the subject-matter and activities currently listed in Article 52(2) would then suddenly become patentable. Discoveries, scientific theories, mathematical methods, aesthetic creations, and purely mental or business acts, in particular, will continue not to be eligible for patent protection as long as they do not involve a technical teaching ... Patentability would continue to depend solely on whether the claimed subject-matter, considered as a whole, had a technical character or not. The task of determining this can be left to the departments of the EPO, its boards of appeal and the national courts, who are best equipped to do it. They are better able than the legislator to take the right decision in each individual case, as well as to take account of technical advances and thus promote the pragmatic development and harmonisation of European patent practice. (Document CA/PL 6/99: 6–7)

At the ninth meeting of the CPL in March 1999 a proposal to make methods of treatment patentable was not approved, but in January 2000 the president made further suggestions for amendment (Document CA/PL 4/00). In the president's proposals of March 1999 the question of the second and further medical uses of pharmaceuticals was addressed.

The acceptability of a Swiss-type use claim to a second indication had been addressed by the first decisions of the EBoA in December 1985, but the validity and enforceability of such claims had remained in doubt and the president and other parties wished to settle this in a manner acceptable to the pharmaceutical industry:

> The national courts and appeal divisions of the patent offices of the contracting states to the EPC have taken issue to various degrees with the case law of the Enlarged Board of Appeal relating to the 'second medical use' in the so-called 'Swiss form of claim', although for the sake of uniform interpretation they have mainly followed the Enlarged Board's decision ... In a more recent decision of the UK High Court handed down in 1998 ... substantial doubts were expressed as to the novelty of 'Swiss claims' ... This legal uncertainty has to be eliminated, as it is difficult to predict with any certainty whether European patents with so-called 'Swiss claims' directed to a 'further medical indication' will ultimately be found to be valid by the national courts in the contracting states to the EPC. Moreover, there are considerable doubts as to whether patents of this type will actually guarantee the intended protection sufficiently and whether they can be enforced accordingly ... It is therefore proposed that Article 54(5) EPC be amended to unambiguously permit patent protection for the second and each subsequent medical use of a substance or composition known for a medical use, in the same way as for its first medical use, in the form of purpose-related product protection. (Document CA/PL 4/00: 2)

The president then proposed a new paragraph for Art. 54 EPC that would allow purpose-limited product claims for drug substances found to have *further* medical uses: 'The provisions of paragraphs 1 to 4 [of Art. 54 EPC] shall not exclude the patentability of any substance or composition, comprised in the state of the art, for use in a method referred to in Article 52, paragraph 4, provided that this use is not comprised in the state of the art' (Document CA/PL 4/00: 3).

This, of course, was not adopted, since it would remove the basis for the very broad first indication claims that were being accepted by the EPO, of 'substance X for use in medicine', and would allow purpose-limited product claims only when the end use was specified narrowly. This was pointed out by epi (the Institute of Professional Representatives before the European Patent Office) (Document Info/2PL 12).

In the meantime, the EPO's Administrative Council had, in June 1999, advised that the EPC Rules were to be amended to bring them into line with the EBD and the new Rules came into effect in September 1999.

At the twelfth meeting of the CPL, in February 2000, the suggestions of the EPO president and of epi were considered. The Austrian and German delegations considered the matter was political and should be referred to the Administrative Council. According to the German delegation: 'protection for later indications [constituted] an encroachment on the therapeutic freedom of the medical practitioner in the performance of his duties' (Document CA/PL PV12: 5).

The EPO president set out the EPO's major proposals (Document CA/PL 25/00: 37–44) for the revision of the EPC in June 2000, in advance of the fourteenth meeting of the CPL in July 2000. The proposed revisions were the insertion of 'in all fields of technology' into Art. 52(1) EPC to achieve compliance with TRIPS, the deletion of Art. 52(2) EPC and the insertion of whatever equivalent was necessary into the Implementing Regulations, the restriction of Art. 53(a) EPC to commercial exploitations that were contrary to morality or 'ordre public', and the displacement of medical methods from Art. 52 EPC to Art. 53 EPC, that is the abandonment of the legal fiction that they were not susceptible of industrial application. Apart from the deletion of Art. 52(2) EPC, this was uncontroversial.

The president explained that Art. 52(1) EPC was to be made TRIPS-compliant, to make 'it plain that patent protection is available to technical inventions of all kinds' and that the exclusions of Art. 52(2) EPC, with the exception of that of computer programs, which was to disappear, were to go into the EPC Rules. On computer programs, he commented that: 'There now appears to be a broad consensus that computer programs should disappear from the list of non-patentable inventions … [R]ecent decisions of the Boards of Appeal (see T-1173/97 [Computer program product/IBM] …) have confirmed that computer programs, as a rule, are patentable subject-matter under the EPC. Therefore, the current exception concerning computer programs has become *de facto* obsolete' (Document CA/PL 25/00: 37).

Again, the president sought to validate the '*technical character*' approach recently adopted by TBoA 3.5.01 in T-1173/97 Computer program product/IBM:

> [T]he transfer of Article 52(2) and (3) EPC would offer a welcome opportunity to combine these provisions with a Rule providing some sort of definition of the term 'invention' as it should be understood throughout the EPC. Such a rule implementing Article 52(1) EPC could read as follows: '"Invention" within the meaning of this Convention shall be understood as being a teaching addressed to a person skilled in the art as to how to solve a technical problem using technical means'. (Document CA/ PL 25/00: 37–9)

On the subject of the exclusion of medical methods, the president commented that: 'While these surgical or therapeutic methods constitute inventions, they have been excluded from patentability by the fiction of their lack of industrial applicability. It is undesirable to uphold this fiction since methods of treatment and diagnostic methods are excluded from patentability in the interests of public health' (Document CA/PL 25/00: 41).

From here on, the *travaux préparatoires* are those for the Munich Diplomatic conference of November 2000. The Administrative Council of the EPO produced its draft revision of the EPC in October 2000 (Document MR/3/00). In Art. 52(1) the words 'all fields of technology' were to be inserted, in Art. 52(2) computer programs were to be deleted, methods of treatment were to be moved from Art. 52(4) to Art. 53(c), 'publication' was to be deleted and 'commercial' inserted in Art. 53(a), and a new second medical use clause, Art. 54(5), was to be added allowing purpose-limited product claims for any specific use when that specific use was not known (Document MR/3/00: 9–11).

On 17 November 2000 the French delegation proposed the reinsertion of the exclusion of programs for computers, giving the reason that:

> A lively debate is under way in Europe about whether and how patent protection for software inventions should develop. The European Commission has also just published a consultation paper on the subject, and the economic stakes are considerable. Simply deleting the words 'and programs for computers' might be interpreted as signalling a wider range of patentable subject-matter. The risk of uncontrolled drift towards patents for business methods in particular must be avoided. Rather than adopt a premature position, and without calling existing EPO practice into question, the French delegation therefore suggests that the decision on amending Article 52(2)(c) be deferred. (Document MR/8/00: 3–4)

This position was supported by the Danish delegation:

> The patentability of software is a highly controversial issue which has considerable economical impact ... We are not convinced that the deletion of the words 'computer programs' from Art. 52(2)(c) EPC is more or less a formality which will have no impact on Board of Appeal decisions. Furthermore, the European Commission has recently launched a consultation within the member states with the purpose of having a thorough discussion of the issue and possibly establishing proper means for harmonisation on this issue within the Community. We find it imperative to await the outcome of the Community initiative before any further action on this matter is taken in relation to the EPC. This issue is considered by our government to be of crucial importance for our assessment of the Basic proposal as a whole. (Document MR/15/00: 1)

The exclusion of computer programs was reinserted (Document MR/3/00 Rev. 1).

Later in November 2000, the Swiss delegation proposed a new wording for the novelty exemption for purpose-limited product claims to cover second and further medical uses. The actions of the Swiss in this area are important to note since they appear to have misled the delegates from the other countries as to the effect of their proposed changes. The proposed wording would have had Art. 54(5) EPC read:

> Notwithstanding paragraphs 2 and 3, the provisions of this article shall not exclude the patentability of any substance or composition referred to in paragraph (4) for any specific use in any method referred to in Article 53(c), provided that such use is not comprised in the state of the art. (Document MR/18/00)

More specifically, the Swiss delegation suggested that:

> The new Article 54(5) EPC eliminates any legal uncertainty on the patentability of further medical uses. It unambiguously permits purpose-related product protection for each further new medical use of a substance or composition already known as a medicine. This protection is equivalent, as far as the further uses are concerned, to that offered by the 'Swiss type claim'. In contrast to previous Article 54(5), now Article 54(4) EPC, providing broad (generic) protection for use in a medical method for the inventor of such use for the first time, new Article 54(5) is expressly limited to a specific use. This limitation is intended to match as closely as possible the scope of protection to the scope provided by a 'Swiss type claim'. (Document MR/18/00: 2)

As will be explained in Chapter 5, however, allowing purpose-limited product claims for second and further medical uses worsened the position of the physician seeking to use a generic medicine in place of the patented equivalent.

The Drafting Committee put forward a draft revised text on 27 November 2000, incorporating the 'TRIPS-compliance' amendment to Art. 52(1) EPC to refer to 'all fields of technology', placing medical methods into Art. 53 EPC, incorporating a purpose-limited second and further medical use exemption into Art. 54 EPC, but maintaining all of the Art. 52(2) EPC exclusions (Document MR/DCD 1/00).

The Diplomatic Conference at which the amendment of the EPC was agreed took place in Munich from 20 to 29 November 2000. The chairman, the director of the Swiss Patent Office, Roland Grossenbacher, opened the conference stating in relation to the revision process that: 'There are ... several "tough nuts to crack", to coin a phrase. Some of these are major legal issues, whilst others have extended beyond the purely legal aspects and thus taken on a strategic importance; one example is the proposal to delete the exclusion of computer programs, which is really only intended to codify existing practice' (Document MR/24/00: 4–6).

As a proposal for an EU Directive relating to the patenting of computer-related inventions was then under discussion, the question of the retention of computer programs in the exclusions list of Art. 52(2) EPC was prominent. The head of the German delegation, in his opening statement, commented that: 'the draft Revision Act contains one proposal whose effects in our view have not yet been fully explored and which we believe should be postponed to a later date. I am referring to the proposal to delete computer programs as such from the list of non-patentable inventions in Article 52(2) EPC' (Document MR/24/00: 9). The head of the Irish delegation commented that the computer programs provision needed at least some clarification. However, in view of the European Commission consultation process, Ireland felt that a deletion was not desirable at this stage. Luxembourg concurred. The Dutch delegation considered that the computer program exclusion was 'obsolete in the eyes of the Netherlands' but that they would 'not go along with patenting business methods as such'. The Belgian delegation said that their country had always supported the removal of the computer programs exclusion, but in view of the EU's consultation exercise it felt that the status quo should be maintained. The Danish delegation felt it imperative not to take any decision on programs for computers until the outcome of the EU's consultation process was known. In the end, France, Denmark, Germany, Finland, Monaco, Sweden, Ireland, Italy, Belgium, Spain, Luxembourg, Cyprus, Portugal and the UK wanted to keep the computer program exclusion; Switzerland, Liechtenstein, Austria and The Netherlands wanted to see it go; and Turkey would not vote on the subject (Document MR/24/00: 17–38).

The TRIPS-compliance amendment to Art. 52(1) EPC was agreed. The limitation of the morality clause (Art. 53(a) EPC) to inventions that were contrary to morality or 'ordre public' when *commercially* exploited went through. Moving the medical methods exclusion from Art. 52 to Art. 53 EPC was agreed. The Swiss proposal to allow purpose-limited product claims was accepted after the Swiss had argued that:

> [A]s regards second or further medical uses, the case law evolved by the EPO Enlarged Board of Appeal should be enshrined in the Convention. For the sake of transparency and legal certainty the aim of the Basic Proposal was to keep the legal status quo for medical uses … The proposed reform satisfied the demand users had long been making for the existing loophole in respect of the patenting of the second and further medical uses to be closed. The Basic Proposal met this demand without extending protection beyond the legal status quo. (Document MR/24/00: 71–72)

The revised EPC came into force in December 2007 and since then there have been no major legislative changes. Arts. 52 and 53 EPC now read as follows:

Article 52 – Patentable inventions

(1) European patents shall be granted for any inventions, in all fields of technology, provided that they are new, involve an inventive step and are susceptible of industrial application.
(2) The following in particular shall not be regarded as inventions within the meaning of paragraph 1:
  (a) discoveries, scientific theories and mathematical methods;
  (b) aesthetic creations;
  (c) schemes, rules and methods for performing mental acts, playing games or doing business, and programs for computers;
  (d) presentations of information.
(3) Paragraph 2 shall exclude the patentability of the subject-matter or activities referred to therein only to the extent to which a European patent application or European patent relates to such subject-matter as such.

Article 53 – Exceptions to patentability

European patents shall not be granted in respect of:
  (a) inventions the commercial exploitation of which would be contrary to 'ordre public' or morality; such exploitation shall not be deemed to be so contrary merely because it is prohibited by law or regulation in some or all of the Contracting States;
  (b) plant or animal varieties or essentially biological processes for the production of plants or animals: this provision shall not apply to microbiological processes or the products thereof;
  (c) methods for the treatment of the human or animal body by surgery or therapy and diagnostic methods practised on the human or animal body; this provision shall not apply to products, in particular substances or compositions, for use in any of these methods.

The Art. 52(2) EPC exclusions are governed by the 'as such' qualification of Art. 52(3) EPC and, with one exception, are covered in Chapter 2. The exception is the exclusion of discoveries, which has been directly affected by the EBD and which is dealt with in Chapter 4. The Art. 53 EPC exclusions are dealt with individually in Chapters 5 to 8.

3 Computer programs

> [T]he boards of appeal cannot assume the role of legislator. They have to apply the law as it stands and cannot strive to meet wishes which are incompatible with the provisions of the European Patent Convention ... There are those who would like to see Article 52(2) EPC removed in order to allow protection to be obtained for a computer program as recorded ... In its current version, the EPC is not believed to be interpretable in such a way as to afford that degree of protection.
>
> (van den Berg[1] 1996: 45)

> [I]t by no means follows that because of pressure from applicants, the grant of patents for excluded categories should be allowed or that the excluded categories (particularly ... computer programs) should be construed narrowly. Just as with arms, merely because people want them is not sufficient reason for giving them.
>
> (Jacob LJ in *Aerotel Ltd* v. *Telco Holdings Ltd & Ors*
> (UK-Aerotel 2006: para. 19)

3.1 Introduction

The exclusion from patent-eligibility of computer programs 'as such' is governed by Arts. 52(2) and (3) EPC, which were unchanged during the 2000 revision of the EPC and read in relevant part as follows:

(2) The following in particular shall not be regarded as inventions within the meaning of paragraph 1: ... (c) ... programs for computers; ...
(3) Paragraph 2 shall exclude the patentability of the subject-matter or activities referred to therein only to the extent to which a European patent application or European patent relates to such subject-matter or activities as such. (EPO 2010a: 106)

The EPC contains no definition of what an invention is, merely a list of examples in Art. 52(2) EPC of things that are not to be regarded as

[1] Former chairman of TBoA 3.5.01 and member of the EBoA.

inventions. Art. 52(1) EPC specifies that inventions are patentable if they are new, involve an inventive step and are susceptible of industrial application, so these three characteristics cannot be required characteristics of an invention, merely of a *patentable* invention.

Since the list in Art. 52(2) EPC is not exhaustive, as was made clear during the negotiations leading to the adoption of the EPC (see Chapter 2), and is emphasised by the presence of the words 'in particular', two opportunities to broaden the set of exclusions exist: firstly, where subject-matter is considered equivalent in nature to one or more of the subjects listed in Art. 52(2) EPC; and second where a quality common to all the excluded subject-matter can be identified, which, if possessed by any other subject-matter, characterises that other subject-matter as not being an 'invention'. For the second of these opportunities to be available, such a common quality must exist, and its existence is doubtful in view of the very different nature of the two distinct sources of the topics listed in Art. 52(2) EPC: Art. 2 SPC; and the subject-matter which, possibly for purely practical reasons was added during the drafting of the EPC in 1969–1973. Pila (2005a: 185–6) has commented on the likely impossibility of such a common quality being found.

The only clear guidance that is to be found in the EPC as to what is not patent-eligible under Art. 52(2) EPC is in the words 'in particular' in Art. 52(2) EPC itself, and in the words 'as such' in Art. 52(3) EPC, terms that must be interpreted in the same way for each of the listed exclusions since they do not discriminate between the exclusions.

There are clearly several ways in which an exclusion from patent-eligibility can be interpreted. The most obvious are perhaps the following:

(a) If a claim has excluded subject-matter as a feature, the claim is unacceptable (the *contamination* approach).
(b) If a claim encompasses excluded subject-matter, the claim is unacceptable (the *novelty* approach).
(c) If a claim has any features that are not excluded subject-matter, the claim is acceptable (the *anything added* approach).
(d) If a claim uses a generic definition that encompasses, but is not limited to, excluded subject-matter, the claim is acceptable (the *higher taxonomic level* approach).
(e) If the subject-matter of the claim has a technical character, then *even if it belongs to an excluded class*, it is not excluded (the *technical character* approach).

In addition, a number of tests are possible for subject-matter that escapes the Art. 52(2) EPC exclusion:

(1) If the novelty or inventiveness of the claim lies in an area of excluded subject-matter, the claim is unacceptable (the *technical contribution* test).
(2) The novelty or inventiveness of the claim may only be assessed with reference to features that have *technical character* (the *COMVIK* test).
(3) Where the novelty or inventiveness of the claim lies in an area of excluded subject-matter, the excluded subject-matter must achieve an extra technical effect beyond that inherent in being the excluded subject-matter (e.g. a computer program the *further technical effect* test).
(4) If the claim comprises a combination of excluded and non-excluded subject-matter, then the claim is unacceptable if that combination is a mere 'collocation' but acceptable if there is synergy between the excluded and non-excluded components (the *synergy* test).[2]

These will be discussed further in Chapter 9. However, we would briefly note here that the *contamination* and *higher taxonomic level* approaches are not appropriate for the Art. 52(2) EPC exclusions.

Since the EPC entered into force in 1978, the nature of technology-based industry has changed remarkably, in particular with the growth of the biotechnology and computer industries. Accordingly, two of the Art. 52(2) EPC exclusions have become particularly contentious, those of discoveries and of computer programs. Discoveries are discussed in Chapter 4. In this chapter we will cover the other exclusions of Art. 52(2) EPC, concentrating in particular on computer-implemented inventions, especially on computer programs, a field that overlaps with the mathematical methods, business methods, rules for games and mental acts exclusions.

Discoveries aside, most of the EPO case law on Art. 52(2) EPC derives from only a very few TBoAs, and indeed the major contribution has been from one single Board, Electricity I (TBoA 3.5.01), and especially from that Board under the chairmanship of Paul van den Berg and subsequently Dr Stefan Steinbrener. Other TBoAs, notably Physics I and Mechanics IV (i.e. 3.4.01 and 3.2.04), have diverged from TBoA 3.5.01, a tension between different Boards that is also seen in relation to other exclusions, as will be described in Chapters 5 and 7.

[2] A combination is referred to as a collocation where the effect of the combination is no more than the sum of the expected effects of the individual components or as a synergistic combination where there is an inter-relationship between the components such that their combined effect is greater than their sum.

The discussion of the development of the case law below will thus focus first on the achievements of TBoA 3.5.01 before considering the contributions of the other TBoAs and of the EBoA.

Much of the case law development, quite naturally in view of the 'as such' provision of Art. 52(3) EPC, has been concerned with 'mixed' claims, that is claims specifying the combination of a feature excluded under one of the provisions of Art. 52(2) EPC and a feature that is not so excluded, for example a claim to a computer programmed with a particular program, or to a method of carrying out business using a machine.

3.2 The TBoA 3.5.01 (Electricity I) story

The Board's story begins in December 1985 with T-16/83 FRANCERIES (Chairman Korsakoff), where it decided that a method of regulating traffic flow, and an apparatus for performing such a method that comprised a computer, were both excluded under Art. 52(2) and (3) EPC as a method of doing business as such, despite the fact that certain features in the apparatus claims were technical means. The Board considered that the apparatus claims were nothing more than a reformulation of the unpatentable method claims and were equally unpatentable under Art. 52(2) and (3) EPC. This is in effect the *technical contribution* test that later dominated the Board's decisions until T-1173/97 Computer program product/IBM in 1999.

In March 1986, in T-51/84 Coded distinctive mark/ STOCKBURGER, the Board considered a method of protecting products by applying a distinctive mark, where the mark was formed by coding data characteristics of the product. No technical means for carrying out the process steps was recited and the forming by coding could have been a purely mental act. The method was rejected as concerning 'an act which under Article 52(2)(c) EPC is not patentable, namely the activity as such referred to in Article 52(3) EPC' (T-51/84: 228).

The true beginning of the TBoA 3.5.01 approaches was in July 1986 with T-208/84 Computer-related inventions/VICOM. An application with claims to a method for digitally processing images and to apparatus for carrying out that method, that is a computer running a special computer program, had been rejected by the Examining Division on the basis that the method claims related to 'a mathematical method which is not patentable by virtue of Article 52(2)(a) and (3) EPC' and that the apparatus claims were not novel. Moreover, the Examining Division considered that 'the normal implementation of the claimed methods by a program run on a known computer could not be regarded as an invention in view of Article 52(2)(c) and (3) EPC' (T-208/84: 15).

The Board considered that there was a difference between a mathematical method and a technical process, since a mathematical method is carried out on numbers, provides a result in numerical form and produces no direct technical result, while if used in a technical process carried out on a physical entity and implemented by some technical means, the process provides as its result a certain change in that entity (T-208/84: 19). Thus: 'even if the idea underlying an invention may be considered to reside in a mathematical method a claim directed to a technical process in which the method is used does not seek protection for the mathematical method as such' (T-208/84: 19).

A method which involved excluded subject-matter was therefore not excluded if it was a technical process that caused some physical change, an approach somewhat akin to the Federal Circuit's 'Machine or transformation of matter' test in the USA. This reasoning was applied to methods involving the use of a computer program: 'a claim directed to a technical process which ... is carried out under the control of a program ... cannot be regarded as relating to a computer program as such ... as it is the application of the program ... for which ... protection is sought' (T-208/84: 20).

On the apparatus claims, the Board concluded that claims to a 'computer set up to operate in accordance with a specified program ... for controlling or carrying out a technical process cannot be regarded as relating to a computer program as such' and that it 'would seem illogical to grant protection for a technical process controlled by a suitably programmed computer but not for the computer itself when set up to execute the control' (T-208/84: 21–2).

Nevertheless, the Board noted that a computer program itself was not claimed and stated that: '[i]ndeed such a program would not be patentable' (T-208–84: 22).

This decision followed a 'normal' interpretation of the words 'as such' – excluded subject-matter may be one of the features of a claim but it must not *itself* be the subject of the claim, thus a *technical* method involving the use of a computer program is not excluded, nor is a computer that is 'set up to operate in accordance with a ... program'. Alternatively put, 'mixed' claims should be permissible. This decision was compatible with both the *technical contribution* and *anything added* approaches later developed by this Board and clearly rejected the *contamination* approach that became favoured for Art. 53 EPC. The decision, however, is not compatible with the *technical character* approach later developed by this Board.

In September 1988, in T-115/85 Computer-related invention/IBM, TBoA 3.5.01 (now chaired by Paul van den Berg) considered that '[e]ven if the basic idea underlying [an] … invention might be considered to reside in [a] … computer program … a claim directed to its use in the solution of a technical problem cannot be regarded … as seeking protection for the program as such' (T-115/85: 34). However, the Board did warn that computer programs would not *necessarily* constitute technical means, that is that referring to the use of a program was not automatically sufficient to guarantee patent-eligibility. This decision thus suggests that a 'mixed' claim is permissible if a technical problem is solved using technical means.

In October 1988 the Board began the development of its *technical contribution* approach, an approach that was to be dominant for a decade. T-22/85 Document abstracting and retrieving/IBM was concerned with an application rejected on the basis that the contribution to the art resided solely in a computer program, and that '[c]onsequently, this subject-matter was not a patentable invention within the meaning of Article 52(1) EPC, *in whatever form it was claimed*' (T-22/85: 12, emphasis added).

Rather than turning to the meaning of the words 'as such', the Board sought to find a common feature to the exclusions of Art. 52(2) EPC, finding that '[w]hatever their differences, these exclusions have in common that they refer to activities which do not aim at any direct technical result but are rather of an abstract and intellectual character' (T-22/85: 17). This led to the development of an early form of the *technical contribution* approach:

> The requirement that an invention must have a technical character *or in other words, must provide a technical contribution to the art* is at the basis of a long-standing legal practice in at least the majority of Contracting States of the EPO. Neither from the terms of Article 52 EPC, nor from the legislative history of that Article as appearing from the preparatory documents can it be deduced that these Contracting States would have intended to deviate from their national laws and jurisprudence in this respect. On the contrary, it seems to be borne out by the list of exceptions in Article 52(2)(a) to (d) EPC that they did not wish to do so. (T-22/85: 17, emphasis added)

Interestingly, the Board sought support for this position in the EPC Rules, which cannot of course broaden or narrow the scope of any of the EPC's exclusions to patentability.

The *technical contribution* approach requires that the contribution, that is the point of novelty of the claimed subject-matter, must lie outside the fields excluded by Art. 52(2) EPC. Thus:

> the mere setting out ... of the sequence of steps necessary to perform the activity in terms of functions or functional means to be realised with the aid of conventional computer hardware elements does not import any technical considerations and can, therefore, neither lend a technical character to that activity nor to the claimed subject-matter considered as a whole, no more than solving a mathematical equation could be regarded as a technical activity when a conventional calculating machine is used and thereby overcome the exclusion from patentability ... *The contribution to the art and the effects obtained are only in the area of the excluded activity* and the true nature of the invention remains the same, whether or not a technical terminology is used in expressing it ... In the opinion of the Board it cannot have been intended by the Contracting States to the EPC that express exclusions from patentability could be circumvented simply by the manner in which the invention is expressed in a claim. (T-22/85: 18–19, emphasis added)

With regard to T-208/84 Computer-related invention/VICOM, the Board cautioned that it was not necessarily the case that 'any manner of bringing about a change in a physical entity would ipso facto qualify as a technical process' (T-22/85: 20).

This decision is notable for setting the foundation for this Board's later interpretation of 'as such' as meaning 'only if not technical in nature', based on its conclusion that the subject-matter excluded by Art. 52(2) EPC was not technical but abstract and intellectual. Despite referring to the legislative history, no particular documents were cited to support the TBoA's importation into the EPC of a requirement for technical character or the 'long-standing legal practice in at least the majority of the Contracting States of the EPO' (T-22/85: 17).

In February 1989, in T-38/86 Text processing/IBM, a case relied upon for years afterwards, the TBoA was faced with a 'mixed'-method claim which had been rejected *for lack of inventive step* as a 'collocation' of the technical but known (a word processor) and the excluded (a mathematical method). Rather than following the *synergy* test and leaving the acceptability of 'mixed' claims to be judged under Art. 56 EPC for inventive step, the TBoA essentially finalised its *technical contribution* approach. Thus while the Board accepted that specifying the use of a technical means could transform a method into 'a technical process ... and therefore ... one which is not excluded from patentability', it did not accept that all such mixes were patent-eligible: '[s]ince patentability is excluded only to the extent to which the patent application relates to excluded subject-matter or activities as such, it appears to be the intention of the EPC to permit patenting in those cases in which the invention involves a *contribution to the art in a field not excluded from patentability*' (T-38/86: 391, emphasis added).

Some confusion still reigned, however, as the Board indicated that its *technical contribution* approach led to rejection for lack of inventiveness (Art. 56 EPC) rather than for not being an invention (Art. 52(2) EPC): 'the method according to Claim 1 of the present application does not contribute to the art anything involving an inventive step in a field not excluded from patentability by Article 52(2)(c) EPC' (T-38/86: 392).

The decision also addressed the patentability of computer programs, giving an indication that the predictable effects of a collocation cannot result in patentability, but again applying the *technical contribution* test and warning against allowing clever claim-drafting to circumvent the legislators' intentions:

> While it cannot be denied that there is an interaction between the programs and the hardware, since the programs without the hardware or the hardware without the programs could do nothing, but together they make it possible to perform the method claimed in Claim 1, this fact alone cannot confer patentability on either the method or the apparatus. Since the only conceivable use for a computer program is the running of it on a computer, the exclusion from patentability of programs for computers would be effectively undermined if it could be circumvented by including in the claim a reference to conventional hardware features, such as a processor, memory, keyboard and display, which, in practice, are indispensable if the program is to be used at all. (T-38/86: 394)

This is a clear statement that the Board considered that its own later *technical character* and *anything added* approaches were not in line with the legislators' intentions.

In March 1989, in T-163/85 Colour television signal/BBC, the Board addressed the patent-eligibility of a colour television *signal*. The Board had contemplated finding that such a signal was merely a presentation of information, unpatentable under Art. 52(2)(d) EPC, but found that it was not a presentation of information 'as such' since it was 'defined in terms which inherently comprise the technical features of the TV system in which it occurs' (T-163/65: 383). This would appear to allow minimal specification of implicit 'technical features' to cause the Art. 52(2) EPC exclusions to be evaded and this decision is an early glimpse of the Board's later *technical character* doctrine. The Board again interpreted the subject-matter excluded by Art. 52(2) EPC to be 'abstract' and 'non-technical', and again bolstered its reasoning by reference to one of the Implementing Regulations: 'the exclusion might arguably be generalised to subject-matter which is essentially abstract in character, which is non-physical and therefore is not characterised by technical features in the sense of Rule [43(1)]

EPC'[3] (T-163/85: 383). The claimed signal can be viewed as a 'mixed' invention, the combination of technical and non-technical components, and so this decision did not replace the *technical contribution* approach the Board had developed in T-22/85 Document abstracting and retrieving/IBM and T-38/86 Text processing/IBM.

In October 1992, in T-167/92 IBM, the Board, considering a 'mixed'-method claim, and, applying its *technical contribution* approach, confirmed that features within an excluded field could only make such a contribution if they impact on non-excluded subject-matter by contributing to a technical effect or the solution of a technical problem.

The Board's view that claims to computer programs per se should not be accepted was still being held in April 1993, when in T-110/90 Editable document form/IBM it commented that it agreed:

> with the ... view that a computer program claimed by itself is not patentable, *irrespective of its content*. Although in the exclusions from patentability under Article 52(2), a general tendency might be detected to suggest that only abstract and non-technical subject-matters are excluded as such (Article 52(3)), *it seems worthwhile to note that computer programs not having an abstract, or non-technical 'content' must be considered also to fall within the exclusion*, as long as they are claimed as such. (T-110/90: 568, emphasis added)

In the same month, in T-236/91 TEXAS INSTRUMENTS, the Board reconfirmed its belief that the purpose of Art. 52(2) EPC was to exclude the non-technical: 'The feature common to most of the matters excluded by the non-exhaustive list of Article 52(2) is generally qualified as "non-technical"' (T-236/91: para. 4.1). This was qualified by an acknowledgement that the exclusion of computer programs 'did not necessarily concern non-technical subject-matter' (T-236/91: para. 4.2). Thus we have reached the stage where the Board is tacitly acknowledging that being technical in character is not sufficient to escape the Art. 52(2) EPC exclusion if only the *technical contribution* approach is applied. Moreover, in this decision the Board once again implicitly admits that the *technical contribution* approach relates to the assessment of inventive step via a *synergy* approach to 'mixed' claims rather than to patent-eligibility: 'In deciding the present case it will therefore be necessary to deal with these excluded matters only insofar as there is an "interrelationship" between any of them and the main issue to be decided, namely the involvement of an inventive step' (T-236/91: para. 4.3).

[3] Formerly Rule 29(1) EPC 1973. Rules and Articles are as numbered in EPC 2000 unless otherwise stated.

On the same day, in T-833/91 IBM, we see the Board begin to pride itself upon having established clear criteria as to how the exclusions of Art. 52(2) and (3) EPC should be interpreted:

> In accordance with the *consistent* case law, it can be said that the technical contribution to the art rendering a claimed invention an invention in the sense of Article 52(1) and thus patentable, may lie either in the problem underlying, and solved by, the claimed invention, or in the means constituting the solution of the underlying problem, or in the effects achieved in the solution of the underlying problem. (T-833/91: para. 3.1, emphasis added)

The Board's discomfort with its own belief that Art. 52(2) EPC only excluded the non-technical and its awareness of the technical nature of computer programs continued. Later in the same month, in T-164/92 Electronic computer components/ROBERT BOSCH, it commented that '[t]he fields excluded from patentability by virtue of Article 52(2) EPC are mostly non-technical fields. This is not the case, however, for computer programs as such, for they are excluded even when their "content" is of a technical nature' (T-164/92: 315–16).

Regarding 'mixed' claims, the Board became more explicit in acknowledging that the source of the 'technical contribution' might lie in the excluded subject-matter:

> it seems to the board that in the claimed subject-matter ... a computer program ... contributes ... to the clear technical character of the subject-matter since the [program] ... produces a technical effect consisting of considerably reducing the operating time of the computer component and thus undoubtedly improving the effectiveness of the device ... The said [computer program] ... should therefore be regarded as a technical means for carrying out the invention. (T-164/92: 316)

By October 1993, in T-204/93 AT&T, the Board had considered and rejected an alternative understanding of the Art. 52(2) EPC exclusions as being of subject-matter not susceptible of industrial application. This of course would have made no sense, for at the time methods of therapy, surgery and diagnosis were excluded on this basis but yet had been separated from the Art. 52(2) EPC exclusions during the drafting of the EPC. Nevertheless, the Board's belief that computer programs were unpatentable continued: 'computer programs as such ... are not patentable irrespective of their content, i.e. even if that content happened to be such as to make it useful, when run, for controlling a technical process' (T-204/93: para. 3.13).

The nature of the *technical contribution* required of a 'mixed' claim was elaborated on further in May 1994 in T-769/92 General purpose management system/SOHEI, a case relating to a method of doing business:

If, for instance, a non-patentable (e.g. mathematical, mental or business) method is implemented by running a program on a general-purpose computer, the fact alone that the computer consists of hardware does not render the method patentable ... However, if a contribution to [the computer] art can be found either in a technical problem (to be) solved, or in a technical effect achieved by the solution, said mix may not be excluded from patentability ... In the board's view the non-exclusion from patentability also applies to inventions, where technical considerations are to be made concerning the particulars of their implementation ... The very need for such technical considerations implies the occurrence of an (at least implicit) technical problem to be solved ... and (at least implicit) technical features ... solving that technical problem. (T-769/92: 535–6)

Thus the *anything added* approach that was later adopted was apparently still unacceptable at this stage. Nonetheless, in the same decision the Board went on to contradict itself on this very point:

More particularly, the teaching to provide, in the memory, the afore mentioned five files intended for different purposes ... and to cause the processing unit to perform the afore mentioned five functions would clearly require technical *considerations* ... It follows ... that subject-matter is not excluded from patentability if it involves, or implies, at least one aspect, or component, which is not excluded. (T-769/92: 538–9, emphasis added)

Although this is merely a first stage of a more elaborate implementation of the *technical contribution* approach – if a feature involves technical *considerations*, then it might result in a *technical contribution* and so the claim cannot automatically be rejected – the passage shows perhaps that the Board was beginning to think that if 'claimed subject-matter involves a feature which is not excluded', then it passes the Art. 52(2) and (3) EPC barrier, and if it also makes an inventive *technical contribution*, it then passes the Art. 56 EPC barrier too.

By October 1995 the Board was acknowledging an interrelationship between patent-eligibility under Art. 52(2) EPC and inventive step under Art. 56 EPC, or more correctly that its favoured approach was in fact a mixture. Thus in T-190/94 MITSUBISHI it commented that 'there is nevertheless some relationship between the ... issue of exclusion or not from patentability (Article 52(2)/(3)) and the issue of lack or not of inventive step (Article 56) ... On the other hand, this does not detract from the necessity to consider the two issues separately, one after the other' (T-190/94: para. 4).

This brings us to the last major decisions on patent-eligibility made by the Board while under the chairmanship of Paul van den Berg, the decisions in which the *technical contribution* approach was discarded as flawed and in which one of the two now dominant approaches, the *technical character* approach, was explicitly adopted. T-1173/97 Computer program product/IBM is dated July 1998, but was not issued until 1 March 1999.[4] The claims at issue were directed to computer programs as such, or on a carrier, more particularly:

20. A computer program product directly loadable into the internal memory of a digital computer, comprising software code portions for performing the steps of ... when said product is run on a computer.
21. A computer program product stored on a computer usable medium, comprising: computer readable program means for causing a computer to control an execution of an application. (T-1173/97: 610–11)

These claims had been rejected on the grounds that the subject-matter was a computer program as such. The Examining Division had argued that:

> Since the data medium and the program recorded thereon were not technically related, except for features which were already known from the prior art, the technical character of the computer program could not be derived from the physical character of the storage medium on which it was recorded. The technical character could also not be derived from the method or system in which the computer program was used. (T-1173/97: 612)

IBM had argued that the TRIPS Agreement did not exclude the patenting of computer programs and that the US and Japanese Patent Offices allowed claims to computer program products. In its summons to oral proceedings, the Board:

> pointed out that on the basis of the rules of interpretation according to Article 31 of the Vienna Convention on the Law of Treaties, Article 52(2) and (3) EPC could be understood to mean that computer programs claimed as such were excluded from patentability, regardless of their technical or non-technical content. Technical character became relevant only when a computer program was claimed within the framework of a method or an apparatus ... With reference to paragraph 4 of Article 31 of the Vienna Convention, *giving a special meaning to any of the terms of Article 52 EPC would not be an appropriate way to overcome the exclusion provisions.* (T-1173/97: 612–13, emphasis added)

According to IBM: 'for an invention to be patentable under Article 52(1) to (3) EPC it only has to have a technical character, be novel, involve an inventive step and be industrially applicable' and that the 'technical character of the invention according to the present application, which is essentially defined by the command sequence as specified in the stored program ... could not be lost for the sole reason that the

[4] An almost identical decision, T-935/97 Computer program product II/IBM was dated February 1999, but again it issued on 1 March 1999.

invention was claimed in a different format, like the format of claims 20 and 21' (T-1173/97: 613–14).

IBM specified this *technical character* approach, saying that:

In view of the technical problem and the technical solution required by Rules [42 and 43] EPC and the fact that the person skilled in the art is addressed in several provisions of the EPC, an invention must be understood to have a technical character in order to be patentable ... Article 52(2)(c) EPC gives a non-exhaustive list of negative examples, including computer programs. Since this paragraph also mentions activities which are clearly outside the realm of technology, the exclusion of computer programs as such can only be understood as intending to exclude these programs to the same extent as these other activities, which all concern non-technical subject-matter. A 'program as such' (excluded from patentability) would therefore in fact be a non-technical program. (T-1173/97: 614, emphasis added)

In other words, according to IBM, despite clearly saying that computer programs are excluded, despite having no definition of 'invention', and despite having no requirement of *technical character* for subject-matter to be an 'invention', the EPC should be interpreted as considering all technical subject-matter to be patent-eligible. This submission must be placed in the context of the entry into force of TRIPS, which, from 1994, in its Art. 27, mandated that inventions in all fields of technology (other than those covered by the current form of Art. 53 EPC) should be patentable. Should the EPC be non-compliant with TRIPS, it would have to be amended or its use abandoned in fields where there was non-compliance, and, as the adoption of EPC 2000 showed, amendment could be a lengthy process, risking the viability of the EPO if the EPC were not to be TRIPS-compliant during the process.

IBM directly attacked the Board's *technical contribution* approach, arguing that while the technical character of an invention might result from its field of application, it might equally well result from using technology to solve a problem in a non-technical field. It also argued: 'Like the relationship between a plug and a socket, the technical interface between computer and program ... ensures that the technical character of the method or system is maintained if the computer program is claimed by itself as a product' (T-1173/97: 615).

The Board accepted the significance of TRIPS but was not convinced that it applied to the EPC, although it was important to take TRIPS into consideration: 'since it is aimed at setting common standards and principles concerning the availability, scope and use of trade-related intellectual property rights, and therefore of patent rights. Thus TRIPS gives a clear indication of current trends' (T-1173/97: 616). In a similar vein, while emphasising that US and Japanese patent laws did not have counterparts to Art. 52(2) and (3) EPC, the Board commented that developments there 'represent a useful indication of modern trends. In the Board's opinion they may contribute to the further highly desirable (world-wide) harmonisation of patent law' (T-1173/97: 617). Maintaining the *technical contribution* approach risked both TRIPS non-compliance and the EPO becoming a backwater in the development of patent law in step with the development of new technologies. The EBD, which gave a green light to the relaxation of the EPO's approach to biotechnological inventions, despite the provisions of Art. 53 EPC, was finalised at the same time as the Board was revising its approach to computer-related inventions in T-1173/97 Computer program product/IBM. As a result, and in an extraordinary piece of logic requiring a perverse interpretation of the words 'as such' in Art. 52(3) EPC, the Board decided that the:

> combination of the two provisions (Article 52(2) and (3) EPC) demonstrates that the legislators did not want to exclude from patentability all programs for computers. In other words the fact that only patent applications relating to programs for computers as such are excluded from patentability means that patentability may be allowed for patent applications relating to programs for computers where the latter are not considered to be programs for computers as such. (T-1173/97: 618–19)

This required the Board to determine what 'as such' must mean, as this might 'result in the identification of those programs for computers which, as a result of not being considered programs for computers as such, are open to patentability' (T-1173/97: 619).

At this stage, the Board began to concretise its *technical character* approach, as in earlier decisions illegitimately relying on the Rules and 'general acceptance':

> Within the context of the application of the EPC the technical character of an invention is generally accepted as an essential requirement for its patentability. This is illustrated, for instance, by Rules [42 and 43] EPC ... The exclusion from patentability of programs for computers as such ... may be construed to mean that such programs are considered to be mere abstract creations, lacking in technical character. The use of the expression 'shall not be regarded as inventions' seems to confirm this interpretation ... This means that programs for computers must be considered as patentable inventions when they have a technical character. (T-1173/97: 619)

Having decided that all that was required to escape the exclusion was *technical character*, the nature of technical character for a computer program had to be resolved, as computer programs could not have technical character simply by virtue of being computer programs, since that would render the exclusion meaningless. Thus, the Board continued:

This means that physical modifications of the hardware … deriving from the execution of the instructions given by programs for computers cannot per se constitute the technical character required for avoiding the exclusion of those programs … Although such modifications may be considered to be technical, they are a common feature of all those programs for computers which have been made suitable for being run on a computer, and therefore cannot be used to distinguish programs for computers with a technical character from programs for computers as such. (T-1173/97: 620)

In other words, a *further technical effect*, beyond that implicit to any of the excluded subject-matter, was required. This, the Board said:

could be found in the further effects deriving from the execution (by the hardware) of the instructions given by the computer program. Where said further effects have a technical character or where they cause the software to solve a technical problem, an invention which brings about such an effect may be considered an invention, which can, in principle, be the subject-matter of a patent … Consequently a patent may be granted … in every case where a program for a computer is the only means, or one of the necessary means, of obtaining a technical effect within the meaning specified above, where, for instance, a technical effect of that kind is achieved by the internal functioning of a computer itself under the influence of said program … In other words, on condition that they are able to produce a technical effect in the above sense, all computer programs must be considered as inventions within the meaning of Article 52(1) EPC, and may be the subject-matter of a patent if the other requirements provided for by the EPC are satisfied. (T-1173/97: 620–1)

This then was the new test to be applied in respect of the Art. 52(2) and (3) EPC exclusions, the *technical character* approach according to which, should the excluded subject-matter implicitly have technical character, then the required *technical character* should result from a *further technical effect*. The reader will appreciate that this results in certain categories of subject-matter excluded by Art. 52(2) EPC, in particular discoveries, computer programs and methods of doing business, being treated differently from the others, in direct contradiction to the Board's statement that '[w]ith reference to paragraph 4 of Article 31 of the Vienna Convention, *giving a special meaning to any of the terms of Article 52 EPC would not be an appropriate way to overcome the exclusion provisions*' (T-1173/97: 613, emphasis added).

The Board then dropped its long-standing *technical contribution* approach by saying that 'Determining the technical contribution an invention achieves with respect to the prior art is … more appropriate for the purpose of examining novelty and inventive step than for deciding on possible exclusion under Article 52(2) and (3)' (T-1173/97: 623).

Since a computer program only has effect when run, the Board considered that a computer program product as such merely possessed the *potential* to produce the required *further technical effect*, but it saw no good reason to distinguish between a direct technical effect and the potential to produce a technical effect. A computer program product could therefore possess a technical character because it had the potential to cause a *further technical effect*.

The Board then had to show how this peculiar interpretation of the words 'as such' met with the requirements of the Vienna Convention, in particular Art. 31(1) VC which states: 'A treaty shall be interpreted in good faith in accordance with the ordinary meaning to be given to the terms of the treaty in their context and in the light of its object and purpose'; and Art. 31(4), which states: 'A special meaning shall be given to a term if it is established that the parties so intended.'

The Board felt that its interpretation was in full agreement with the Vienna Convention and that it had 'not gone beyond the ordinary meaning given to the terms of the EPC. The meaning it has attributed to the expression "as such" in Article 52(3) EPC is, in its opinion, not a special meaning within the meaning of Art. 31(4) VC, which would have required the consent of the parties to the EPC' (T-1173/97: 627). No explanation was given as to why this was not a 'special meaning'.

The Board then summarised its conclusions allowing claims to computer programs as such and when recorded on a carrier by virtue of technical character through technical effect:

> a computer program claimed by itself is not excluded from patentability if the program, when running on a computer or loaded into a computer, brings about, or is capable of bringing about, a technical effect which goes beyond the 'normal' physical interactions between the program (software) and the computer (hardware) on which it is run … *Furthermore, the Board is of the opinion that with regard to the exclusions under Article 52(2) and (3) EPC, it does not make any difference whether a computer program is claimed by itself or as a record on a carrier.* (T-1173/97: 632, emphasis added)

In other words, interestingly, claims to computer programs per se were not to be considered to be excluded by the language of Art. 52(2) EPC.

In September 2000, in T-931/95 Controlling pension benefits system/PBS PARTNERSHIP, the Board expanded on the new *technical character* approach: 'an invention may be an invention within the meaning of Article 52(1) if for example a technical effect is achieved by the invention or if technical considerations are required to carry out the invention' (T-931/95: 448–9).

However, in the case at issue the Board found that all the steps of the method claim were non-technical and while the claim referred to data processing and computing means:

> The feature of using technical means for a purely non-technical purpose and/or for processing purely non-technical information does not necessarily confer technical character to any such individual steps of use or to the method as a whole: in fact, any activity in the non-technical branches of human culture involves physical entities and uses, to a greater or lesser extent, technical means … The board notes that the mere occurrence of technical features in a claim does thus not turn the subject-matter of the claim into an invention within the meaning of Article 52(1). Such an approach would be too formalistic and would not take due account of the term 'invention'. (T-931/95: 450)

The reader will note that, at this stage, the Board had not yet accepted its later *anything added* approach.

The apparatus for performance of a method of doing business was not objectionable and the Board considered that a distinction with regard to patentability between a method for doing business and an apparatus suited to perform such a method was justified by the wording of Art. 52(2)(c) EPC:

> according to which 'schemes, rules and methods' are non-patentable categories in the field of economy and business, but the category of 'apparatus' in the sense of 'physical entity' or 'product' is not mentioned in Article 52(2) EPC. This means that, if a claim is directed to such an entity, the formal category of such a claim does in fact imply physical features of the claimed subject-matter which may qualify as technical features of the invention concerned and thus be relevant for its patentability. (T-931/95: 452)

This of course is an interpretation of 'as such' that gives those words their normal meaning – an apparatus cannot be a method 'as such'.

Obviously feeling a little nervous of its new *technical character* approach, the Board commented that: '[i]t may very well be that … the meaning of the term "technical" or "technical character" is not particularly clear … In the board's view the fact that the exact meaning of a term may be disputed does in itself not necessarily constitute a good reason for not using that term as a criterion, certainly not in the absence of a better term: case law may clarify the issue' (T-931/95: 454). The Board went on to congratulate itself that the German Courts had very recently adopted a similar approach: 'it seems appropriate to mention here the decision of the German Federal Court of Justice [DE-Sprachanalyseeinrichtung 2002] … which, although it points out that "technical character" as a distinctive criterion between patentable and non-patentable subject-matter is a rather vague notion, applies it itself' (T-931/95: 455).

The decision is also notable for its suggestion that non-technical features in a claim should become part of the formulation of the problem when inventive step is assessed using the problem-solution approach, in effect considering the non-technical features to be part of the state of the art (as opposed to neither part of the state of the art nor contributory to inventive step as the Board would later decide):

> the improvement envisaged by the invention according to the application is an essentially economic one, i.e. lies in the field of economy, which, therefore, cannot contribute to inventive step. The regime of patentable subject-matter is only entered with programming of a computer system for carrying out the invention. The assessment of inventive step has thus to be carried out from the point of view of a software developer or application programmer, as the appropriate person skilled in the art, *having the knowledge of the concept and structure of the improved pension benefits system and of the underlying schemes of information processing as set out for example in the present method claims* ... Regarding that the technical features of the apparatus claimed are functionally defined by precisely those steps of information processing which form part of the knowledge of the skilled person and that the application of computer systems in the economic sector has already been a general phenomenon at the priority date (filing date) of the application, it must be concluded that the claimed subject-matter does not involve an inventive step. (T-931/95: 456–7, emphasis added)

In March 2002, in T-49/99 Informational modeling/ INTERNATIONAL COMPUTERS, the Board (now chaired by Dr Stefan Steinbrener) began to take a fresh approach to the Art. 52(2) EPC exclusions. In a glimpse of its later *COMVIK* approach, the Board confirmed that: '[i]f the invention as claimed relates to non-technical subject-matter or activities, only those aspects or elements of the invention which contribute to its technical character are to be given significance in assessing inventive step' (T-49/99: para. 5). The case at issue related to information modelling, which the Board held to be non-technical, despite not being one of the exclusions listed in Art. 52(2) EPC:

> Information modelling is a formalized process carried out by a system engineer or a similar skilled person ... Although information modelling embodies useful concepts and methods in developing complex software systems, it is as such an intellectual activity having all traits typical for non-technical branches of knowledge and thus being closely analogous to the non-inventions listed under Article 52(2)(a) and (c) EPC ... In examining inventive step, it should hence be treated like any other human activity in a non-technical field, which is, as such, not an invention for the purposes of Article 52(1) EPC. Only the purposive use of information modelling in the context of a solution to a technical problem ... may contribute to the technical character of an invention. (T-49/99: para. 7)

Thus, the 'purposive use' of a non-technical technique in the solution of a 'technical problem' may contribute to the *technical character* of an invention and so demonstrate the presence of an inventive step. In other words *technical character* seems to be a feature required not only for subject-matter to qualify as an invention but also for a development over the prior art to involve an inventive step.

Although the next relevant decision in date order from the Board is T-1177/97 Translating natural languages/SYSTRAN, a decision dated July 2002, that decision did not in fact issue in written form until July 2003, by which time what is one of the most important decisions of the Board under the chairmanship of Stefan Steinbrener, T-641/00 Two identities/COMVIK, had issued in written form. T-641/00 Two identities/COMVIK issued in September 2002 following oral proceedings in January 2002.

T-641/00 Two identities/COMVIK sets out the Board's realisation that moving to the *technical character* approach and separating patent-eligibility from inventive step still leaves problems, problems which the Board tried to solve by arguing that non-technical features cannot be taken into account when assessing inventive step. This is not yet a *synergy* approach but a step in that direction. The decision has caused immense confusion for the manner in which it suggested this be done and the implications to the meaning of 'the state of the art', the body of prior knowledge defined in Art. 54 EPC against which novelty and inventive step are assessed. To be generous to the *COMVIK* approach, it could be understood as meaning only that things without technical character or impact on technical character *cannot* contribute to inventive step. In its most basic and original form (it was 'tweaked' later), the *COMVIK* approach is substantially equivalent to the previously scrapped *technical contribution* approach.

The decision went further, however, by excluding the published but non-technical from the state of the art. Thus:

> Article 56 EPC states in its English text that an invention shall be considered to involve an inventive step if, having regard to the state of the art, it is not obvious to a person skilled in the art. The equally authentic French and German texts are somewhat more informative in that they can best be rendered in English as stating that an invention shall be considered as based on inventive activity if a skilled person cannot derive it in an obvious manner from the *state of technology*. (T-641/00: 356, emphasis added)

Thus the 'state of the art' encompasses only technological knowledge. If this seems an unreasonable interpretation of the passage quoted above, we can only say that it is the Board's own interpretation:

as explained in the COMVIK decision ... the term 'state of the art' ... should ... be understood as 'state of technology', which in the context of the EPC does not include the state of the art in commerce and business methods ... It can hardly be assumed that the EPC envisaged the notional person skilled in the (technological) art to take notice of everything, in all fields of human culture and regardless of its informational character. A consistent construction of the patentability provisions requires the term 'everything' in Article 54(2) EPC to be understood as concerning such kind of information which is relevant to some field of technology ... From these considerations it follows that anything which is not related to any technological field or field from which, because of its informational character, a skilled person would expect to derive any technically relevant information, does not belong to the state of the art to be considered in the context of Articles 54 and 56, even if it had been made available to the general public before the relevant priority date. (T-172/03: paras. 8–10)

T-172/03 Order management/RICOH is discussed further below in its proper turn. However, we should plant our flag and declare that this assertion, that things that are public do not form part of the state of the art, is one of the most egregious, and unnecessary, misinterpretations of the clear language of the EPC that we have ever encountered.

Accepting its own earlier *technical character* approach to Art. 52(2) EPC, the Board also grounded the *COMVIK* approach to inventive step in the acceptance of a 'mixed' claim in an early decision (T-26/86 X-ray apparatus/KOCH & STERZEL) from its 'rival' board 3.4.01:

The legal definition of Article 56 EPC is to be put into context with the remaining patentability requirements of Articles 52 to 57 EPC, these articles implying the general principles that patents shall be available for inventions in all fields of technology ... and that technical character is a sine qua non for an invention in the sense of the EPC (see, for example, decision T 931/95 [Controlling pension benefits system/PBS PARTNERSHIP] ...) ... On this approach it is legitimate to have a mix of technical and 'non-technical' features (i.e. features relating to non-inventions within the meaning of Article 52(2) EPC) appearing in a claim, even if the non-technical features should form a dominating part. Thus in T 26/86 [X-ray apparatus/KOCH & STERZEL] ... a mix of technical and non-technical features was considered as a matter of principle to be patentable even if the technical was not the dominating part of the invention. As reasoned by the Board, 'the teaching (might, otherwise, be made) unpatentable in its entirety if the greater part is non-technical and even though the technical aspect which is found to be subordinate is in fact judged to be novel and to involve inventive step' ... It follows that the Board, although allowing a mix of technical and non-technical features to be claimed, *considered the technical part of the invention as the basis for assessing inventive step*. (T-641/00: 356–7, emphasis added)

The Board continued:

Further, where a feature cannot be considered as contributing to the solution of any technical problem by providing a technical effect it has no significance for the purpose of assessing inventive step ... In the present Board's view, this finding is entirely consistent with the general requirement for an invention to have technical character, leading to the conclusion that an invention in the sense of Article 52 EPC can only be made up of those features which contribute to said technical character. (T-641/00: 358)

In T-1177/97 Translating natural languages/SYSTRAN, issued in writing in July 2003, the Board followed T-641/00 Two identities/COMVIK, but softened it by accepting that the non-technical may be considered when assessing inventive step if its use or format has technical character:

Features of the invention which do not form part of the technical solution to the technical problem have to be disregarded in the assessment of inventive step (see for example decision T 641/00 [Two identities/COMVIK] ...) ... Hence, in accordance with [EPO] ... jurisprudence it seems to be common ground that the use of a piece of information in a technical system, or its usability for this purpose, may confer a technical character on the information itself in that it reflects the properties of the technical system, for instance by being specifically formatted and/or processed. Such information when used in or processed by the technical system may be part of a technical solution to a technical problem and form the basis for a technical contribution of the invention to the prior art ... The Board thus comes to the conclusion that information and methods related to linguistics may in principle assume technical character if they are used in a computer system and form part of a technical problem solution ... The implementation of the information and methods related to linguistics as a computerized translation process ... requires technical considerations and thus provides a technical aspect to per se non-technical things such as dictionaries ... Features or aspects of the method which reflect only peculiarities of the field of linguistics, however, must be ignored in assessing inventive step. (T-1177/97: para. 3)

By November 2003, in T-172/03 Order management/RICOH, the Board was firmly focused on the technical, considering that:

the patentability of an invention, for which inventive step is a requirement, must arise from features and aspects of the invention from which a technical solution to a technical problem can be inferred and which are thus of a technical character ... In the case of a mixed-type invention (including non-technical aspects), examination for patentability normally requires an analysis of the invention and the construction of the claims to determine the technical content of the claims as a prerequisite step. (T-172/03: para. 3)

However, as mentioned above, this brought the Board to consider that non-technical features were neither part of the state of the art nor features that should be considered when assessing inventive step.

In April 2004 the Board took a further major step in setting forth an alternative to the *technical character* approach to Art. 52(2)/(3) EPC, although as mentioned above this alternative was also used in T-1173/97 Computer program product/IBM. Thus, in T-258/03 Auction method/ HITACHI the Board progressed from its *technical character* approach to its *anything added* approach to 'mixed' claims:

it is often difficult to separate a claim into technical and non-technical features, and an invention may have technical aspects which are hidden in a largely non-technical context ... Such technical aspects may be easier to identify within the framework of the examination as to inventive step, which, in accordance with the jurisprudence of the boards of appeal, is concerned with the technical aspects of an invention ... Thus, in addition to the restrictive wording of Article 52(3) EPC limiting the applicability of Article 52(2) EPC, there may be practical reasons for generally regarding mixes of technical and non-technical features as inventions in the meaning of Article 52(1) EPC. (T-258/03: 583)

Accepting that there was an inconsistency with T-931/95 Controlling pension benefits system/PBS PARTNERSHIP, the Board decided that, to be consistent with scrapping the *technical contribution* approach, which involved considering the prior art when applying Art. 52(2) EPC:

there should be no need to further qualify the relevance of technical aspects of a method claim in order to determine the technical character of the method. In fact, it appears to the Board that an assessment of the technical character of a method based on the degree of banality of the technical features of the claim would involve remnants of the contribution approach by implying an evaluation in the light of the available prior art or common general knowledge. (T-258/03: 584)

The Board considered that for methods and apparatus for putting methods into effect the same treatment under Art. 52(2) EPC was required:

What matters having regard to the concept of 'invention' within the meaning of Article 52(1) EPC is the presence of technical character which may be implied by the physical features of an entity or the nature of an activity, or may be conferred to a non-technical activity by the use of technical means. In particular, the Board holds that the latter cannot be considered to be a non-invention 'as such' within the meaning of Article 52(2) and (3) EPC. Hence, in the Board's view, activities falling within the notion of a non-invention 'as such' would typically represent purely abstract concepts devoid of any technical implications ... The Board is aware that its comparatively broad interpretation of the term 'invention' in Article 52(1) EPC will include activities which are so familiar that their technical character tends to be overlooked, such as the act of writing using pen and paper ... It is therefore concluded that, in general, a method involving technical means is an invention within the meaning of Article 52(1) EPC. (T-258/03: 585)

This is in effect the *anything added* approach.

In June 2006 the Board handed down six, almost identically worded, decisions relating to a method of operating a computer and a computer program on a carrier. Here we will refer to only one of these, T-424/03 Clipboard formats/MICROSOFT. The program on a carrier claim read as follows: 'a computer-readable medium having computer-executable instructions adapted to cause the computer system to perform the method of one of claims 1 to 4' (T-424/03: para. IV).

On the subject of the patent-eligibility of the method claims under Art. 52(2) EPC, the Board followed T-258/03 Auction method/HITACHI and accepted that the method was not excluded since it used technical means, for example a clipboard memory. However, the Board chose to go further:

Moreover, the Board would like to emphasise that a method implemented in a computer system represents a sequence of steps actually performed and achieving an effect, and not a sequence of computer-executable instructions (i.e. a computer program) which just have the potential of achieving such an effect when loaded into, and run on, a computer. Thus, the Board holds that the claim category of a computer-implemented method is distinguished from that of a computer program. Even though a method, in particular a method of operating a computer, may be put into practice with the help of a computer program, a claim relating to such a method does not claim a computer program in the category of a computer program. Hence, present claim 1 cannot relate to a computer program as such. (T-424/03: para. 5.1)

It will be appreciated that this represents an interpretation of the phrase 'as such' in Art. 52(3) EPC as having its ordinary common sense meaning: a method is not a computer program, a computer is not a computer program, and so on. We term this the *anything added* approach and it is indeed the approach that we consider to be correct as there is no need to give these words anything other than their ordinary, literal meaning.

The Board also considered the method steps to contribute to the technical character as they solved a technical problem by technical means in that functional data structures (clipboard formats) were used independently of any cognitive content to enhance the internal operation of a computer system. The method steps were therefore considered to provide the computer with a further functionality. This was of relevance since in this way the method steps could be considered when assessing inventive step using the *COMVIK* approach.

Regarding the program-on-carrier claim, the Board considered that its subject-matter had:

technical character since it relates to a computer-readable medium, i.e. a technical product involving a carrier (see decision T 258/03 [Auction method/

> HITACHI] ...) ... Moreover, the computer-executable instructions have the potential of achieving the above-mentioned further technical effect of enhancing the internal operation of the computer, which goes beyond the elementary interaction of any hardware and software of data processing (see T 1173/97 [Computer program product/IBM] ...) ... The computer program recorded on the medium is therefore not considered to be a computer program as such, and thus also contributes to the technical character of the claimed subject-matter. (T-424/03: para. 5.3)

Thus a program-on-carrier is not excluded when the *anything added* approach of T-258/03 Auction method/HITACHI is followed and moreover the program itself is not excluded since, by contributing a *further technical effect*, it is not a program as such in accordance with T-1173/97 Computer program product/IBM. From here on, neither programs nor programs on carriers need to be excluded if the Board's case law is followed (although different interpretations of what 'as such' means are of course being applied) and the requirement for an inventive step only provides a hurdle if no *further technical effect* can be determined and if the perverse exclusion of the non-technical in the *COMVIK* approach has to be followed.

On the subject of inventive step, having found the method steps to provide technical character, the claims to the program-on-carrier were held to involve an inventive step since they referred to the method, that is the program had the potential to put the method into effect and so had technical character and had to be taken into account when assessing the inventive step of the program plus carrier combination using the *COMVIK* approach.

In March 2006 one of the other Electricity Boards, 3.5.02, had made a gentle challenge to the *anything added* approach of the Board in T-258/03 Auction method/HITACHI, to the effect that the claim must explicitly mention the hardware rather than rely on its presence or use being implied. In June 2006 in T-928/03 Video game/KONAMI, the Board again confirmed that implicit use was sufficient. The opportunity was also taken, however, to justify the *COMVIK* approach to inventive step by allowing non-technical features to be included in the formulation of the technical problem:

> The Board would like to add that applying the Comvik approach (i.e. treating non-technical aspects as constraints in the formulation of the technical problem) in a fair manner must bear in mind its purpose: on the one hand, the approach is to make sure that non-technical aspects do not support a finding of inventiveness; on the other hand, actual contributions to the technical character by any feature of an invention must be taken into account when assessing inventive step. (T-928/03: para. 5.3.3)

The *COMVIK* approach was referred to in October 2006 by the England and Wales Court of Appeal as 'intellectually dishonest'. In his judgment, in *Aerotel* v. *Telco Holdings* (UK-Aerotel 2006), Jacob LJ suggested that the president of the EPO should put the following points to the EBoA in order to clarify the Art. 52(2) EPC exclusions:

1. What is the correct approach to adopt in determining whether an invention relates to subject matter that is excluded under Article 52?
2. How should those elements of a claim that relate to excluded subject matter be treated when assessing whether an invention is novel and inventive under Articles 54 and 56?
3. And specifically:
   (a) Is an operative computer program loaded onto a medium such as a chip or hard drive of a computer excluded by Art. 52(2) unless it produces a technical effect, if so what is meant by 'technical effect'?
   (b) What are the key characteristics of the method of doing business exclusion? (UK-Aerotel 2006: para. 76)

Alain Pompidou, the then president of the EPO, declined Jacob LJ's invitation:

I am writing to you to let you know that the above-mentioned decision has led to a discussion within the EPO as to the possibility of referring questions regarding the exclusions to patentability set out in Article 52(2) EPC to the Enlarged Board of Appeal.

On the basis of these discussions I have decided that at the moment there is an insufficient legal basis for a referral under Article 112(1)(b) EPC. Leaving aside Board of Appeal case law the line of reasoning of which has been abandoned by later case law, I believe there are insufficient differences between current Board of Appeal decisions dealing with Article 52 EPC exclusions on important points of law that would justify a referral at this stage. (Pompidou: 2007)[5]

In November 2006, at the oral proceedings in T-154/04 Estimating sales activity/DUNS LICENSING ASSOCIATES, the appellants asked the Board to refer Jacob's questions to the EBoA, together with two further questions:

4. Is a system for estimating product distribution for non-reporting outlets based on weighing factors that are a function of the distance between the non-reporting outlets and sample reporting outlets and the characterisation, e.g. size, of the non-reporting and reporting outlets of a technical nature?

5(a). Are the exclusions of Article 52 to be treated differently from each other in the way that obviousness is assessed?

[5] This letter is referred to in G-3/08 Programs for computers as being dated 22 February 2007.

5(b). Are inventions alleged to be within Article 52 to have a different test for obviousness than other inventions not alleged to be within Article 52? (T-154/04: 53)

The Board's written decision was issued in May 2007 and set out at length its justification for its position. In doing so, it referred to the 'constant' jurisprudence of the Boards as having seven principles, of which the following are relevant here:

(B) Having technical character is an implicit requisite of an 'invention' within the meaning of Article 52(1) EPC …
(C) Article 52(2) EPC does not exclude from patentability any subject matter or activity having technical character, even if it is related to the items listed in this provision since these items are only excluded 'as such' (Article 52(3) EPC).
(E) For examining patentability of an invention in respect of a claim, the claim must be construed to determine the technical features of the invention, i.e. the features which contribute to the technical character of the invention.
(F) … Novelty and inventive step, however, can be based only on technical features … Non-technical features, to the extent that they do not interact with the technical subject matter of the claim for solving a technical problem, i.e. non-technical features 'as such', do not provide a technical contribution to the prior art and are thus ignored in assessing novelty and inventive step.
(G) For the purpose of the problem-and-solution approach, the problem must be a technical problem which the skilled person in the particular technical field might be asked to solve at the relevant priority date. The technical problem may be formulated using an aim to be achieved in a non-technical field, and which is thus not part of the technical contribution provided by the invention to the prior art. This may be done in particular to define a constraint that has to be met (even if the aim stems from an a posteriori knowledge of the invention). (T-154/04: 60–1)

The Board pointed to the legislative history of the adoption of Art. 52(3) EPC to support its argument that the exclusions were to be interpreted narrowly:

The second paragraph of Article 52 EPC is merely a negative, non-exhaustive list of what should not be regarded as an invention within the meaning of Article 52(1) EPC. It was the clear intention of the contracting states that this list of 'excluded' subject matter should not be given a too broad scope of application, as follows from the legislative history of Article 52 (2) EPC … amended on initiative of the German delegation with the reasoning: 'This could lead to the erroneous conclusion that a broad interpretation should be given to items not limited in this way in paragraph 2' (see … [Document] M/11 … and … [Document] M/PR/I …). Paragraph 3 of the present Article 52 EPC was introduced as a bar to such a broad interpretation of Article 52(2) EPC. (T-154/04: 62–3)

The Board referred to various earlier decisions to show that *technical character* had long been accepted by the Boards as a requirement for patentability. However, this glossed over the fact that 'character A is required for X to be a patent-eligible invention' does not equate to 'the possession of character A makes X a patent-eligible invention'. (The fact that a heartbeat is required for a dog to be alive does not mean that possession of a heartbeat makes the possessor a live dog.)

More interestingly, the Board claimed that the common applicability of an exception to the exclusion (i.e. of Art. 52(3) EPC) meant that the exclusions of Art. 52(2) EPC had a common criterion, again of course *technical character*:

> The mere fact that the Article 52(2) list of items not to be regarded as inventions is non-exhaustive ('in particular') is indicative of the existence of an exclusion criterion common to all those items and allowing for additions to the list that were thought possible. The enumeration of typical non-inventions in Article 52(2) EPC covers subjects whose common feature is a substantial lack of technical character. The formulation of the law ultimately derives from the classical notion of invention adopted, which distinguishes between practical scientific applications and intellectual achievements in general. The connection of the notions of invention and technical character of the invention arises immediately, because the list of exclusions in Article 52(2) EPC, with its reference to Article 52(1) EPC, must be viewed as a negative definition of the notion of invention. This connection is also inherent in other provisions of the EPC, such as Articles 18 and 56 and Rules [42(1) and 43(1)] EPC, which clearly express this underlying principle of patent law. (T-154/04: 64–5)

Rather weakly, the Board then sought to confirm this by reference to the amendment of Art. 52(1) EPC which had been agreed in the 2000 revision (whereby the clause had been supplemented by a reference to 'all fields of technology'). Although the amendment had nothing to do with the Board's case law and everything to do with making the EPC TRIPS-compliant, the Board commented:

> The technical character as a legal requirement of invention was expressly confirmed by the Conference of the Contracting States to Revise the European Patent Convention of 20 to 29 November 2000. Revised Article 52(1) EPC was approved by the contracting states on the basis of the Basic Proposal for the Revision of the European Patent Convention, [D]ocument MR/2/00, which is hence – as part of a subsequent agreement between the contracting states concerning the EPC – a valid instrument for construing the Convention according to the traditional rules of interpretation. (T-154/04: 65)

Had the intention of the legislators of the EPC 2000 revision been to enshrine the then extremely recent and substantial reclassification by TBoA 3.5.01 of the words 'as such' in Art. 52(3) EPC as meaning 'to the extent the subject-matter does not have or have the potential to have technical character', we might have expected Art. 52(3) EPC to be revised or even deleted. No such revision occurred, despite the deletion of the exclusion of computer programs being discussed at length.

While never quite addressing the *synergy* approach to inventive step for 'mixed' claims, the Board again got close: 'non-technical features to the extent that they do not interact with technical features to produce a technical effect cannot establish novelty or inventive step' (T-154/04: 72–3).

The self-inflicted problems of the combination of the EPO's problem/solution and *COMVIK* approaches to inventive step received some further attention:

> for the purpose of the problem-and-solution approach developed as a test for whether an invention meets the requirement of inventive step, the problem must be a technical problem ... The definition of the technical problem, however, is difficult if the actual novel and creative concept making up the core of the claimed invention resides in the realm outside any technological field as it is frequently the case with computer implemented inventions. Defining the problem without referring to this non-technical part of the invention, if at all possible, will generally result either in an unintelligible vestigial definition, or in a contrived statement that does not adequately reflect the real technical contribution provided to the prior art ... The Board, therefore, allowed in COMVIK an aim to be achieved in a non-technical field to appear in the formulation of the problem as part of the framework of the technical problem that is to be solved, in particular as a constraint that is to be met ... Such a formulation has the additional, desirable effect that the non-technical aspects of the claimed invention, which generally relate to non-patentable desiderata, ideas, and concepts and belong to the phase preceding any invention, are automatically cut out of the assessment of inventive step and cannot be mistaken for technical features positively contributing to inventive step. Since only technical features and aspects of the claimed invention should be taken into account in assessing inventive step, i.e. the innovation must be on the technical side, not in a non-patentable field ... it is irrelevant whether such a non-technical aim was known before the priority date of the application, or not. (T-154/04: 73–4)

In other words, the *COMVIK* approach is only an artefact; it does not actually change what is or is not prior art.

In December 2006, following the *technical character* approach in T-1227/05 Circuit simulation I/INFINEON TECHNOLOGIES, the Board accepted a claim to a computer program per se: 'The computer program according to claim 4 has the potential for a technical effect going beyond basic hardware/software interaction in a standard computer. Loaded onto a computer it provides for automatic simulation and evaluation of noise-affected circuits. The computer program thus does not come under the program exclusion' (T-1227/05: 584).

It will be appreciated that most physical objects, including aesthetic creations and discoveries, have the *potential* for achieving technical effects and that claims to such objects per se cover all uses of the objects and not just those in which the potential for technical effect is realised.

The Board still clearly felt that further exoneration of the *COMVIK* approach was required and in March 2007, in T-1284/04 Loan system/KING, added:

> The Board would nevertheless like to add that the COMVIK approach does not consider the non-technical constraints as belonging to the prior art, but rather as belonging to the conception or motivation phase normally preceding an invention since they may lead to a technical problem without contributing to its solution. (T-1284/04: para. 3.1)

The written decision in T-154/04 Estimating sales activity/DUNS LICENSING ASSOCIATES was handed down in May 2007. In July 2007 a new president of the EPO (Alison Brimelow) was appointed, and in October 2008 she referred the following questions to the EBoA in an attempt to get clarification on the law as it concerned exclusions:

1. Can a computer program only be excluded as a computer program as such if it is explicitly claimed as a computer program?

2(A). Can a claim in the area of computer programs avoid exclusion under Art. 52(2)(c) and (3) merely by explicitly mentioning the use of a computer or a computer-readable data storage medium?

2(B). If question 2(A) is answered in the negative, is a further technical effect necessary to avoid exclusion, said effect going beyond those effects inherent in the use of a computer or data storage medium to respectfully execute or store a computer program?

3(A). Must a claimed feature cause a technical effect on a physical entity in the real world to contribute to the technical character of the claim?

3(B). If question 3(A) is answered in the positive, is it sufficient that the physical entity be an unspecified computer?

3(C). If question 3(A) is answered in the negative, can features contribute to the technical character of the claim if the only effects to which they contribute are independent of any particular hardware that may be used?

4(A). Does the activity of programming a computer necessarily involve technical considerations?

4(B). If question 4(A) is answered in the positive, do all features resulting from programming thus contribute to the technical character of a claim?

4(C). If question 4(A) is answered in the negative, can features resulting from programming contribute to the technical character of a claim only when they contribute to a further technical effect when the program is executed? (Correspondence *Brimelow* 2008)

In May 2010, just before Brimelow ceased to be president of the EPO, the Enlarged Board replied, rejecting the referral. The referral opinion is discussed below in section 3.5.

3.3 What the other Boards were doing

3.3.1 Board 3.4.01 (Physics I)

The most active of the other Boards was Physics I, TBoA 3.4.01, which began in May 1987 with a decision that TBoA 3.5.01 later repeatedly had to find a way around, T-26/86 X-ray apparatus/KOCH & STERZEL (Chairman Lederer). At this stage, the only major decision in place was T-208/84 Computer-related invention/VICOM.

The patent at issue had claims that covered known X-ray imaging apparatus operating under the control of a novel computer program. Following T-208/84 Computer-related invention/VICOM, this would be patentable, but one of the opponents argued that such a narrow interpretation of Art. 52(3) EPC would:

> have the effect of undermining Article 52(2) EPC, since it would mean that any computer program designed for a general-purpose computer would meet the patentability requirements because of the technical effect of generating signals ... In other words, Article 52(2) EPC should be regarded as applying whenever the essence of the subject-matter was not of a technical character (as when the essence of the teaching was a computer program). (T-26/86: 21)

Board 3.4.01 took a robust and straightforward approach, in essence the *anything added* approach:

> [t]o decide whether the subject-matter of claim 1 is or is not an invention within the meaning of Article 52(2) EPC, it is necessary to determine whether or not it is a computer program as such ... Claim 1 relates neither to a computer program on its own ... nor a computer program in the form of a recording on a data carrier, nor a known, general-purpose computer in combination with a computer program. It is in fact [directed to apparatus] ... incorporating a data processing unit operating in accordance with a [program]. (T-26/86: 22)

In July 1988, in T-366/87 Harmonic vibrations/STERNHEIMER, TBoA 3.4.01 considered an application relating to a method for generating sound and apparatus for performing such a method. The Board found the Art. 52(2) EPC exclusions to have in common the characteristic of not comprising technical means or involving the use of technical means to achieve a concrete technical effect, for example of changing the structure or properties of an object.

The apparatus claims involved technical means producing a technical effect, but the method claim had to be examined to see if it involved the use of technical means or the production of a technical effect. The Board found that certain steps of the method were of a technical nature and that therefore the claims could not be rejected. This decision thus seems to anticipate the *technical character* approach later adopted by TBoA 3.5.01 and again to employ something similar to the *anything added* approach.

Returning to the topic in December 1989 in T-158/88 Character form/SIEMENS, Board 3.4.01 referred back only to its own earlier decision T-26/86 X-ray apparatus/KOCH & STERZEL. The case concerned a method for displaying characters on a visual display unit (computer screen). The Board considered that the method claim:

> essentially describes not a technical operating procedure for a computer and its visual display unit but an idea for a program, i.e. general instructions on how to program a software-controlled computer to achieve the desired effect … The statement that technical means … are to be used to carry out the claimed process … is not alone sufficient to render patentable within the meaning of Article 52(1) EPC a process which in essence constitutes a computer program as such. A computer program is not considered part of a technical operating procedure if the claimed teaching merely modifies the data and produces no effects beyond information processing. (T-158/88: 569–70)

The Board considered that the result of the claimed process was not technical in nature and thus that the process could only be patent-eligible if it solved a technical problem using technical means.

On the subject of the computer program implicitly used in the claimed process, the Board found that its purpose as an information carrier involved nothing technical and that it could not: 'be considered part of a technical teaching on the basis of the result achieved' (T-158/88: 572). The method claim was therefore to be considered as relating to the program as such.

To summarise, Board 3.4.01 looked for technical means, a technical result, the solution of a technical problem and a technical teaching. The use of a visual display unit or a computer program was not enough and by implication the *technical contribution* approach was followed, requiring the prior art to be considered before the applicability or otherwise of Art. 52(2) EPC could be known.

In July 1990, in T-603/89 Marker/BEATTIE, Board 3.4.01 indicated that it was following its own earlier decisions T-26/86 X-ray apparatus/KOCH & STERZEL and T-158/88 Character form/SIEMENS as well as TBoA 3.5.01's decision T-115/85 Computer-related invention/IBM. The subject-matter at issue was a marker to facilitate the playing of a keyboard instrument. The Examining Division had rejected this under the mental acts and presentations of information provisions of Art. 52(2) EPC. The claim was thus a 'mixed' claim and Board 3.4.01

confirmed its earlier approach to such mixed claims: 'that the subject-matter of a "mix" claim is not excluded from patentability under Article 52(2) and (3) EPC *when, but only when, the non-technical elements interact with the known technical elements in order to produce a technical effect*' (T-603/89: 236, emphasis added). This, we suggest, is similar to the *synergy* approach that we feel is the correct manner to deal with 'mixed' claims (under inventive step). More particularly, the Board set out its requirement for technicality:

> the Board considers that when there is an interaction between the technical and non-technical elements, and the mix as a whole solves a technical problem, it is not excluded from patentability ... In the absence of such an interaction – when the technical elements are only a support for the non-technical elements but do not otherwise co-operate therewith – the invention does not make use of technical means and cannot therefore be granted. (T-603/89: 236)

In the case at issue, no technical means were found to have been used and no technical problem was solved, so the marker was excluded under Art. 52(2) EPC.

In T-854/90 Card reader/IBM in July 1992, Board 3.4.01 (Chairman Paterson) was faced with an application concerning a method of operating an automatic self-service machine in which a prospective user inserts a card carrying his identifying information. Where the card is presented for the first time, the Board considered it to be in effect equivalent to an application form and the method to be one of deciding whether that card should thereafter be recognised by the machine as an authorised card. This the Board considered to be part of a business operation. While the claimed method did include the use of technical means, 'the presence of such technical components does not alter the fact that the claimed method is a business method as such, rather than a technical method (just as the use of a typewriter to perform a business activity would not change such an activity into a technical method)' (T-854/90: 676). In this decision, Board 3.4.01 confirmed that the mere fact of being a 'mixed' claim did not automatically give the claimed subject-matter technical character.

In a frequently quoted decision from July 1994, T-1002/92 Queueing system/PETTERSSON, Board 3.4.01 had to consider a patent relating to an apparatus for determining the queue sequence for serving customers, that is a business method using hardware operating under the control of software. The opponent relied on Board 3.5.01's *technical contribution* approach of T-38/86 Text processing/IBM. Board 3.4.01, however, indicated that this approach misunderstood the relationship between Art. 52 and Art. 56 EPC:

In a case such as the present, a first question to be considered is whether the Appellant is correct in his contention that the subject-matter of Claim 1 does not constitute an 'invention' within the meaning of Article 52(1) EPC. If, contrary to the Appellant's contention, such subject-matter is not excluded from being patentable under Article 52 EPC, a further and separate question, also raised by the Appellant, is whether the claimed subject-matter involves an inventive step. (T-1002/92: 612–13)

Commenting that '[a] common characteristic of [the Art. 52(2) EPC] ... excluded categories is that their subject-matter is abstract in nature' (T-1002/92: 613), the Board developed its own early version of the *technical character* approach: 'The claimed apparatus is clearly technical in nature ... and has practical application to the service of "customers". The fact that one such practical application of such apparatus concerns the service of customers of "a business equipment" does not mean that the claimed subject-matter must be equated with a method of doing business, as such' (T-1002/92: 613).

By October 1996 Board 3.4.01 seemed to be applying an early version of the *COMVIK* approach to inventive step. In T-599/93 SIEMENS, Board 3.4.01 considered that characterising features of a claim that lay in a field excluded from patentability under Art. 52(2)(d) EPC could not contribute to inventive step (T-599/93: para. 4). This led to the bizarre conclusion that the subject-matter lacked inventive step and 'therefore is not allowable under Art. 52(1) and (2d) in conjunction with Art. 56 EPC' (T-599/93: para. 6).

By July 2005, with the *technical character* test now dominant, in T-914/02 Core loading arrangement/GENERAL ELECTRIC Board 3.4.01 (Chairman Schachenmann) commented on 'technical considerations' as these relate to the establishment of technical character of what would otherwise be an excluded activity. The case concerned a method of designing a core loading arrangement for a reactor. The position is summarised as follows:

The claimed method ... consists in a series of steps which may be purely abstract, as at no stage the use of any technical means is implied. The whole method may be performed mentally ... Moreover, as a result, the claimed method provides a design ... which may be a purely mental, abstract scheme ... rather than a concrete, physical [structure] ... In the appellant's view, however, the claimed method has technical character and, therefore, does not constitute a method for performing a mental act as such ... The appellant sees this technical character being given in that the claimed method addresses a technical problem ... involves technical considerations, lies in the field of technology in general and leads to a solution providing a technical contribution. (T-914/02: paras. 2.3.1–2.3.2)

The Board accepted the proposition that an invention in the sense of Art. 52(1) EPC must implicitly have *technical character* and that the method claimed must involve 'technical considerations'. However, involving technical considerations did not automatically mean having *technical character*, but required, for a method, technical implementation:

In the board's opinion, however, the involvement of technical considerations is not sufficient for a method which may exclusively be carried out mentally to have technical character. In fact, other non-inventions listed in Article 52(2) EPC, such as scientific theories, but also computer programs, typically involve technical considerations. In the present case, rather, technical character would be provided through the technical implementation of the method, resulting in the method providing a tangible, technical effect ... The claimed method, however, lacks such a technical implementation. (T-914/02: para. 2.3.3)

The Board accepted the position of T-258/03 Auction method/ HITACHI that a method must always have *technical character* when it involves the use of technical means but would not allow the main request where such means were not recited. The Board then took on the magnum opus of TBoA 3.5.01, T-1173/97 Computer program product/IBM, where excluded matter was not itself 'as such' if it had *technical character*. This is important since TBoA 3.5.01's position had been developed by ignoring the exclusions in Art. 52(2) EPC other than computer programs yet proposing an interpretation of the words 'as such' in Art. 52(3) EPC that should inevitably apply to the other exclusions (see Sterckx and Cockbain 2010a and Cockbain and Sterckx 2011a). The passage thus deserves quoting at length:

The appellant has also made reference to decision T 1173/97 [Computer program product/IBM] ... in which a distinction was made between programs for computers as such, excluded from patentability in accordance with Articles 52(2)(c) and 52(3) EPC, and programs for computers having technical character. By analogy, it was argued that a distinction should be made in the present case between methods of performing a mental act 'as such' and methods of performing a mental act having technical character, the claimed method pertaining to the latter ... In the board's view it may be questioned, whether the distinction made in the decision referred to above for programs for computers can be sensibly extended to the other entities and activities listed in Article 52(2) EPC, or whether rather the particular character of programs for computers should be acknowledged in this respect ... The distinction between methods of performing a mental act 'as such' and methods of performing a mental act having technical character may be drawn where the method provides a tangible technical effect, such as the provision of a physical entity as the resulting product or a non-abstract activity, such as through the use of technical means. (T-914/02: para. 2.3.6)

While the auxiliary request, which recited technical means, was accepted following TBoA 3.5.01's *anything added* approach of T-258/03 Auction method/HITACHI, the Board used TBoA 3.5.01's *COMVIK* approach to cast doubt on the patentability of the subject-matter.

3.3.2 Board 3.2.04 (Mechanics IV)

A newcomer to the fray, in June 2007 Board 3.2.04 (Mechanics IV) has diverged from the dominant Board's position in T-1543/06 Game machine/GAMEACCOUNT (Chairman Ceyte). In this, and two other decisions (T-336/07 IGT and T-859/07 DEQ SYSTÈMES), Board 3.2.04 seems to propose a *synergy* approach to 'mixed' claims.

The Board explained the current *technical character* approach:

> The most liberal approach (from the applicant's point of view) is that first adopted in T 931/95 [Controlling pension benefits system/PBS PARTNERSHIP] … and refined in T 258/03 [Auction method/HITACHI] … according to which … technical character results either from the physical features of an entity or (for a method) from the use of technical means. While an invention as a whole may possess technical character, it may nevertheless legitimately include both technical and non-technical features. (T-1543/06: para. 2.2)

The Board then confirmed that it accepted the *COMVIK* approach to assessing inventive step of 'mixed' claims, but reformulated the approach:

> the principle as expressed in T 641/00 [Two identities/COMVIK] may also be reformulated as follows: an invention which as a whole falls outside the exclusion zone of Article 52(2) EPC (i.e. is technical in character) cannot rely on excluded subject matter alone, even if novel and non-obvious (in the colloquial sense of the word), for it to be considered to meet the requirement of inventive step. The Board is of the firm belief, that it cannot have been the legislator's purpose and intent on the one hand to exclude from patent protection such subject matter, while on the other hand awarding protection to a technical implementation thereof, where the only identifiable contribution of the claimed technical implementation to the state of the art is the excluded subject-matter itself. It is noted that here the term 'contribution' encompasses both means (i.e. tangible features of the implementation) and effects resulting from the implementation. In that case Article 52(2) EPC would be reduced to a mere requirement as to form, easily circumvented. The Board believes it is intended as substantive in nature, whatever considerations may have been the source of this exclusion at the time of its adoption. (T-1543/06: para. 2.5)

From this, the Board concluded that mere technical implementation of an excluded method is not enough:

It follows from the above that the mere technical implementation of excluded subject-matter per se cannot form the basis for inventive step. The Board concludes that inventive step can be based only on the particular manner of implementation. To this end it is therefore necessary to ask how the per se excluded subject-matter (e.g. a game or business method) is implemented. In the context of the problem-solution approach this can be rephrased as a fictional technical problem in which the per se excluded subject matter appears as an aim to be achieved ... Where such excluded subject matter is novel such a formulation of the problem seemingly implies that such matter may be regarded as a given in the assessment of inventive step, which thus appears to depart from what is in fact a hidden starting point. The Board views this fiction as an artefact of the systematic use of the problem-solution approach for assessing inventive step and the need to differentiate between excluded and non-excluded matter. This should not detract from the basic tenet that excluded subject-matter cannot form the sole basis for a patentable invention. (T-1543/06: para. 2.6)

The Board rightly concluded that, where excluded subject-matter implicitly has some technical nature, *further technical effect* is required:

The explicit requirement of a 'further' technical effect has been first formulated for computer-related inventions in decisions T 1173/97 [Computer program product/IBM] ... but the same principle holds also for other categories of excluded subject-matter which may inherently possess some 'technical' effect. In fact, inherent and arguably technical effects may be easily identified for practically all excluded subject-matter ... This is why it needs to be stressed that the 'further' technical effect can not be the same one which is inherent in the excluded subject-matter itself. (T-1543/06: para. 2.8)

Thus for an invention relating to rules for a game (doing business, and so on): 'inventive step cannot be based on the mere technical implementation of these rules' (T-1543/06: para. 5.1).

Here, ostensibly applying the *COMVIK* approach, the Board seemed to arrive at a reasonable approach to assessing inventive step for 'mixed' claims: 'The Board is unable to identify any effects other than those inherent in the game rules themselves or those connected to the carrying out of functions by a computer with a processor and display. *There is also no identifiable synergic effect between the game rules and the technical implementation*' (T-1543/06: para. 5.4, emphasis added).

3.3.3 The other Boards

In March 1998, in T-72/95 Ionizing liquid/IBBOTT and in three other very similar decisions, Board 3.3.05 (Chemistry V – Chairman

Spangenberg), mused on the subject of what an 'invention' was, deciding that it must have *technical character* to be patentable and that features without technical relevance should not be considered when assessing inventive step:

[T]he Board wants to emphasize that the notion of 'non-obviousness' is related to the concept of 'invention'. The concept of 'invention' implies a technical character. This follows directly from the wording of Article 56 EPC, wherein the expressions 'invention' and 'obvious' are linked with 'state of the art' and 'a person skilled in the art' ... In the Board's judgment, technically non-functional modifications are therefore irrelevant to inventive step, even if the skilled person would never think of such a modification. A parallel can be drawn here with a new design based on a known technical concept. That new design might be a surprise and thus 'not obvious' for professional designers. Nevertheless if the modifications have no technical relevance and are, from a technical point of view, arbitrary, the new design is not patentable and does not involve an inventive step within the meaning of Article 56 EPC. (T-72/95: para. 5.4)

This is compatible both with the *COMVIK* approach and a *synergy* approach.

In March 2000, in T-1194/97 Data structure product/PHILIPS, Board 3.5.02 (Electricity II – Chairman Wheeler) seemed to apply a *technical character* approach to presentations of information, namely that a presentation of functional information rather than of information with merely cognitive or aesthetic content is not a presentation of information as such. This line of reasoning was followed by Board 3.5.03 in August 2005 in T-858/02 Structured voicemail messages/LUCENT.

In March 2006, in T-619/02 Odour selection/QUEST INTERNATIONAL, Board 3.4.02 (Chairman Klein) considered a case relating to odour selection and thus mental acts:

[T]he method also involves physical activities, i.e. activities in the physical world such as the fact of presenting the test person with odours and stimuli which do not constitute mental acts. In addition ... the selection method relies on the 'implicit odour memory' of the test person, i.e. on non-conscious associative recollection of odours as opposed to explicit memory. Consequently, not even the perceptual processes in the mind of the test person constitute mental acts within the meaning of Article 52(2)(c) EPC. Such perceptual processes (emotions, impressions, feelings, etc.) are psychological in nature and relate to – at least to a predetermined degree – subconscious processes that take place in the human mind, in contrast to the abstract nature of mental acts within the meaning of Article 52(2)(c) EPC which ... are primarily based on cognitive, conceptual or intellectual processes conducted by the human mind. (T-619/02: 72–3)

3.4 The legislative history

Before turning to the EBoA decision in G-3/08 Programs for computers, we feel we must emphasise that the interpretation of the exclusion developed by TBoA 3.5.01 is unsupported by the *travaux préparatoires*. For further discussion of the *travaux préparatoires* see Kolle (1974), Zipse (1973), Pila (2005a, 2005b and 2010) and Sterckx and Cockbain (2010a).

Although, as mentioned in Chapter 2, the question of what subject-matter might not be eligible for the grant of European patents was considered very early in the activities of the CoE's Committee of Experts on patents, with a questionnaire to be sent to the Member States being drawn up in January 1953 and the results being summarised in Roger Gajac's report of January 1955 (Document EXP/Brev (53) 18 rev), the SPC proceeded without any definition of subject-matter that the Member States should consider not to be inventions. It was at a relatively late stage of the drafting of the CEPL, at the twelfth meeting of the EEC's Patents Working Party (PWP) in February/March 1964, that the German and Dutch delegations were asked to draw up a list of the unpatentable. The result, reported in Document 9663/IV/64, was an extended version of the listing proposed by the German experts in the CoE's Committee of Experts in October 1956 (Document EXP/Brev (56) 8), which was adopted at the fifteenth meeting of the PWP in October 1964 and was incorporated into the last draft version of the CEPL of January 1965 (Document 2335/IV/65-E).

Although the CEPL was one of the starting points for the drafting of the EPC, we should note that the 'as such' provision of Art. 52(3) EPC was missing and that computer programs and presentations of information had not yet appeared in the list of excluded subject-matter.

When the first meeting of Working Party I (WP-I) took place in May 1969, computer programs and presentations of information were still not in place as possible exclusions; nonetheless the very existence of an Article specifying exclusions was challenged by the UK and Swedish delegations. WP-I disagreed, believing that 'it was a substantial provision fixing the conditions for the grant of patents' (Document BR/7/69: 9–10).

The appearance of computer programs followed their mention in July 1969 in a draft of Rule 39.1 PCT (Document PCT/DC/5), which set out subject-matter that did not have to be searched by international searching authorities. However, whether computer programs should be excluded from patentability under the EPC remained uncertain.

Thus, at the second Intergovermental Conference (IGC) in January 1970, it was considered that 'the present state of developments did not allow it to be determined whether computer programmes could be the subject of a patent' (Document BR/26/70: 7). At the seventh meeting of WP-I, in January 1971, the forerunner to Art. 52 EPC was quite extensively revised. At that meeting, WP-I had agreed that the paragraph 'should first and foremost be adapted to the corresponding provision of the Regulations under the PCT (Rule 39.1), although the regulations in question were not in fact identical' (Document BR/94/71: 10).

At its ninth meeting, in October 1971, WP-I considered several amendments to paragraph 2. On the subject of computer programs, the UK argued that these should not be patentable and that a program 'was merely the mathematical application of a logical series of steps in a process which was no different from a mathematical method excluded under [sub-paragraph](a). However some form of protection might be desirable for computer programmes but this, which might be considered by WIPO, called for some new form and not under existing patent laws.' The UK's definition was not adopted, the decision being to leave this to the EPO and the national courts. It was considered that some protection might be given to computer programs but not patent protection. WP-I agreed that computer programs should be excluded (Document BR/135/71: 47–50).

Once more the UK delegation proposed that paragraph 2 should be deleted and that exclusions should be set out in the EPC Rules (which do not require unanimity among the Contracting States for their amendment but simply a majority decision by the EPO's Administrative Council). However, WP-I disagreed: 'Amendments to the rules [*sic*] on patentability were of such importance that it was undesirable to allow the provisions to be amended by the [EPO's] Administrative Council. The development of patent law should be left to the courts and the question of amendment should be left to revision by a Diplomatic Conference' (Document BR/135/71: 51).

At fifth IGC in January/February 1972, the conference also rejected a request for paragraph 2 to be deleted 'since it considered it necessary, from the entry into force of the system, to create the greatest possible legal certainty in this field', stating that '[s]ubject to final drafting, paragraph 2 will thus remain in the Convention, and it may only be amended by means of a revision of the Convention'. Certain delegations had thought it 'was inappropriate to insert a fundamental subject such as that of patentability in the Implementing Regulations which were subordinate to the Convention'. A request that the list of exclusions in paragraph 2 be made exhaustive was rejected 'so as to retain the flexibility necessary to the system'. The exclusion of presentations of information was agreed but WP-I was instructed to consider further amendment to paragraph 2 (Document BR/168/72: 10–12).

Thus paragraph 2 returned to WP-I for discussion at its eleventh meeting in February/March 1972 where, after some discussion, computer programs were moved to sub-paragraph (d) as an exclusion to 'the use of computers' (Document BR/177/72: 2–3). This, after consideration by the Drafting Committee, resulted in the May 1972 form of paragraph 2 (Document BR/199/72: 56).

In the run-up to the Munich Diplomatic Conference, in March 1973 the German delegation suggested revision of Art. 52 EPC (then Art. 50 of the draft), proposing a new clause stipulating that the exclusions of paragraph 2 extended only to the subject-matter 'as such'.

At the Munich Diplomatic Conference itself, in Main Committee I, the chairman commented on the exclusion of programs for computers, saying that at the Luxembourg Diplomatic Conference the attempt to define programs had been in vain and that '[t]he European Patent Office would simply have to be relied upon subsequently to interpret this expression unequivocally' (Document M/PR/I: 28).

Various parties, in particular the United Kingdom and Ireland, yet again proposed putting the paragraph 2 exclusions into the EPC Rules. The German delegation, however, 'thought it was inadmissible, as a matter of principle, for the question of the patentability of such subject-matter or activities to be left to the Administrative Council to decide'. The French delegation pointed out that 'Article [52] was a fundamental Article of the Convention. The provisions governing patentability should not be left to the Administrative Council; the latter ought not to be able, irrespective of the legal and technical means employed, to amend the individual provisions on its own responsibility' (Document M/PR/I: 28).

On the proposal from Germany (Document M/11), Main Committee I agreed to specify in paragraph 3 that 'the patentability of the subject-matter and activities listed in paragraph 2 was excluded only to the extent to which an application or patent related to the subject-matter or activities as such' (Document M/PR/I:29).

And thus the wording of the Art. 52(2)/(3) EPC exclusions was settled. Although amendment to Art. 52(2) EPC was considered during the negotiations leading to EPC 2000, no change to the wording of Art. 52(2) or (3) EPC was agreed. These provisions thus retain their original meaning from 1973.

Writing in the year after the EPC was signed, Gert Kolle[6] commented on the absence of a requirement for technicality as a prerequisite for acknowledgement of invention in the EPC:

> [T]he Diplomatic Conference abstained from limiting the concept of 'invention' by the attribute 'technical' or such similar characteristics as was once proposed. There are good reasons for this approach. The concept of technical invention as it has been developed in the German-language countries is in no way common to other national patent systems. Thus, for instance, Art. 6 of the French Patent Law of 1968 speaks of '*caractère industriel*', and Sec. 101 of the British Patents Act of 1949 speaks of the 'manner of manufacture'. Even if these definitions of invention and the concept of technical invention led to essentially analogous results at least for the delimitation of unprotectable subject matter from patentable inventions, a further limitation of patentable inventions to 'technical' inventions would simply thrust difficulties in understanding on the remaining contracting states ... the existence of the exceptions list brings to the forefront that the general concept of invention should remain fully open. Neither the contents and the arrangement of the provision nor its genesis therefore authorizes the conclusion that patentability is only for the technical inventions ... Further, this cannot be derived from the characteristics of industrial application as laid down in Art. 57 [EPC]. (Kolle 1974: 145–6, footnotes omitted)

It seems clear, therefore, that TBoA 3.5.01's invocation of national practice, and even of the Rules, to support its repeated allegation that Art. 52(2)/(3) EPC is no more than a requirement for *technical character* and has no support in the clear wording of Art. 52 EPC or in the *travaux préparatoires*.

3.5 The Enlarged Board Opinion – G-3/08 Programs for computers

3.5.1 Should the president's referral have been admitted?

In accordance with Art. 112(1)(b) EPC, '[i]n order to ensure uniform application of the law, or if a point of law of fundamental importance arises', the president of the EPO 'may refer a point of law to the Enlarged Board of Appeal where two Boards of Appeal have given different decisions on that question' (EPO 2010a: 176–8). Thus for a president's referral on a point of law to be accepted by the EBoA, it must meet two criteria: first, two Boards must have given different decisions on the point; and, second, the point must be of fundamental importance or the referral must be needed to ensure uniform application of the law.

[6] Later the EPO's Principal Director of International Legal Affairs.

Although there was some argument about the first criterion, G-4/98 Designation fees had already established that having divergent decisions from two Boards of the same name or number (e.g. 3.5.01) but with different Board members was sufficient. Thus, unless the decisions referred to by the president could be found not to be different, the EBoA would have had to decide (a) whether the issue was of fundamental importance or (b) whether the existing case law could lead to non-uniform application of the law, a positive answer to either making it necessary for the Board to reply to the president's questions.

The issue was clearly of fundamental importance given the importance of computer programs in industry. Moreover, TBoAs other than 3.5.01 had 'strayed' from the path laid down by 3.5.01, so the key question facing the EBoA in G-3/08 Programs for computers was whether the decisions given by TBoA 3.5.01 and cited by the president in her referral gave different interpretations of the exclusions. Given the history of TBoA 3.5.01 sketched out above, this would seem to be a clear yes. It was not. To reopen the question of the interpretation of the exclusions risked not only the interests of the computing industry but also those of the biotechnology industry (for Art. 52(2)/(3) EPC also relates to discoveries) and the attractiveness of the EPO as a forum for having patent applications examined and granted (since reinterpretation risked the possibility of the EPC being found non-compliant with one or both of TRIPS and the EBD). The stakes were therefore extremely high.

3.5.2 The divergent decisions

All of the decisions that were supposedly divergent were from TBoA 3.5.01. However, where decisions were said to diverge, the compositions of the Board were different. For questions 1, 2 and 3, the divergence was between van den Berg and Steinbrener decisions, while for question 4 the divergence was between early, pre-*technical character* van den Berg decisions on the one hand and the lead *technical character* decision from van den Berg and an early, pre-*anything added, technical character* decision from Steinbrener on the other.

3.5.3 The Enlarged Board's reasoning

As mentioned above, in order to decide whether the referral was admissible, the EBoA had to address three points: (1) fundamental importance/ensuring uniform application; (2) whether the decisions of *two* Boards were at issue; and (3) whether those decisions were 'different'.

On the first of these, the Enlarged Board admitted that 'Given the economic significance of such inventions [i.e. computer-implemented inventions] in many technical fields, plus the consequent heated public debate on their patentability and the many cases before the EPO's Technical Boards and various national courts, *the fundamental importance of the general subject addressed by the questions referred is not open to serious doubt*' (G-3/08: para. 4.2, emphasis added).

On the second question, as to whether two decisions from TBoA 3.5.01 where the Board members were different qualified as decisions from two Boards, the EBoA followed its own earlier decision G-4/98 Designation fees to agree that the answer was in the affirmative.

The EBoA thus had to consider what was meant by 'different' decisions and after much deliberation commented that 'The "different decisions" criterion would appear to show that the president is only intended to be allowed to refer a question to the Enlarged Board when there is a divergence or, better, conflict in the case law making it difficult if not impossible for the Office to bring its patent granting practice into line with the case law of the Boards of Appeal' (G-3/08: para. 7.2.6).

However, the EBoA was cautious as to when 'divergence' was merely 'development' as opposed to 'disagreement' or 'conflict' (helpfully reminding the audience that '[w]hen judiciary-driven legal development meets its limits, it is time for the legislator to take over' (G-3/08: para.7.2.7). Thus:

> Development of the law is an essential aspect of its application, whatever method of interpretation the judge applies, and is therefore inherent in all judicial activity. In that light an element of legal development can even be seen whenever a specific case is subsumed under an abstract regulation … Consequently, legal development as such cannot on its own form the basis for a referral, only because case law in new legal territory does not always develop in linear fashion, and earlier approaches may be abandoned or modified … While the development of the law may superficially appear to give rise to different decisions within the meaning of that provision, on its own it cannot justify a referral to the Enlarged Board. A referral is justified only if at least two Board of Appeal decisions come into conflict with the principle of legal uniformity. The object and purpose of Article 112(1)(b) EPC is to have an Enlarged Board decision re-establish legal uniformity when it has clearly been disrupted, not to intervene in legal development … [E]ven a radical shift in jurisprudence need not necessarily be construed as a different decision within the meaning of Article 112(1)(b) EPC vis-à-vis earlier case law, provided that the Board corrects itself and – mostly in explicit fashion – declares its earlier practice to be no longer relevant. The President does not acquire the right of referral simply because he prefers the earlier decision … Such corrections are a normal part of the application and development of the law and do not constitute a difference that could be corrected by means of a presidential referral to

> the Enlarged Board, overriding the interpretative power of the Boards ... The same should apply where the Boards' case law has developed over an extended period and in the course of several decisions has gradually arrived at solutions which clearly and justifiably move away from the initial premise, even if the public and the patent granting authority have found earlier solutions acceptable. In that way, too, legal development has followed a course which, while not entirely linear, as long as it is transparent does not justify speaking of different decisions that could be grounds for a referral ... [T]he Enlarged Board must also consider whether the divergent decisions might not be part of a constant development, possibly still ongoing, in jurisprudence on recent patent law issues, in the course of which older decisions have lost their significance and so can no longer be considered in connection with newer decisions. Such putative differences do not justify presidential referrals, legal development being one of the principal duties of the Boards of Appeal, in particular in new territory. (G-3/08: paras. 7.3.1–7.3.8)

To paraphrase: a referral by the president is not admissible if divergences in decisions stem from 'the development' of the legal interpretation by the Boards of Appeal; or more succinctly: only if different Boards disagree or if a Board is erratic is a referral welcome. Where, as is the case with Art. 52(2) EPC, one TBoA has dominated the development of the legal interpretation of the exclusions, thereby reducing the likelihood of another TBoA referring the interpretation to the EBoA, we feel that the reluctance of the EBoA to review the development of the law with fresh eyes was most unfortunate.

3.5.4 The questions

3.5.4.1 Question 1: Can a computer program only be excluded as a computer program as such if it is explicitly claimed as a computer program?

As noted earlier, the 'divergence' in the case law referred to in the president's referral was between T-1173/97 Computer program product/IBM and T-424/03 Clipboard formats/MICROSOFT.

The EBoA noted that in T-1173/93 Computer program product/IBM it had been said that a computer program which, by achieving a *further technical effect* when run, met the *technical character* test for escaping exclusion, was thus not itself excluded under Art. 52(2)/(3) EPC. Commenting on the *technical character* approach, the EBoA stated that:

> By taking this position the Board consciously abandoned the so-called 'contribution approach' which had been applied, somewhat inconsistently, in the earlier case law. This was clearly a deliberate development of the case law (the inconsistency of the previous case law having previously been identified in [van den Berg (1996)]). *To our knowledge no decision of the Boards of Appeal has since*

challenged this choice by the Board … It therefore stands as the established case law, and cannot be overturned by this Opinion. (G-3/08: para. 10.4, emphasis added)

Thus far, the position is therefore that *technical character* has been Board 3.5.01's unchallenged interpretation of the Art. 52(2)/(3) EPC exclusions since T-1173/97 Computer program product/IBM (when its earlier *technical contribution* approach was explicitly abandoned) and thus, as legitimate legal development, it could not be overturned.

The key to this comparison between T-1173/97 Computer program product/IBM and T-424/03 Clipboard formats/MICROSOFT is to investigate whether there is a conflict between the *anything added* approach to a claim to a program-on-carrier in T-424/03 Clipboard formats/MICROSOFT and the *technical character* approach of T-1173/97 Computer program product/IBM. We suggest that such a conflict does exist since the *technical character* acknowledged in T-424/03 Clipboard formats/MICROSOFT was that of the *carrier*, whereas T-1173/97 Computer program product/IBM made it clear that what made the program-on-carrier claim acceptable was the *further* potential technical effect of the otherwise excluded subject-matter, the computer program.

The EBoA, however, found instead that T-424/03 Clipboard formats/MICROSOFT simply applied the logic of T-1173/97 Computer program product/IBM to find the requirement for a *further technical effect* for the program to be unnecessary. Nonetheless, the EBoA correctly noted that *technical character*, when viewed in this way, moves the consideration of how to give teeth to the Art. 52(2) EPC exclusions over to the examination for inventive step, something which Board 3.5.01 realised with its introduction of the *COMVIK* approach in T-641/00 Two identities/COMVIK. Accordingly, the EBoA continued:

The question whether the program itself caused a 'further technical effect' when run, and would therefore also qualify as technical means, only assumed importance for the question of inventive step – in parallel to these decisions [investigating the *technical character* approach] the Board had been developing the [*COMVIK*] approach to the appraisal of inventive step taking into account the fact that some of the features of a claim might, considered alone, fall under the exclusions of Article 52(2) EPC … For this approach it is important which features contribute to the technical character of the claimed subject-matter, since only such features are taken into account for the assessment of inventive step. In the particular case of T 424/03 [Clipboard formats/MICROSOFT], both the computer-readable medium and the program itself were features which gave the subject-matter of the particular claim as a whole a technical character, and were both therefore to be taken into account for the assessment of its inventive step. (G-3/08: para. 10.7.1)

The EBoA therefore considered that, although T-424/03 Clipboard formats/MICROSOFT did deviate from a view expressed in T-1173/97 Computer program product/IBM, this itself was 'a legitimate development of the case law' and not a divergence that would make the referral admissible (G-3/08: para. 10.12).

On inventive step, the EBoA commented that:

> We note, in passing, that it is somewhat surprising that the referral does not address any of its questions to the validity of this way of judging an inventive step, an issue which is surely of general interest ... The Board can only speculate that the President could not identify any divergence in the case law on this issue, despite the fact that (at present) approximately seventy decisions issued by a total of fifteen different Boards (in the sense of organisational units) cite T 641/00 [Two identities/COMVIK] ... and over forty decisions by eight Boards cite T 258/03 [Auction method/HITACHI] ... the decisions which essentially defined the approach. Nor is the Enlarged Board aware of any divergence in this case law, suggesting that the Boards are in general quite comfortable with it. (G-3/08: para. 10.13.2)

3.5.4.2 Questions 2, 3 and 4

For question 2, the allegedly divergent decisions were T-1173/97 Computer program product/IBM (which established the *technical character* approach) and T-258/03 Auction method/HITACHI (which established the *anything added* approach, which, as we have seen above, the EBoA considered to be a legitimate legal development of the understanding of the *technical character* approach). It will come as no surprise that no sufficient divergence to make the referral admissible was found.

For question 3, the allegedly divergent decisions were T-163/85 Colour television signal/BBC, T-190/94 MITSUBISHI, from the days when TBoA 3.5.01 applied the now defunct *technical contribution* approach, T-424/03 Clipboard formats/MICROSOFT and T-125/01 Gerätesteuerung/HENZE from the era of the now properly understood *technical character* approach. Once again no divergence was found.

For the last question, the decisions were T-1173/97 Computer program product/IBM and T-172/03 Order management/RICOH on one side, which represented the as yet unembellished *technical character* approach, and T-833/91 IBM, T-204/93 AT&T and T-769/92 General purpose management system/SOHEI, which came from the *technical contribution* era on the other. Again, no divergence was found.

3.6 Conclusion

The current position is therefore that, at a first level, the *anything added* approach applies to the exclusions under Art. 52(2) and (3) EPC, that is that in a 'mixed' claim the inclusion of anything *not* excluded (i.e. with *technical character*) is sufficient to qualify the subject-matter of the claim as an invention for the purposes of Art. 52(1) EPC. With this we find no fault.

For an 'unmixed' claim directed to subject-matter which, prima facie, seems to be excluded by Art. 52(2) EPC, for example a computer program claimed as a computer program, the 'overarching' *technical character* approach from T-1173/97 Computer program product/IBM applies, with the result that the subject-matter qualifies as an invention for the purposes of Art. 52(1) EPC if it has (or has the potential to have) a *technical effect*. This approach, in our view, derives from blatant disregard and misconstruction of Art. 52(3) EPC by TBoA 3.5.01 in T-1173/97 Computer program product/IBM.

For both 'mixed' and 'unmixed' claims, the subject-matter must still be examined for novelty and inventive step before being judged patentable. TBoA 3.5.01's current approach to this is the *COMVIK* approach of T-641/00 Two identities/COMVIK in which subject-matter that has no technical effect, is not a technical means, and so on, cannot be taken into consideration as contributing to novelty or inventive step (or even is considered to form part of the state of the art or alternatively not able to form part of the state of the art). Following Jacob LJ in UK-Aerotel (2006), we find this approach to be intellectually dishonest and we note that the Boards, not just TBoA 3.5.01, have been writing apologia for it since it first appeared. Moreover, we note with interest the EBoA's surprise that the president of the EPO failed to challenge the *COMVIK* approach in her G-3/08 Programs for computers referral letter.

4 Discoveries

> A discovery may be brilliant and useful, and not patentable. No matter through what long, solitary vigils, or by what importunate efforts, the secret may have been wrung from the bosom of Nature, or to what useful purpose it may be applied. Something more is necessary.
>
> (US-Morton 1862: 884)

> Theorists have long argued for the existence of a robust entity known as 'the public domain', and many contend that it should include much of the genetic realm. From their perspective, something that has the attributes of public domain material – a product of nature, for example – has a claim to inviolability. Those who would capture it as private property must meet a substantial burden. Yet over the last twenty years of biotechnology patent law development the public domain has rarely risen to the level of an afterthought. It has certainly not been treated as a well-defined realm that can be invaded only for good cause.
>
> (Conley and Makowski 2004: 6, references omitted)

4.1 Introduction

Art. 52(2)(a) EPC provides that 'The following in particular shall not be regarded as inventions … discoveries' (EPO 2010a: 106).

In the context of patent law, this is particularly interesting since Article 1, Section 8 of the US Constitution, in apparent contradiction, empowers Congress: 'To promote the Progress of Science and useful Arts, by securing for limited Times to … Inventors the exclusive Right to their … Discoveries.'

The question thus arises: what does 'discovery' mean, and more particularly, what does it mean in the context of Art. 52(2) EPC?

At the time the US Constitution was drafted, the meaning of the term 'discovery' was different from its current meaning. What it meant at that time would have been well known to the drafters of the Constitution, not least since it is set out in the then dominant and new

English dictionary: the revealing of something that had been (kept) secret (Johnson 1755: 604).

In current usage, however, 'discovery' normally means *to find something that was pre-existing and the properties of which were already taking effect at the time of discovery* – one discovers a previously unknown plant or mineral, or one discovers that energy is proportional to mass squared or that the square on the hypotenuse equals the sum of the squares of the lengths of the other two sides of a right-angled triangle, or indeed that a gene sequence codes for a protein. To the extent that native genes, their variants and their correlation with disease states are *pre-existing*, identification of the gene and its variants represents a *discovery* in the current sense of the term.

A third meaning of discovery which is highly relevant to patent law relates to situations where *something is identified that had not previously been in operation* (i.e. had not been in effect). Where a product of a marine microorganism, if injected into the human brain, can slow the progress of Alzheimer's, for example, then to use the product to treat Alzheimer's would involve the *application* of a 'discovery' that had not previously been in effect.

The *travaux préparatoires* give guidance as to what was intended by the framers of the EPC, or more specifically of the SPC and CEPL as the term had appeared in the discussions while those conventions were being negotiated and was not changed during the drafting of the EPC itself or in the 2000 revision of the EPC. Thus, from the earliest discussions, discoveries were seen as different from patentable inventions: 'As a general rule, a patent can only protect an invention (a creation) and not a discovery, i.e. the mere becoming aware of a pre-existing reality' (Document EXP/Brev (53) 18 rev: 4, authors' translation from French). From this, it is clear that the discoveries that were not to be patent-eligible according to Art. 52(2) EPC were discoveries with the second meaning set out above.

However, all or almost all inventions have a discovery at their base, and this too was recognised from the start: 'a patentable technical indication may be based on a discovery' (Document EXP/Brev (53) 18 rev: 4, authors' translation from French).

What is required to transform an unpatentable discovery into a patentable invention is perhaps not so clear. However, guidance may be found in the Guidelines for Examination in the European Patent Office, the EPC Rules and the EPO case law from the TBoAs.

The current (2011) version of the Guidelines for Examination in the European Patent Office mentions the following on the meaning of 'discovery':

> *If a new property of a known material or article is found out, that is mere discovery* and unpatentable because discovery as such has no technical effect and is therefore not an invention within the meaning of Art. 52(1). If, however, that property is put to practical use, then this constitutes an invention which may be patentable. For example, the discovery that a particular known material is able to withstand mechanical shock would not be patentable, but a railway sleeper made from that material could well be patentable. *To find a previously unrecognised substance occurring in nature is also mere discovery* and therefore unpatentable. However, if a substance found in nature can be shown to produce a technical effect, it may be patentable. An example of such a case is that of a substance occurring in nature which is found to have an antibiotic effect. In addition, if a microorganism is discovered to exist in nature and to produce an antibiotic, the microorganism itself may also be patentable as one aspect of the invention. Similarly, a gene which is discovered to exist in nature may be patentable if a technical effect is revealed, e.g. its use in making a certain polypeptide or in gene therapy. (EPO 2011: C.IV.2–3, emphasis added)

From this, it is clear that two positions are being advocated – first that the *application* of a discovery may be patentable, and second that, if it has technical effect, the discovery *itself* may be patentable. The first seems to be in line with the *travaux préparatoires*, while the second is an application of the *technical character* approach developed by TBoA 3.5.01 in connection with computer programs and discussed in Chapter 3.

Turning now to the Rules, two relevant Rules were introduced in September 1999 in order to make the EPC compliant with the EBD: Rules 27(a) and 29(2) EPC. Rule 27(a) EPC, which is based on Art. 3(2) EBD, provides that 'Biotechnological inventions shall also be patentable if they concern: … biological material which is *isolated* from its natural environment or *produced by means of a technical process* even if it previously occurred in nature' (EPO 2010a: 330, emphasis added). Whereas, according to Rule 29(2) EPC, which is based on Art. 5 EBD: 'An element *isolated* from the human body or otherwise *produced by means of a technical process*, including the sequence or partial sequence of a gene, may constitute a patentable invention, even if the structure of that element is identical to that of a natural element' (EPO 2010a: 332, emphasis added).

Here we encounter a third way of turning a discovery into an invention, by *isolation* or by (technical) *synthesis*. The product claimed remains the discovery itself; all that is added is a restriction specifying the manner in which the product is produced. Claims might be to 'an isolated DNA molecule' or 'a recombinant DNA molecule' or 'an artificially synthesised DNA molecule'. These are termed 'product-by-process' claims, and it is interesting to note what the Guidelines for Examination in the European Patent Office have to say on the subject:

Claims for products defined in terms of a process of manufacture are allowable only if the products as such fulfil the requirements for patentability, i.e. inter alia that they are new and inventive. A product is not rendered novel merely by the fact that it is produced by means of a new process (see T 150/82 [Claim categories/IFF]). A claim defining a product in terms of a process is to be construed as a claim to the product as such. The claim may for instance take the form 'Product X obtainable by process Y'. Irrespective of whether the term 'obtainable', 'obtained', 'directly obtained' or an equivalent wording is used in the product-by-process claim, it is still directed to the product per se and confers absolute protection upon the product (see T 20/94 [Amorphous TPM/ENICHEM]). (EPO 2011: C.III.11–12)

Rules 27(a) and 29(2) EPC thus clearly appear to be in conflict not only with Art. 52(2) EPC but also with Art. 54 EPC, which sets out the requirements for novelty. As Art. 164(2) EPC makes clear, when Rules conflict with Articles, the Articles override the Rules.

Finally, of course, the clearest guidance for the interpretation of how a discovery may be transformed into an invention is given in Art. 52(3) EPC, which qualifies the exclusion of Art. 52(2) EPC by providing that 'Paragraph 2 shall exclude the patentability of the subject-matter or activities referred to therein only to the extent to which a European patent application or European patent relates to such subject-matter *as such*' (EPO 2010a: 106, emphasis added). At first sight, this would support the first technique mentioned above – the *application* of a discovery may be an invention, that is the *anything added* approach discussed in Chapter 3. This is also the approach that the British courts seem to have reached when considering the patentability of a human protein in *Genentech Inc.'s Patent* (UK-Genentech (1987) and UK-Genentech (1989)). To quote from the judgment of Whitford J in the Patents Court: 'It is trite law that you cannot patent a discovery, but if on the basis of that discovery you can tell people how it can be usefully employed, then a patentable invention may result' (UK-Genentech 1987: 566).

Other than to acknowledge that discoveries may lie behind inventions, few Board of Appeal decisions have addressed the exclusion of discoveries. We will now discuss the relevant TBoA decisions in chronological order.

4.2 T-877/92 Removal of carcinogenic hydrocarbons/EXXON

In January 1988 Exxon Chemical Patents filed a patent application (Brownawell *et al.* 1988) relating to a method for removing carcinogenic agents (polynuclear aromatic compounds or PNAs) from the lubricating oil circulating in a combustion engine by using a sorbent. The aim was that the used oil would no longer be hazardous if the toxic agents were removed.

In January 1990 the Examining Division said it had doubts as to whether the claimed subject-matter met the requirements of Articles 52(2) and 52(3) EPC. Not convinced by Exxon's response, in the summons to oral proceedings the Examining Division observed that the subject-matter of the use claims was a discovery:

> Although the Application may have greatly contributed to the art by pointing out the inherent absorption of PNAs with the activated carbon ... the Examining Division can only note ... that the industrial application of this property does not involve any modification of the already existing use of the absorbent ... Therefore, the Examining Division considers that at least the subject-matter of claims 1 to 7 is merely a discovery that using the sorbent according to the teaching of [a prior art document] was implying the absorption of the PNAs. (Correspondence *EPO* 1991: 4)

In March 1992 the Examining Division refused the application on the grounds of novelty and inventive step, but noted that it could also be refused under Art. 52(2) EPC. Exxon appealed.

The claim of concern read: 'Use of a sorbent for removing ... PNAs ... from lubricating oil circulating in an internal combustion engine and passing in contact with the sorbent.'

In its decision of November 1995, TBoA 3.3.01 (Chairman Nuss) noted, with regard to the 'discovery' issue, that the Examining Division had already accepted that 'the function of achieving the technical effect to remove the toxic PNAs from the lubricating oil is a technical feature of [the claim]' (T-877/92: para. 3). The Board agreed with this. Moreover, the Board considered that the claims did not 'relate to a discovery as such ... since [they were] not directed to the discovered property of activated wood based charcoal, but to a technical use of the discovered property. Therefore, the claimed subject-matter is not excluded from being an "invention"' (T-877/92: para. 4.8).

The case was remitted to the Examining Division and the patent was granted in July 1997. Thus the TBoA held that a claim to the application of a discovery was not excluded. The accepted claim format satisfies the *anything added* approach, which ascribes a normal meaning to the words 'as such' in Art. 52(3) EPC.

4.3 T-869/95 NISSAN MOTOR

In June 1988 Nissan Motor and Ichikoh Industries filed a patent application relating to a projector-type headlamp for use on cars, which was said to provide an ideal luminous intensity distribution pattern preventing the driver of a vehicle running in the opposite direction from being dazzled.

The patent (Yamagishi *et al.* 1993) was granted in April 1993 and oppositions were filed by Hella, Robert Bosch and BMW. In May 1995 the oppositions were rejected by the Opposition Division. All three opponents appealed, and it was argued that the claimed subject-matter related to a discovery. Claim 1 read: 'A projector-type head lamp for vehicles, comprising: a reflector ...; a shade; and ... a lens means of converging the light beam shaped by said shade and having a focal plane near the other focus of said reflector.'

TBoA 3.2.03 (Chairman Wilson), in a communication annexed to the summons to oral proceedings, observed that it disagreed with the opponents' arguments concerning Art. 52(2)(a):

> [BMW] puts forward that according to the [Opposition Division's] decision the patentability of Claim 1 is supported exclusively on the effect indicated by the [patent holder] that an iridescent zone developed near the light-dark limit of the luminous intensity pattern of a projector-type head lamp can be avoided. Further according to [BMW], as the [patent holder] does not offer an explanation of why this effect occurs and as the effect of the protected combination takes place automatically, the subject-matter of Claim 1 has to be regarded as a discovery ... It seems to be clear that Claim 1 is not directed to a technical effect constituting a discovery per se but to a concrete technical teaching ... Claim 1 does not appear to relate to a discovery as such. (Correspondence *EPO* 1997b: 1–2)

In its decision of October 1997 the Board reconfirmed this: '[T]he claim is not directed to a technical effect constituting a discovery per se, but to a technical instruction concerning a technical apparatus ... Since Claim 1 does not concern a discovery as such as outlined above, its patentability cannot be excluded' (T-869/95: para. 2). Nonetheless, the Board revoked the patent for lack of sufficient disclosure. Once again, the TBoA followed what was essentially an *anything added* approach.

4.4 T-272/95 Relaxin/HOWARD FLOREY INSTITUTE

In December 1983 the Howard Florey Institute (HFI) filed a patent application relating inter alia to DNA fragments encoding the human protein H2-preprorelaxin, sub-units of such DNA, processes for isolating these DNA fragments, processes for synthesising human H2-preprorelaxin, synthetic human H2-preprorelaxin and human H2-preprorelaxin analogues. The contribution made by the patent applicants was said to be the production of recombinant human relaxin in a potentially therapeutically useful form, to alleviate complications associated with labour induction and caesarean section.

The Examining Division observed inter alia that 'in the absence of *specific structural features* or *parameters*, the designation H2 *per se* as used in the various claims is meaningless because a distinction between the H1 and H2 forms of relaxin (or their precursors) and between the H1/ H2 relaxins and the *known* human relaxin merely on the basis of the biological activity is not possible. In fact the activity is identical for all forms of relaxin' (Correspondence *EPO* 1988: 2, emphasis in original).

In response, HFI introduced the term 'isolated' into some of the claims to differentiate the H2-preprorelaxin gene from the naturally occurring chromosomal gene. The patent (Hudson *et al.* 1991) was granted in April 1991 and an opposition was filed on behalf of the faction of the 'Greens' in the European Parliament and its President Mr Paul Lannoye, inter alia on the basis of Art. 52(2)(a) EPC.

The granted patent included the following claims:

1. A DNA fragment encoding human H2-prorelaxin, said H2-prorelaxin having the amino acid sequence …
19. Synthetic human H2-prorelaxin having the amino acid sequence … (Hudson *et al.* 1991: 16–20)

According to the opponents, since nobody could invent genes, the claimed DNA fragment was a discovery and not an invention, and thus unpatentable. They argued that isolating and purifying a gene did not change that – the gene performed the same function as it does in the human body. Even if the method for analysing the structure of a gene could be inventive, this would not make the gene itself patentable (Correspondence *Aglietta et al.* 1992: 5).

HFI responded by sketching the background to the case and stated that 'It was a surprising discovery, by the Patentees, that human relaxin is encoded by two separate genes, now designated as the H1-relaxin gene and the H2-relaxin gene, which genes give rise to the separate H1-relaxin and H2-relaxin polypeptide products. The discovery of the H2-relaxin gene was totally unexpected' (Correspondence *Howard Florey* 1993: 2). It was further added that '[T]he DNA fragments claimed are not the same as the gene for human H2-relaxin … [They] … are all coding sequences, uninterrupted by introns [i.e. non-coding sequences], which are essential for utility' (Correspondence *Howard Florey* 1993: 6).

In its decision, the Opposition Division referred to the Guidelines for Examination in the European Patent Office and noted that these clearly allowed patentability in this case: 'Human H2-relaxin had no previously recognized existence. The [patent] Proprietor has developed a process for obtaining H2-relaxin and the DNA encoding it, has characterised these products by their chemical structure and has found a use for the protein. The products are therefore patentable under Article 52(2) EPC' (Correspondence *EPO* 1995: 10).

The Opposition Division decided to maintain the patent as granted. The opponents appealed. Their arguments regarding 'discovery' were as follows:

> In simple terms, the Proprietor obtained a 'code book' from the donors (the genetic material) and 'cracked the code' (discovered the number and sequence of human relaxin genes). That is no more than a discovery of the characteristics of a substance which is old ... In essence what the patentee has done is discovered something about the human body – that there are two relaxin genes and their sequences – and has sought to claim a monopoly in that sequence and proteins derived therefrom ... The gene and the proteins encoded by it are substances which have existed in nature, probably for many thousands of years. In so far as the Proprietor has given anything to the art it is only the discovery of the existence and sequence of the gene and the proteins. There is no element of invention beyond that mere discovery. There is no suggestion that there is any degree of invention in applying the coding information to the making of the relevant proteins ... [T]he patent relates to a discovery as such. (Correspondence *Aglietta et al.* 1995: 3–4)

TBoA 3.3.04 (Chairman Kinkeldey) issued its decision in October 2002. This Board had recently been slapped down by the EBoA for its interpretation of the Art. 53(b) EPC exclusion of plant varieties that had been at variance with the EBD and the EPC Rules introduced in 1999 to make the EPC EBD-compliant (see the discussion of T-1054/96 (I) Transgenic plant/NOVARTIS and G-1/98 Transgenic plant/NOVARTIS II in Chapter 7). The Board referred to the amendment of the EPC Rules in 1999 and noted that, in view of Art. 164(2) EPC, it had to examine 'whether or not the new rules insofar as they relate to *Article 53(a) EPC* are in conformity with this article' (T-272/95: para. 5, emphasis added). Sadly, the Board did *not* say that it had to do the same in relation to Art. 52(2) or Art. 54 EPC. Reference was made to G-1/98 Transgenic plant/NOVARTIS II, which had found that there was no conflict between a Rule relevant to Art. 53(b) EPC and the Article itself, and that the Rule was only interpretative. It was then added that 'The present Board adopts this view, considers that the same holds true for the new rules as far as they relate to the interpretation of *Article 53(a) EPC* and, thus, will apply [Rule 29 EPC] to the present case' (T-272/95: para. 5, emphasis added).

On that basis, instead of addressing the arguments raised by the Appellant and investigating whether the patented subject-matter constituted a discovery, the Board merely referred to Rule 29 EPC and concluded that no further assessment was needed:

> [The claims which] directly or indirectly relate to DNAs encoding the human protein preprorelaxin or to the human preprorelaxin per se ... are described in the patent in suit ... as having been obtained by technical processes. They, thus, answer the definition of patentable elements of the human body given in Rule [29(2)] EPC. Accordingly, they do not fall within the category of inventions which may not be patented for being discoveries ... *Thus, the Appellants' arguments ... are answered by* [Rule 29] EPC. (T-272/95: paras. 7–9, emphasis added)

TBoA 3.3.04 dismissed the appeal, leaving the patent unamended. The Board did not adopt or suggest any approach to the interpretation of the exclusion of discoveries set out in Art. 52(2) EPC. It simply and slavishly followed an EPC Rule without checking whether that Rule changed the scope of exclusion from patentability set out in the Articles of the EPC. As was made clear by the EBoA in G-2/07 Broccoli/PLANT BIOSCIENCE (discussed in Chapter 6), it is not the case that all the EPC Rules introduced in September 1999 to achieve compliance with the EBD compliance are EPC-compliant. Rule 29 EPC clearly is not.

4.5 T-338/00 Multimeric receptors/SALK INSTITUTE

In December 1992 the Salk Institute for Biological Studies filed a patent application (Evans *et al.* 1993) relating to combinations of steroid/thyroid receptor proteins and methods of using such combinations. The claim of concern here read: 'A heterodimeric receptor comprising one member selected from isoforms of RXR and one different member of the steroid/thyroid superfamily of receptors.'

In October 1999 the Examining Division rejected the application for lack of inventive step. The Salk Institute appealed and, in July 2002, in an annex to the summons to oral proceedings, TBoA 3.3.08 (Chairman Galligano) referred to G-10/93 Scope of examination in ex parte appeal/SIEMENS and noted that Art. 52(2)(a) EPC needed to be discussed.

In its decision, dated November 2002, the Board began by asserting that all the items mentioned in Art. 52(2) EPC as not to be regarded as an invention 'have in common that they refer to activities which do not aim at any direct technical result but are rather of an abstract and intellectual character' (T-338/00: para. 1). With regard to the 'discoveries' issue, it was observed that:

> [T]he board felt it necessary to examine whether ... what is described is merely an interesting research result that might yield a yet to be identified industrial application. These questions are directly linked to the question whether the disclosed interaction of receptors to form heterodimers is a mere 'discovery', i.e. the result of purely intellectual activity with no practical or technical character. (T-338/00: para. 2)

However, the Board considered that 'The activities and products disclosed in the application are not aimed at an abstract or intellectual character but at a direct technical result *that may clearly be applied in an industrial activity* ... Thus, the board considers that the claimed subject matter fulfils the requirements of ... Article 52(1) and (2) EPC' (T-338/00: para. 3).

The Board remitted the case to the Examining Division with an order to grant a patent on the basis of a claim to 'A heterodimeric receptor comprising one member selected from isoforms of RXR and COUP-TF' (T-338/00: para. VII). However, the application was later deemed to be withdrawn. The claim accepted by the Board appears to represent a claim to a *combination* of components that *individually* might have been discoveries.

4.6 T-1538/05 ZAGYANSKY

In March 2001 Professor Yuly Zagyansky filed a patent application (Zagyansky 2000) with the initial claim directed to 'The "magnetic" (magnetic) force characterized in that it is born as a result of the mutual deformations of the electric fields (of only existing electric charges) due to their relative movements'. The Examining Division refused the application in July 2005, on the basis that the subject-matter was not of a technical character, contravened Art. 52(2) EPC and consequently did not meet the basic requirement of Art. 52(1) EPC of being an 'invention'.

Professor Zagyansky appealed and, in his Statement of Grounds of Appeal, argued that the physical theories set out in his application were correct and that the employees of the EPO had colluded against him in order not to grant a patent on a 'new famous magnetic force' and a 'revolutionary scientific theory'. In response to a communication from TBoA 3.2.04 (Chairman Ceyte), explaining that the claimed subject-matter related to a discovery of a scientific theory and that it lacked industrial applicability, Professor Zagyansky accused the EPO of criminal intent and censorship and of being a united mafia.

In its decision of October 2006 the Board noted that:

> In most general terms, an invention must be of a technical character and must solve a technical problem with – at least partially – technical means ... The appellant claims to have discovered a magnetic force that was hitherto unknown, and as a consequence thereof, established theories such as the Heisenberg uncertainty principle as well as Einstein's theory of relativity should be wrong. These are scientific theories or discoveries of the law of nature different from those currently established. Neither the claims, nor the description, nor the numerous letters sent by the applicant give any indication about a clear technical teaching ... The above deficiencies thus make the invention unpatentable under Article 52 EPC. (T-1538/05: para. 4)

The Board dismissed the appeal. While this is one of the few decisions that decided that the claims were directed to a discovery (or scientific theory), it adds little to the manner of interpreting Art. 52(2) EPC, largely because of the format of the claims and the unproven nature of the subject-matter.

4.7 T-1213/05 Breast and ovarian cancer/ UNIVERSITY OF UTAH

In August 1995 Myriad Genetics (a spin-off from the University of Utah), the University of Utah Research Foundation (UURF) and the United States of America[1] filed a patent application relating inter alia to isolated DNA coding for BRCA1 (a breast cancer gene) or modified forms of it which are functionally equivalent or associated with a predisposition to breast or ovarian cancer, corresponding RNA, probes and primers for this DNA and corresponding RNA, methods of producing the DNA, genetic tests to diagnose a predisposition to breast or ovarian cancer, DNA substantially homologous and substantially similar in function to the 'wild-type' (i.e. naturally occurring) DNA for use in gene therapy, and methods for screening cancer drugs. After a long period of back-and-forth argument between the Examining Division and the patent applicants regarding inter alia novelty but not morality, the patent (Skolnick *et al.* 2001a) was granted in November 2001. Myriad would later assign its title to the patent to UURF.

Relevant claims included the following:

1. An isolated nucleic acid which comprises a coding sequence for the BRCA1 polypeptide defined by the amino acid sequence ...
6. A nucleic acid probe wherein the nucleotide sequence of said probe comprises the DNA sequence ...

[1] The US National Institutes of Health had been involved in the research.

7. A hybridization probe wherein the sequence of said probe comprises a portion of a coding sequence for a mutant BRCA1 polypeptide ...
8. An isolated nucleic acid comprising at least 15 contiguous nucleotides of a coding sequence for a mutant BRCA1 polypeptide ...
15. An isolated human BRCA1 polypeptide corresponding to the amino acid sequence ...
17. An isolated mutated human BRCA1 polypeptide obtainable by expression of a mutated form of the nucleotide sequence ...
27. A wild-type BRCA1 gene nucleic acid which encodes a BRCA1 polypeptide having the amino acid sequence ...
29. A wild-type BRCA1 polypeptide defined by the amino acid sequence ... (Skolnick *et al.* 2001a: 123–5)

Eight parties opposed the patent: Sozialdemokratische Partei der Schweiz (Switzerland); Greenpeace (Germany and Austria); Institut Curie (France); Assistance Publique – Hôpitaux de Paris (France); Institut Gustave Roussy (France); Belgian Society of Human Genetics (as well as thirteen other genetics and cancer societies); Dr Rolf Wilhelms (Germany) and The Netherlands (represented by its Minister of Health).

At the oral hearing in January 2005, two opponents (Greenpeace and Dr Wilhelms) argued that the patent contravened Art. 52(2) EPC since genes are discoveries and thus non-patentable (Correspondence *EPO* 2005e: 8–9). The central concept underlying the patent application, according to Greenpeace, was the discovery of a link between a gene and a disease. Dr Wilhelms noted that the claimed sequence could be found in nature and was thus a discovery. The patentee did not respond to this, but had pointed out at the start of the oral proceedings that the case law of the EPO demonstrated that genes could be patented. The Opposition Division rejected this objection, arguing that:

The subject-matter claimed is directed to nucleic acid probes comprising specific sequences. The claimed probes cannot be reduced to a presentation of information. The fact that a link between the claimed probes, BRCA1 and breast cancer exists does not preclude the claimed probes to be patentable ... Moreover, Rule [29(2)] EPC explicitly states that 'elements isolated from the human body or otherwise produced by means of a technical process including the sequence or partial sequence of a gene may constitute patentable invention even if the structure of that element is identical to that of a natural element'. Since the nucleic acid probes were described in the opposed patent ... as having been obtained by technical processes, they fulfill the definition of patentable elements of the human body given in Rule [29(2)] EPC. The probes as claimed cannot therefore be considered as mere discoveries (see T 272/95 [Relaxin/HOWARD FLOREY INSTITUTE]). (Correspondence *EPO* 2005b: 26)

The Opposition Division decided to maintain the patent in amended form. Both the patentee and one of the opponents (the Swiss Social-Democratic Party) appealed. Oral proceedings took place in September 2007.

In its decision from September 2007, TBoA 3.3.04 (Chairman Kinkeldey), the Board responsible for the flawed T-272/95 Relaxin/HOWARD FLOREY INSTITUTE decision, argued that:

> According to the case law of the Boards of Appeal (see decision T 272/95 [Relaxin/HOWARD FLOREY INSTITUTE]), Article 52(2)(a) EPC is to be interpreted in accordance with [Rule 29 EPC] ... Claims 1 to 3 relate to nucleic acid probes comprising partial DNA sequences of the human BRCA1 gene, which are described in the patent in suit as having been obtained by technical processes ... These probes are thus isolated elements of the human body as defined in Rule [29(2)] EPC and thus patentable subject-matter. Accordingly, the subject-matter of claims 1 to 3 does not fall within the category of inventions which may not be patentable as being discoveries. (T-1213/05: paras 44–5)

The appeal was dismissed and the patent reissued in amended form in August 2008. As is clear, the Board simply applied its own earlier flawed reasoning to reject the objection to the claims under Art. 52(2) EPC.

4.8 T-666/05 Mutation/UNIVERSITY OF UTAH

In August 1995, on the same day as the previous case, Myriad Genetics, the Centre de Recherche du Chul (Canada) and the Cancer Institute (Tokyo) filed a patent application with claims directed inter alia to isolated DNA coding for BRCA1 mutations and polymorphisms, probes, methods of producing the DNA, and methods for diagnosing a predisposition for breast and ovarian cancer in humans by determining whether a BRCA1 mutation indicative of it was present.

The patent (Shattuck-Eidens *et al.* 2001) was granted in May 2001 and six oppositions were filed, namely by: Institut Curie, Assistance Publique – Hôpitaux de Paris, Institut Gustave Roussy, Vereniging van Stichtingen Klinische Genetica (VVSKG, together with the German, Danish and Belgian Society for Genetics, a German Cancer Society and Belgium, represented by its Ministers of Health, Social Affairs and Economic Affairs and Scientific Research), The Netherlands (represented by its Minister of Health) and Greenpeace.

Greenpeace invoked Art. 52(2)(a) EPC, arguing that genes were discoveries rather than inventions (Correspondence *Greenpeace* 2002: 10–11). The Opposition Division, in its comments accompanying the summons to oral proceedings, rejected these arguments, referring to Rule 29(2) EPC, adding that 'for this reason alone an objection under Art. 52(2) EPC must fail' (Correspondence *EPO* 2004b: 6). In its written decision, the Opposition Division argued:

> The very wording of [Rule 29(2) EPC] contradicts [the opponent's] submission. There is no fundamental bar to the patenting of complete or partial human gene sequences (cf. also [T-272/95 Relaxin/HOWARD FLOREY INSTITUTE]). Claims 1 to 3 directly or indirectly relate to DNAs encoding parts of the human BRCA1 protein, which is described throughout the patent in suit as having been obtained by technical processes ... They, thus, meet the definition of patentable elements of the human body given in Rule [29(2)] EPC. Accordingly, they do not fall within the category of inventions which may not be patented for being discoveries (Article 52(2)(a) EPC). (Correspondence *EPO* 2005d: 15)

The Opposition Division decided to maintain the patent in amended form. UURF appealed. The Institut Curie, the Assistance Publique – Hôpitaux de Paris and the Institut Gustave Roussy also (jointly) appealed.

TBoA 3.3.04 (Chairman Kinkeldey) essentially followed the same reasoning as in the case discussed in section 4.7 and concluded that:

> [The contested claim] relates to a nucleic acid probe comprising partial DNA sequences of the human BRCA1 gene, which is described in the patent in suit as having been obtained by technical processes. This probe is thus an isolated element of the human body as defined in Rule 29(2) EPC and thus patentable subject-matter. Accordingly, the subject-matter of [the claim] does not fall within the category of inventions which may not be patentable as being discoveries. (T-666/05: para. 76)

In November 2008 the Board remitted the case to the Opposition Division with an order to maintain the patent in amended form. Again, the Kinkeldey Board simply followed its own earlier flawed reasoning.

4.9 T-80/05 Method of diagnosis/UNIVERSITY OF UTAH

In August 1995, on the same date as the two previous cases, Myriad Genetics, UURF and the United States of America filed a patent application with the initial claim relating to 'A method for diagnosing a predisposition for breast and ovarian cancer in a human subject which comprises determining whether there is a germline alteration in the sequence of the BRCA1 gene or a BRCA1 gene regulatory sequence in a tissue sample of said subject, said alteration being indicative of a predisposition to said cancer'.

The patent (Skolnick *et al.* 2001b) was granted in January 2001 with some amendments to the claims in response to comments from the Examining Division regarding lack of novelty and inventive step, as well as lack of clarity and support of the patent claims. Oppositions were filed by the Institut Curie, Assistance Publique – Hôpitaux de Paris, the Institut Gustave Roussy, the Belgian Society of Human Genetics, and an Italian cancer research organisation (Associazione Angelaserra per la ricerca sul cancro).

The Belgian Society of Human Genetics argued that the primary claim of the patent could be analysed as involving three steps, which were all excluded from patentability under Art. 52(2) EPC:

(1) the discovery of a relationship which exists in nature between mutations which exist in human beings and a disease;
(2) the discovery of a mutation in the genome of a human who exists in nature; and
(3) deducing from steps 1 and 2 that the human subject has a predisposition for ovarian or breast cancer, i.e. a method of performing a mental act excluded by Art. 52(2)(c) EPC. (Correspondence *Belgian Society of Human Genetics* 2001)

The Opposition Division decided, in November 2004, to revoke the patent inter alia on the basis of lack of inventive step and lack of clarity of the claims. This decision was appealed by the patent holders in January 2005. In June 2005 the case was transferred from TBoA 3.3.08 to TBoA 3.3.04 (Chairman Kinkeldey), in view of certain technical aspects of the appeal. According to the Board in its decision from November 2008:

The methods of the patent in suit are performed on a tissue sample of a human subject and relate to a specific gene, namely the BRCA1 gene. The diagnostic methods make use of the knowledge of the open reading frame coding for the BRCA1 polypeptide, and identify frameshift mutations in the patient's sample ... In order to get the knowledge required to carry out the claimed diagnostic methods, it was necessary to isolate the gene of interest from the human body ... According to the case law of the Boards of Appeal (see decision T 272/95 [Relaxin/HOWARD FLOREY INSTITUTE]), Article 52(2)(a) EPC is to be interpreted in accordance with ... Rule 29(2) EPC) which states that an element isolated from the human body or otherwise produced by means of a technical process may constitute a patentable invention ... This finding applies to claims relating to products, here genes, and is a fortiori applicable to the method claims here at issue ... Accordingly, the subject-matter of claims 1 to 7 does not fall within the category of inventions which may not be patentable as being discoveries. (T-80/05: para. 59)

The Board remitted the case to the Opposition Division with an order to maintain the patent in amended form. The patent was reissued in

August 2009. Although the Kinkeldey Board referred to T-272/95 Relaxin/HOWARD FLOREY INSTITUTE, this acceptance of the patent's method claims is more akin to the early decisions accepting that applications of a discovery are not excluded as discoveries 'as such'.

4.10 Comments

Some have argued that the exclusion from patentability of discoveries is a 'soft', that is easily circumvented, exclusion. In a decision from the British Patents Court from 2005, for example, it was argued that:

> [I]t cannot be ruled out in advance that some of the exclusions [from patentability] are 'soft' and others are 'hard': a matter of degree. All of the excluded items are information about something, and the harder the exclusion, the more it is the policy of the law to insist that the use of the information be not foreclosed under patent law ... An instance of a 'soft' exclusion is a discovery. It is well-settled law that, although you cannot patent a discovery, you can patent a useful artefact or process that you were able to devise once you had made your discovery. *This is so even where it was perfectly obvious how to devise the artefact or process, once you had made the discovery.* The detractors of your patent are not allowed to say: the discovery does not count and the rest was obvious. They are not allowed to dissect your invention in that way. The discovery is an integral and all-important part of your invention. The law does not object to that. It objects only when you try to monopolise your discovery for all purposes i.e. divorced from your new artefact or process. For that would enable you to stifle the creation of further artefacts or processes which you yourself were not able to think of. (UK-CFPH 2005: paras 9–10, emphasis added)

However, as rightly argued by the opponents in T-272/95 Relaxin/HOWARD FLOREY INSTITUTE, the exclusion of discoveries is of great importance:

> There is a sound policy reason for excluding patentability of ... discoveries and why the EPC should not be construed so as to permit them. The overriding purpose of the patent system is to promote research and the development of new and advantageous inventions. Permitting the acquisition of monopoly rights in the information encoded in already existing genes and gene fragments does not do this. It is likely to lead to the reverse, since other researchers are thereby hampered in their ability to make real inventions (rather than discoveries) using the genetic information sought to be monopolized by the patentee. This is a point which has been made by [various] scientific organizations. (Correspondence *Algietta et al.* 1995: 4)

Not only is the exclusion of great importance, but it has been present since the early days of the *travaux préparatoires* and all attempts to delete it (and the other Art. 52(2) EPC exclusions) were firmly rebuffed, as described in Chapter 2.

The EPO case law on discoveries is scarce; however, the exclusion corresponds closely to the exclusion from patent-eligibility under US case law of phenomena of nature. For this reason, we shall draw upon the case law of the US Supreme Court to illustrate the importance of the exclusion of discoveries. We do this also since in December 2011 an application[2] was made to the US Supreme Court to consider the patent-eligibility of 'isolated DNA', that is subject-matter that Rule 29(2) EPC would have us believe is not excluded under Arts. 52(2) or 54 EPC.

As far as natural products and phenomena are concerned, the patent-eligibility test, the test under Section 101 of the US Patent Law (i.e. 35 USC 101), is well illustrated by the 1980 US Supreme Court decision in *Diamond* v. *Chakrabarty*:

> [We are not suggesting] that [35 USC 101] has no limits or that it embraces every discovery. The laws of nature, physical phenomena, and abstract ideas have been held not patentable. Thus, a new mineral discovered in the earth or a new plant found in the wild is not patentable subject matter. Likewise, Einstein could not patent his celebrated law that $E = mc^2$; nor could Newton have patented the law of gravity. Such discoveries are 'manifestations of ... nature, free to all men and reserved exclusively to none'. (US-Diamond (1980), quoting from US-Funk (1948))

The claims under consideration in *Diamond* v. *Chakrabarty* related to a genetically engineered microorganism that was not naturally occurring. Finding those claims acceptable, the Supreme Court distinguished over its 1948 decision in *Funk Bros. Seed Co* v. *Kalo Inoculant Co*:

> Concluding that the patentee had discovered 'only some of the handiwork of nature', the [Funk] Court ruled the product [a combination of known bacterial species] nonpatentable: 'No species acquires a different use ... The bacteria perform in their natural way. Their use in combination does not improve in any way their natural functioning. They serve the same ends nature originally provided and act quite independently of any effort by the patentee.' ... Here, by contrast, the patentee has produced a new bacterium with markedly different characteristics from any found in nature and one having the potential for significant utility. *His discovery is not nature's handiwork, but his own; accordingly it is patentable subject matter* under [35 USC 101]. (US-Diamond 1980, emphasis added)

[2] An application by the Association of Molecular Pathology, made following a decision of the Federal Circuit in July 2011, itself a decision following an appeal by Myriad Genetics from a decision of the District Court of the Southern District of New York (US-AMP 2010). In March 2012, the US Supreme Court ordered the Federal Circuit to vacate its decision on the AMP case and reconsider it in view of the Supreme Court's March 2012 decision in *Mayo* v. *Prometheus* (US-Mayo 2012). The Federal Circuit is due to hear oral arguments in July 2012.

As rightly noted by Conley and Makowski, the product of nature doctrine developed by the US Supreme Court, as it stands today, implies that 'If something is a product of nature, it should be held to be unpatentable, without ever reaching the questions of its novelty, utility or non-obviousness' (Conley and Makowski 2004: 25–6). Likewise, under the EPC, if something is excluded subject-matter, for example a discovery, it is held to be a priori unpatentable, regardless of potential novelty, inventive step or susceptibility of industrial application.

In the AMP case (US-AMP 2010), one of the main questions at issue was whether the claims to DNA failed the judiciary-made law as being claims to naturally occurring substances, that is discoveries that are essentially similar to 'products of nature'. Obviously, DNA does not exist in nature in isolated form. However, isolation or purification of native DNA does not change the fact that the claimed DNA *itself* is a product of nature. As with the 'isolated DNA' claims considered in the UURF cases by TBoA 3.3.04, the question arises as to whether the *wording* of a claim (e.g. as an isolated, purified or synthetic version of a natural product) can make the claim patent eligible. As we have explained in section 4.1, such wording simply places the claims in product-by-process format. To be acceptable in that format, the product *itself*, and not simply the process for making it, should be patentable, that is neither lacking novelty nor being excluded as a discovery.

In the case of 'isolated DNA', where the DNA as a natural product is the discovery, it is itself still the subject-matter of the claim, and thus such claims must still fail as being directed to discoveries as such. If somebody removes a painting by Picasso from its wrappings, the 'painting as revealed' is still Picasso's painting, his product and not that of the unwrapper. Any properties or characteristics that non-patentable discoveries acquire implicitly, by virtue of being isolated or extracted, *cannot* contribute to the patentability of the material itself. Consider, for example, a pecan nut extracted from its shell: the kernel is, as it always was, a product of nature, even though it now has the new characteristic of edibility. As Conley and Makowski rightly note:

> [I]f a claimed invention is nothing more than a product of nature, its source is irrelevant. *If the product itself is substantially the same as its natural counterpart, it [is not patent-eligible], regardless of how it is produced ... [W]ords such as 'isolated', 'purified' and 'synthesized' should not be accorded talismanic status ... Because the distinction between a [patentable] invention and a [non-patentable] product of nature is one of substance rather than form, cases should not be resolved on the basis of incantations*. Rather, there should be a fact-specific inquiry into the materiality of the differences that are created by the processes such as isolation, purification and synthesis. (Conley and Makowski 2004: 34, emphasis added)

The position should be even clearer in Europe than the USA since investigating or purifying or isolating a discovery can itself reveal a discovery. If the pecan nut referred to above is a discovery, then so, upon removing the shell and 'isolating' the kernel, is the kernel.

Conley and Makowski explain this further:

> [D]espite its nominal chemical distinctiveness, [isolated DNA/RNA] is functionally indistinguishable from natural DNA and RNA. It contains exactly the same genetic information as its natural counterpart. It can do precisely the same work as a naturally occurring gene – protein synthesis – and it employs precisely the same processes to do it, whether in the body or in the laboratory. ... In other words, what is claimed is whatever it is that does the work of the naturally occurring ... gene ... [T]he non-coding regions do not participate in doing the work.
>
> In evaluating the materiality of the differences between claimed DNA sequences and their natural counterparts, we are left with chemical distinctions versus informational and functional identity. Critically, it is these informational and functional properties that are the whole reason for seeking DNA patents. Researchers isolate, purify and synthesize DNA both as an intermediate step in the process of gene identification and as a tool for building proteins. Thus, [the] DNA [for which patents are granted] is identical to its natural counterpart with respect to the qualities that researchers deem most significant, and distinct in ways that can be fairly characterized as incidental. (Conley and Makowski 2004: 35)

It is interesting to reconsider, in this light, the statement quoted earlier from the US Supreme Court in *Funk Bros Seed Co* v. *Kalo Inoculant Co*, approved in *Diamond* v. *Chakrabarty*, that some 'discoveries are manifestations of nature, free to all men and reserved exclusively to none', a statement which was made in the following context:

> [The patent applicant] does not create a state of inhibition or of non-inhibition in the bacteria. Their qualities are the work of nature. Those qualities are of course not patentable. For patents cannot issue for the discovery of the phenomena of nature ... The qualities of these bacteria, like the heat of the sun, electricity, and or the qualities of metals, are part of the storehouse of knowledge of all men. *They are manifestations of laws of nature, free to all men and reserved exclusively to none. He who discovers a hitherto unknown phenomenon of nature has no claim to a monopoly of it which the law recognizes. If there is to be invention from such a discovery, it must come from the application of the law of nature to a new and useful end.* (US-Funk 1948: 130, emphasis added)

What is meant in US patent law by an unpatentable discovery, and what is meant by a discovery in Art. 52(2) EPC, we would suggest, is a discovery in the sense of *something already in existence and effect* (e.g. the law of gravity, that energy and matter are interrelated, a newly found mineral, a newly found plant, and other products, phenomena or 'handiwork' of nature).

However, if the exclusion of discoveries is not to be circumvented by clever claim-drafting, if such discoveries are to be 'free to all men', then so too must be their applications in manners which would have been obvious had their existence been known. Otherwise, their exclusion from patentability would be substantially ineffective as their discoverer could patent all those obvious uses. Put differently, where a use of a discovery is obvious, then simply proposing that use and seeking to patent it would prevent the discovery from being 'free to all men'.

While the Art. 52(2)(a) EPC exclusion can be overcome by combining the discovery in a 'mixed' claim with something non-excluded, as we explain in Chapter 9 the subsequent examination of the claim for inventive step should only acknowledge the existence of an inventive step if there is a *synergistic* interaction between the excluded and non-excluded components of the mixed claim.

Thus, an *application* of a non-patentable discovery, for example a product incorporating it as one of its several elements, or a process using it in one of its several steps, may be an invention and so may indeed be patent-eligible. However, any claim that de facto encompasses *all* applications of a non-patentable discovery is effectively a claim to the discovery itself and thus should not be permissible. In other words, an act of invention or human ingenuity is required to transform an unpatentable discovery into a patentable invention. Mere isolation or purification cannot do the trick.

In this regard, it is also instructive to quote at length some arguments and analogies from the *amicus curiae* brief of the USA in the AMP case before the Federal Circuit:

> Genomic DNA itself ... is a product of nature that is ineligible for patent protection, whether or not claimed in 'isolated' form. We acknowledge that this conclusion is contrary to the longstanding practice of the Patent and Trademark Office ... The district court's judgement in this case [US-AMP 2010], however, prompted the United States to reevaluate the relationship between [patents in the past sought and obtained for isolated genomic DNA] ... and the settled principle under Supreme Court precedent that the patent laws do not extend to products of nature ...
>
> The basic composition claims at issue in this case are directed not to the wild-type or mutated BRCA genes in situ but to 'isolated' DNA molecules that have the same chemical structure and function but have been extracted from the cellular environment. The 'isolated' limitation must therefore carry the entire weight of these claims ... Yet the fact of 'isolation' is inadequate for this task. The fact that genes do not occur in 'isolated' form in nature does not provide principled basis for patent-eligibility ... Many natural products – coal beneath the earth, cotton fibers mixed with cotton seeds, the stigmas of the saffron flower – must be physically separated, i.e., 'isolated', from

their natural environments before becoming useful to mankind, but few would doubt that coal, cotton, and saffron are products of nature and not patent-eligible. Likewise the unique nucleotide sequence that induces human cells to express the BRCA1 protein is no more an invention of appellants ... when captured in a test tube than in its natural context in the human body ... [T]he isolated DNA segment itself remains, in structure and function, what it was in the human body. Common sense would suggest that a product of nature is not transformed into a human-made invention merely by isolating it ... *The fundamental question ... is whether the inventor has created something through the application of human ingenuity or merely exposed something previously unappreciated in nature* ... In this case, the answer is the latter ... [Myriad] urge[s] that isolated genomic DNA has practical uses that native DNA has not, and that [the patent law] should be construed in a manner that provides an incentive for companies to identify, describe, and develop those uses into commercial applications that promote the public welfare. This contention, however, rests on several erroneous premises. First, while isolated genomic DNA may have more potential applications than human genes in their natural context, the same is equally true of mined coal, separated cotton fibers, pure metallic lithium, ductile uranium, and other products of nature whose industrial value to mankind likewise arises when they are extracted from their naturally occurring environments. (USA 2010, emphasis added, footnotes omitted)

To sum up, in order to be patentable, a product must be a human-made invention, the result of human ingenuity – rather than the revelation of something unappreciated but naturally occurring, that is it must not be a product of nature, whether or not extracted, purified or isolated – and, if related to a product of nature, it must be transformed or altered to become something man-made. This, in our view, is the correct position, whereas the approach of the EPO to the exclusion of discoveries, following the EBD, is logically untenable and boils down to an emasculation of the exclusion.

5 Methods of medical treatment and diagnosis

> Medical and veterinary practitioners should be free to use their skills and knowledge of the best available treatments to achieve the utmost benefit for their patients uninhibited by any worry that some treatment might be covered by a patent.
>
> (G-1/07: 174)

5.1 Introduction

In this chapter we will consider the exception to patentability of methods of therapy, surgery and diagnosis ('medical methods') set out in Art. 53(c) EPC as well as the two well-established ways of evading this exception: the use of purpose-limited product claims and the, now defunct, Swiss-type use claims. We will begin, however, with the medical methods exception that appeared in Art. 52(4) EPC 1973 but that, in the 2000 revision of the EPC, was transferred to Art. 53(c) EPC, a place where it sits much more happily. Art. 53(c) EPC reads as follows:

> European patents shall not be granted in respect of ... methods for treatment of the human or animal body by surgery or therapy and diagnostic methods practised on the human or animal body; this provision shall not apply to products, in particular substances or compositions, for use in any of these methods. (EPO 2010a: 108)

In its previous incarnation, the exclusion relied on the legal fiction that medical methods were not susceptible of industrial application. As is clear from the *travaux préparatoires* (see Chapter 2), this legal fiction can be disregarded – the exclusion was and remains based on social, ethical and political grounds. Nonetheless, for the sake of completeness, we should mention that the exclusion in its original form, Art. 52(4) EPC 1973, read as follows:

> Methods for treatment of the human or animal body by surgery or therapy and diagnostic methods practised on the human or animal body shall not be regarded as inventions which are susceptible of industrial application within

the meaning of paragraph 1. This provision shall not apply to products, in particular substances or compositions, for use in any of these methods. (EPO 2006: 70)

For our present purposes, the explanatory second part of the provision needs little comment – it is there to make it clear that the medical methods exemption is not so broad as to apply to materials and apparatus used in the performance of a medical method, although these still have to meet the conventional hurdles of novelty, inventive step and susceptibility of industrial application in order to be patentable, that is they are patent-eligible unless excluded by other provisions of Arts. 52(2) and 53 EPC.

The purpose, or *ratio legis*, of Art. 53(c) EPC has been interpreted from the earliest days of the Boards of Appeal as being to permit physicians and veterinarians to carry out their professional tasks without fear of patent infringement suits. Thus, in the first decision from the Enlarged Board of Appeal, G-5/83 Second medical indication/EISAI, in December 1984, this was expressed as: 'The intention of Article [53(c)] EPC … is only to free from restraint non-commercial and non-industrial medical and veterinary activities' (G-5/83: 66). By December 2005, when the Enlarged Board gave its opinion in G-1/04 Diagnostic methods, this explanation of the basis for Art. 53(c) EPC had expanded to read:

[T]he exclusion from patentability of [medical] methods under Article [53(c)] EPC seems actually to be based on socio-ethical and public health considerations. Medical and veterinary practitioners should be free to take the actions they consider suited to diagnose illnesses by means of investigative methods. Consequently, the policy … appears to be aimed at ensuring that those who carry out diagnostic methods as part of the medical treatment of humans or veterinary treatment of animals are not inhibited by patents (cf. T 116/85 [Pigs I/WELLCOME]). (G-1/04: 348)

By February 2010 and the most recent of the relevant Enlarged Board of Appeal decisions, G-1/07 Treatment by surgery/MEDI-PHYSICS, the purpose was still viewed in the same light:

Even if it was true that national legislations like the US law allowing patenting but providing that no sanctions may be issued with respect to a medical practitioner's performance of a medical activity that 'constitutes an infringement' provide better solutions, the European legislator did not adopt it. On the contrary, in the EPC revision the European legislator deliberately maintained the exclusions under Article [53(c)] EPC … *Thereby the principle has been confirmed that medical and veterinary practitioners' freedom to use the best available treatments to the benefit of their patients uninhibited by any worry that some treatment might be covered by a patent is protected by excluding these activities from patentability*

... [T]he Travaux Préparatoires do not reveal a specific legal purpose for the introduction of the exclusion of surgical treatments in the EPC. By contrast, as regards the general purpose of the exclusion of therapeutic, diagnostic and surgical methods from patentability, already under the EPC 1973 it was commonly accepted that *the real reason for excluding the defined methods from patentability were socio-ethical considerations and considerations of public health ... Medical and veterinary practitioners should be free to use their skills and knowledge of the best available treatments to achieve the utmost benefit for their patients uninhibited by any worry that some treatment might be covered by a patent.* (G-1/07: 174, emphasis added)

In between these cases, numerous TBoA decisions have agreed with this interpretation. However, the purpose of Art. 53(c) EPC is not, and has never been, to protect the medical practitioner from *any* accusation of patent infringement since, as the final part of Art. 53(c) EPC and the *travaux préparatoires* make clear, the tools of the medical practitioner, drugs and equipment, may themselves be patentable.

The key questions to be addressed in determining the scope of the exclusion in Art. 53(c) EPC are thus:

(1) What is a method of therapy, surgery or diagnosis?
(2) What does 'practised on the human or animal body' require in the context of a diagnostic method?
(3) Does the exclusion only apply to methods actually performed by a physician or veterinary surgeon?
(4) May a claim be accepted if, in some contexts, the method covered constitutes therapy, surgery or diagnosis while in others it does not?
(5) Are mixed claims requiring both a medical step and a non-medical step excluded?

To a large extent these questions have been addressed and answered in the case law of the EPO Boards of Appeal. Particular reference in this regard should be had to the recent Enlarged Board of Appeal decisions G-1/04 Diagnostic methods and G-1/07 Treatment by surgery/MEDI-PHYSICS. Grey areas do remain, however, and some of the decisions are inconsistent or less than satisfactory. The question of diagnostic methods is particularly problematic since the act of diagnosis is (or is equivalent to) a mental act, and omission of the actual act of diagnosis from a claim otherwise clearly directed to a diagnostic method *can* be sufficient to render the method patentable.

Any analysis of what is excluded begins by determining what is meant by therapy, surgery and diagnosis. It proceeds by asking whether the claimed method must or can fall within such definitions, and, in the latter case, continues by asking whether the chosen claim wording allows the method to avoid exclusion.

We shall review the case law relating to the five questions mentioned above before returning to the *travaux préparatoires* and considering whether the intentions of the framers have been met.

5.2 What is therapy?

This question itself splits into several sub-questions. Is a method of treatment to guard against a disease or ailment (e.g. vaccination or application of a sunscreen to prevent sunburn) therapy? Is a method of treatment to reduce, terminate or prevent something that is not a disease or ailment (e.g. appetite, life or pregnancy) a method of therapy? Is a method of treatment that does not change or even worsens current or future body function (e.g. the taking of lifestyle drugs) therapy? Must a method of therapy involve treatment with a 'therapeutic agent' (e.g. radiation or a drug)? Is treatment to reduce or avoid infestation by a parasite a method of therapy of the host animal, and does it make a difference whether the treatment is of an external parasite (e.g. lice) or of an internal parasite (e.g. tapeworms)? Can a cosmetic treatment method which can have therapeutic effects be saved from exclusion (a) by specifying that it is a cosmetic treatment, (b) if it would not normally have a significant therapeutic effect, (c) by requiring conditions where there would be no therapeutic effect, (d) by specifying that no therapeutic effect occurs, or (e) never?

The question of what is therapy, as opposed to cosmetic treatment, was considered by TBoA 3.3.01 (Chairman Kahn) in March 1986 in T-144/83 Appetite suppressant/DU PONT, which related to the use of a drug to suppress appetite. The Board considered that the exclusions of Art. 53(c) EPC:

> *should not apply to treatments which are not therapeutic in character.* As far as the language of the main claim is concerned, it clearly covers a method of cosmetic use and is unrelated to the therapy of human or animal body in the ordinary sense ... Cosmetic treatment is 'designed to beautify hair, skin, complexion etc. ... or intended to improve appearance' ... *Therapy, on the other hand, clearly relates to the treatment of a disease in general or to a curative treatment in the narrow sense as well as the alleviation of the symptoms of pain and suffering.* (T-144/83: para. 3, emphasis added)

In T-81/84 Dysmenorrhea/RORER, in May 1987, TBoA 3.3.02 (Chairman Lançon) was considering a method of relieving pain and discomfort associated with menstruation:

> *In the view of the Board, the concept of therapy should not be confined narrowly.* There are many chemical agents which are used by physicians to relieve pain,

discomfort and incapacity. Although at least some of such and similar experiences may have been caused by natural circumstances (e.g. menstruation, pregnancy or age etc.) or by a reaction to situations in the human environment (e.g. atmospheric conditions provoking tiredness, headaches, etc.), these overlap with and are often indistinguishable from symptoms of a disease or an injury ... The use of medicaments may be called for whenever the human body is suffering from a disease, illness, pain or discomfort or incapacity, and the administration thereof could provide or contribute to either full or partial healing, or relief or restoration of fitness. These are part of the everyday therapeutic activities of the medical profession ... Contrary to other situations where the boundaries with the non-medical handling of the human body are not at all clear in view of the involvement of different specialists (e.g. cosmeticians), the treatment of pain normally is a matter exclusively reserved for the physician ... For these reasons *it is the view of the Board that irrespective of the origin of pain, discomfort or incapacity, its relief, by the administration of an appropriate agent, is to be construed as 'therapy' or 'therapeutic use'* in the sense of Article [53(c)] EPC. (T-81/84: paras. 3–5, emphasis added)

In October 1987 Chemistry I TBoA 3.3.01 (Chairman Jahn) handed down a decision, T-19/86 Pigs II/DUPHAR, concerning prophylactic (i.e. preventative) treatment:

The treatment of the pigs in the present case is prophylactic rather than curative. In the Board's view both prophylactic and curative treatments of disease should be regarded as falling within the meaning of the word 'therapy' in the sense that that word is used in Article [53(c)] EPC since both are directed to the same objective, i.e. *the maintenance or restoration of health.* (T-19/86: para. 7, emphasis added)

In November 1988 Mechanics II TBoA 3.2.02 (Chairman Delbecque) again had pigs to consider, in T-58/87 Pigs III/SALMINEN, where the claims covered a method for preventing piglet suffocation involving blowing air when their mother stood up. The Board held that this could not 'reasonably be called a treatment by therapy' and was more akin to a method of preventing accidents. More relevantly, the Board agreed that the word 'therapy' covered 'any non-surgical treatment which is designed to cure, alleviate, remove or lessen the symptom of, or prevent or reduce the possibility of contracting any malfunction of the animal body ... and also – relates to the treatment of a disease in general or to a curative treatment in the narrow sense as well as the alleviation of the symptoms of pain and suffering' (T-58/87: para. 2.1).

TBoA 3.2.02 (Chairman Szabo) returned to the question of what 'treatment', in this case by surgery, should be deemed to be, in July 1993 in T-182/90 Blood-flow/SEA-SHELL, a case relating to a method of measuring blood flow:

According to [Schwalm(1980)] ... the term 'medical treatment' means any non-insignificant intentional physical or psychic intervention performed directly or indirectly by one human being ... on another (or, by analogy, on animals) using means or methods of medical science ... The term 'treatment' as used in Article [53(c)] EPC and in [Schwalm (1980)] is not restricted to methods serving a direct therapeutic (including prophylactic) purpose. (The latter purpose is introduced by the express reference to 'therapy' in Article [53(c)] EPC.) According to the above definition (see [Schwalm 1980: 6–8]), the term 'medical treatment' may also include treatments for other, non-curative purposes such as cosmetic treatment, the termination of pregnancy, castration, sterilisation, artificial insemination, embryo transplants, treatments for experimental and research purposes and the removal of organs, skin or bone marrow from a living donor ... It is clear that the general term embraces a variety of possibilities including some which have been recognised as patentable, e.g. cosmetic treatment with substances (cf. T 36/83 [Thenoyl peroxide/ROUSSEL-UCLAF], and T 144/83 [Appetite suppressant/DU PONT]). It is therefore necessary to consider the specific characteristics of the further relevant term in the Article [i.e. surgery, therapy or diagnosis]. (T-182/90: para. 2.2)

This decision went on to confirm that methods which have as their goal the death of the subject of treatment are not excluded by the provisions of Art. 53(c) EPC (although Art. 53(a) EPC, the morality and 'ordre public' exclusion, might of course apply).

In May 1994, considering a case relating to laser treatment of the eye, T-24/91 Cornea/THOMPSON, TBoA 3.2.02 (Chairman Seidenschwartz) provided a particularly concise definition of therapy: 'The meaning of the term "therapy" is not restricted to curing a disease and removing its causes. Rather, this term covers any treatment which is designed to cure, alleviate, remove or lessen the symptoms of, or prevent or reduce the possibility of contracting any disorder or malfunction of the human or animal body' (T-24/91: para. 2.7).

TBoA 3.2.02 (Chairman Seidenschwartz) returned to therapy in June 1997 with T-329/94 Blood extraction method/BAXTER, which concerned external limb stimulation in a method of blood extraction:

This ... does not produce any therapeutic or prophylactic effect on the donor himself, that is with a view to maintaining or restoring his health by preventing or curing diseases (T 19/86 [Pigs II/DUPHAR]). In other words, *there is no functional link or physical causality between the measure implemented and any therapeutic effect produced on the body to which this measure is applied* ... Again, the purpose of the claimed blood extraction assistance method is not of therapeutical or surgical, but merely of technical nature, with the sole aim of improving the efficiency of taking blood from a donor. This method is clearly distinguishable from a therapeutic or diagnostic effect. (T-329/94: paras. 7–8, emphasis added)

The following month, Chemistry II TBoA 3.3.02 (Chairman Lançon) considered a case relating to the reduction in the perception of fatigue resulting from exercise, T-469/94 Perception of fatigue/MIT:

> The condition of fatigue induced by the performance of exercises is a transitory physiological condition caused by natural circumstances and removable by simple rest … *Pain or serious suffering do not appear to be manifestations of fatigue, which therefore is not comparable with the pathological state typical of a disease or an injury. The treatment for reducing the perception of fatigue is not even comparable with the relief of pain, discomfort and incapacity* considered in decision T 81/84 [Dysmenorrhea/RORER]. (T-469/94: para. 4.2, emphasis added)

Back to TBoA 3.2.02 (Chairman Weiß), which, in T-592/98 UNIVERSITY OF MANITOBA in October 2001, considered claims relating to controlling gas flow to a patient and set out clearly its understanding of the scope and purpose of the therapeutic exclusion: 'The term "therapy" within the meaning of Article [53(c)] EPC is not restricted to curing a disease or to removing its causes *but it covers also any treatment designed to alleviate or reduce the symptoms of any malfunction of the human body*. This is the case here' (T-592/98: para. 2, emphasis added).

In October 2004 TBoA 3.2.02 (Chairman Kriner) returned to the subject of therapy in T-383/03 Hair removal method/THE GENERAL HOSPITAL, a case relating to hair removal by optical irradiation. Examining the *ratio legis* for the exclusion of Art. 53(c) EPC, the Board found:

> Evidently the exclusion aims at protecting curative activities … [C]urative activities are those activities aimed at maintaining and restoring the health, the physical integrity, and the physical well-being of a person (and also preventing diseases). The same applies to activities performed on animals … *It follows that the intention of the legislator was that only those treatments by therapy or surgery are excluded from patentability which are suitable for or potentially suitable for maintaining or restoring the health, the physical integrity, and the physical well being of a human being or an animal and to prevent diseases.* (T-383/03: para. 3.2, emphasis added)

Thus to conclude this section, the Boards of Appeal appear to have come round to the definition of 'therapy' as being an action to maintain or restore health, physical integrity, and physical and mental well-being, or, to quote from T-24/91 Cornea/THOMPSON, 'any treatment which is designed to cure, alleviate, remove or lessen the symptoms of, or prevent or reduce the possibility of contracting any disorder or malfunction of the human or animal body' (T-24/91: para. 2.7).

5.3 What has been found to be, or not to be, therapy?

The decided cases divide between those relating to treatments which are potentially physically beneficial to the 'patient', those which are neither beneficial nor harmful (e.g. some cosmetic treatments), and those where the treatment is positively harmful or even fatal. In the first case, such methods have been deemed therapeutic and in the last they have not. For the second group, unless a therapeutic side effect is inevitable, the treatments have been considered not to be therapeutic. In some cases it was in the interests of the patentee (or applicant) for the method in question to be deemed to be therapeutic, as this would open the way to the medicament in question being patented using a Swiss-type use claim or a purpose-limited product claim.

Thus the first category of potentially beneficial treatments has included vaccination and other prophylactic treatments to prevent disease (see for example T-19/86 Pigs II/DUPHAR and T-708/02 Sea lice infestation/VERICORE), treatment to combat hair loss (see for example T-143/94 Trigonelline/MAI), treatment of parasitic infestation (see T-116/85 Pigs I/WELLCOME), treatment of pain and discomfort (see T-81/84 Dysmenorrhea/RORER), and treatment or prophylaxis relating to sun damage of the skin (see T-1077/93 UV radiation protection/L'OREAL).

The second category, of neither beneficial nor harmful treatments, has included cosmetic treatments to control weight or hair loss (see T-144/83 Appetite suppressant/DU PONT, T-453/95 Chelating agent/REDKEN and T-383/03 Hair removal method/THE GENERAL HOSPITAL), chemical methods of contraception (see T-820/92 Contraceptive method/THE GENERAL HOSPITAL and T-74/93 Contraceptive method/BRITISH TECHNOLOGY GROUP), methods of dealing with muscle fatigue (T-469/94 Perception of fatigue/MIT) or snoring (T-584/88 Anti-snoring means/REICHERT) or enhancing comfort by cooling (T-385/09 LELY ENTERPRISES), methods of improving breeding efficiency (T-1223/01 AJINOMOTO) or yield (T-774/89 Efomycin/BAYER), methods of cleansing (T-36/83 Thenoyl peroxide/ROUSSEL-UCLAF and T-290/86 Cleaning plaque/ICI), methods of improving muscle performance (T-1230/05 Increasing energy in vivo/BIOENERGY), methods of improving blood extraction (T-329/94 Blood extraction method/BAXTER), and methods of promoting weight gain (T-438/91 Feeds/MEIJI).

In the last category, of harmful or fatal treatments, there have been cases relating to euthanasia (T-866/01 Euthanasia compositions/

MICHIGAN STATE UNIVERSITY) and animal slaughtering (T-182/90 Blood flow/SEA-SHELL).

5.4 What is surgery?

For this section, the following questions in particular arise:

(a) Does surgery have to involve penetrating living tissue, or indeed the body in general?
(b) Does any action involving such penetration constitute surgery?
(c) Does surgery have to involve improving or maintaining health, physical integrity or physical or mental well-being?
(d) Must the performer of surgery be a surgeon?

While much of the doubt concerning what is or is not surgery for the purposes of Art. 53(c) EPC has been dispelled by G-1/07 Treatment by surgery/MEDI-PHYSICS, it is instructive to see how the definition of 'surgery' developed in the earlier case law from the TBoAs, once again mostly Mechanics II TBoA 3.2.02.

The earliest major decision, fittingly from TBoA 3.2.02 (Chairman Szabo), came in January 1993 in T-182/90 Blood-flow/SEA-SHELL, which concerned measuring blood flow within animal tissue. After noting that treatment under Art. 53(c) EPC must be of a living body, the Board addressed the meanings of 'surgery' and 'treatment by surgery'. After first noting that the term 'surgery' can cover non-curative procedures, the Board noted that the then current Guidelines for Examination in the European Patent Office stated:

> that the term 'surgery' defines the *nature* of the treatment rather than its *purpose*. This may, however, not be true in all cases ... According to [Landau *et al.* (1986: 2762)], the term 'surgery' means 'that branch of the art, science, and practice of medicine that deals with the diagnosis and correction of bodily defects resulting from injury or disease and the relief of suffering by manual and instrumental procedures'. This term even comprises 'closed surgery' which, according to said dictionary, means the 'manipulation of a part, organ, or tissue without making a skin incision' ... Similarly, [Brockhaus (1987: 520)] defines 'surgery' as the branch of medicine concerned with the healing of disease, accidental injury or bodily defects by operating on the living body – including both conservative (non-invasive) procedures such as repositioning, and the far more numerous operative (invasive) procedures using instruments ... [Reifferscheid and Weller (1989: 131–2)] defines an operation as direct or indirect treatment of any kind performed on the structure of an organism – including endoscopy, puncture, injection, excision, and opening of the bodily cavities. Catheter insertion is also considered as an intensive surgical technique

... This inclusion of endoscopy, puncture, injection, excision and catheterisation in the definition of 'surgical interventions' is also consistent with the definition of 'chirurgie' given in the French dictionary [Rey (1985: 577–88)] ... The reference to healing in some of the preceding definitions of the term 'surgery' appears to be inconsistent with the fact that, in today's medical and legal linguistic usage, the non-curative treatments mentioned at the [beginning of this quote] ... are, if carried out by surgery, regarded as surgical treatments ... Apparently, the term 'treatment by surgery' has undergone a change in meaning insofar as it nowadays may also comprise particular treatments which are not directed to the health of the human or animal body. (T-182/90: paras. 2.3–2.4, emphasis added)

However, addressing the facts of the case at hand, the Board refused to stretch the meaning of 'treatment by surgery' so far as to cover *all* manual or instrumental intervention by a human on another human or an animal:

Although the term 'surgical treatment' is not restricted to a treatment serving a curative purpose ... the distinction between surgical and non-surgical procedures cannot be so broadly drawn that 'surgical treatment' includes any kind of manual or instrumental intervention by one human being on another, or on an animal. Clearly, the guillotining of people, or the slaughter of animals, is not a form of surgical treatment (indeed, methods for the slaughter of animals have traditionally been considered patentable). In the Board's view, methods consciously ending in the laboratory animal's death ... are not in their nature methods of surgical treatment, even if some of the steps they involve may have a surgical character ... In other words, the semantic change in the terminology mentioned in [the previously quoted passage] cannot extend so far that the opposite of the original meaning falls within its scope, i.e. that a method involving the deliberate killing of the laboratory animal should represent a surgical treatment ... It appears that the matter of such and similar destructive purposes was discussed in the preparatory stage of the European Patent Convention (cf. [Document] BR/177/72 ...). It was agreed that these methods were not to be excluded from patentability and that, however, there was no need to expressly mention this in the Article ... Hence, a method which includes a surgical step practised on a living laboratory animal and, in addition, a step of sacrificing said animal, which step is also necessary to carry out the method, cannot be regarded in its entirety as a method for treatment of the animal by surgery in the sense of Article [53(c)] EPC. (T-182/90: para. 2.5)

Thus the story opens with the requirements that the subject of surgery be alive and that the purpose need not be curative but must not be to kill. Beyond that, the intervention need not be penetrative, but tissue-penetrative operations (such as injections) would count as surgery. As will become clear below, the view of all tissue-penetrative operations as being surgical has changed – the other comments, however, still hold good.

In September 1999 TBoA 3.2.02 (Chairman Weiß) returned to the subject in T-35/99 Pericardial access/GEORGETOWN UNIVERSITY, a case relating to catheter insertion into the heart, and expanded upon the discussion of the meaning of 'surgery':

> [A] first category [of physical interventions on the human or animal body] embraces those interventions which, whatever their specific purpose, *give priority to maintaining life or health of the human or animal body on which they are performed. This applies both to healing and to cosmetic surgery, and generally to all physical interventions aimed at altering functions of the living body* (e.g. castration to bring about changes in body functions linked to sex), as well as to the removal of body parts (e.g. for transplantation) ... The application of procedures of [this] category is in general [risky and complex]. The absolute imperative to maintain life and health, especially those of a human being, has to be considered against the background of the complexity and individuality of human and animal life in its biological and mental constitution. Therefore, the effects of surgical and therapeutic measures on the life and health of the treated body, whether intended or not, cannot be foreseen with certainty; in critical situations, such as life-threatening illnesses or injuries, decisions must be taken and treatments given even if they involve a great risk under extreme time pressure. Such problems do not arise in the case of technical procedures not designed to maintain the life or health of a human being or animal; but they are inherent in all activities in the fields of diagnosis, surgery and therapy. (T-35/99: paras. 2–8, emphasis added)

This decision contains the third approach to determining whether a method constitutes surgery – the risk to the patient.

In October 2004 TBoA 3.2.02 (Chairman Kriner) returned to the question of what constituted a method of surgery in T-383/03 Hair removal method/THE GENERAL HOSPITAL, which related to hair removal by light exposure. After reviewing the existing EPO case law, the Board addressed the issue as to whether non-curative or non-protective treatments were excluded (since that same Board had found that, in the therapeutic context, they were not – see T-24/91 Cornea/THOMPSON above). Thus, the Board commented:

> Although it emerges from [earlier] decisions that methods of treatment which are not directed to improving or maintaining the health of a human being or an animal may be patentable, the case is not so clear where the treatment involves manual and/or instrumental procedures (treatment by surgery) ... It is therefore necessary to examine whether ... a therapeutic effect plays a decisive role in determining which interventions are excluded from patentability as stated for example in T 329/94 [Blood extraction method/BAXTER]. The answer to this question is all the more important as the term 'surgery' has undergone a change in meaning as explained in T 182/90 [Blood flow/SEA-SHELL]. (T-383/03: para. 3)

After considering the purpose and history of Art. 53(c) EPC, the Board decided that:

Even if in medical linguistic usage the term 'treatment by surgery' nowadays also comprises treatments which are not directed to the health of human beings or animals, *they do not fall within the exclusion from patentability if they are not covered by the ratio legis of Article [53(c)] EPC* … Thus, *treatments by surgery which are clearly neither suitable nor potentially suitable for maintaining or restoring the health, the physical integrity, or the physical well-being of human beings or animals do not fall within the exclusion from patentability of Article [53(c)] EPC*. (T-383/03: para. 3, emphasis added)

This represented a significant divergence from the earlier decisions, for example suggesting that *invasive* cosmetic surgery might be patentable. This was a clear statement of the *purpose* approach to defining what might be surgery.

In May 2005 TBoA 3.2.02 (Chairman Kriner) confirmed this interpretation of the meaning of 'surgery' in T-1172/03 THERMAGE, a case relating to a 'cosmetic' method of skin tightening by heat treatment. However, the Board suggested that the meaning of surgery might change with time:

The Board cannot follow the opinion of the appellant that the meaning of a word ('surgery') used in law should always remain that which it meant at the moment of entry into force of the law … On the contrary, the law must be adapted to the current situation keeping in mind the aim of the legislator when he wrote the law, the so called 'ratio legis'. This adaptation is particularly important in a field such as patent law, in which the technology is rapidly developing so that the legislator could never foresee all the possible applications of the law … The Board … considers that a claim must be judged for the purpose of Article [53(c)] EPC on the basis of substantive and not of formal aspects of the claim (T 775/97 [EXPANDABLE GRAFTS]). As stated in decision T 1077/93 [UV radiation protection/L'OREAL], *the exclusion under Article [53(c)] EPC cannot be simply avoided by a wording of the claims defining the method as a cosmetic method in a formal way, if in substance the method is a therapeutic one* … It follows that … patentability must be excluded if the cosmetic use is not expressed as a technical feature inherent in the claimed method, but only expressed in the claim as a mere intention of the applicant … In the present case, the cosmetic effect is not distinguishable from the therapeutic one for the following reasons … [T]he thermal induction of scar collagen deposition as a reaction to inflammation induced by thermal injury has a therapeutic reconstructive effect. Thus, the claimed method can be regarded as restoring the patient's physical integrity. This effect is not distinguishable from the aesthetic effect of skin tightening, resulting from the subsequent contraction of both the existing and the produced nascent scar collagen … Therefore, it is not a technical feature of the method which renders it cosmetic and different from a therapeutic method, but only the intention of the person using the method for cosmetic purposes. (T-1172/03: paras 2.1–2.3, emphasis added)

In December 2005, in an opinion on diagnostic methods (G-1/04 Diagnostic methods), the EBoA again raised the *risk* approach to defining surgery: 'Methods of surgery within the meaning of Article [53(c)] EPC include any physical interventions on the human or animal body in which maintaining the life and health of the subject is of paramount importance … [W]ithin the meaning of Article [53(c)] EPC, a claim including the feature "performing a lumbar puncture to deliver epidural injections" is to be considered to relate to a method of surgery' (G-1/04: 352).

In T-5/04 CAMTECH in January 2006, however, TBoA 3.2.02 (Chairman Kriner), considering a case involving the placement of sensors within the body, reverted to the *nature* approach of defining surgery:

For a method to be regarded as a method for surgical treatment and as such excluded from patentability under Article [53(c)] EPC, it is not necessary that the intervention be invasive or that tissues be penetrated. *The mere catheterisation or the insertion of components of a device into the body is already prohibited by Article [53(c)] EPC as constituting a surgical step of the method* (see T 35/99 [Pericardial access/GEORGETOWN UNIVERSITY]) … What actually counts for the assessment of Article [53(c)] EPC is that the sensors are placed inside the body and that this feature is part of the method as claimed … It results therefrom that the method as claimed involves at least one surgical step within the meaning of the case law of the boards of appeal. (T-5/04: para. 2)

In October 2006 Physics I TBoA 3.4.01 (Chairman Schachenmann), hearing the case T-992/03 (I) Treatment by surgery/MEDI-PHYSICS, which related to a method of magnetic resonance imaging that could involve injection of polarised xenon (Xe) into the heart, brought the matter to a head. The Board summarised the previous and possible approaches to defining what a method must involve in order to be excluded as a method of surgery:

In the Guidelines for Examination in the European Patent Office (June 2005) it is stated that 'surgery defines the nature of the treatment rather than the purpose' … This approach corresponds to that adopted in decisions T 182/90 [Blood flow/SEA-SHELL] and T 35/99 [Pericardial access/GEORGETOWN UNIVERSITY] … On the other hand, in case T 383/03 [Hair removal method/THE GENERAL HOSPITAL] the fact that the claimed method did not aim at maintaining or restoring the health, the physical integrity or the physical well-being of a person or animal played a decisive role in determining which inventions were excluded from patent protection under Article [53(c)]

EPC. The nature of the physical intervention on the body ... was secondary ... The jurisprudence of the boards of appeal concerning the interpretation of 'methods for treatment of the human or animal body by surgery' in Article [53(c)] EPC does not appear to be consistent. Whereas one approach is based on an assessment of the nature of the physical intervention on the body, the other concentrates on whether the physical intervention is suitable for maintaining or restoring the health, the physical integrity or the physical well-being of a person or an animal ... In the Board's view, the approach based on the purpose may give rise to opposing judgements as to the exclusion from patent protection of one and the same physical intervention. For example, an injection of a medicament for treating a disease would be excluded but an injection of a substance reducing wrinkles for cosmetic purposes might not be considered to constitute a treatment by surgery within the meaning of Article [53(c)] EPC because it is not suitable for maintaining or restoring health. In both cases, the physical intervention on the body would be substantially the same, i.e. an injection ... *Besides the nature and the purpose of the physical intervention other approaches are conceivable ... An approach may be related to the medical risk involved in the physical intervention.* This *risk* is linked to the further issue of whether a medical or veterinary practitioner should be responsible for carrying out the method steps. In this context, the approach based on the nature of the physical intervention appears to be more suitable than that based on its purpose, at least for those methods whose execution would require professional medical expertise and would thus fall under the competence of a medical or veterinary practitioner ... [I]n the present case it is reasonable to assume that an injection into the heart should be carried out by a medical or veterinary practitioner. (T-992/03 (I): para. 4, emphasis added)

Thus there were three approaches to determining whether a method was a method of surgery, which respectively involved considering the *nature*, the *purpose* and the *risk* of the intervention.

The Board decided to refer several questions to the EBoA, of which only the first is relevant to this section:

Is a claimed ... method for a diagnostic purpose ... which comprises or encompasses a step consisting in a physical intervention practised on the human or animal body (in the present case, an injection of a contrast agent into the heart), to be excluded from patent protection as a 'method for treatment of the human or animal body by surgery' pursuant to Article [53(c)] EPC if such step does not per se aim at maintaining life and health? (T-992/03 (I): Order)

These questions were answered in February 2010 in G-1/07 Treatment by surgery/MEDI-PHYSICS. The EBoA first commented on the *travaux préparatoires*:

The only document [in the *travaux préparatoires*] explicitly addressing the issue as to whether surgical treatment of animals not intended for therapeutic purposes, but on the contrary for destructive purposes (e.g. the sterilisation of insects) was included in the provision, is the ... Report on the 11th meeting of Working Party I held in Luxembourg from 28 February to 3 March 1972, [Document] BR/177 e/72. It is noted therein in point 9(d): 'The Working Party was of the opinion that treatment of this kind was not in fact intended to be included in this provision, but did not consider it necessary to draft a text stating this explicitly' ... Hence, it appears that the question of the patentability of certain kinds of treatments of animals was perceived as being more generally concerned with finding an appropriate distinction between methods for the industrial exploitation of animals which should be patentable and methods for the therapeutic treatment of animals which were to be excluded from patentability on humanitarian grounds and in the interest of public health ([Document] BR/168 e/72 ...). However, *neither [D]ocument BR/177/ e/72 nor any other document from the Travaux Préparatoires ... reflect the general view that only such surgical methods as are of a therapeutic nature were intended by the legislator to be excluded from patentability by the wording chosen in Article [53(c)] EPC* ... Hence, what would be the normal reading of the wording of Article 53(c) EPC as a provision containing three alternatives, i.e. that these alternatives are different in scope, and that, as a consequence, *the exclusion of 'treatments by surgery' cannot be seen as limited to surgery which is performed for a therapeutic purpose, since it would then already be entirely covered by the exclusion of therapeutic methods from patentability*, appears not to be in conflict with but rather to be supported by the course of the preparatory work for the EPC 1973. (G-1/07: 182–4, emphasis added)

The Board then considered the *purpose* approach further:

At least with respect to humans a limitation of the exclusion to such surgical methods which serve a therapeutic purpose does not take full account of and does not give full effect to the purpose of the exclusion. In particular as regards serious and risky surgical interventions, e.g. in cosmetic surgery, organ transplantation, embryo transfer, sex change operations, sterilisation and castration, i.e. surgical methods which require considerable professional medical expertise to be carried out and involve serious health risks even when carried out with the required professional care and expertise, the ratio legis of the exclusion, i.e. to free practitioners from being potentially hampered by patents in the application of the best possible treatment on their patients, does apply, is important and calls for their exclusion from patentability ... Summarising the above, neither the legal history nor the object and purpose ('ratio legis') of the exclusions from patentability in Article 53(c) EPC justify a limitation of the term 'treatment by surgery' to curative surgery, contrary to what the ordinary meaning of the word 'surgery' implies and contrary to the fact that Article 53(c) EPC defines three separate alternative exclusions thereby suggesting that these are not merely identical in scope ... *Hence, the Enlarged Board concludes that the meaning of the term 'treatment by surgery' is not to be interpreted as being confined to surgical methods pursuing a therapeutic purpose.* (G-1/07: 189–93, emphasis added)

The *purpose* approach was thus rejected. The *nature* approach was considered next:

> The advances in safety and the now routine character of certain, albeit invasive techniques, at least when performed on uncritical parts of the body, have entailed that many such techniques are nowadays generally carried out in a non-medical, commercial environment like in cosmetic salons and in beauty parlours and it appears, hence, hardly still justified to exclude such methods from patentability. This applies as a rule to treatments such as tattooing, piercing, hair removal by optical radiation, micro abrasion of the skin … If so, that can also not be ignored when it comes to the application of routine interventions in the medical field … Considering this technical reality, excluding from patentability also such methods as make use of in principle safe routine techniques, even when of invasive nature, appears to go beyond the purpose of the exclusion of treatments by surgery from patentability in the interest of public health. (G-1/07: 195–6)

The *nature* approach was therefore also dismissed and a better understanding of 'treatment by surgery' was sought:

> The exclusion serves the purpose of, in the interests of public health and of patients, specifically freeing the medical profession from constraints which would be imposed on them by patents granted on methods for surgical or therapeutic treatment, thus any definition of the term 'treatment by surgery' must cover the kind of interventions which represent the core of the medical profession's activities, i.e. the kind of interventions for which their members are specifically trained and for which they assume a particular responsibility. … *These are the physical interventions on the body which require professional medical skills to be carried out and which involve health risks even when carried out with the required medical professional care and expertise.* It is in this area that the ratio legis of the provision to free the medical profession from constraints by patents comes into play. Such a narrower understanding rules out from the scope of the application of the exclusion clause uncritical methods involving only a minor intervention and no substantial health risks, when carried out with the required care and skill, while still adequately protecting the medical profession. (G-1/07: 196, emphasis added)

The question put to the EBoA was thus answered as follows:

> A claimed … method, in which, when carried out, maintaining the life and health of the subject is important and which comprises or encompasses an invasive step representing a substantial physical intervention on the body which requires professional medical expertise to be carried out and which entails a substantial health risk even when carried out with the required professional care and expertise, is excluded from patentability as a method for treatment of the human or animal body by surgery pursuant to Article 53(c) EPC. (G-1/07: 210)

It is thus clear that the *risk* approach was dominant. An intervention (which may or may not be invasive, and may or may not be beneficial to the patient) is a method of treatment by surgery if it 'entails a substantial health risk even when carried out with the required professional care and expertise'.

5.5 The aftermath of the Enlarged Board decision on 'surgery'

Following the Enlarged Board's decision in G-1/07 Treatment by surgery/ MEDI-PHYSICS, Physics I, TBoA 3.2.02 (Chairman Schachenmann) resumed its consideration of the Medi-Physics case and in November 2010 issued its decision T-992/03 MEDI-PHYSICS, agreeing to grant a patent with claims which were amended to remove references to risky procedures such as injections into the heart.

In March 2011 Physics I TBoA 3.4.01 (Chairman Schachenmann) again contributed to the discussion, in T-663/02 PRINCE, a case which related to a method of magnetic resonance imaging involving catheterisation of an artery. Explaining that such tasks were frequently delegated, the TBoA found that the use of catheterisation did not make a method unpatentable:

> As a matter of fact, the placement of an intravenous catheter is one of the most common invasive procedures performed in hospitals and consulting rooms. Physicians are traditionally responsible for this intervention. But the increasing qualification level of paramedical professionals ... has led to the adoption in national healthcare systems of regulations allowing physicians to delegate some activities which were in the past of their exclusive pertinence ... Therefore, it appears that in current healthcare systems a physician may delegate medical acts, for example intravenous injections, to paramedical professionals duly trained and qualified for carrying out the delegated act ... The delegating physician usually evaluates the risks to the patient, delegates only those acts for which a paramedical professional has been specifically trained, and supervises the work of the delegated professional. De facto, qualified hospital nurses are today entrusted with taking venous blood probes, giving infusions and making intravenous injections ... In view of this development, *delegated acts can hardly be considered as belonging to the core of medical activities.* (T-663/02: para. 3.2.4, emphasis added)

5.6 What would be found to be or not to be surgery?

With the *risk* approach, set out in G-1/07 Treatment by surgery/MEDI-PHYSICS and developed in T-663/02 PRINCE, it would seem that interventions such as massage, tattooing, tanning, shaving, ear-piercing, blood-drawing, and routine injection or catheterisation will not classify as excluded methods of surgery. However, bone-setting, castration, vasectomy, embryo implantation and cosmetic surgery involving anaesthetics seem likely to be excluded.

5.7 What is diagnosis?

After therapy and surgery, diagnosis should come as a relief to the reader (in terms of European patent law that is). In view of a divergence in interpretation between TBoA decisions T-385/86 Non-invasive measurement/BRUKER and T-964/99 Device and method for sampling substances using alternating polarity/CYGNUS (both from the Physics I board 3.4.01, but chaired by Lederer and Davies respectively), the then president of the EPO, Ingo Kober, asked the EBoA in December 2003 to answer, inter alia, the following question:

> Are ... 'diagnostic methods ...' within the meaning of Article [53(c)] EPC ... only those methods containing *all* the procedural steps to be carried out when making a medical diagnosis, i.e. the *examination phase* involving the collection of relevant data, the comparison of the examination data thus obtained with the standard values, the finding of any significant deviation (a symptom) during that comparison and, finally, the attribution of the deviation to a particular clinical picture (the deductive *medical decision phase*), or ... is a claimed method a 'diagnostic method' even if it only contains *one* procedural step that can be used for diagnostic purposes or relates to the diagnosis? (G-1/04: 335–6, emphasis added)

The Enlarged Board's answer was simple – a diagnostic method is implicitly a two or more step process involving first data-gathering or data comparison and second the (mental) act of diagnosis. Without the step of diagnosis, a method *cannot* be excluded from patentability under Art. 53(c) EPC.

The story on what constituted 'diagnosis' had started with four earlier decisions from Mechanics I TBoA 3.2.01. In November 1983, considering a medical imaging method in T-61/83 Diagnostic method/ THOMSON, TBoA 3.2.01 (Chairman Anderson) had decided that a method had to refer to the diagnosis to be made in order to qualify as a diagnostic method. In August 1984, in T-208/83 Diagnostic method/ THOMSON, TBoA 3.2.01 followed its earlier line of reasoning, adding that a diagnostic method 'comprises not only the method of analysis allowing one to arrive at a specific result, but also the diagnosis that is the result of the analysis'.

When Physics I, TBoA 3.4.01 (Chairman Lederer), faced the question of what diagnosis was, in September 1987 in T-385/86 Non-invasive measurement/BRUKER, they turned to the *travaux préparatoires*:

According to an initial proposal, processes used in the laboratory for the purpose of diagnosis were definitely not to be patentable where they involved treatment by doctors (see [Document] BR/135/71 ...). The subsequent proposal of a general exclusion of all diagnostic methods brought objections from interested circles who claimed that advances in technology had indeed led to the evolving of diagnostic methods which were not of a specifically medical nature (see [Document] BR/169/72 ...). Following a proposal from the French delegation, the term 'diagnostic methods' was later defined more precisely by the addition of the words 'applied to the human or animal body' (see [Document] BR/177/72 ...). ... The Board is therefore convinced that the only diagnostic methods to be excluded from patent protection are those whose results immediately make it possible to decide on a particular course of medical treatment. This means that to answer the question whether a method is a diagnostic method for the purposes of Article [53(c)], first sentence, *it is necessary to ascertain whether the method claimed contains all the steps involved in reaching a medical diagnosis. Methods providing only interim results are thus not diagnostic methods in the meaning of Article [53(c)], first sentence, even if they can be utilised in making a diagnosis.* (T-385/86: 310–11, emphasis added)

Gathering data and results that could be used in a method of diagnosis was again confirmed not to represent diagnosis by TBoA 3.4.01 in 1988 and 1990, in T-83/87 SIEMENS (Chairman Lederer) and T-400/87 NRDC. This line of reasoning was followed by TBoA 3.4.02 (Physics II – Chairman Turrini) in T-530/93 GENERAL ELECTRIC in 1996. Then, in T-964/99 Device and method for sampling substances using alternating polarity/CYGNUS, in June 2001, Physics I, TBoA 3.4.01 (Chairman Davies), came up with a different definition of diagnosis. The Board commented on its earlier line of reasoning, stating that it:

equates the meaning of the expression 'diagnostic methods practised on the human or animal body' in Article [53(c)] EPC with the conventional meaning of the term 'diagnosis' and thus implies that 'diagnostic methods' cover activities which are not normally practised on the body but predominantly involve mental acts, i.e. activities of non-technical nature performed by a medical professional, such as the steps of comparing the data with normal values and recording any significant deviation and of attributing the deviation to a particular clinical picture. (T-964/99: 12–13)

While accepting that the reasoning followed in T-385/86 Non-invasive measurement/BRUKER would exclude a fully automated diagnostic method, the Board found that it would not exclude certain activities typically considered to be diagnostic procedures, 'like percussion, auscultation or palpation could ... because they do not constitute a complete diagnosis' (T-964/99: 13). This, the Board considered, went against the spirit of Art. 53(c) EPC. While accepting that arriving at a diagnosis required all the steps mentioned in T-385/86 Non-invasive measurement BRUKER, the Board considered that for a method to be a 'diagnostic method' within the meaning of Art. 53(c) EPC it need not contain all the steps involved in reaching a medical diagnosis.

In March 2002 TBoA 3.3.04 (Chemistry IV – Chairman Kinkeldey) happily followed T-385/86 Non-invasive measurement/BRUKER in their decision T-1038/00 Apoptopic cells/NEXINS RESEARCH. Similarly, in April 2003 Chemistry VIII (TBoA 3.3.08 – Chairman Galligani) found it unnecessary to follow T-964/99 Device and method for sampling substances using alternating polarity/CYGNUS in their decision T-310/99 Down syndrome/MACRI. As a result of the conflicting approaches of the Technical Boards as to what was 'surgery', in December 2003 Ingo Kober, the president of the EPO, referred his questions to the EBoA resulting in the issue of opinion G-1/04 Diagnostic methods in December 2005.

The EBoA plumped squarely for the earlier approach, that of T-385/86 Non-invasive measurement/BRUKER. The EBoA analysed what 'diagnosis' must mean before explaining why 'diagnostic methods' must involve diagnosis:

> Diagnosis in connection with the patent exemption for diagnostic methods practised on the human or animal body under Article [53(c)] EPC is the determination of the nature of a medical or veterinary medicinal condition intended to identify or uncover a pathology ... As the deductive medical or veterinary decision phase, diagnosis for curative purposes in itself is an intellectual exercise ... As an intellectual exercise, pursuant to Article 52(2) EPC, the deductive decision phase is not regarded as an invention within the meaning of Article 52(1) EPC ... [I]t follows that, in a situation where the deductive medical or veterinary decision phase is a purely intellectual exercise ... such a method must necessarily further include preceding steps ... of a technical nature, in order to satisfy the requirements of Article 52(1) EPC ... Article [53(c)] EPC mentions 'diagnostic methods practised on the human or animal body'. The provision does not make reference to particular steps pertaining to such methods, nor does it contain a wording such as 'relating to diagnosis' or 'of value for diagnostic purposes'. Thus, the text of the provision itself already gives an indication towards a narrow interpretation in the sense that, in order to be excluded from patentability, the method is to include all steps relating to it. (G-1/04: 349-50)

Thus, omitting the data-gathering step prevents a method from being a diagnostic method. However, more importantly, omitting the step of diagnosis has the same effect:

> If diagnosis as the deductive medical or veterinary decision phase is a purely intellectual exercise ... the feature pertaining to the diagnosis for curative

purposes and the features relating to the preceding steps which are constitutive for making the diagnosis represent the essential features of a diagnostic method within the meaning of Article [53(c)] EPC ... Intermediate findings of diagnostic relevance must not be confounded with diagnosis for curative purposes stricto sensu ... which consists in attributing the detected deviation to a particular clinical picture. It follows that a method for obtaining such results or findings does not constitute a sufficient basis for denying patentability by virtue of Article [53(c)] EPC. (G-1/04: 353)

This insistence on the inclusion of the (mental) act of diagnosis raised the problem of how such a step could be practised on the patient's body. The solution was found – it was that the steps of a technical nature must be practised on the patient's body, or at least with that body present:

The criterion 'practised on the human or animal body' is to be considered only in respect of method steps of a technical nature. Thus, it does not apply to the diagnosis for curative purposes stricto sensu, i.e. the deductive decision phase, which as a purely intellectual exercise cannot be practised on the human or animal body. Also, in a diagnostic method, the preceding steps which are constitutive for making a diagnosis for curative purposes may, in addition to method steps of a technical nature, include method steps such as comparing data collected in the examination phase ... with standard values belonging to the common general knowledge of the person skilled in the art. These activities are predominantly of a non-technical nature and, in any event, are not normally practised on the human or animal body ... Article [53(c)] EPC does not require a specific type and intensity of interaction with the human or animal body. Thus, each of the method steps of a technical nature referred to ... above is either invasive or non-invasive. The non-invasive method steps may involve direct physical contact with the human or animal body or may be practised at a certain distance to it. Furthermore, the performance of each one of these method steps may or may not involve the use of data collecting devices and/or diagnostic equipment for measurement and analysis purposes. *It follows that each and every one of these method steps satisfies the criterion 'practised on the human or animal body' if its performance implies any interaction with the human or animal body, necessitating the presence of the latter.* (G-1/04: 356–7, emphasis added)

The president's question was then answered as follows:

In order that the subject-matter of a claim relating to a diagnostic method practised on the human or animal body falls under the prohibition of Article [53(c)] EPC, the claim is to include the features relating to:

(i) the diagnosis for curative purposes stricto sensu representing the deductive medical or veterinary decision phase as a purely intellectual exercise,
(ii) the preceding steps which are constitutive for making that diagnosis, and
(iii) the specific interactions with the human or animal body which occur when carrying those out among these preceding steps which are of a

> technical nature ... In a diagnostic method under Article [53(c)] EPC, the method steps of a technical nature belonging to the preceding steps which are constitutive for making the diagnosis for curative purposes stricto sensu must satisfy the criterion 'practised on the human or animal body' ... Article 52(4) EPC does not require a specific type and intensity of interaction with the human or animal body; a preceding step of a technical nature thus satisfies the criterion 'practised on the human or animal body' if its performance implies any interaction with the human or animal body, necessitating the presence of the latter. (G-1/04: 360–1)

Since opinion G-1/04 Diagnostic methods issued in December 2005, the TBoAs seem to have had no difficulty in following it, usually finding the claimed methods not to be excluded. Two examples where exclusion was found, T-238/06 LEXION MEDICAL and T-1197/02 THE AUSTRALIAN NATIONAL UNIVERSITY, both decisions from TBoA 3.2.02 (Chairman Kriner), seem more to have been the result of careless claim drafting than anything else.

5.8 What would be found to be or not to be diagnosis?

The EBoA decision in G-1/04 Diagnostic methods is sufficiently clear to make this section almost redundant. Nonetheless, imaging methods and ex vivo diagnostic tests would not normally be excluded. Indeed, exclusion is rarely going to be found unless the data gathering is necessarily performed on or in the presence of the patient *and* the claim requires a diagnosis to be reached by a human or a machine. As a fig leaf to cover the fact that it is now possible to claim most diagnostic methods simply by omitting the actual step of diagnosis from the claim, the EBoA has indicated that the claim should recite all the steps necessary in the performance of the method – however, if framed as a data-gathering method, then the step of diagnosis itself can be omitted and the exclusion is avoided. Where the novelty of a method resides only in the diagnostic decision (e.g. using conventional data gathered by conventional means), exclusion is likely.

5.9 Does the identity of the performer matter?

EPO case law is consistent in this regard. The answer is that the identity of the performer is not decisive; however, where the *safety* of the patient requires a step recited in a method claim to be performed by a physician, the likelihood that the method is excluded is greater.

5.10 What happens when the treatment claimed could overlap with an excluded method?

EPO case law is clear and consistent in specifying that where a therapeutic (or surgical) effect is the *inevitable result* of performing a claimed method, then simply specifying in the claim that the method is cosmetic (or non-therapeutic or non-surgical) is insufficient to avoid exclusion (see for example T-245/87 Flow measurement/SIEMENS, and T-82/93 Cardiac pacing/TELECTRONICS). However, where the 'medical' effect is not inevitable, then the method will escape the exclusion if worded appropriately. This may involve restrictive wording (e.g. referring to the method as 'cosmetic'), or 'general' wording (e.g. referring to a contrast agent as being 'administered' to the patient in a diagnostic imaging method rather than as being 'injected into the heart'). This 'generalised' wording does *not* equate to the *higher taxonomic approach* mentioned in Chapter 3, but instead is a recognition that where there are many patentable and some unpatentable ways of doing X, then as long as the patentee has suggested a patentable way in the patent text, she is entitled to refer in her claim to the step of 'doing X'.

This does raise the question as to whether, if a method is performed in which a step, defined in the patent claim in 'generalised' terms, is actually a surgical or therapeutic step, then can there be infringement? The answer, we feel, must be no. There must be an implicit disclaimer of the unpatentable. This holds, too, for the morality provisions, as we will explain in Chapter 8.

5.11 The *travaux préparatoires*

Right from the earliest days of the *travaux préparatoires*, it was clearly the intention of the framers to exclude methods of medical treatment from patentability. With the exception of a short period when the precursor to Art. 52(2) EPC was first being formulated as Art. 9(2) CEPL (see Document 2335/IV/65-E), the exclusion of methods of medical treatment has been on societal and ethical grounds rather than on the basis that such methods could not be 'inventions'. This has been repeatedly acknowledged by the Technical and Enlarged Boards of Appeal, as explained in section 5.1 above.

However, in the most recent relevant decision of the Enlarged Board from February 2010, G-2/08 Dosage regime/ABBOTT RESPIRATORY, even the same explanation of the *ratio legis* showed the imperfection of the analysis that the Boards of Appeal had used:

> [I]t would be improper to consider the second sentence of Article 53(c) EPC as a lex specialis to be interpreted narrowly, rather on the contrary it is appropriate to give both provisions the same weight, and draw the general conclusion that in respect of claims directed to therapy, *method claims are absolutely forbidden in order to leave the physician free to act unfettered*, whereas product claims are allowable provided their subject-matter be new and inventive. (G-2/08: para. 5.7, emphasis added)

It has long been clear that ex vivo diagnostic methods (e.g. diagnostic tests performed on blood samples) as well as the substances and equipment used by physicians and veterinary surgeons in the course of diagnosis, therapy and surgery, were not and are not excluded from patentability. This is clear from the *travaux préparatoires* (see Chapter 2) and from the presence of the final clause in Art. 53(c) EPC: 'this provision shall not apply to products, in particular substances or compositions, for use in any of these methods' (EPO 2010a: 106).

The option of freeing physicians from fear of allegations of patent infringement by specifying within the EPC that their activities could not constitute patent infringement was considered by the legislators, but was not adopted (see Chapter 2).

Nonetheless, since a physician, operating within a commercial context, *can* infringe European patents in the course of carrying out her professional tasks, the conclusion can only be that the legislators' intention was *not* 'to leave the physician free to act unfettered', or to leave physicians 'free to use their skills and knowledge of the best available treatments to achieve the utmost benefit for their patients uninhibited by any worry that some treatment might be covered by a patent', or to ensure 'that those who carry out diagnostic methods as part of the medical treatment of humans or veterinary treatment of animals are not inhibited by patents', or even 'to free from restraint non-commercial and non-industrial medical and veterinary activities', to quote from the four Enlarged Board decisions mentioned in section 5.1. The intention can only be understood if it was to leave the physician free of fear of allegations of patent infringement in unplanned, or unpremeditated, medical treatments of her patients. Premeditation, in the sense of making a patented product without a licence or buying an infringing product with the intention of using such a product when the need arose, was not to be acquiesced to, but otherwise when medical need arose the physician would be free to use whatever was available and in the best interests of her patient yet without fear of infringing. Such freedom is clearly ethically and socially desirable, while still respecting the rights and interests of patentees.

Unfortunately, within one limited sphere of action, that of generic substitution, the medical practitioner has lost this freedom to act unpremeditatedly with the revision to the EPC in 2000. The EPC revision introduced a new clause, Art. 54(5) EPC, which permits purpose-limited product claims for compounds and compositions found to have a second or further medical use. Such product protection was vigorously opposed during the EPC 1973 negotiations but was introduced in the revised version of the EPC, following the misleading statements from the Swiss delegation to the effect that the amendment did no more than codify the then current position whereby Swiss-type use claims afforded second indication protection. Swiss-type use claims could *not* be infringed by a medical practitioner in the normal course of her job. Purpose-limited product claims can, however, be infringed if the medical practitioner uses a drug which was legitimately available for a different treatment (Sterckx and Cockbain 2010c). This change in the law was acknowledged in the Enlarged Board's decision in G-2/08 Dosage regime/ABBOTT RESPIRATORY.

5.12 The *contamination* approach

From the outset, the EPO Boards of Appeal have applied the *contamination* approach to the interpretation of the exclusion of Art. 53(c) EPC, that is if the claimed method includes a step which itself is a method of surgery, then the method is unpatentable. To have done otherwise would have made a mockery of the exclusion – if cutting off a man's leg is surgery, then does giving him a cup of tea afterwards mean he has not undergone surgery? Moreover, to have done otherwise would have been to cause the medical practitioner to risk allegations of patent infringement, not necessarily for having carried out *all* the steps of the claimed method on his own, but for having carried out all those steps together with co-infringers.

The *contamination* approach is, we suggest, the only possible correct approach to the exclusions of Art. 53(c) EPC, for this exclusion is not 'softened' in the same way as those of Art. 52(1) EPC since Art. 53 EPC has no equivalent to the 'as such' provision of Art. 52(3) EPC. In this regard, we can refer, for example, to T-820/92 Contraceptive method/THE GENERAL HOSPITAL, where the Board commented on a contraceptive method involving administration of two substances, one of which had a therapeutic effect. Although contraception was not therapy, the claimed method had to be excluded:

In the case of a method involving administration of two or more substances, the question for the purposes of Article [53(c)] EPC is not whether the main or even the only reason for carrying out the whole of the claimed method is non-therapeutic. Rather a method claim falls under the prohibition of Article [53(c)] EPC already if the administration of one of the substances is a treatment by therapy, and the administration of this substance is a feature of the claim. (T-820/92: para. 5.9)

5.13 Patenting known drug substances

5.13.1 Second and further indications

Novel drug substances are clearly patentable per se under the EPC. In the drafting of EPC 1973, a special exemption (to the novelty provisions) was introduced to allow purpose-limited product protection (e.g. 'compound X for use in medicine') in relation to compounds and compositions that were known but not known to have any medical use. This special exemption, Art. 54(4) EPC, reads as follows:

Paragraphs 2 and 3 [which define the state of the art against which novelty is measured] shall not exclude the patentability of any substance or composition, comprised in the state of the art, for use in a method referred to in Article 53(c), provided that its use for any such method is not comprised in the state of the art. (EPO 2010a: 110)

Such protection for new drugs and compounds newly found to have a use as drugs left a loophole. What about compounds known to be useful as drugs for treating one condition but newly found to have pharmaceutical efficacy against another condition, a 'second medical indication'? Perhaps the best known such drug recently is Viagra®. The expense of clinical trials and obtaining regulatory approval may be less for a second indication, but it is still high. The pharmaceutical industry thus pressed for the grant of patents for second medical indications from the earliest days of the operation of the EPO.

A problem, however, lay in the wording that claims for second indications might take. The invention, if there was one, lay in the new method of medical treatment, a claim to which would be excluded by Art. 53(c) EPC. The solution adopted in Germany, which was to accept claims in the format 'use of known drug X for new treatment Y', required the ridiculous presumption that such use included the steps up to but not including the actual use that was claimed. The Swiss Patent Office came up with a 'compromise', the 'Swiss-type' use claim that has the format 'use of known drug X for the known manufacture of a known medicament for use in the new treatment Y'. Such a claim, like the purpose-limited product claim, permitted when a *first* medical indication was found for a known compound or composition, would derive its novelty from the intended new use for which the medicament was manufactured.

TBoA 3.3.01, in seven appeals, referred *the same question* on this topic to the EBoA. The seven referrals were consolidated, and in December 1984 the EBoA gave its first decision, G-5/83 Second medical indication/ EISAI. The Swiss-type use claim became accepted by the EPO. This was a thoroughly unconvincing decision on patentability from the EBoA.

Following G-5/83 Second medical indication/EISAI, a disagreement arose between two of the Chemistry TBoAs, 3.3.02 under Pierre Lançon and 3.3.04 under Ursula Kinkeldey. Could a *method* or *process* claim, framed in the same terms as a Swiss-type use claim, be equally acceptable as a Swiss-type *use* claim? Thus, for example, TBoA 3.3.04 (the Kinkeldey Board), in a decision in June 1994, rejected a process claim in the form 'A process for the manufacture of a medicament for use in treatment X comprising mixing Y with a carrier and/or diluent' as lacking novelty, while at the same time accepting that, under G-5/83 Second medical indication/EISAI, the equivalent Swiss-type use claim ('Use of Y for the manufacture of a medicament for use in treatment X') was novel. Since a use claim *is* a process claim,[1] this decision would seem bizarre without the following justification given by the TBoA: 'the novelty of the intended use of the product can only be taken into account as a technical feature limiting the claim where the claim takes the form of a use claim as approved of in decision G 5/83' (T-51/93: 7). This is a statement that the Swiss-type use claim belongs to a category apart from other process claims, and one to which the normal rules of novelty do not apply. TBoA 3.3.02 (the Lançon Board) disagreed, and considered that formulation of a claim explicitly as a process was equally acceptable as formulation as a Swiss-type use. (See, for example, T-958/94 Anti-tumoral agent/THERAPEUTIQUES SUBSTITUTIVES and T-853/94 Benanomicin A/ZAIDAN.)

The matter came to a head when in T-1319/04 (I) Dosage regime/ KOS LIFE SCIENCES, TBoA 3.3.02 (now chaired by Oswald) referred the question of the acceptability of Swiss-type use claims, in which the point of novelty was not the nature of the ailment or of the intended patients but of the quantity and timing of drug dosage, to the Enlarged Board. The result was an Enlarged Board decision in February

[1] See, however, Cockbain and Sterckx (2011b) for our comments on G-2/88 Friction reducing additive/MOBIL III, in which a 'use' claim was unbelievably found to be a product claim.

2010, G-2/08 Dosage regime/ABBOTT RESPIRATORY, in which the Enlarged Board tacitly accepted that the Swiss-type use claim format did not confer novelty, and declared that claims in the Swiss-type use format should stop being accepted by the EPO.

The major problem with the Swiss-type use claim format was of course that the novelty of the claimed subject-matter derived from the *intended end use* of the drug, and, the first indications of Art. 54(4) EPC aside, purpose-limitation has generally not been considered to confer novelty on a product. Product X for use Y is interpreted as covering product X *in a form suitable for* use Y, and if the old drug formulation could be used in the new treatment then the Swiss-type use claim would lack novelty.

However, the claim format also poses problems when it comes to determining whether infringement has occurred. This may be illustrated by the drug acetyl salicylic acid (aspirin), which for decades has been available over the counter (i.e. not requiring a prescription) in tablet form as an analgesic. Recently, aspirin has been suggested to be useful in reducing the occurrence of cancers. In the Swiss-type claim form, this could have been claimed as: 'The use of acetyl salicylic acid for the manufacture of a medicament for use in prophylactic treatment against cancer.' Consider then three cases where a patient has taken aspirin tablets for this purpose: the first where the patient has bought the tablets over the counter in a package from company A labelled as for analgesic use (a form that had been available from long before the new indication was found); the second where the tablets were made by company B, bought by company C in bulk and packaged for analgesic *or* cancer prophylaxis use; and the third where the tablets were made and packaged by company D for analgesic *or* cancer prophylaxis use.

In the first case, the tablets only became 'for use in prophylactic treatment against cancer' when they were purchased and consumed by the patient. Company A had no control over the intentions and actions of the purchaser and clearly could not be held to infringe. In the second case, bulk manufacturer B had no control over the actions of its customer C or the intentions of the end user – it was simply continuing to do something (tablet manufacture) which it may have been doing for years and again seems unlikely to be found to infringe. Even in the third case, since the tablets were packaged for two alternative uses and since actual consumption could only be for one of these uses, the tablets again only become 'for use in prophylactic treatment against cancer' when they were purchased *and* consumed by the patient.

If an action can only become infringement when a drug is consumed, it would seem that the process covered by the claim would have to be interpreted as including the act of consumption, which would make the process unpatentable as a method of medical treatment. Thus it would appear that a Swiss-type use claim is only infringed if the *manufacturer* of the tablets, at the time of manufacture, intended (all) the tablets to be used for the new indication.

Philip Grubb has noted that: 'At best, a patent containing a Swiss-type claim may be used to prevent a competitor from actively promoting the compound for the new use, by advertisements, package inserts, etc., but it cannot prevent doctors from prescribing for the patented new use a generic product which is already on the market for an earlier indication' (Grubb 2004: 243).

Besides direct infringement, there may be contributory infringement of a patent claim – where the infringer supplies something that can be used by the recipient to put the invention into effect. However, since, in the case of a Swiss-type use claim, the 'invention' claimed is the process for manufacturing the tablets, a bulk manufacturer such as company B could not be guilty of contributory infringement as it supplied the product of the process and not a means for putting the process into effect.

The situation concerning patent protection for *second and further* medical indications changed with the revision of the EPC in 2000, when Art. 54(5) EPC was added, allowing purpose-limited product per se claims for drugs found to be useful in new treatments. Art. 54(5) EPC was introduced at the suggestion of Switzerland (Document CA/PL PV14). The submissions made by the Swiss delegation in support of the new clause, to the effect that it did no more than transpose into statute law the effects of G-5/83 Second medical indication/EISAI, were misleading and incorrect. This was apparently not picked up by the other delegates to the Munich Conference at which the adoption of Art. 54(5) EPC was approved. We have discussed the misleading nature of the Swiss submissions elsewhere (Sterckx and Cockbain 2010c). It was also discussed in an *amicus curiae* brief filed by one of the present authors in G-2/08 Dosage regime/ABBOTT RESPIRATORY, and, at length, at the EBoA oral proceedings. Put briefly, the position regarding patent infringement by medical practitioners at least is worsened by the adoption of Art. 54(5) EPC. This was acknowledged in the EBoA decision: 'It appears that the rights conferred on the patentee by the claim category under Article 54(5) EPC are likely broader, and could, in particular, lead to possible restrictions on the freedom of medical practitioners to prescribe or administer generics' (G-2/08: 490).

More to the point, however, in G-2/08 Dosage regime/ABBOTT RESPIRATORY the EBoA decided that Swiss-type use claims were no longer necessary, and should no longer be allowed, in view of the adoption of Art. 54(5) EPC:

> Article 54(5) EPC now permits purpose-related product protection for any further specific use of a known medicament in a method of therapy. Therefore … the loophole existing in the provisions of the EPC 1973 [whereby there was no clear basis in the EPC for allowing patent protection for drugs found to have a second (or further) medical use] was closed … In other words '*cessante ratione legis, cessat et ipsa lex*', when the reason of the law ceases, the law itself ceases … The cause of the praetorian approach ceasing, the effect must cease. (G-2/08: 492)

In patent law in general, the applicant is free to define her invention as she wishes. The claim she decides upon is examined for patent-eligibility under Art. 52(2) and Art. 53 EPC, and then for novelty, inventive step, susceptibility to industrial application, sufficiency of disclosure and clarity. Apart from the addition of Art. 54(5) EPC, these gatekeepers to the patentability of further medical indication inventions were essentially unchanged in the 2000 revision. Why, then, should an applicant no longer be free to use Swiss-type use claims? The key is to be found in the EBoA's references to 'praetorian' law in the G-2/08 Dosage regime/ABBOTT RESPIRATORY decision.

Praetorian law is judicially made law and can go beyond the simple 'interpretation' of statute law that courts are required to engage in. The EPC, however, is an international treaty for which amendment to the definitions of what is and is not patentable requires ratification by all the Member States (as was done with EPC 2000). The following questions thus arise:

(1) Did the EBoA, in G-5/83 Second medical indication/EISAI, extend the scope of the subject-matter for which European patents could be granted beyond the scope permitted by EPC 1973?
(2) If it did not, then why are Swiss-type use claims no longer to be permitted?
(3) If it did, then are the European patents that have been granted with Swiss-type use claims invalid?

Before commenting on these issues, we would draw attention to the 'breathing space' that EPO Boards of Appeal have to create new law. First, we should quote Paul van den Berg, the erstwhile chairman of TBoA 3.5.01 and for a long time a member of the EBoA: '[EPO] boards of appeal cannot assume the role of legislator. They have to apply the law as it stands and cannot strive to meet wishes which are incompatible with the provisions of the European Patent Convention' (van den

Berg 1996: 45). Further, we would draw attention to the powers of the Boards of Appeal to 'interpret' the EPC as set out in Art. 23(3) EPC: 'In their decisions the members of the Boards ... shall comply ... with the provisions of the [EPC]' (EPO 2010a: 69). Finally, we would refer to the minutes of the Munich Diplomatic Conference of 1973, the conference at which the wording of EPC 1973 was agreed, and in particular to two comments relating to Art. 54(4) EPC, the clause that permits purpose-limited claims to a known compound that has been found for the first time to have a medicinal use:

> The Netherlands delegation proposed that the wording of [Art. 54(4) EPC] ... should be improved. It said that on no account did it wish, with its proposal, to break away from the principle that only the first application of the use of a known substance or composition in a method for treatment of the human or animal body by surgery or therapy is patentable, and not the second and subsequent applications ... The Chairman replied to the Yugoslav delegation and said that, in his opinion, the aim in [Art. 54(4) EPC] was to make it clear that a known substance (or a known composition) which, since it formed part of the state of the art, was no longer patentable, nevertheless could be patented for the first use in a method for the treatment of the human or animal body by surgery or therapy; however, a further patent could not be granted if a second possible use were found for the same substance, irrespective of whether the human or animal body was to be treated with it ... The Chairman noted that his views were shared by the Government delegations. (Document M/PR/I: 29)

From this, it seems clear that the intention of the legislators of EPC 1973, unlike that of the legislators of EPC 2000, was to provide a loophole (to the exclusion from patentability of methods of medical treatment) *only* for compounds found for the *first* time to have a medicinal use. G-5/83 Second medical indication/EISAI went against this intention by allowing claims (Swiss-type use claims) to second and subsequent indications.

We must now turn to the texts of the G-5/83 Second medical indication/EISAI and G-2/08 Dosage regime/ABBOTT RESPIRATORY decisions.

5.13.2 The G-5/83 Second medical indication/EISAI Decision

In the EISAI decision, the justification given for accepting Swiss-type use claims was as follows:

> As is rightly recognised ... Article 52(1) EPC expresses a general principle of patentability for inventions which are industrially applicable, new and inventive and it is clear that in all fields of industrial activity other than those of making products for use in surgery, therapy and diagnostic methods, a new use for a

known product can be fully protected as such by claims directed to that use … This is in fact the appropriate form of protection in such cases as the new and non-obvious use of the known product constitutes the invention and it is the clear intention of the European Patent Convention that a patent be granted for the invention to which a European patent application relates … Article [54(4)] EPC provides an exception to this general rule, however, so far as the first use of medicaments is concerned, in respect of which the normal type of use claim is prohibited by Art. [53(c)] EPC. In effect, in this case the required novelty for the medicament which forms the subject-matter of the claim is derived from the new pharmaceutical use. (G-5/83: 66)

Thus far, nothing much new or groundbreaking: where an invention resides in a new use for a known thing, that invention can be claimed as: 'A method of doing new thing X using known thing Y.' Where the method is a medical treatment with a drug, however, such claims are not allowed and an alternative claim format is required. Where the drug is new, the claim can be to the drug as such. Where the drug is a known substance, but not a substance known to have medicinal properties, Art. 54(4) EPC provides a special exception, allowing the alternative format to be a purpose-limited product claim.

Art. 54(4) EPC states that the provisions of the rest of the Article, which say that an invention will be considered to be new if it does not form part of the state of the art, 'shall not exclude the patentability of any substance or composition, comprised in the state of the art, for use in a method [of treatment] … provided that its use for any such method [of treatment] … is not comprised in the state of the art'. Since the drug compound as such is comprised in the state of the art, the first indication *invention* (Compound Y for use in medicine) is novel because 'for use in medicine' provides novelty, that is in some way distinguishes over the drug as such and in some way is limitative.

Art. 54(4) EPC thus provides a special exception to the general rule that a purpose limitation does not provide novelty over a known product *in a form suitable for that purpose* – the special exception, however, is relatively limited for, as a matter of fact, medicines do have to be made under special conditions, and a compound that is known, but not known to have any medicinal use, would rarely be in a form suitable for use as a medicine. The same logic would *not* apply to a second or further medical indication, as the drug would very likely form part of the state of the art in a form suitable for the new use.

The Enlarged Board continued: 'It seems justifiable by analogy to derive the novelty for the process which forms the subject-matter of the type of use claim now being considered from the new therapeutic use of the medicament and this irrespective of the fact whether any pharmaceutical use of the medicament was already known or not' (G-5/83: 66). The analogy, however, is not so direct. In the Swiss-type use claim, which is directed to a *process* for preparing a product, the *invention* as claimed is a process, but the purpose limitation is not on the process (the subject-matter of the claim) but on the product. The process claimed may be identical to a known process in all process aspects. In other words, strictly speaking, the invention forms part of the state of the art and therefore lacks novelty according to Art. 54 EPC. The Enlarged Board itself does mention in relation to Swiss-type use claims that 'there may be a problem concerning the novelty of the invention' (G-5/83: 66). The UK Patents Court, in *John Wyeth's and Schering's Applications*, felt similarly:

> there can be no objections to the patenting in the Swiss form of claim of an invention directed to a second or subsequent medical use of a known pharmaceutical if the statutory requirement of novelty can be met ... However, that stated, had the matter to be considered on the wording of sections 1 to 4 of the UK statute (the 1977 Act) and without regard to the position, as it has developed, under the corresponding provisions of [EPC 1973], we think the better view would be that a claim in the Swiss form to an invention directed to the use of a known pharmaceutical to manufacture a medicament, not in itself novel, for a second or subsequent and novel medical use would not be patentable as lacking the required novelty. It has to be recognised that it would have been a simple matter to provide for the patenting of such an invention directed to a second medical use by the omission of the word 'any' in section 2(6) [i.e. the section corresponding to Art. 54(4) EPC], if it had been the intention of the legislature that a novel second or further use of a known pharmaceutical should be patentable. (UK-Wyeth 1986: 565)

The UK Patents Court then reviewed the EISAI approach to the novelty of Swiss-type use claims and concluded that:

> [The EBoA's] approach to the novelty of the Swiss type of use claim directed to a second, or subsequent, therapeutic use is equally possible under the corresponding provisions of the [UK] 1977 Act and, notwithstanding the opinion expressed earlier [i.e. the opinion quoted immediately above] as to the better view of the patentability of such a Swiss type claim under the material provisions of the [UK 1977] Act considered without regard to the position, as it has developed, under the corresponding provisions of the [EPC 1973], having regard to the desirability of achieving conformity, the same approach should be adopted to the novelty of the Swiss type of claim now under consideration under the material provisions of the [UK 1977] Act. (UK-Wyeth 1986: 567)

Put differently, the EBoA was wrong, but for the sake of uniformity its decision had to be followed, at least until it was overturned by a higher court or by the EBoA itself.

Turning back to G-5/83 Second medical indication/EISAI, the EBoA commented on the exclusion from patentability of methods of medical treatment and, reassuring itself that its view was also held by the German Federal Supreme Court, stated that 'The intention of Article [53(c)] EPC is only to free from restraint non-commercial and non-industrial medical and veterinary activities' (G-5/83: 66).

The Enlarged Board minimised the reach of the exclusion: 'To prevent the exclusion from going beyond its proper limits, it seems appropriate to take a special view of the concept of the "state of the art" ... Article [54(4)] EPC alone provides only a partial compensation for the restriction on patent rights in the industrial and commercial field resulting from [the exclusion]' (G-5/83: 66).

At the Munich Diplomatic Conference in 1973, the French and German delegations had made it abundantly clear (Document M/PR/I: 28) that the scope of what was or was not patentable subject-matter was too important to be left to the EPO's Administrative Council to decide; in other words, it was only for the EPC Member States to agree that scope. One wonders whether the delegations would have been comfortable with the scope of the patentable being broadened by the EBoA.

The EISAI Board then left credibility behind:

> It should be added that the Enlarged Board does not deduce from the special provision of Article [54(4)] EPC that there was any intention to exclude second (and further) medical indications from patent protection other than by a purpose-limited product claim. The rule of interpretation that if one thing is expressed the alternative is excluded ... is a rule to be applied with very great caution as it can lead to injustice. No intention to exclude second (and further) medical indications can be deduced from the terms of the European Patent Convention: nor can it be deduced from the legislative history of the articles in question. (G-5/83: 66)

As mentioned above, at the Munich Diplomatic Conference in 1973 the delegates had clearly taken a very different position:

> The Netherlands ... said that on no account did it wish, with its proposal, to break away from the principle that only the first application of the use of a known substance or composition in a method for treatment of the human or animal body by surgery or therapy is patentable, and not the second and subsequent applications ... The Chairman ... said that, in his opinion, the aim in [Art. 54(4) EPC] was to make it clear that a known substance (or a known composition) which, since it formed part of the state of the art, was no longer patentable, nevertheless could be patented for the first use in a method for the treatment of the human or animal body by surgery or therapy; however, a further patent could not be granted if a second possible use were found for the same substance, irrespective of whether the human or animal body was to

be treated with it ... The Chairman noted that his views were shared by the Government delegations. (Document M/PR/I: 29)

The EISAI Board then approved the use of Swiss-type use claims, that is it found that purpose limitation could render an otherwise anticipated claim novel. This was praetorian law, in other words the EBoA deciding that it was entitled to *supplement* or *correct* the EPC.

The answer to the questions whether the EBoA, in EISAI, extended the scope of the subject-matter for which European patents could be granted beyond the scope permitted by EPC 1973, is clearly yes. This is confirmed by the G-2/08 Dosage regime/ABBOTT RESPIRATORY Board's references, discussed in the next section, to G-5/83 Second medical indication/EISAI as representing praetorian law. This makes redundant the question as to why Swiss-type use claims should no longer be permitted since the format does *not* confer novelty.

5.13.3 G-2/08 Dosage regime/ABBOTT RESPIRATORY decision

In G-2/08 Dosage regime/ABBOTT RESPIRATORY the EBoA revisited the topic of the Swiss-type use claims and argued as follows:

It has been established practice under the EPC 1973 that a patent related to a further medical indication of a known medicament could only be granted for a claim directed to the use of a substance or composition for the manufacture of a medicament for a specified therapeutic application ... Since the medicament *per se* was not new the subject-matter of such a claim was rendered novel by its therapeutic application ... This *praetorian* approach was a 'special approach to the derivation of novelty' ... and therefore constituted a narrow exception to the principles governing the novelty requirements which was not intended to be applied in other fields of technology. (G-2/08: 491, emphasis added)

The description of the EISAI board as having adopted a *praetorian* approach, that is one which goes beyond the law as agreed by the EPC 1973 legislators, appears to be a clear admission that the EISAI Board's acceptance of Swiss-type use claims was bad law, which should be followed no longer. The G-2/08 Dosage regime/ABBOTT RESPIRATORY Board proceeded first to explain how the 'praetorian' approach had come about, before explicitly stating that it no longer had its place in European patent law:

That *praetorian* ruling found its cause in the fact that a claim directed to the use of the substance or composition for the treatment of the human body by therapy had to be regarded as a step of treatment ... A claim of that kind was forbidden. On the other hand only the first medical indication of a known composition in the form of a medicament was by virtue of Article [54(4) EPC] entitled to be drafted in the form of a purpose-related product claim. And since the intention of the legislator was clearly not to exclude second therapeutic indications of a known medicament from the field of patentability the so-called Swiss-type claim constituted the adequate but exceptional solution … Article 54(5) EPC now permits purpose-related product protection for any further specific use of a known medicament in a method of therapy. Therefore, as mentioned in the preparatory document ([Document] MR/24/00 …) the loophole existing in the provisions of EPC 1973 was closed … In other words '*cessante ratione legis, cessat et ipsa lex*', when the reason of the law ceases, the law itself ceases … The cause of the *praetorian* approach ceasing, the effect must cease. (G-2/08: 491–2, emphasis added)

Note, however, that the ABBOTT RESPIRATORY Board merely *repeated* the EISAI Board's incorrect statement that 'the intention of the legislator was clearly not to exclude second therapeutic indications of a known medicament from the field of patentability', *without* this time stating that it had studied the *travaux préparatoires*.

5.13.4 The Implications of the G-2/08 Dosage regime/ABBOTT RESPIRATORY decision

If the EBoA decides that something previously thought to be patentable is not, do the owners of patents or applicants for patents claiming such subject-matter have a 'legitimate expectation' that their patents will be held to be valid or that their applications will be granted, despite the new decision? Normally, one would expect not – the interests of the public must be guarded against the grant of unwarranted monopolies, regardless of the interests of the investors and patentees who may have benefited for many years from an unjustified monopoly. Monopolies are an exception to business practice in Europe and one which requires justification to the public who, as a result of such monopolies, must pay prices for goods and services which are higher than those which might apply were there to be free and open competition. In a decision in December 2010, in G-1/08 Tomatoes/STATE OF ISRAEL, the EBoA addressed this very point: 'There can be no "legitimate expectation" that an interpretation of a substantive provision governing patentability given in a decision of the boards of appeal will not be overruled in the future by the Enlarged Board of Appeal, since recognising such an expectation as legitimate would undermine the function of the Enlarged Board of Appeal' (G-1/08: para. 2.5). It seems, therefore, that European patent claims which derive their novelty from purpose limitations, when subject-matter suitable for that purpose was known, might be invalid. The answer to the question, whether European patents that have been granted with Swiss-type use claims are invalid, indeed seems to be yes, validity (or more precisely novelty) is not conferred on such claims by the 'for use' purpose limitation. This, of course, may upset many users of the patent system.

The G-2/08 Dosage regime/ABBOTT RESPIRATORY decision honours the law agreed to by the legislators, and by recognising that Swiss-type use claims arose out of praetorian law, 'the cause of [which] ceasing, the effect must cease', the EBoA has dispatched into oblivion a claim format which should never have been permitted.

6 Essentially biological processes for the production of plants and animals

> [G]iven that there is a certain tendency to ever broaden the technical field covered by a patent by drafting claims directed to all envisaged contexts in which the invention might potentially be used, the fact that the legislator did not want such an extension of protection in the field considered here is still a valid consideration to be respected.
>
> (G-2/07: para. 6.4.2.3)

6.1 Introduction

There is much confusion surrounding the scope of the exclusion that is the subject of this chapter. According to Llewelyn and Adcock, the 'essentially biological processes' provision:

> was introduced to ensure that private rights were not granted over i) those processes which occurred naturally and ii) those processes commonly used by plant breeders which might involve some human intervention but which predominantly rely on nature to effect the desired result ... The first matter for consideration is the fact that some believe that the patent system only protects the results of modern biotechnology and not the results of conventional plant breeding. The apparent basis for this belief lies in part in the perceived inability of such products to meet the patent law threshold of novelty and inventive step, but it also lies in a misunderstanding of the scope of the exclusion of essentially biological processes. The problem with the exclusion of essentially biological processes is that it is thought (in some quarters) to extend to the results achieved through the use of an essentially biological process ... The second issue ... relates to the degree of technical intervention necessary to turn an essentially biological process into a microbiological one. The crux of the problem is whether the reference to 'essentially' means that the process must in the main be biological but it need not be wholly biological in form or function. (Llewelyn and Adcock 2006: 465–6, reference omitted)

In 1991 Rainer Moufang referred to the exclusion as being unclear and, in legal policy terms, questionable (Moufang 1991: 62).

6.2 The law

Art. 53(b) EPC excludes the patenting of essentially biological processes in the following terms: 'European patents shall not be granted in respect of ... essentially biological processes for the production of plants or animals; this provision shall not apply to microbiological processes' (EPO 2010a: 108). The equivalent German and French texts refer respectively to '*Verfahren zur Züchtung*' and '*procédés d'obtention*' in place of 'processes for the production' (EPO 2010a: 108–9). This provision was not amended with the adoption of EPC 2000.

The Implementing Regulations for the EPC give some guidance as to how this exclusion might be interpreted in Rule 26(5) EPC: 'A process for the production of plants or animals is essentially biological if it consists *entirely* of natural phenomena such as crossing and selection' (EPO 2010a: 328, emphasis added). This corresponds to Rule 23b(5) EPC 1973, which was introduced in September 1999 when the EPO's Administrative Council sought to bring the EPC into compliance with the EBD. It cannot, however, serve to broaden or narrow the interpretation of Art. 53(b) EPC in view of Art. 164(2) EPC, which states that 'In case of conflict between the provisions of this Convention and those of the Implementing Regulations, the provisions of this Convention shall prevail' (EPO 2010a: 248).

6.3 The key issues

There are several points at issue relating to this exclusion, in particular:

(1) does the exclusion *only* apply to processes for producing new varieties of plant or animal;
(2) can the exclusion be escaped by *specifying* the plant or animal at a higher taxonomic level than the lowest;
(3) does the inclusion of *any non-biological step* in the process as claimed allow the process to escape the exclusion;
(4) does the inclusion of *any biological step* in a claim to a multi-step process cause that process to be excluded; and
(5) if the answers to (3) and (4) are no, then will the inclusion of *certain types of non-biological step* allow the process to escape exclusion, and, if so, which types.

6.4 Key decisions

The key decisions by the EPO in relation to this clause are the pair of decisions handed down by the Enlarged Board of Appeal in December

2010 following consolidation of two sets of proceedings, G-2/07 Broccoli/PLANT BIOSCIENCE and G-1/08 Tomatoes/STATE OF ISRAEL.

G-2/07 Broccoli/PLANT BIOSCIENCE arose from T-83/05 (I) Broccoli/PLANT BIOSCIENCE and concerned European Patent No. 1069819 (the 'Broccoli patent') which had been opposed by Syngenta and Limagrain, both major players in the agrochemical industry. The claims[1] of the Broccoli patent, as considered by TBoA 3.3.04 (Chairman Kinkeldey) in T-83/05 (I) Broccoli/PLANT BIOSCIENCE, related to a method for the production of broccoli with elevated glucosinolate levels which involved crossing certain different broccoli species, selecting hybrids with elevated glucosinolate levels, backcrossing and selecting plants which also expressed elevated glucosinolate levels, and selecting a line with this characteristic. Selection in this method involved the use of, or rather detection of, molecular markers. In other words, the crossing and selection were standard crop breeding techniques with the alleged technical character lying in the use of the molecular markers to enable appropriate selection.

G-1/08 Tomatoes/STATE OF ISRAEL arose from T-1242/06 (I) Tomatoes/STATE OF ISRAEL and concerned European Patent No. 1211926 (the 'Tomato patent') which had been opposed by Unilever. The claims[2] of the Tomato patent, as considered by TBoA

[1] The version of the claim given here is heavily abridged. Claim 1 in the granted patent was directed to 'a method for the production of Brassica oleracea with elevated levels of 4-methylsulfinylbutyl glucosinolates, or 3-methylsulfinylbutyl glucosinolates, or both, which comprises: (a) crossing wild Brassica oleracea species with Brassica oleracea breeding lines; and, (b) selecting hybrids with levels of 4-methylsulfinylbutyl glucosinolates, or 3-methylsulfinylpropyl glucosinolates, or both, elevated above that initially found in Brassica oleracea breeding lines'. Claim 9 was directed to 'an edible Brassica plant produced according to the method of any one of claims 1 to 6'. Claim 10 was directed to 'an edible portion of a broccoli plant produced according to the method of any one of claims 1 to 6'. Claim 11 was directed to 'seed of a broccoli plant produced according to any one of claims 1 to 6'. Claim 13 to 'a broccoli plant having elevated levels of 3-methylsulfinylpropyl gucosinolates, or 4-methylsulfinylbutyl glucosinolates, or both; wherein the broccoli plant is a hybrid plant following crossing of broccoli breeding lines with wild species and, the levels of 4-methylsulfinylbutyl glucosinolates, or 3-methylsulfinylpropyl glucosinolates, or both, are elevated above that initially found in broccoli breeding lines'.

[2] The version of the claim given here is heavily abridged. Claim 1 of the granted patent was directed to 'a method for breeding tomato plants with reduced fruit water content comprising the steps of: crossing at least one Lycopersicon esculentum plant with a Lycopersicon spp. to produce hybrid seed; collecting the first generation of hybrid seeds; growing plants from the first generation of hybrid seeds; pollinating the plants of the most recent hybrid generation; collecting the seeds produced by the most recent hybrid generation; growing plants from the seeds of the most recent hybrid generation; allowing plants to remain on the vine past the point of normal ripening; screening for

3.3.04 (Chairman Kinkeldey), related to a method for breeding tomato plants that produces tomatoes with a reduced water content, which involved crossing tomato plants to produce hybrid seed, growing plants from the hybrid seed, growing at least one further generation, allowing the fruit to remain on the vine past normal ripening and screening for reduced water content as indicated by extended preservation and wrinkling of the skin. Again, this amounted to crossing and selecting as is normal in plant breeding, with the alleged technical character lying in the preservation/wrinkling selection criteria.

In accordance with Art. 9 of the Rules of Procedure of the EBoA, the president of the EPO (Alison Brimelow) was asked to comment on the cases. Some of the president's comments deserve quoting:

> Even if it is considered that Rule 26(5) EPC changed, i.e. narrowed the scope of application of Article 53(b) EPC, no legitimate expectations or acquired rights can be affected since Rule 26(5) EPC remains within the framework of what could have been decided with respect to Article 53(b) EPC by the departments entrusted with the procedure ... [N]otwithstanding the intrinsic ambiguities of the wording of Rule 26(5) EPC, the approach to be adopted should be based on a dynamic and harmonised interpretation of the process exclusion under Article 53(b) EPC ... A process for the production of plants is essentially biological if it consists entirely of natural phenomena, these being understood as those which are uncontrollable and/or occur without human intervention, including the methods used by traditional plant breeders, such as sexual crossing or natural selection. Given that, for example, selection may be technical and cannot always be considered a 'natural' phenomenon, crossing and selection must be construed as constituting possible examples of natural phenomena only if they are of a non-technical nature ... The term 'essentially biological' comprises both a quantitative and a qualitative element. The quantitative element requires at least one non-biological feature, whilst the qualitative element requires that such a feature have a genuine technical effect. The Article should be interpreted to the effect that the process exclusion does cover processes which comprise, in addition to natural phenomena, features of an insubstantial or insignificant technical nature. In order to escape the process exclusion, an additional feature of a technical nature should have a technical effect, provided by human intervention, on the process as such or on the product

reduced fruit water content as indicated by extended preservation of the ripe fruit and wrinkling of the fruit skin'. Claim 15 was directed to 'a tomato fruit characterized by a capability of natural dehydration while on a tomato plant, natural dehydration being defined as wrinkling of the skin of the tomato fruit when the fruit is allowed to remain on the plant after a normal ripe harvest stage, said natural dehydration being generally unaccompanied by microbial spoilage'. Claim 16 was directed to 'a tomato fruit characterized by an untreated skin which permits dehydration of the fruit so as to obtain wrinkling of the skin, said dehydration being generally unaccompanied by microbial spoilage'.

obtained therefrom. If the non-biological feature can be omitted without losing the desired effect, the process is not patentable. (G-2/07: 25–6)

Roughly interpreted, the president was saying: (a) that patents already granted because of the word 'entirely' in Rule 26(5) EPC should not be retroactively deemed invalid; (b) that the interpretation of the exclusion should move with the times, acknowledging that plant breeding now uses sophisticated technology; and (c) that inclusion of a required technical step should be sufficient to escape the exclusion.

The first point is not germane to this chapter; however, the Enlarged Board's response was clear: 'There can be no "legitimate expectation" that an interpretation of a substantive provision governing patentability given in a decision of the boards of appeal will not be overruled in the future by the Enlarged Board, since recognising such an expectation as legitimate would undermine the function of the Enlarged Board of Appeal' (G-2/07: 32). In other words, such patents *may* be invalid.

Many *amicus curiae* briefs were filed with the Enlarged Board, including a brief by one of the present authors, which was subsequently published in revised form (Sterckx 2009).

Besides processes, both the Tomato and the Broccoli patents claimed direct and indirect products of the claimed processes. Those product claims are of concern not only to the plant breeder, but also to the farmer, in view of the following question: where an invention lies in a process for producing plants and animals, can patent coverage extend to the progeny of the direct product of the process?

The earlier Board of Appeal decisions that were relevant to the case were T-320/87 Hybrid plants/LUBRIZOL, T-19/90 Oncomouse/HARVARD, T-356/93 Plant cells/PLANT GENETIC SYSTEMS, T-1054/96 (I) Transgenic plant/NOVARTIS, G-1/98 Transgenic plant/NOVARTIS II, and T-315/03 Transgenic animals/HARVARD, of which T-320/87 Hybrid plants/LUBRIZOL is the most pertinent.

In decision T-320/87 Hybrid plants/LUBRIZOL (Chairman Lançon) the exclusion was commented on as follows:

There is in the preparatory documents no clear guidance as to the interpretation of the concept of 'essentially biological'. It has in this respect to be born in mind that at the time when the exception was drafted, the knowledge of the potential development in the field of biotechnology was rather limited … The Board takes the view that whether or not a (non-microbiological) process is to be considered as 'essentially biological' within the meaning of Article 53(b) EPC has to be judged on the basis of the essence of the invention taking into account the totality of human intervention and its impact on the result achieved. It is the opinion of the Board that the necessity for human intervention alone is not yet a sufficient criterion for its not being 'essentially biological'. Human intervention may only mean that the process is not a 'purely biological' process, without contributing anything beyond a trivial level. It is further not a matter simply of whether such intervention is of a quantitative or qualitative character. (T-320/87: 76–7)

However, the supposed lack of clear guidance in the *travaux préparatoires* is amply shown to be false by the thorough analysis of them, presumably prepared by the Board's legal member Dr Rainer Moufang, set out in T-83/05 (I) Broccoli/PLANT BIOSCIENCE. We will come back to this in the section on the *travaux préparatoires* below.

T-19/90 Onco-mouse/HARVARD (Chairman Lançon) adds little relevant to this chapter. A process involving insertion of a gene into a vector and injection of that vector into an early stage embryo was considered not to be 'essentially biological'.

TBoA 3.3.04 (Chairman Kindeldey) in T-356/93 Plant cells/PLANT GENETIC SYSTEMS took the matter a little further forward, drawing on the *travaux préparatoires* for inspiration:

The historical documentation shows that, when drafting Article 53(b) EPC, the EPC Working Party recognised that even if protection of new plant varieties and processes for producing new plants was to be excluded under European patent law, European patents still had to be granted for processes which, while applicable to plants, were of a technical nature (see [D]ocument IV/2071/61-E, page 6, first paragraph). Processes for producing new plants by irradiation of the plants themselves or the seed with isotopes were cited as an example of such processes (ibid., loc. cit.). The board observes that the example given is one in which plants or seeds undergo genetic modifications due to irradiation … In order to provide a distinction between inventions resulting from non-technical processes for the production of plants (e.g. essentially biological processes such as selective breeding), which were to be excluded, and inventions resulting from technical processes for the production of plants, which were considered patentable, the legislator introduced in Article 53(b), first half sentence, EPC the exclusion from patentability of 'essentially biological processes for the production of plants' … As is derivable from the example given in the quoted document of the EPC Working Party … this provision gives rise to the legal consequence that processes of a technical nature for producing plants, including processes involving genetic modification of plants, are patentable … Based on the above considerations, it follows that a process for the production of plants comprising at least one essential technical step, which cannot be carried out without human intervention and which has a decisive impact on the final result … does not fall under the exceptions to patentability under Article 53(b), first half sentence EPC. (T-356/93: 571–3)

As will be clear from the discussion below, the TBoA in T-83/05 (I) Broccoli/PLANT BIOSCIENCE found far more pertinent documents in the *travaux préparatoires* than simply Document IV/2071/61-E, which was referred to by the TBoA in T-356/93 Plant cells/PLANT GENETIC SYSTEMS.

There are two TBoA decisions bearing the number T-1054/96, one from 13 October 1997 (Transgenic plant/NOVARTIS – an interlocutory decision, here referred to as T-1054/96 (I), which referred certain questions to the Enlarged Board of Appeal, questions which were partially answered in G-1/98 Transgenic plant/NOVARTIS II), and one from 6 December 2000 (the final decision – Anti-pathogenic compositions/NOVARTIS III) holding that, since the essence of the claimed process involved the performance of genetic engineering steps, the process was not 'essentially biological'. In the referring decision, TBoA 3.3.04 had put forward three possible interpretations of the exclusion: (1) that, analogously to methods of medical treatment, the inclusion of a single biological step would render a process claim unpatentable; (2) the interpretation suggested in T-320/87 Hybrid plants/LUBRIZOL and T-356/93 Plant cells/PLANT GENETIC SYSTEMS discussed above; and (3) that the inclusion of a single non-biological step would render a claim patentable. In G-1/98 Transgenic plant/NOVARTIS II, the EBoA side-stepped the interpretation of 'essentially biological', saying that '[t]o offer guidance in this respect without having a sound factual basis for doing so is inappropriate' (G-1/98: 29).

Decision T-315/03 Transgenic animals/HARVARD (Chairman Davison-Brunel) moves us forward very little in the sole relevant comment that '[i]t is self-evident that a process which includes genetic manipulation does not consist entirely of natural phenomena' (T-315/03: 81).

6.5 The *travaux préparatoires*

Art. 53(b) EPC was unchanged in the 2000 revision of the EPC. Art. 53(b) EPC 1973 derives from Art. 2(b) SPC, which was adopted as the first text for Art. 53(b) EPC when the drafting of the EPC began. Art. 2(b) SPC specifies that 'The Contracting States shall not be bound to provide for the grant of patents in respect of ... plant or animal varieties or essentially biological processes for the production of plants or animals; this provision does not apply to micro-biological processes and the products thereof'.

Accordingly, for assistance in interpreting Art. 53(b) EPC, one must turn to the *travaux préparatoires* for the SPC and for the first attempt at a European Community patent law, the Convention relating to a European Patent Law or CEPL (see Document 2335/IV/65-E).[3]

[3] The *travaux préparatoires* relating to Art. 53(b) EPC are discussed at length in Pila (2009).

Discussions began first for the SPC, a Council of Europe project, and parallel discussions on the CEPL began in 1961 but came to an end at the end of 1964. Since several countries were members of both the European Community and the Council of Europe, efforts were made to ensure the exclusions from patentability were the same in the SPC and the CEPL. Since Art. 53(b) EPC was agreed long before the deliberations concerning the EBD and Rule 26(5) EPC, since no revision of Art. 53(b) EPC has occurred, and since the scope of its exclusion can neither be broadened nor narrowed by the EBD or the Rule, discussion of the *travaux préparatoires* relating to the EBD is quite simply not relevant for the purpose of determining the scope of the exclusion.

First it should be noted that, in the same sentence, Art. 53(b) EPC excludes plant and animal *varieties* and essentially biological processes for the production of plants or animals. The process exclusion is not limited to plant or animal *varieties* and more specifically it is not limited to *new* varieties. If it were, then it would be clear that the process exclusion related to the breeding of new varieties (which we will generally refer to as 'breeding' here) and not to the growing of existing varieties (which we will generally refer to as 'farming' here). The difference in wording had been commented upon in 1983 by TBoA 3.3.01 (Chairman Cadman) in T-49/83 Propagating material/CIBA-GEIGY: 'The very wording of Article 53(b) EPC before the semi-colon precludes the equation of plants and plant varieties, which would also be at variance with the general sense of the provision' (T-49/83: 115). This difference in the wording of the two exclusions led the Enlarged Board in G-2/07 Broccoli/PLANT BIOSCIENCE to say:

> [I]n the absence of any indication in the legislative history that the term 'plants' was meant to signify only 'plant varieties', and in view of the importance of the difference in legal meaning of the term 'plant' on the one hand and 'plant variety' on the other, as demonstrated by the Enlarged Board's decision G 1/98 [Transgenic plant/NOVARTIS II], any interpretation of the term 'plant' as meaning, contrary to its wording, only 'plant varieties' is ruled out. Hence, the Enlarged Board concludes that the exception of 'essentially biological processes for the production of plants' cannot be read as only applying where the result of such a process is a plant variety. In other words, it cannot be read as being limited to processes for the production of plant varieties. (G-2/07: 53)

This gives rise to two interpretations of decision G-2/07 Broccoli/PLANT BIOSCIENCE. Either the exclusion is not avoided by specifying the plant or animal at a taxonomic level above the lowest (i.e. the *higher taxonomic level* approach should not be followed), or the exclusion can also exclude processes which do not result in a new variety (i.e. it can exclude farming processes).

The precise meaning turns on the meaning of the words 'production', '*Züchtung*' and '*obtention*'. The English word 'production' would clearly cover both breeding and farming. The German word '*Züchtung*', while normally used in relation to breeding, also can be and is sometimes used in relation to farming (e.g. of bees). The French word could also cover both. The Enlarged Board declined to decide this issue, since both cases related to breeding, which would be covered by either interpretation. Since the Enlarged Board declined to decide, the passage quoted above must presumably mean that the exclusion is not escaped by specifying the plant or animal at a taxonomic level above the lowest, that is the *higher taxonomic level* approach was rejected.

One of the earliest reports in the drafting history of the SPC, a comparative study of patentability across Europe presented in November 1955, saw problems with agricultural inventions, especially breeding and cultivation methods, as not being sufficiently 'industrial' to be patentable (see Document EXP/Brev (53) 18 rev: 3–7). By the time of the Haertel Study of July 1960, it had been recognised that some agricultural activities were technical and might be patentable (Document Haertel 1960: 18). In a memorandum on the unification of the legislation from November 1960, it was suggested that 'it would be inexpedient to try to impose a common solution for the highly controversial question of the patentability of new plant varieties' and that the 'only sensible and practicable endeavour would thus seem to be towards harmonising European legislation on the patentability of "purely agricultural" processes' (Document EXP/Brev (60) 7).[4] Thus, in the preliminary draft of the SPC from early 1961, the equivalent exclusion stood as 'the contracting states shall not be bound to provide for the grant of patents in respect of new plant or animal species or of purely biological, horticultural or agricultural (agronomic) processes' (Document EXP/Brev (61) 2 rev: 26).

In contrast, the first preliminary draft of the CEPL of 14 March 1961 (Document IV/2071/61-E) proposed a precursor to the essentially biological processes exclusion reading as follows: 'European patents shall not be granted in respect of … inventions relating to the production of or a process for producing a new plant variety or a new animal species. This provision shall not apply to processes of a technical nature' (Document IV/2071/61-E, Section 13: 3).

In Section 14 of the same document, setting out comments on the first preliminary draft, it was commented that 'European patents will … have to be granted for processes which, while being applicable to plants, are of a technical nature, e.g. processes for producing new plants

[4] Quoted from Pila (2009).

by irradiation of the plants themselves or the seeds with isotopes ... But it should be noted that ... in particular, purely agricultural processes are not regarded as patentable in all countries' (Document IV/2071/61-E, Section 14: 6–7).

By the end of April 1961, following the first meeting of the EEC's Patents Working Party, the text of the exclusion in the CEPL had been modified to become: 'European patents shall not be granted in respect of ... new plant varieties or new animal species and purely biological processes for producing them' (Document IV/2498/1/61-E: 3).

In May 1961 the CoE's Committee of Experts began drafting the SPC, and in November 1961 the exclusion in the draft SPC was substantially amended to delete 'horticultural or agricultural (agronomic)' and to change 'purely' biological to 'essentially' biological. This was explained in a memorandum:

> The processes for the 'production of plants or animals' referred to in the new text include those which may produce known varieties as well as those which may produce new ones ... Selection or hybridisation of existing varieties may be mentioned as examples of such processes (in the vegetable kingdom). The new text specifies that the processes which may be ineligible for patent protection are essentially (and no longer purely) biological. It was evident that the exclusion should be extended to cover processes which were fundamentally of this type even if, as a secondary feature, 'technical' devices were involved (use of a particular type of instrument in a grafting process, or of a special greenhouse in growing a plant), it being understood that such technical devices may perfectly well be patented themselves, but not the biological process in which they are used. (Document EXP/Brev (61) 8: 4–5)

The same rationale was presented in July 1962 (Document CM (62) 160: 4).

From 1957 to 1961 a convention providing *sui generis* protection for new plant varieties was under discussion, namely the International Convention for the Protection of New Varieties of Plants (UPOV 1961), which was agreed in December 1961. In Art. 5(1) UPOV 1961 the effect of the right granted was specified to be such that the breeder's prior authorisation was required for the production, for commercial marketing, of the reproductive or vegetative propagating material of the new variety and for the offering for sale or marketing of such material. Art. 5(3) UPOV 1961, however, provided a 'breeder's exemption' whereby authorisation by the rights holder was not required by breeders using the new variety to create still further new varieties.[5]

[5] By March 1991 UPOV had been revised to incorporate the 'farmers' privilege' under Art. 15(2) UPOV 1991 whereby the breeder's rights could be restricted to 'permit farmers to use, for propagating purposes, on their own holdings, the product of the

By May 1962 the first published draft of the CEPL had been prepared. The wording of the exclusion was brought into line with the SPC wording: 'European patents shall not be granted in respect of ... plant or animal varieties or essentially biological processes for the production of plants or animals' (Document 4488/IV/62-E). As Pila notes, faced with the divergence between the draft texts of the SPC and the CEPL: 'the EEC states had the following choice: adhere to the text which they had drafted with the intent that it be restrictive in scope, or adopt the text of the Strasbourg framers to ensure consistent patent regimes. They chose the latter, affirming their decision the following year by incorporating the microbiological exemption despite earlier concerns regarding its terms' (Pila 2009: 442, footnotes omitted). The desire for uniformity is easy to understand given that there was considerable overlap between the membership of the Council of Europe's Committee of Experts on Patents and that of the European Economic Community's Patents Working Party.

The CoE's Committee of Experts reviewed the draft SPC in July 1962. As indicated above, an exemption to the exclusion – the exception of microbiological processes and the products thereof – was now in the draft. In November 1963 the SPC was signed.

At the tenth meeting of the EEC's Patents Working Party in September 1963, the exemption of microbiological processes was also agreed for the CEPL (see Document 9081/IV/63-E-Final: 65). By January 1965 the final text of the CEPL was reached, with the exclusion reading: 'European patents shall not be granted in respect of ... plant or animal varieties or essentially biological processes for the production of plants or animals; this provision does not apply to microbiological processes or the products thereof' (Document 2335/IV/65-E). This is of course effectively the same as Art. 2(b) SPC.

When discussions on a European patent law resumed in 1969, they began from Art. 2(b) SPC and that wording was maintained until EPC 1973 was finalised.[6] Moreover, as noted earlier, Art. 53(b) EPC was not discussed in the EPC 2000 *travaux préparatoires*. It seems abundantly clear, therefore, that since the wording of the exclusion derives from the SPC, since the *travaux préparatoires* of the SPC show that 'production' of plants or animals was intended to cover both breeding and farming,

harvest which they have obtained by planting, on their own holdings, the protected variety'.

[6] Nonetheless, in the *travaux préparatoires* for the EPC, Document BR/135/71 reports the UK delegation seeking unsuccessfully to have 'essentially biological processes' deleted from Art. 53 EPC on the basis that it was unclear and that only processes for treating humans should be excluded.

and since this is a normal reading of the words used, the *travaux préparatoires* would seem to confirm that this is the correct reading.

6.6 Possible types of claims and their acceptability in view of the exclusion

There can be only three forms of claims to the production of plants and animals: where only technical steps are recited; where only biological steps are recited; and where a mixture of technical and biological steps are recited, that is a 'mixed' claim. At first sight, the first form would seem clearly not to be excluded while the second form does seem to be excluded. Until G-2/07 Broccoli/PLANT BIOSCIENCE, this appeared to be the position adopted by the EPO.

Regarding the third ('mixed') claim format, on the question as to whether the inclusion of a single biological step is in and of itself enough to render the claim unallowable – that is the *contamination* approach adopted in relation to methods of surgery or therapy as discussed in Chapter 5 – the Enlarged Board in G-2/07 Broccoli/PLANT BIOSCIENCE held that the presence of the word 'essentially' precluded this. This tallies with the interpretation of van Empel, in one of the earliest commentaries on the EPC (van Empel 1975: 71), who stated that '[i]t appears that the word "essentially" is meant to convey the meaning that not only 100% biological processes are concerned … but also those processes that are fundamentally of this type'. In this context, van Empel referred to Document CM (62) 160, a document of the SPC *travaux préparatoires* mentioned above.

On the question as to whether a single technical step causes a claim to escape the exclusion – that is the *anything added* approach adopted in relation to computer program-related inventions as discussed in Chapter 3 – in G-2/07 Broccoli/PLANT BIOSCIENCE the Enlarged Board, correctly to our minds, rejected this, pointing out that such an approach is only valid for computer programs because of the 'as such' provision of Art. 52(3) EPC, a provision which has no analogue in Art. 53 EPC.

The third claim format (mixture of biological and technical steps) comprises two categories: where a technical step causes a genetic change; and where no genetic change is caused by a technical step. Of these, the second category seems clearly to be ruled out by the *travaux préparatoires* unless the product's characteristics are markedly changed, while the first might seem to be patentable if the mixed claim is to a process that is not 'essentially biological'. However, it should be kept in mind that the 'production' of plants and animals (i.e. growing them from fertilised cell to harvestable seed, plant or animal) in a process claim that may recite further *treatment* process steps (e.g. the coating of a seed) is itself very likely a conventional biological process, and so the overall claim is very likely dominated by an 'essentially biological process for the production' of a plant or animal. As TBoA 3.3.04 (Chairman Kinkeldey) commented in T-356/93 Plant cells/PLANT GENETIC SYSTEMS: 'A whole plant cannot be assimilated to a plant cell or tissue for the sole reason that it has acquired its characterising feature during the initial "microbiological" step of transforming the plant cell or tissue' (T-356/93: 582).

T-320/87 Hybrid plants/LUBRIZOL (Chairman Lançon) had provided several criteria for assessing whether a claimed process was 'essentially biological', including the requirement that '[t]he totality and the sequence of the specified operations neither occur in nature nor correspond to the classical breeders' processes' (T-320/87: 76–7). The Enlarged Board correctly rejected the approach taken in this decision:

> Basically, any approach that makes the decision on whether a claimed process for the production of plants is essentially biological and therefore excluded from patentability, or technical and therefore patentable, dependent on criteria which are determined by reference to the state of the art is flawed because it conflates the considerations which are relevant for patentability with those relevant for novelty and inventive step. Furthermore, such an approach is detrimental to legal certainty, since the qualification of a process as being patentable subject-matter or, on the contrary, excluded from patentability could then change with every new state of the art that comes to be considered in the various procedural stages which an application and a patent granted on it may run through during the whole lifetime of the patent. (G-2/07: 56)

The Enlarged Board noted that, with Art. 52(2) EPC exclusions, the effect of Art. 52(3) EPC was to allow one to determine whether claimed subject-matter was excluded without reference to the prior art and said that the same should apply for the essentially biological process exclusion. A similar approach had already been adopted by the Tribunal of Commerce of the Canton of Bern (Switzerland) in its 'Tetraploide Kamille' decision (CH-Tetraploide Kamille 1995).

To determine the meaning of the exclusion, the Enlarged Board felt that it was necessary to consider the purpose of the exclusion. Sadly, the Enlarged Board could not clearly identify that purpose from the text of the EPC but considered that the exclusion's position within Art. 53(b) EPC: 'only allows the conclusion that some kinds of processes must be excluded even though they are inventions, and that, hence, the exclusion must not be interpreted in such a way that it would be entirely deprived of any field of application and thereby rendered obsolete'

(G-2/07: 62). This sentiment, we hope, will spread to all future decisions on exclusions.

Reviewing the *travaux préparatoires*, in particular the passage from the 1961 Document EXP/Brev (61) 8 and the 1961 first preliminary draft of the CEPL, and noting that at that stage UPOV, which would give plant breeders *sui generis* rights to new plant varieties, was under discussion (it was adopted in December 1961), the Enlarged Board concluded that the legislators' intention was to exclude conventional plant breeding processes based on the sexual crossing of plants and the subsequent selection of plants having the desired traits – processes 'characterised by the fact that the traits of the plants resulting from the crossing were determined by the underlying natural phenomenon of meiosis' (G-2/07: 66).

The example of special greenhouses quoted above, according to the Enlarged Board:

> shows that the legislator did not wish breeding processes to be patented in which the technical measures used are only means serving to bring about processes for the production of plants which are otherwise based on biological forces. This is made abundantly clear by the additional remark in the explanatory notes that such technical devices may perfectly well be patented in themselves but not so the biological process in which they are used. (G-2/07: 66–7)

On the question as to whether the exclusion had become obsolete in view of the advance in technology, the Enlarged Board felt that the fact that the legislator did not want an extension of patent protection in the field of plant production was still a valid consideration. Thus the Board concluded that a process for the production of plants that is based on the sexual crossing of whole genomes and on the subsequent selection of plants, in which human intervention serves to enable or assist the performance of the process steps, remains excluded from patentability as essentially biological. Where a technical step by itself introduces a trait into the genome or modifies a trait in the genome, the Enlarged Board considered that the process has left the realm of plant breeding and is not excluded by Art. 53(b) EPC.

At this stage, the words of the Enlarged Board decision need to be quoted at some length, as they appear to make it clear that processes for the genetic modification of plants (or animals) cannot be claimed in such a way that progeny of the modified plants can receive protection as direct products of the claimed process:

> [The escape from the exclusion] applies only where [the gene modification] step is performed within the steps of sexually crossing and selection, independently from their number of repetitions. Otherwise the exclusion of sexual

crossing and selection processes from patentability under Article 53(b) EPC could be circumvented simply by adding steps which do not properly pertain to the crossing and selection process, being either upstream steps dealing with the preparation of the plant(s) to be crossed or downstream steps dealing with the further treatment of the plant resulting from such crossing and selection process. Any such additional technical steps which are performed either before or after the process of crossing and selection should therefore be ignored when determining whether or not the process is excluded from patentability under Art. 53(b) EPC. For the previous or subsequent steps per se patent protection is available. This is the case, for example, for genetic engineering techniques ... However, in such cases the claims should not, explicitly or implicitly, include the sexual crossing and selection process. As a result this means that, while the presence in a claim of one feature which could be characterised as biological does not necessarily result in the claimed process as a whole being excluded from patentability under Article 53(b) EPC, this does not apply where the process includes sexual crossing and selection. (G-2/07: 69–70)

So what does this conclusion mean? A mixed claim, that is one containing both technical and biological steps, cannot explicitly or implicitly include a crossing and selection unless the technical step is within the crossing and selection step and serves to genetically modify the plant (or animal). Where the technical step is a genetic engineering step, the product obtained directly from the claimed process cannot therefore be downstream progeny.

6.7 Implications

Where does G-2/07 Broccoli/PLANT BIOSCIENCE leave us? If a process does not involve technically modifying the genome during a crossing and selection step, it cannot be claimed in a way that covers a subsequent crossing and selection step. In other words, it cannot cover breeding true after a technical genome modification. Moreover, since crossing and selection is no more 'essentially biological' than planting and harvesting, it would seem that, according to G-2/07 Broccoli/PLANT BIOSCIENCE, the activities of the farmer are untouched by process claims. The actions of the breeder are only affected if she carries out the technical genome-altering step. In the Broccoli and Tomato patents, the process claims did not involve as the technical step a gene-modifying one, thus these claims should be revoked.

Where a technical step is simply one which improves yield or the like, for example the application of a fertiliser, as farming is no less essentially biological than breeding and as the *travaux préparatoires* show that the exclusion is not intended to be restricted to breeding processes, the process must be unpatentable if claimed as a method of producing plants or animals (rather than as a method of killing weeds or fertilising crops, etc.). The technical tool used must instead be patented in itself and not in use in a process. This interpretation of the exclusion is in line with the intention expressed in UPOV and the EPC *travaux préparatoires* to provide special treatment to farmers and breeders. Whether *plants and animals themselves* may properly be patented as products is the subject of the next chapter.

So, turning once more to the questions listed at the beginning of this chapter as to the correct interpretation of the exclusion, the answers would seem to be:

(1) Does the exclusion *only* apply to processes for producing new varieties of plant or animal? No.
(2) Can the exclusion be escaped by *specifying* the plant or animal at a *higher taxonomic level* than the lowest? No.
(3) Does the inclusion of *any non-biological step* in the process as claimed allow the process to escape the exclusion? No.
(4) Does the inclusion of *any biological step* in a claim to a multi-step process cause that process to be excluded? No.
(5) If the answers to (3) and (4) are no, then will the inclusion of *certain types of non-biological step* allow the process to escape exclusion, and, if so, which types? A claim can only be accepted if either the only or final step is a technical genome-modifying step, or the only step is a crossing and selection step within which a technical act serves to modify the genome (and not simply a pollen transfer since there the genome-modification occurs subsequently by natural means).

This is a rather unexpected but uplifting conclusion.[7]

As to Rule 26(5) EPC, clearly this is not in accordance with Art. 53(b) EPC. This was confirmed by the Enlarged Board in G-2/07 Broccoli/PLANT BIOSCIENCE (G-2/07: 31) and will of course lead to problems because the EPC is thus not compliant with the EBD. We can therefore expect an industry-led drive to amend EPC 2000 to permit patenting of all processes that are not entirely biological.

6.8 Products of 'essentially biological processes'

Art. 64 (2) EPC guarantees the holders of patents with process (or method or use) claims the ability to sue for infringement in relation to the direct product of the claimed process, whether or not that product is

[7] The Board's conclusion approximates to and even goes beyond the suggestion in Sterckx (2009) that process claims should only be accepted if the final step is technical.

itself patentable: 'If the subject-matter of the European patent is a process, the protection conferred by the patent shall extend to the products directly obtained by such process' (EPO 2010a: 120). This is of particular concern having regard to the Art. 53(b) EPC exclusion of 'essentially biological processes'. The subject was raised in the third question put to the EBoA in T-1054/96 (I) Transgenic plant/NOVARTIS: 'Should the provisions of Article 64(2) EPC be taken into account when considering what claims are allowable?' (T-1054/96 (I): 553).

In its referring decision, TBoA 3.3.04 (Chairman Kindeldey) commented that the practice of the EPO was to ignore this provision when assessing the patentability of process claims 'on the basis that this is a provision addressed not to patent offices but only to courts in the Contracting States concerned with considering alleged infringements' and that the 'drafters of the EPC saw no conflict here with the requirement under Articles 52(1) and 54 EPC that patents shall be granted for inventions that are new. The extension of the protection conferred on the patented process to cover a known product, was not considered a violation of the provisions of Articles 52 and 54 EPC.' The referring Board itself saw 'no conflict between on the one hand the plant variety indirectly enjoying patent protection as the direct product of a process under Article 64(2) EPC and on the other hand the plant variety as such not being patentable under Article 53(b) EPC' (T-1054/96 (I): 546).

While a proposal had been made in the drafting of the EPC to limit the product protection by the addition of the words 'insofar as such product is not a plant or animal variety excluded from patent protection under Article 53 of the European patent convention', this proposal was not followed through. Accordingly, the referring Board's position was that 'applicants in the field of plant breeding by recombinant-DNA-technique have … protection for plants produced by the method as long as they are *direct* products of the method claimed' (T-1054/96 (I): 548, emphasis added).

In response, the EBoA commented as follows:

For the avoidance of any doubt, question 3 is answered in conformity with the established case law according to which the protection conferred by a process patent is extended to the products obtained directly by the process, even if the products are not patentable per se (Case Law of the Boards of Appeal of the EPO … [current edition EPO 2010b]). This practice takes account of the purpose of the provision and is in accordance with its location in the EPC. The requirements on patentability to be examined by the EPO are contained in Part II, Chapter I EPC (Articles 52 to 57); Article 64(2) EPC belongs to Part II, Chapter III, containing provisions concerning the effects of patents and patent applications and is to be applied by the Courts responsible for deciding on infringement cases. The referring Board also comes to the conclusion that Article 64(2) EPC does not affect the examination of claims for the manufacture of plants ... The protection of the product obtained by a patented process is of particular importance in situations where product protection is not available. (G-1/98: 137)

Thus far, there seems to be total agreement. However, neither the referring decision nor the EBoA decision took explicit notice of the practice of patent applicants of drafting process claims which require one or more conventional process steps subsequent to the novel and inventive step in order that the direct product of the claimed process be the product of the last of those conventional steps, that is in order to cause the product protection to reach through to a downstream product, the process for the production of which may be essentially biological, for example a growing step. This omission, however, seems to have been redressed by the EBoA in the recent G-2/07 Broccoli/PLANT BIOSCIENCE decision:

[T]he exclusion of sexual crossing and selection processes from patentability under Article 53(b) EPC could be circumvented simply by adding steps which do not properly pertain to the crossing and selection process, being either upstream steps dealing with the preparation of the plant(s) to be crossed or downstream steps dealing with the further treatment of the plant resulting from such crossing and selection process ... *[I]n such cases the claims should not, explicitly or implicitly, include the sexual crossing and selection process.* (G-2/07: para. 6.4.2.3, emphasis added)

The answer would seem to be clear – a plant production process may not be claimed using a claim format, for example a reach-through claim, which makes the Art. 64(2) EPC 'direct product' protection extend beyond the product produced directly by a novel technical process step.

Besides coverage by reach-through process claims, the product of an essentially biological process could perhaps be claimed as a product per se or as a product-by-process (i.e. using a claim of the format 'novel plant or animal *obtainable by* the following essentially biological process'). In either case, the product must of course be new so the option is only available for products of breeding rather than farming.

The patentees in the Broccoli and Tomatoes cases took this approach following the issue of decisions G-2/07 Broccoli/PLANT BIOSCIENCES and G-1/08 Tomatoes/STATE OF ISRAEL, deleting the process claims and requesting maintenance of their patents with claims to the broccoli and tomatoes themselves. The opponents in the Broccoli case, the agrochemical companies Limagrain and

Syngenta, were prepared to accept this and the TBoA (3.3.04) likewise seemed to be willing to maintain the product claims and cancelled the oral proceedings that had been scheduled for October 2011.

In the Tomatoes case, however, the opponent (Unilever – a huge corporation, but not an agrochemical company) was not prepared to accept this. At the oral proceedings in November 2011, TBoA 3.3.04 (chaired by Romolo Gramaglia) decided to refer a further set of questions to the Enlarged Board, this time relating to the patentability of the products of an essentially biological process. Before posing its questions to the EBoA, the TBoA noted that: '[d]isregarding the process exclusion in the examination of product claims altogether would have the general consequence that for many plant breeding inventions patent applicants and proprietors could easily overcome the process exclusion of Article 53(b) EPC by relying on product claims providing a broad protection which encompasses that which would have been provided by an excluded process claim. At least *prima facie* this would appear to be at odds with a purposive construction of Article 53(b) EPC' (T-1242/06 (I2): para. 47). The Board continued, arguing that the exclusions from patent-eligibility: 'demonstrate that situations exist where an exclusion referring to specific processes ... may negatively affect the allowability of product claims' (T-1242/06 (I2): para. 52). In particular, the Board asserted that the finding of G-1/98 Transgenic plant/NOVARTIS II: 'can therefore not simply be extrapolated to the present case' (T-1242/06 (I2): para. 59). The wording of those questions referred to the EBoA are thus:

1. Can the exclusion of essentially biological processes for the production of plants in Article 53(b) EPC have a negative effect on the allowability of a product claim directed to plants or plant material such as a fruit?
2. In particular, is a claim directed to plants or plant material other than a plant variety allowable even if the only method available at the filing date for generating the claimed subject-matter is an essentially biological process for the production of plants disclosed in the patent application?
3. Is it of relevance in the context of questions 1 and 2 that the protection conferred by the product claim encompasses the generation of the claimed product by means of an essentially biological process for the production of plants excluded as such under Article 53(b) EPC? (T-1242/06 (I2): Order)

Shortly before the November 2011 hearing, one of the authors submitted an *amicus curiae* brief commenting as follows:

a patent claim to a product is *also infringed* by performance of a process for the production of that product. Accordingly, should you agree that these patents be maintained with the claims proposed by the patentees, then the public will be in no better situation than had the process claims been allowed. This cannot have been the intention either of the Enlarged Board or of the legislators of Art. 53 EPC … The problem arises since the plant products may be new. Normally where a new product X can be produced by an excluded process Y and by a non-excluded process Z, one might expect that claims to product X and non-excluded process Z might be permitted. However, where, *as is the case here*, product X can *only* be produced (on the basis of the patentees' disclosure)[8] by the *excluded* process Y, then, *if the Art. 53(b) EPC exclusion is to have any effect*, neither claims to X or Y should be permitted. Were the exclusion of 'essentially biological processes' to be interpreted in any other way, then it would only have effect in relation to the production of *known* plants and animals, i.e. farming rather than breeding. It should be noted that this explanation is unaffected by the development of genetic engineering techniques. (Correspondence *Sterckx* 2011: 3)

This decision to refer further questions to the EBoA represents a volte-face for TBoA 3.3.04, which, under the chairmanship of Christopher Rennie-Smith, had decided in May 2010, in T-1854/07 Oil from seeds/CONSEJO SUPERIOR, to ignore the relevance of the EBoA's decisions in G-2/07 Broccoli/PLANT BIOSCIENCE and G-1/08 Tomatoes/STATE OF ISRAEL and to accept claims to sunflowers obtainable by conventional breeding processes. The Board based its acceptance of those claims on the earlier EBoA decision G-1/98 Transgenic plant/NOVARTIS II:

Claim 1 refers to a product defined in terms of the process by which it is produced. Such 'product by process' claim remains a product claim irrespective of the process it refers to … [Opponent Greenpeace's] argument, that claim 1 refers to an essentially biological process for the protection of plants which is excluded from patentability according to Article 53(b) EPC, must therefore fail … G 1/98 [Transgenic plant/NOVARTIS II] makes clear beyond doubt that, whether or not a plant is considered to be a plant variety depends only on whether or not it meets the criteria set out in the definition in Rule 26(4) EPC … The method for its production, be it by recombinant gene technology or by a classical plant breeding process, is not relevant for answering this question. (T-1854/07: paras. 4–10.4)

The question as to whether novel plants, obtainable at the filing date only by an 'essentially biological process', can be protected by a

[8] In the case of a biological organism, e.g. a 'plant with property *X obtainable* by biological process Y', the *same* plant is *not* 'obtainable by' a genetic engineering process which modifies the plant's genetics to introduce property X. Thus a claim of this format is most likely neither infringed by, nor supported by, the production of a plant with this property by genetic engineering.

product claim has in the meantime been considered by the Dutch courts (NL-Taste of Nature 2012). The answer was that they probably could not (see Cockbain and Sterckx 2012). The case is under appeal with the patentee relying heavily on G-1/98 Transgenic plant/NOVRTIS II and T-1854/07 Oil from seeds/CONSEJO SUPERIOR.

It will be some time before the answer becomes clear – has the EBoA changed its spots after all?

6.9 The status quo

As of June 2011 the Guidelines relating to the exclusion of essentially biological processes for the production of plants and animals read as follows:

> When a process for the production of a plant variety is examined, Art. 64(2) is not to be taken into consideration (see G 1/98 [Transgenic plant/NOVARTIS II] ...). Hence a process claim for the production of a plant variety (or plant varieties) is not a priori excluded from patentability merely because the resulting product constitutes or may constitute a plant variety ... A process for the production of plants or animals which is based on the sexual crossing of whole genomes and on the subsequent selection of plants or animals is excluded from patentability as being essentially biological, even if other technical steps relating to the preparation of the plant or animal or its further treatment are present in the claim before or after the crossing and selection steps. To take some examples, a method of crossing, inter-breeding, or selectively breeding, say, horses involving merely selecting for breeding and bringing together those animals (or their gametes) having certain characteristics would be essentially biological and therefore unpatentable. This method remains essentially biological and unpatentable even if it contains an additional feature of a technical nature, for example, the use of genetic molecular markers to select either parent or progeny. On the other hand, a process involving inserting a gene or trait into a plant by genetic engineering does not rely on recombination of whole genomes and the natural mixing of plant genes, and is hence patentable. However, a claim to such a process may not contain crossing and selection steps. A process of treating a plant or animal to improve its properties or yield or to promote or suppress its growth, e.g. a method of pruning a tree, would not be essentially biological since although a biological process is involved the essence of the invention is technical; the same applies to a method of treating a plant characterised by the application of a growth-stimulating substance or radiation. The treatment of soil by technical means to suppress or promote the growth of plants is also not excluded from patentability. (EPO 2011: C-IV 10–11)

The EPO examiners may thus not yet have grasped the full implications of the G-2/07 Broccoli/PLANT BIOSCIENCE decision.

7 Plant and animal varieties

> A claim is not allowable if the grant of a patent in respect of the invention defined in said claim is conducive to an evasion of a provision of the EPC establishing an exception to patentability.
>
> (T-356/93: 581)

> [It] is the generally expressed view that the duty of the judges is to apply and not to create the law.
>
> (T-1054/96 (I): 530–1)

7.1 Introduction

The question as to whether plants and animals are a proper subject for patent rights remains highly controversial and has been addressed by the courts in several jurisdictions. In this chapter we will explain how the EPC's exclusion of plant and animal varieties has been side-stepped by the EPO and why this has problematic implications.

Art. 53(b) EPC provides that:

European patents shall not be granted in respect of:

...

(b) plant or animal varieties or essentially biological processes for the production of plants or animals; this provision shall not apply to microbiological processes or the products thereof. (EPO 2010a: 106)

This Article was not amended when the EPC was revised in 2000. However, in September 1999 amendments to the EPC Rules entered into force as a result of a decision by the Administrative Council of the EPO.[1] Some of the new Rules are relevant to the exclusion from patentability of plant and animal varieties. However, we should emphasise once again that, although Rules may be used to assist the interpretation

[1] The Rules were renumbered in EPC 2000 and, unless mentioned otherwise, we will refer to the numbers from EPC 2000 (EPO 2010a: 265–558). The new Rules that are relevant to the present chapter will be set out, where relevant, in footnotes.

of EPC Articles, they cannot change the scope of the Articles, hence they cannot broaden or narrow the scope of the exclusions from patentability under the EPC. If a conflict arises between a Rule and an Article, the Article prevails according to Art. 164(2) EPC.

We will first give an overview of the important TBoA and EBoA decisions on the exclusion of plant and animal varieties. This will be chronological, that is decisions regarding animals will be discussed 'amidst' plant cases, as Boards deciding on plant cases have sometimes relied on arguments from decisions in animal cases and vice versa. A chronological discussion will allow the reader to see how the arguments used by the different Boards have changed or continued to be repeated. The most important decisions will be described in greater detail. We will then provide our own comments on the ways in which this exclusion has been interpreted, and make some observations regarding the decision-making trends of particular TBoAs.

7.2 Plants: T-49/83 Propagating material/CIBA-GEIGY

Ciba-Geigy filed a patent application (Sturm *et al.* 1980) in August 1979 concerning a chemical treatment of plant propagating material (e.g. seeds) to provide resistance to agricultural chemicals. In April 1982 the Examining Division informed Ciba-Geigy that claim 13 ('Propagating material for cultivated plants, treated with an oxime derivative') and claim 14 ('Propagating material according to claim 13, characterised in that it consists of seed') were contrary to Art. 53(b) EPC.

In August 1982 Ciba-Geigy responded, arguing that no new plant variety was produced by the chemical treatment, since the genetic material was not altered and nothing was obtained that could be protected by plant breeders' rights. Consequently, Ciba-Geigy argued, the claimed propagating material could not be excluded by Art. 53(b) EPC. According to Ciba-Geigy, the legislator of the EPC did not intend to exclude plants and animals *as such* from patent protection, but only to forbid the patenting of new plant varieties that were protectable by special laws (e.g. UPOV). The claimed propagating material was said to be analogous to other industrial materials, for example brewing yeast (Correspondence *Ciba-Geigy* 1982: 1–3).

In October 1982 the Examining Division issued its decision, rejecting the application. The Examining Division observed that claims 13 and 14 related to the propagating material of *any* cultivated plants that had been chemically treated in a particular way, including that of known plant varieties, and that Art. 53(b) EPC applied not only to new but also to known plant varieties.

Ciba-Geigy appealed, arguing that only plant 'varieties' were excluded by Art. 53(b) EPC and that the use by the legislator of the different terms 'plant varieties' and 'plants' implied that they could not have the same meaning. Moreover, according to Ciba-Geigy, the term 'plant variety' related to products of biological breeding, whereas their invention was not an 'essentially biological' but an 'essentially technical' invention. Reference was made to Art. 64(2) EPC, which provides that, if the subject-matter of a European patent is a process, the protection extends to the products directly obtained by that process. This was said to apply, in accordance with the Guidelines for Examination in the European Patent Office, to the products of technical processes for treating plants and animals to improve their properties. Rainer Schulte's commentary on German patent law and the EPC was referred to, according to which a plant that cannot be patented *as such* under Art. 53(b) EPC could nonetheless get patent protection as a direct product of a patented non-biological process (Schulte 1981: 120). The legislator had not intended to exclude 'essentially technical' inventions involving plants and animals, Ciba-Geigy argued, and their invention had to be patentable as it concerned a technical process and its direct products. The claimed treatment only affected the treated individuals and was not transferred to subsequent generations. The term 'variety' was said to have no relevance since the definition of a 'plant variety' identified a particular taxonomic level (Correspondence *Ciba-Geigy* 1983).

TBoA 3.3.01 (Chairman Cadman) overruled the Examining Division and commented as follows on the meaning of the term 'plant variety':

> The skilled person understands the term 'plant varieties' to mean a multiplicity of plants which are largely the same in their characteristics and remain the same within specific tolerances after every propagation or every propagation cycle. This definition is reflected in [UPOV 1961], which is intended to give the breeder of a new plant variety a protective right ... *Plant varieties in this sense are all cultivated varieties, clones, lines, strains and hybrids which can be grown in such a way that they are clearly distinguishable from other varieties, sufficiently homogeneous, and stable in their essential characteristics* ... The legislator did not wish to afford patent protection under the European Patent Convention to plant varieties of this kind, whether in the form of propagating material or of the plant itself. (T-49/83: 114, emphasis added)

According to the Board: '[e]ven if certain known varieties of wheat, millet and barley are mentioned in the examples in [the patent specification], *the subject-matter* of claims 13 and 14 *is not an individual variety of plant distinguishable from any other variety*, but the claims relate to any cultivated plants in the form of their propagating material which have been chemically treated in a certain way' (T-49/83: 115, emphasis added). The Board concluded from this that Art. 53(b) EPC did not prohibit the patenting of the subject-matter of these claims, for this Article 'prohibits only the patenting of plants or their propagating material in the genetically fixed form of the plant variety' (T-49/83: 115).

It was further noted that the first half-sentence of Art. 53(b) EPC implied that the concepts of 'plants' and 'plant varieties' cannot have the same meaning. Plant varieties were to be excluded 'mainly because' several of the signatory states to the EPC had developed *sui generis* protection for plant breeding (T-49/83: 115). The Board observed that the wording of Art. 53(b) EPC had been copied from Art. 2(b) SPC and added: 'Even at that time the majority of the States represented on the Council of Europe were already of the opinion that plant varieties should be protected not by patents but by a special industrial property right ... *By contrast, the innovation claimed here does not lie within the sphere of plant breeding, which is concerned with the genetic modification of plants*' (T-49/83: 115, emphasis added). It was also suggested that Art. 53(b) EPC was intended to exclude from patentability *only* new plant varieties that could be protected by plant breeders' rights:

> The new parameter for the propagating material, namely treatment with an oxime derivative, is not a criterion which can be characteristic of a plant variety as far as the protection of varieties is concerned. There is therefore no conflict between the protection of varieties or the patent as different forms of protection for propagating material treated in this way. In fact, patent protection is the only possibility ... If plant varieties have been excluded from patent protection because specifically the achievement involved in breeding a new variety is to have its own form of protection, it is perfectly sufficient for the exclusion to be left restricted, in conformity with its wording, to cases in which plants are characterized precisely by the genetically determined peculiarities of their natural phenotype ... On the other hand, innovations which cannot be given the protection afforded to varieties are still patentable if the general prerequisites are met. (T-49/83: 115–16)

On the basis of these arguments, the Board decided in July 1983 that Art. 53(b) EPC did not preclude the patenting of the claimed propagating material.[2] The case was remitted to the Examining Division for further prosecution and the patent (Sturm *et al.* 1985) was granted in March 1985.

[2] At about the same time, the same TBoA came to essentially the same conclusions in another Ciba-Geigy case (T-34/83 CIBA-GEIGY).

7.3 Plants: T-320/87 Hybrid plants/LUBRIZOL

Lubrizol Genetics filed a patent application in July 1981 (Lawrence and Hill 1982) which was refused by the Examining Division in May 1987. Claims 1, 10 and 17 related to processes for rapidly developing hybrids and commercially producing hybrid seeds in general (Claims 1 and 10) or belonging to the genus *Brassica* (Claim 17). According to the Examining Division, these claims were directed at essentially biological processes for the production of plants, which are excluded from patentability under Art. 53(b) EPC. We will not elaborate on that ground here, as it is addressed in Chapter 6.

Lubrizol appealed and filed new claims during the oral proceedings before TBoA 3.3.02 (Chairman Lançon) in November 1988. Claim 20 read as follows:

> Hybrid seed that yields plants that are phenotypically uniform, said seed having been produced by a process comprising: (a) selecting a heterozygous first parent plant and selecting a second parent plant; (b) crossing said first parent plant with said second parent plant to obtain original-parent-derived hybrids that are phenotypically uniform; (c) cloning said first parent plant to produce a first cloned parental line; (d) crossing plants of said first cloned parental line with said second parent plant ... to obtain hybrid seeds which yields hybrids that are phenotypically uniform ... and (e) repeating steps (c) and (d) as required to obtain hybrid seed that yields phenotypically uniform hybrid plants. (T-320/87: 73)

Claim 21 was directed to: 'Phenotypically uniform hybrid plants produced from hybrid seed according to Claim 20.' According to Lubrizol, these products were not protectable by breeders' rights since they were hybrid populations and not varieties. Consequently, denying patent protection would leave these products unprotected (T-320/87: 74).

The TBoA noted that the product claims were drafted as 'product-by-process' claims and observed that, since the claimed products were not 'individually definable biological entities, which could be characterised by their physiological or morphological features', there was no way of defining the seeds and plants other than by the processes for their production (T-320/87: 75–6).

As to the question whether the claimed plants and seeds were to be considered as 'plant varieties' and hence as unpatentable, the Board first noted that:

> The term 'variety' is not defined in the European Patent Convention at all. There is further no generally recognised taxonomic definition for 'variety' as there is for 'species' or 'genus'. In the case of the particular exception to

patentability with regard to plant varieties, the legal history of Article 53(b) EPC makes it clear that plant varieties were excluded from patent protection under the EPC *mainly because* several of the Signatory States had developed special legal protection for plant breeding at national and international level (UPOV Convention) and were of the opinion that *such special protection was better adapted to meet the interests of plant breeders*. (T-320/87: 79, emphasis added)

The Board referred to the description of 'plant varieties' in T-49/83 Propagating material/CIBA-GEIGY, discussed earlier, and concluded that the characteristics of 'homogeneity' and 'stability' were prerequisites for a 'plant variety' (T-320/87: 79). That approach led the Board to argue that:

[As the claims are] defined by general processes in which at least one of the parent plants used as a source for the whole processes is heterozygous with respect to a certain trait and therefore will never breed true, it appears that the claimed hybrid seeds or plants, *considered as a whole generation population*, are not stable ... and therefore cannot be considered as a 'variety'. As emphasized by [Lubrizol] during the whole procedure, stability ... is not aimed at, let alone guaranteed. On the contrary, the invention relies on going back repeatedly to the parent plants for further propagation by cloning because the hybrids resulting from the crossing of the parent plants ... do not provide plants which, when further sexually propagated, remain stable with respect to certain desired features. Even if the totality of the hybrid generation resulting from the crosses of the cloned selected parent plants were to comprise single individual plants which would be stable for a certain trait when further crossed and propagated, this fact does not in itself contradict the stated non-stability of the population taken as a whole. Furthermore, such single individual plants are not to be construed as embraced within the subject-matter of the product claim. (T-320/87: 79–80, emphasis added)

This is an example of the *higher taxonomic level* approach referred to in Chapter 3.

Consequently the Board decided in November 1988 that the claimed seed and plants could not be regarded as 'plant varieties' within the meaning of Art. 53(b) EPC. The case was remitted to the Examining Division but was later deemed to be withdrawn because Lubrizol did not reply to a communication from the Examining Division.

7.4 Animals: T-19/90 Onco-mouse/HARVARD

A patent application (Leder and Stewart 1986) was filed in June 1985, by the president and fellows of Harvard College, concerning animals whose germ and somatic cells contained an activated oncogene sequence inserted into the animal, or an ancestor, at an embryonic stage. The presence of such an oncogene increases the probability that the animals develop tumours. It was thought that such 'onco-animals' could be used to test materials thought to cause cancers, by exposing the animals to the material in question and subsequently determining neoplastic growth as an indicator of carcinogenicity. The patent specification also mentioned that the animals could be used to test materials that were thought to confer protection against tumour growth. It was explicitly stated that 'any species of transgenic animal can be employed' (Leder and Stewart 1986: 18).

The main product claim initially was claim 17: 'A transgenic non-human eukaryotic animal [i.e. one whose cells contain a nucleus] whose germ cells and somatic cells contain an activated oncogene sequence introduced into said animal, or an ancestor of said animal, at an embryonic stage' (Leder and Stewart 1986: 21).

After oral proceedings, the application was rejected by the Examining Division in July 1989, inter alia on the grounds of Art. 53(b) EPC. The following reasons were given:

> Article 53(b) EPC ... is interpreted by the Examining Division to refer not only to cases where a specifically designated variety is claimed but also to cases where varieties are covered by a claim ... The restrictive interpretation of the exclusion of plant varieties [in T-49/83 Propagating material/CIBA-GEIGY and T-320/87 Hybrid plants/LUBRIZOL] is ... justified by the limited purpose of the provision to exclude from patent protection only such subject-matter which is eligible for plant variety protection ... No similar situation exists in the field of animals ... *The idea behind the [exclusion of animal varieties] was that animal varieties are not an appropriate subject-matter for patent protection* ... Moreover, if Article 53(b) EPC is considered in the three official languages it is apparent that with regard to plants the legislator used identical designations in all three languages whereas this is not the case with respect to animals ... *This is a further indication that the legislator's intention was not the exclusion of some particular group of animals but rather the exclusion of animals in general* ... [The second part of Art. 53(b) EPC] has to be interpreted in the light of the first part; if the product of a process is something which falls under the manifest exclusion of the first part of said article, the second part cannot be interpreted as setting aside the first part. (Correspondence *EPO* 1989: 4–8, emphasis added)

In the case of animals, the Examining Division was thus applying what was referred to in Chapter 3 as the *novelty* approach, that is that claims should be rejected if they encompass excluded subject-matter.

Harvard appealed and in October 1990, in T-19/90 Onco-mouse/HARVARD, TBoA 3.3.02 (Chairman Lançon) first noted that a comparison of the German, French and English texts of Art. 53(b) EPC revealed that the German term ('*Tierarten*') was broader than the French and English terms ('*races animales*' and 'animal varieties') and that their common meaning had to be established through interpretation of the EPC (T-19/90: 486).

The Board considered that the Examining Division had not taken into account that any exception to patentability 'must ... be narrowly construed' (T-19/90: 486). In the Board's view, Art. 53(b) EPC applied to certain categories of animals ('animal varieties') but not to animals 'as such'. TBoA 3.3.02, as in its earlier decision T-320/87 Hybrid plants/LUBRIZOL, was thus applying the *higher taxonomic level* approach once again.

Moreover, the Board suggested that, in view of the second half-sentence of Art. 53(b) EPC, animals were patentable if they were the product of a microbiological process:

> The Examining Division did not decide whether the present invention involves a microbiological process, taking the view that Article 53(b), second half-sentence, EPC does not apply if the product (in this case the animal) is excluded under the first half-sentence on the grounds that the second part of the provision cannot be interpreted in a manner which would set aside the first part. The Board does not share this view ... [T]he general principle of patentability under Article 52(1) EPC is restored for inventions involving microbiological processes and the products of such processes. Consequently, patents are grantable for *animals* produced by a microbiological process. The Examining Division must therefore consider, should the case arise, whether the claimed processes constitute microbiological processes within the meaning of Article 53(b) EPC.[3] (T-19/90: 489–90, emphasis added)

The case was remitted to the Examining Division to determine whether the claimed genetically modified animals fell within the meaning of the term 'animal varieties', as well as to consider the case in the light of Art. 53(a) EPC (the 'morality clause' – see Chapter 8). In December 1990 the Examining Division invited Harvard to comment. Harvard responded in April 1991, noting that the claims were 'generically drafted' and did not 'relate to other than a particular general class of animals' (Correspondence *Harvard* 1991: 4). Reference was also made to T-320/87 Hybrid plants/LUBRIZOL. All the Examining Division needed to do, according to Harvard, was 'to recognise that the animal claims in the present Application are generic claims and do not contain claims to individual varieties' (Correspondence *Harvard* 1991: 4–5).

In support of claims to animal generations after the genetically manipulated animals, Harvard further noted that:

[3] The line of argument that the second half-sentence of Art. 53(b) EPC could overrule the first was later found to be incorrect in G-1/98 Transgenic plant/NOVARTIS II (see section 7.8).

Obviously, on simple practical grounds the extent of protection is unreasonable and of commercially very little significance if it extends only to the direct product of the first genetic manipulation. A reasonable balance, in contrast, is struck by allowing protection for any animal directly derived from the original genetic manipulation step, even if involving a multiplicity of subsequent breeding. Furthermore, society's interest in excluding certain categories of animals is met, it is respectfully submitted, by an exclusion from patentability which reads on to the products of conventional breeding only. (Correspondence *Harvard* 1991: 10)

In May 1992 the patent was granted (Leder and Stewart 1992) with claims directed to a 'transgenic non-human mammalian animal'. Further developments in this case resulted in T-315/03 Transgenic animals/HARVARD, which is discussed in section 7.13.

7.5 Plants: T-356/93 Plant cells/PLANT GENETIC SYSTEMS

Plant Genetic Systems (PGS) applied for a patent in January 1987. The patent (Leemans *et al.* 1990) was granted in October 1990 and related to the genetic engineering of plants to make them resistant to herbicides that operate by the inhibition of glutamine synthetase, an essential enzyme for plant cells. As stated in the patent specification:

[T]he invention also relates to a process, which can be generally defined as a process for producing plants and reproduction material of said plants including a heterologous genetic material *stably integrated therein* ... comprising the non biological steps of producing plant cells or plant tissue including said heterologous genetic material ... regenerating plants or reproduction material of said plants or both from said plant cells or plant tissue including said genetic material and, optionally, biologically replicating said last mentioned plants or reproduction material or both ... and to cause the stable integration of said [genetic material] ... in said plant cells and tissue, as well as in the plant and reproduction material processed therefrom throughout generations ... More generally the invention relates to plant cells, reproduction material, particularly seeds, as well as plants containing a foreign or heterologous DNA fragment stably integrated in their respective genomic DNAs, *said fragments being transferred throughout generations of such plant cells, reproduction material, seeds and plants.* (Leemans *et al.* 1990: 7–8, emphasis added)

In the description of the experiments carried out on tobacco plants, the patent mentions inter alia that 'resistant F1 [i.e. first generation] seedlings are grown to maturity and seeds are harvested. F2 seedlings are grown ... and tested for ... resistance [by spraying a herbicide]. Some of the F1 plants produce F2 seedlings which are all ... resistant showing that these plants are homozygous for the resistance gene' (Leemans *et al.* 1990: 19).

The patent included claims to processes for producing plants and reproduction material of plants, as well as to plant cells, seeds and plants per se. We will only focus on the latter here. Claim 21 was directed to a 'Plant, non biologically transformed, which possesses, *stably integrated in the genome of its cells*, a foreign DNA nucleotide sequence encoding a protein having a non-variety-specific enzymatic activity capable of neutralizing or inactivating a glutamine synthetase inhibitor under the control of a promoter recognized by the polymerases of said cells' (Leemans *et al.* 1990: 24, emphasis added).

Greenpeace opposed the patent, inter alia on the basis of Art. 53(b) EPC. As to the issue of 'plant varieties', Greenpeace referred to the definition provided in T-49/83 Propagating material/CIBA-GEIGY and T-320/87 Hybrid plants/LUBRIZOL, discussed above, and also argued that:

> It is impossible to make technical or legal sense of the exclusion from patenting of plant varieties ... while at the same time permitting the patenting of plants, cells and seeds ... In fact the invention might be almost useless in economic terms if applied to a multiplicity of plants not being a variety. This view is supported by the fact that the claimed invention has already been applied to varieties during field trials ... The Opponents deny the applicability of the decisions taken in Lubrizol ... and Ciba-Geigy ... In contrast to the claims in these decisions, the aforementioned claims are of potential economic importance far beyond the F1 generation. (Correspondence *Greenpeace* 1991: 10–11)

In response, PGS argued that the claims to plants were not prohibited by Art. 53(b) EPC as none of the claims was 'directed to' a plant variety or referred to 'a specific plant variety or phenotype'. Moreover, according to PGS, the plants in question were the products of 'microbiological processes' and 'hence not subject to any exclusion from patentability under Art. 53(b)' EPC (Correspondence *Plant Genetic Systems* 1992: 13).

The Opposition Division agreed with PGS and maintained the patent as granted. Greenpeace appealed, arguing inter alia that:

> It is axiomatic that if a thing within the scope of a claim is not patentable, it cannot be made patentable by extending the claim to cover other things ... If a plant variety is within the claim (as is admitted [by the Patentee as well as the Opposition Division]), it plainly cannot be said that the claim does not claim a plant variety because it also claims other things. (Correspondence *Greenpeace* 1993: 8–9)

Greenpeace were thus arguing for the *novelty* approach.

TBoA 3.3.04 (Chairman Kinkeldey) investigated the meaning of the concept of 'plant varieties' and noted that, in T-49/83 Propagating material/CIBA-GEIGY and T-320/87 Hybrid plants/LUBRIZOL, this concept had been interpreted with reference to UPOV. The Board provided the following definition of 'plant varieties' for the purposes of Art. 53(b) EPC:

[A]ny plant grouping within a single botanical taxon of the lowest known rank which, irrespective of whether it would be eligible for protection under the UPOV Convention, is characterised by at least one single transmissible characteristic distinguishing it from other plant groupings and which is sufficiently homogeneous and stable in its relevant characteristics ... *Plant cells* as such, which modern technology allows to culture much like bacteria and yeasts, cannot be considered to fall under the definition of a plant or of a plant variety ... plant cells are considered to be 'microbiological products' in the broad sense under the current practice of the EPO ... *A product claim which embraces within its subject-matter 'plant varieties' as just defined ... is not patentable under Article 53(b) EPC*, first half-sentence. (T-356/93: 571, emphasis added)

The Board was thus approving the *novelty* approach and, applying this line of reasoning to claim 21 qucted above, the Board noted that:

The subject-matter of [this claim] differs decisively from the subject-matter dealt with in decisions T 49/83 [Propagating material/CIBA-GEIGY] and T 320/87 [Hybrid plants/LUBRIZOL] ... in that it relates to genetically modified plants which remain stable in their modified characteristic(s). The stated characterising feature of the claimed plant is, in fact, transmitted in a stable manner in the plants and seeds throughout succeeding generations ... The working examples in the patent in suit relate to the production of transformed plants from known varieties ... It is shown with tobacco plants that the plants transformed in this way display normal fertility and that the second generation seedlings are homozygous for the resistance gene. Thus, the transformed plants or seeds of the working examples, *irrespective of whether they would meet the conditions for the grant of a breeder's right*, are plant varieties as they [are] distinguishable, uniform and stable in their relevant characteristics. ... Claim 21 defines plants which, regardless of whether or not they belong to any particular variety, are distinguished from all other plants by the stated specific characteristic which is transmitted in a stable manner to the progeny ... [T]he practical forms of realisation of the invention according to claim 21 are 'genetically transformed' plant varieties ... *even though this claim is not drafted in terms of a variety description.* (T-356/93: 579–80, emphasis added)

Hence, the Board concluded that the genetically modified plants *were* plant varieties and that claims to such plants could only be allowable if they were the product of a microbiological process. However, the Board argued that this was not the case and made the following general comment on the reason underlying the 'exception to the exception':

In the light of the historical documentation, the inclusion of [the second half-sentence] may be explained by the legislator's intention to make it absolutely clear that the EPC must provide patent protection for industrially applicable processes involving micro-organisms and for their products. This clarification was most certainly considered useful in order to prevent the exclusion from patentability from being extended to processes using eukaryotic micro-organisms which could be fitted into the pattern of the plant or animal kingdoms (e.g. some fungi, plant cells, animal cells). (T-356/93: 573)

In this context, the Board also referred to T-19/90 Onco-mouse/HARVARD and noted that it followed from this decision that 'animal varieties' were patentable if they were the product of a microbiological process, and added that this principle applied *mutatis mutandis* to *plant* varieties[4] (T-356/93: 573–4).

As to the interpretation of the term 'micro-organism', the Board noted that it includes 'all generally unicellular organisms with dimensions beneath the limits of vision which can be propagated and manipulated in a laboratory' (T-356/93: 575) (i.e. not only bacteria and yeasts, but also fungi, algae, protozoa, cells of human, animal and plant origin, plasmids and viruses). This was said to imply that 'genetic engineering processes carried out on vegetable cells may be defined as "microbiological processes" and their products, namely *genetically modified vegetable cells and their cultures*, may be defined as "the products thereof"' (T-356/93: 576, emphasis added).

In general terms, according to the Board, the concept of 'microbiological processes' refers to 'processes in which micro-organisms ... or their parts, are used to make or to modify products or in which new microorganisms are developed for specific uses'. The 'products thereof' hence 'encompasses products which are made or modified by micro-organisms as well as new micro-organisms as such' (T-356/93: 576). This then gave rise to the question as to whether a multi-step process for producing plants, including at least one microbiological step, could *as a whole* be regarded as a 'microbiological process' and whether, consequently, the transgenic plants resulting from the multi-step process could be considered as the products of microbiological processes.

The Board, rightly in our view, found that the concept of 'microbiological processes' may *not* be extended to include all the steps of 'technical processes comprising a succession of steps, wherein at least one essential step is of a microbiological nature'. The Board commented that: '"technical processes including a microbiological step" may not simply be equated with "microbiological processes". Nor can the resulting final products of such technical processes (e.g. plant varieties) be

[4] As noted earlier, this view was later considered to be mistaken by the EBoA (see section 7.8).

defined as "products of microbiological processes" within the meaning of Article 53(b), second half-sentence, EPC' (T-356/93: 577). Indeed, the Board is right that even if a microbiological process is involved at some stage in the production of something, that does not necessarily make that something the product of a microbiological process. Otherwise *all* plants and all animals that result from fusion of gametes would qualify as products of microbiological processes and hence the exclusion of varieties and essentially biological processes for the production of plants and animals would have no effect.

With regard to the case at issue, the Board observed that:

> The plant according to claim 21 is produced by a multi-step process ... which, in addition to the initial microbiological process step ... comprises the step of regenerating plants from the transformed plant cells or tissue and the step of reproducing the plant material. The initial microbiological process step undeniably has a decisive impact on the final result because by virtue of this step the plant acquires its characterising feature that is transmitted throughout generations ... However, the board observes that the subsequent steps of regenerating and reproducing the plants have an important added value and contribute, although in a different manner, to the final result as well. These two process steps involve complex phenomena and events such as cell differentiation, morphogenesis and reproduction and may, therefore, not be equated to the much simpler process step of multiplying and propagating transformed plant cells or tissue in culture, which is a typical microbiological process ... It is the controlled performance and/or successful occurrence of all these phases and events which will then allow the 'imprinted' plant cells or tissue to develop into a whole plant. Such a plant is not identical to the initial starting product (the transformed plant cells or tissue) in spite of the fact that it contains the same characterising genetic information. A whole plant cannot be assimilated to a plant cell or tissue for the sole reason that it has acquired its characterising feature during the initial 'microbiological' step of transforming the plant cell or tissue. (T-356/93: 581–2)

Hence the Board concluded that the plants in question could not be regarded as the products of a microbiological process.

The Board did accept that 'modern multi-step processes for producing plants involving genetic engineering techniques' are not excluded from patentability by the first half-sentence of Art. 53(b) EPC (T-356/93: 577). This, however, is an observation with regard to the patentability of certain *processes* for the production of plants. It does *not* imply in any way that, if a multi-step process for the production of plants involving a genetic engineering step produces a plant variety, such a *product* would escape the first half-sentence of Art. 53(b) EPC by the application of the second-half sentence of the provision.

In the end, the PGS patent was maintained in an amended form from which all the claims to seeds and plants had been deleted.

7.6 Plants: G-3/95 Inadmissible referral

Although T-356/93 Plant cells/PLANT GENETIC SYSTEMS was decided by TBoA 3.3.04 in February 1995, the decision was only issued in written form in April 1995. Barely three months later, in July 1995, the president of the EPO (Paul Braendli) referred the following question to the EBoA: 'Does a claim which relates to plants or animals but wherein specific plant or animal varieties are not individually claimed contravene the prohibition on patenting in Article 53(b) EPC if it embraces plant or animal varieties?' (G-3/95: 170). Thus the president was asking whether the *novelty* or the *higher taxonomic level* approach was correct.

Explaining the reasons for his referral, the president argued that he considered that different Boards of Appeal had given different decisions on the referred question. More specifically, he considered that T-356/93 Plant cells/PLANT GENETIC SYSTEMS (issued by TBoA 3.3.04) was in conflict with T-49/83 Propagating material/CIBA-GEIGY (issued by TBoA 3.3.01) and with T-19/90 Onco-mouse/HARVARD (issued by TBoA 3.3.02). The conflict, according to the president, was due to the conclusion of TBoA 3.3.04 in T 356/93 Plant cells/PLANT GENETIC SYSTEMS that a 'product claim which embraces within its subject-matter "plant varieties" ... is not patentable under Article 53(b) EPC', for this conclusion amounted to a general statement of legal principle which contradicted T-49/83 Propagating material/CIBA-GEIGY and T-19/90 Onco-mouse/HARVARD (G-3/95: 174–5). According to the president, Art. 53(b) EPC had to be interpreted in line with T-49/83 Propagating material/CIBA-GEIGY as only excluding a claim that defined *specific* plant varieties *individually* (G-3/95: 175). Clearly, therefore, the president considered the *higher taxonomic level* approach to be correct.

However, the EBoA perceived no conflict between T-356/93 Plant cells/PLANT GENETIC SYSTEMS and T-19/90 Onco-mouse/HARVARD, for, with regard to the referral question, the latter decision only noted that the meaning of the term 'animal variety' (or '*race animale*' or '*Tierart*') differed from the meaning of 'animals as such' and that 'animals as such' were not excluded from patentability under Art. 53(b) EPC (G-3/95: 177).

Regarding any conflict between T-356/93 Plant cells/PLANT GENETIC SYSTEMS and T-49/83 Propagating material/

CIBA-GEIGY, the EBoA paid particular attention to one of the two main arguments put forward by Greenpeace in an *amicus curiae* brief, which became the most prominent argument during the appeal proceedings, namely that the main product claim was directed to plants which had been genetically modified in order to make them herbicide-resistant and that the introduced characteristic of herbicide-resistance was distinctive and stable in subsequent generations. Greenpeace had submitted that, from these facts, it could be concluded that *the genetic modification itself made the plants 'plant varieties' in the UPOV sense of the term* and consequently that they had to be excluded under Art. 53(b) EPC. According to the EBoA, the essential basis for the conclusion in T-356/93 Plant cells/PLANT GENETIC SYSTEMS that the product claim was not allowable was precisely this argument and *not* the argument that the claim *encompassed* known plant varieties (the other of Greenpeace's two main arguments, which was the argument that the president had thought generated a conflict with T-49/83 Propagating material/CIBA-GEIGY and T-19/90 Onco-mouse/HARVARD) (G-3/95: 177–8). Hence the EBoA concluded that there was no conflict between T-356/93 Plant cells/PLANT GENETIC SYSTEMS and T-49/83 Propagating material/CIBA-GEIGY and T-19/90 Onco-mouse/HARVARD, since neither of the latter two were concerned with the point of law that was decided in T 356/93 Plant cells/PLANT GENETIC SYSTEMS (G-3/95: 180). It was therefore decided, in November 1995, that the president's referral was inadmissible.

However, there *was* a conflict between T-356/93 Plant cells/PLANT GENETIC SYSTEMS and T-19/90 Onco-mouse/HARVARD. When TBoA 3.3.02 remitted Harvard's application to the Examining Division, it stated that 'The proper issue to be considered is … whether or not the subject-matter of the application *is an* "animal variety" ("*race animale*", "*Tierart*") within the meaning of Article 53(b) EPC' (T-19/90: 487, emphasis added). This clearly exemplifies the *higher taxonomic level* approach to the exclusion and a denial of the *novelty* approach that was applied by TBoA 3.3.04 in T-356/93 Plant cells/PLANT GENETIC SYSTEMS. The president's referral should therefore have been admitted.

7.7 Plants: T-1054/96 (I) Transgenic plant/NOVARTIS

Novartis filed a patent application (Ryals *et al.* 1991) in March 1991 concerning the control of plant pathogens in agricultural crops. Some of the claims were directed to genetically modified plants comprising in their genomes specific foreign genes, the expression of which resulted in the production of substances that could kill or inhibit the growth of pathogens. As of May 1995, claim 19 read as follows:

A transgenic plant and the seed thereof comprising recombinant DNA sequences encoding

(a) one or more lytic peptides, which is not lysozyme, in combination with;
(b) one or more chitinases; and/or
(c) one or more ß-1,3-glucanases in a synergistically effective amount.

The Examining Division refused the application in June 1996 because, in its view, this claim and three other similar claims were not allowable under Art. 53(b) EPC. In this regard, the Examining Division drew a parallel with T-356/93 Plant cells/PLANT GENETIC SYSTEMS.

Novartis appealed in July 1996, and in its Statement of Grounds of Appeal argued that T-356/93 Plant cells/PLANT GENETIC SYSTEMS was based on an incorrect interpretation of Art. 53(b) EPC. Claim 19, according to Novartis, related to a broadly applicable technical contribution that could only be protected by patents, and discrimination of those who provide such contributions, by refusing them patents, had to be avoided (T-1054/96 (I): 515). This argument was clearly inspired by the words of Art. 27(1) TRIPS.

Novartis did admit that the claim would encompass plant varieties, but argued that Art. 53(b) EPC is concerned with the *form* of a claim, rather than with what the claim *covers*, hence a formal or literal (i.e. *higher taxonomic level*) rather than a substantive (i.e. *novelty*) approach needed to be applied. According to Novartis, as long as the form of the claim was at a *higher taxonomic level* than a variety, the claim could not be rejected under Art. 53(b) EPC. Only claims restricted to a variety are not allowed according to this line of reasoning (T-1054/96 (I): 518).

TBoA 3.3.04 (Chairman Kinkeldey), which in its earlier decision T-356/93 Plant cells/PLANT GENETIC SYSTEMS had supported the *novelty* approach, referred the following four questions to the EBoA:[5]

(1) To what extent should the instances of the EPO examine an application in respect of whether the claims are allowable in view of the provision of Article 53(b) EPC that patents shall not be granted in respect of plant

[5] The referral was made in the TBoA's written decision, which was issued on 6 July 1998, i.e. on the very same day that the EBD was published.

varieties or essentially biological processes for the production of plants, which provision does not apply to microbiological processes or the products thereof, and how should a claim be interpreted for this purpose?

(2) Does a claim which relates to plants but wherein specific plant varieties are not individually claimed ipso facto avoid the prohibition on patenting in Article 53(b) EPC even though it embraces plant varieties?

(3) Should the provisions of Article 64(2) EPC be taken into account when considering what claims are allowable?

(4) Does a plant variety, in which each individual plant of that variety contains at least one specific gene introduced into an ancestral plant by recombinant gene technology, fall outside the provision of Article 53(b) EPC that patents shall not be granted in respect of plant varieties or essentially biological processes for the production of plants, which provision does not apply to microbiological processes or the products thereof? (T-1054/96 (I): 552–3)[6]

In the thorough explanation accompanying this referral, with regard to the first question, the Board distinguished between a 'substantive approach' (i.e. the *novelty* approach) and a 'literal approach' (i.e. the *higher taxonomic level* approach) and noted that:

On [the literal approach], all that is required of the patent office is to check that the words 'plant variety' (or the equivalent French and German terms) do not appear in any claims. If these words do not appear, then Article 53(b) EPC is satisfied in relation to a claim to a plant. This would make examination for conformity with Article 53(b) EPC a very facile procedure …

The Board has difficulty in believing that the drafters of the EPC (and those of the Strasbourg Convention) would have included the provision of Article 53(b) EPC merely to prevent these words appearing in a claim, but without intending the provision to have any substantive function. The purpose suggested for this provision by the Appellant was to achieve harmonisation with UPOV 1961. However, this answer … leaves open the question of what purpose the provision in Article 53(b) EPC excluding animal varieties from the grant of a patent was to achieve. There was no provision for industrial property rights specifically for animal varieties[7] … The Board's conclusion is that the substantive approach is the correct one …

For the EPO to adopt the literal approach would, in effect, be to abdicate any responsibility for examining the substance of the claim, and the outcome of an application

[6] Question 3 relates to an issue that is not the subject of this chapter (even though, in the comments towards the end of this chapter, we will briefly come back to it in the context of decision T-49/83 Propagating material/CIBA-GEIGY). The response given by the EBoA was the following: 'When a claim to a process for the production of a plant variety is examined, Article 64(2) EPC is not to be taken into consideration.'

[7] In this regard the Board also stressed that 'While the existence of a separate protection system for plant varieties on the model sponsored by UPOV was an important reason, it was not the only reason for the legislator to exclude plant varieties from patent protection in the EPC' (T-1054/96 (I): 534).

would depend on the verbal skill of the patent attorney concerned (T-1054/96 (I): 524–5, emphasis added).

As to the question whether a genetically modified plant variety could be considered to be a product of a microbiological process, the Board noted that even if this would be the case, the question would still remain as to whether 'the genetically engineered variety is closer to the original concept of plant variety or closer to the original concept of a product of a microbiological process' (T-1054/96 (I): 529). According to the Board:

The genetically engineered plant variety bears no relation to what was originally meant by the product of a microbiological process ... whereas it is virtually indistinguishable in type from conventionally produced plant varieties ... [T]his leads to the conclusion that genetically engineered varieties are covered by the prohibition of granting patents for plant varieties of Article 53(b) EPC even if they should in some sense be considered as the product of a microbiological process.[8] (T-1054/96 (I): 529)

As to the second question, that is whether a claim that encompasses plant varieties but is not restricted to an individual specific variety escapes the exclusion laid down in Art. 53(b) EPC, Novartis had argued that such a claim should indeed escape the exclusion, for otherwise applicants would be left without protection in this field. However, the Board pointed out that:

[V]arious aspects of the ... technical contribution may be protected in claims of different categories, i.e. in method claims leading to the preparation of the genetically engineered plants, product claims relating to the gene expressing the desired feature, and claims to the vector by which transformation of the plant cells is carried out, none of which according to decision T 356/93 [Plant cells/PLANT GENETIC SYSTEMS] ... falls under an exclusion from patentability. It is, thus, plainly wrong to say that the inventors are deprived of all protection for their technical contribution unless genetically modified plants are patentable. (T-1054/96 (I): 530)

The Board was of course aware of the position of Novartis and various other biotech and agrochemical companies that they wanted product claims for plant varieties. Yet, as the Board noted, the patenting of plant varieties is prohibited and 'it is the generally expressed view that the

[8] The Board also noted that 'Given that processes involving microorganisms, such as fermentation processes or the production of pharmaceuticals had long been patented, and that these processes were to remain patentable, the "exclusion to the exclusion" of Article 53(b) EPC for microbiological processes and their products appears to have been introduced as a precautionary measure to ensure that the terms "plant" or "animal" were not interpreted so broadly as to cover also yeast, bacteria and other microorganisms, processes involving these being already at the time of the Strasbourg Convention considered patentable' (T-1054/96 (I): 536).

duty of the judges is to apply and not to create the law' (T-1054/96 (I): 530–1). In this regard, the Board rightly distinguished between 'dynamically interpreting the law' and 'modifying a convention' (T-1054/96 (I): 531).

Thus the Board's main observation regarding the second question was that 'To deduce from [the] wording of Article 53(b) EPC that a patent shall not be granted for a single plant variety but may be granted if its claims cover more than one variety, does not appear to comply with the normal rules of logic' (T-1054/96 (I): 531). As discussed in Chapter 9, while this appears to be an eminently sensible standpoint, the *novelty* approach is unworkable in relation to the Art. 53 EPC exclusions.[9]

One of Novartis' arguments in favour of the *higher taxonomic level* approach was that this approach was expressed in the (then draft) EBD and ought therefore to be regarded as agreed subsequent practice for the purposes of the Vienna Convention on the Law of Treaties (VC). However, the Board correctly remarked that, in view inter alia of the fact that not all Contracting States of the EPC are EU Member States, 'treating the proposed directive as evidence of any agreed subsequent practice under the EPC seems problematical' (T-1054/96 (I): 545). Moreover, the Board rightly added that:

> [I]t appears that the prohibition of Article 53(b) EPC … does not suggest any intention on the part of the legislator that plant or animal varieties should become patentable according to criteria to be developed by the instances of the European Patent Office, merely because advances in knowledge and technological capabilities might make it easier to create new varieties with particular properties. *Rather it suggests an intention to exclude varieties from patenting until such time as the legislators reconsider the matter.* (T-1054/96 (I): 536, emphasis added)

Indeed, as noted by the Board, the exclusion from patentability of plant and animal varieties is formulated in *absolute terms*, which suggests that even if a plant or animal variety would be an invention, would be susceptible of industrial application, would be new and would involve an inventive step, it would remain unpatentable (T-1054/96 (I): 537).[10]

[9] Patent claims are normally written in general terms and can be read to cover anything that meets the criteria set out in the claim, whether or not other features are present. Thus, as pointed out by Novartis, a claim to a gene construct also covers plant varieties in which that gene construct is present. This being the case, under the *novelty* approach, a claim to a gene construct would have to be rejected since it *encompasses* plant varieties containing that construct.

[10] In this regard the Board also emphasised that it can be inferred from the different wording used in Art. 53(b) EPC and in Art. 52(2) and (3) EPC, as well as from the fact that these exclusions from patentability are in different articles, that there is a *difference in legal category* between the Art. 52(2) EPC exceptions (matter that as such

Finally, as to question 4, that is whether a plant variety that is the outcome of recombinant gene technology falls outside the Art. 53(b) EPC exclusion, the Board saw no reason 'why the mere fact of being derived by genetic engineering should give the producers of such plant varieties a privileged position relative to breeders of plant varieties which meet all the requirements of Article 52(1) EPC but have not been arrived at by genetic engineering' (T-1054/96 (I): 550).

The president of the EPO (Ingo Kober) also provided some comments on the issues that were the subject of the referral. According to him, the subject-matter *excluded* by Art. 53(b) EPC was the same as the subject-matter that is *protectable* under the system of plant breeders' rights. A group of plants merely characterised by one or more single feature(s) did not qualify as a plant variety in his view. Moreover, the president clearly agreed with the *novelty* approach.

7.8 Plants: G-1/98 Transgenic plant/NOVARTIS II

In December 1999, in G-1/98 Transgenic plant/NOVARTIS II, the EBoA answered the questions referred to it in T-1054/96 (I) Transgenic plant/NOVARTIS. The EBoA decided first to address questions 2, 3 and 4, for the answers to those questions would show that question 1 did not need to be answered separately.[11]

Regarding question 2 – whether a claim that encompasses plant varieties but does not individually claim specific varieties, escapes the exclusion – the EBoA started by commenting on the difference between a 'substantive' and a 'literal' approach, that is between the *novelty* and *higher taxonomic level* approaches. With regard to the TBoA's defence of the *novelty* approach (i.e. the view that a patent is granted in respect of plant varieties if a claim encompasses plant varieties), the EBoA agreed with the TBoA that 'it is not the wording but the substance of a claim which is decisive in assessing the subject-matter to which the claim is directed' (G-1/98: 124). However, the EBoA emphasised that, in its view, the *scope* and the *subject-matter* of a claim are different things and that 'In assessing the subject-matter of a claim, the underlying invention has to be identified. In this respect, it is relevant how generic or specific the claimed invention is … If [the inventor] has made an invention

is not regarded as an invention) and the Art. 53 EPC exceptions (matter for which patents shall not be granted).

[11] We agree with the EBoA that question 1 was a very broad question and that the answers to the other questions demonstrate that question 1 did not need a separate answer. We will not go into the EBoA's comments on the relevance of Art. 64(2) EPC (question 3) here, as it is discussed in Chapter 6.

of general applicability, a generic claim is not the consequence of the verbal skill of the attorney ... but of the breadth of application of the invention' (G-1/98: 124). According to the EBoA, the referring decision T-1054/96 (I) Transgenic plant/NOVARTIS did not give any indication that carrying out the invention was restricted to individual varieties to be modified and did not suggest that the result of the modification by genetic transformation was *necessarily* a 'plant variety' (G-1/98: 125).

As to the meaning of the concept of 'plant varieties', the EBoA referred to the definition provided in T-49/83 Propagating material/CIBA-GEIGY and confirmed in T-320/87 Hybrid plants/LUBRIZOL, as well as to the definition provided by UPOV 1991.[12] According to the EBoA, the UPOV criterion 'defined by the expression of the characteristics resulting from a given genotype or combination of genotypes' was 'a reference to the entire constitution of a plant or a set of genetic information' and 'a plant defined by single recombinant DNA sequences is not an individual plant grouping to which an entire constitution can be attributed'. The UPOV definition, the Board noted, is 'an abstract and open definition embracing an indefinite number of individual entities defined by a part of its genotype or by a property bestowed on it by that part' (G-1/98: 125–6).

After admitting that the plants claimed by Novartis were 'defined by certain characteristics allowing the plants to inhibit the growth of plant pathogens', the Board quite astonishingly developed the following reasoning:

> The taxonomic category within the traditional classification of the plant kingdom to which the claimed plants belong is not specified, let alone the further characteristics necessary to assess the homogeneity and stability of varieties within a given species. Hence, it would appear that the claimed invention neither expressly nor implicitly defines a single variety ... This also means that it does not define a multiplicity of varieties which necessarily consists of several individual varieties. In the absence of the identification of specific varieties in the product claims, the subject-matter of the claimed invention is neither limited nor even directed to a variety or varieties. (G-1/98: 126–7)

[12] See Article 1(vi) UPOV 1991. The EBoA noted that an identical definition could be found in Article 5(2) Community Plant Variety Rights Regulation (CPVRR), as well as in Rule 26(4) EPC (which entered into force on 1 September 1999) (G-1/98: 125–6). As far as CPVRR is concerned, it should be noted that, according to the Preamble of this regulation, the definition it provides of 'plant variety' is 'not intended to alter definitions which may have been established in the field of intellectual property rights, especially the patent field, nor to interfere with or exclude from application laws governing the protectability of products, including plants and plant material, or processes under such other industrial property rights'.

The EBoA invoked two further arguments in this regard. First, as Art. 53(b) EPC mentions both 'plant varieties' and '[processes related to the production of] plants', the use of these different terms had to have some purpose and it could not have been the intention of the legislator to exclude 'plants as a group embracing in general varieties' from patentability, for otherwise the word 'plants' would have been used in the product exclusion as well (G-1/98: 127–8). Second, the EBoA agreed with Novartis' assertion that the TBoA's *novelty* approach would apply 'not only to claims for plants embracing plant varieties but also to claims for genes contained in plant varieties'. According to the EBoA, the referring Board's view implied that any genetic material for introduction into a plant would have to be excluded from product patent protection (G-1/98: 128). As we have commented above, this is an appropriate criticism of the *novelty* approach to the exclusions of Art. 53 EPC – nonetheless, it does not make the *higher taxonomic level* approach the correct approach to adopt.

The EBoA agreed with the referring Board that Art. 53(b) EPC was derived from Art. 2(b) SPC. However, an important difference between the two, according to the EBoA, was that, while the EPC opted for the exclusion from patentability of plant varieties, the SPC left it to its Contracting States to decide whether or not to provide for the grant of patents in respect of plant varieties. The approach taken by the SPC had to be understood, the EBoA argued, as an attempt to solve a dilemma for the legislator:

> [O]n the one hand, SPC Contracting States are obliged under Article 1 SPC to grant patents for any inventions which are susceptible of industrial application, which are new and involve an inventive step. On the other hand, UPOV member States were allowed under Article 2(1) UPOV Convention 1961 to recognise the right of the breeder by the grant of either a special plant breeders' right or of a patent; however, simultaneous protection for the same botanical genus or species was not allowed. This so-called ban on dual protection (abandoned in the UPOV Convention 1991) made it necessary for member States of the Council of Europe to exclude patent protection for varieties for which plant breeders' rights were obtainable … Thus, under the SPC, plant varieties were not regarded per se ineligible for patent protection. Rather, this question was left open intentionally. (G-1/98: 129–30)

The Board also noted that 'different European countries' (for example Germany) granted patents for varieties and that several SPC Contracting States (for example Belgium, Germany, France and Spain) excluded patents only for varieties included in the list of varieties annexed to the Plant Varieties Protection Law (G-1/98: 130–1).

The Enlarged Board concluded from this that:

> [I]t is clear from Article 2(b) SPC and its implementation by some of its Contracting States that this provision was not based on the concept that there should be no patent protection for plant varieties. Rather, it was intended to ensure that Contracting States should not be bound to grant patents for subject-matter for which patents were excluded under the ban on dual protection in the UPOV Convention 1961. (G-1/98: 130–1)

The first of these sentences is correct if the word 'national' is inserted before 'patent'. The second sentence is quite misleading, as will be clear from the discussion of the *travaux préparatoires* in Chapter 2 and towards the end of the present chapter. This misleading conclusion led to the further conclusions explained in the following paragraphs.

The Board added that this left open the question whether the purpose of Art. 53(b) EPC was different from the purpose of Art. 2(b) SPC, and then argued that it was not. According to the Board, the purpose of Art. 53(b) EPC was only to exclude inventions that were eligible for protection by plant breeders' rights (G-1/98: 132–4).

The Board concluded from all this that a patent must be refused if a claim is 'directed to' plant varieties, but that such is not the case in 'the absence of the identification of a specific plant variety in a product claim'. Hence, unlike the referring TBoA, the EBoA saw no logical problems with the view that 'a patent shall not be granted for a single plant variety but can be granted if varieties may fall within the scope of its claims' (G-1/98: 136). The EBoA thus approved the *higher taxonomic level* approach and rejected the *novelty* approach.

Based on its observations regarding the purpose of Art. 53(b) EPC, the Board decided that 'The extent of the exclusion for patents is the obverse of the availability of plant variety rights. The latter are only granted for specific plant varieties and not for technical teachings which can be implemented in an indefinite number of plant varieties' (G-1/98: 136).

With regard to question 4 – whether a plant variety that is the outcome of recombinant gene technology falls outside the Art. 53(b) EPC exclusion – the EBoA stated that regarding genetically modified plants as products of microbiological processes in the sense of the second half-sentence of Art. 53(b) EPC would ignore the purpose of the exclusion. As noted earlier, according to the EBoA the purpose of the exclusion is to exclude from patentability subject-matter which may be protected by breeders' rights. On that basis, the EBoA reasoned and concluded as follows:

> Whether a plant variety is the result of traditional breeding techniques, or whether genetic engineering was used to obtain a distinct plant grouping, does not matter for the criteria of distinctness, homogeneity and stability and the examination thereof ... The argument [invoked by Novartis] that the legislator

of the EPC did not envisage the possibility of genetically-modified plant varieties and for this reason could not have had the intention of excluding them from patentability cannot be accepted. Laws are not restricted in their application to situations known to the legislator. Since plant varieties are excluded, the only question is the conditions under which they are excluded. The EBoA supports the view of the referring Board ... that the mere fact of being obtained by means of genetic engineering does not give the producers of such plant varieties a privileged position relative to breeders of plant varieties resulting from traditional breeding only. (G-1/98: 139)

7.9 Plants: T-149/98 Resistance development/BAYER

Plant Genetic Systems (PGS) filed a patent application (Van Meilaert *et al.* 1991)[13] in May 1990 concerning the genetic modification of plants to make them express an insecticidal protein of bacterial origin (*Bacillus thuringiensis* or 'Bt'). The patent (Van Meilaert *et al.* 1994) was granted in August 1994 with claims to processes for producing plants with improved insect resistance, as well as to plant cells and plants per se. We will only focus on the latter.

The patent was opposed by Ciba-Geigy (a predecessor of Novartis and Syngenta) for lack of inventive step and insufficient disclosure. The Opposition Division itself raised an additional objection under Art. 53(b) EPC to the claims to plants, referring to the interpretation of T-356/93 Plant cells/PLANT GENETIC SYSTEMS in G-3/95 Inadmissible referral (Correspondence *EPO* 1997a: 3).[14] As the Opposition Division noted:

If G 3/95 [Inadmissible referral] ... is followed, it can only be concluded that all the transgenic plants disclosed in [the working examples] and the subject-matter of Claims 16, 17 and 19 are to be regarded as plant varieties whether or not the characteristics of the starting plant fulfilled the criteria of stability and uniformity necessary for recognition as a variety, since according to G 3/95 [Inadmissible referral], the introduction of a distinctive, stably-inherited genetic modification into a plant itself makes the modified plant a variety within the meaning of Article 53(b) EPC ... Furthermore in analogy with the findings for the plants dealt with [*sic*] T356/93 [Plant cells/PLANT GENETIC SYSTEMS] ... the present plants cannot be viewed as products of a microbiological process ... In consequence ... the subject-matter of Claims 16, 17, and 19 is excluded from patentability. (Correspondence *EPO* 1997a: 13)

PGS did not agree with the Opposition Division, but did file an auxiliary request (an alternative set of claims) in which the claims to plants had

[13] Bayer, referred to in the title of the decision, was a successor to Plant Genetic Systems.

[14] At this stage, G-1/98 Transgenic plant/NOVARTIS II had not yet issued.

been deleted. The patent was maintained by the Opposition Division on the basis of this auxiliary request (T-149/98: para. II).

Both the patent holder and the opponent appealed. In January 2003 – that is *after* the EBoA had issued decision G-1/98 Transgenic plant/ NOVARTIS II – TBoA 3.3.04 (Chairman Kinkeldey) decided that the patent was to be maintained. With regard to Article 53(b) EPC, the Board merely noted that:

Claims 16, 17 and 19 as granted relate to transgenic plants, without mentioning individual plant varieties. The Board, following the view expressed in decision G 1/98 [Transgenic plant/NOVARTIS II] ... that a claim wherein specific plant varieties are not individually claimed is not excluded from patentability, even though it may embrace plant varieties, concludes that claims 16, 17 and 19 meet the requirements of Article 53(b) EPC (T-149/98: para. 1).

7.10 Plants: T-1054/96 Anti-pathogenic compositions/ NOVARTIS III

In March 2000, after the EBoA's decision G 1/98 Transgenic plant/ NOVARTIS II, TBoA 3.3.04 (Chairman Kinkeldey) communicated to Novartis that the EBoA's decision implied that the four product claims that had previously been regarded by the TBoA (see T-1054/96 (I) Transgenic plant/NOVARTIS) as contravening Art. 53(b) EPC were not excluded by this provision.

In that same month Novartis filed a new set of claims to meet the TBoA's remaining objections to some of the *method* claims, but the wording of the four *product* claims was left unchanged except for the deletion of the words 'and the seeds thereof' from former claim 19.

In December 2000 the TBoA decided with regard to the product claims to plants that:

[These] are directed to transgenic plants and embrace plant varieties. Yet, no plant variety defined by taxonomic name and further variety specific characteristics is individually claimed. In their decision G 1/98 [Transgenic plant/ NOVARTIS II] ... the [Enlarged Board] decided that 'a claim wherein specific plant varieties are not individually claimed is not excluded from patentability under Article 53(b) EPC even though it may embrace plant varieties'. Pursuant to Article 112(2) EPC, this decision is binding in deciding this case and [the claims in question] must be considered as falling outside of the exceptions to patentability laid down in Article 53(b) EPC. (T-1054/96: para. 1)

The TBoA remitted the case to the Examining Division with an order to grant the patent with the claims filed by Novartis in March 2000 and the patent was granted (to Syngenta) in July 2001.

7.11 Plants: T-475/01 Phosphinothricin resistant gene/ BAYER

Bayer CropScience applied for a patent in January 1988 concerning the genetic modification of plants in order to make them resistant to phosphinothricin (a herbicide sold by Bayer as Basta®). The main product claim relating to plants, claim 9, related to plants, plant components and seeds comprising the gene defined in claim 1, 2 or 3. The patent (Strauch *et al.* 1993) was granted in March 1993 and an opposition was filed by Dr Christoph Then, inter alia on the basis that the claims covered plant varieties. The opposition was rejected in a decision from March 2001. According to the Opposition Division, which referred to G-1/98 Transgenic plant/NOVARTIS II, no plant varieties were claimed individually and the operation of the invention was not limited to a particular plant variety.

Dr Then appealed, maintaining his objections under Art. 53(b) EPC. He argued that the Opposition Division had incorrectly interpreted T-356/93 Plant cells/PLANT GENETIC SYSTEMS, T-1054/96 (I) Transgenic plant/NOVARTIS and G-1/98 Transgenic plant/ NOVARTIS II, as well as Rule 27 EPC, and pointed out what he felt was the correct and legally coherent interpretation. Art. 53(b) EPC and Rule 27 EPC implied, in his view, that patents may cover *uses* of plant varieties, but not plant varieties themselves. He also submitted documents concerning the introduction in Germany and the Netherlands of specific varieties of maize which incorporated the gene construct claimed in the patent. Consequently, he argued, claim 9 covered individual, specific plant varieties and the patent should be revoked.

Oral proceedings took place in June 2004. Dr Then's arguments were essentially the following. According to G-1/98 Transgenic plant/ NOVARTIS II, the exclusion from patentability of plant varieties did not apply when only plants with general technical properties rather than varieties in the sense of UPOV were claimed. When examining a claim, one had to consider not the wording but the content of the claim to determine whether it was directed to plant varieties. In the commercial application of the invention, Then asserted, it was inevitable that plants were produced which possessed all the characteristics of a plant variety. The plants covered by the patent could be considered to be 'essentially derived varieties' in the sense of Art. 13 Community Plant Variety Rights Regulation (CPVRR). As the working examples in the patent specification showed, plants produced according to the invention included an individual variety, namely *N. tabacum* Wisconsin 38, and therefore the patent related to 'essentially derived varieties'. Hence, Then concluded, the patent should be revoked.

TBoA 3.3.08 (Chairman Galligani) noted the following as regards Art. 53(b) EPC. In claim 9 plant varieties were not individually claimed and from the patent specification it was not shown that the performance of the invention was or needed to be limited to the production of *N. tabacum* Wisconsin 38. According to G-1/98 Transgenic plant/NOVARTIS II, Art. 53(b) EPC did not therefore preclude the patentability of the subject-matter of claim 9 (T-475/01: para. 6).

The Board found that the decision of the Opposition Division was not based on an incorrect interpretation of T-356/93 Plant cells/PLANT GENETIC SYSTEMS, T-1054/96 (I) Transgenic plant/NOVARTIS and G-1/98 Transgenic plant/NOVARTIS II. It was also noted that T-356/93 Plant cells/PLANT GENETIC SYSTEMS had been overruled by G-1/98 Transgenic plant/NOVARTIS II (T-475/01: para. 7).

Although Then had argued that the performance of the invention led to the production of essentially derived varieties, the Board observed that, following G-1/98 Transgenic plant/NOVARTIS II, the claims of the patent were not directed to individual plant varieties, and considered that there was no relevant difference between the plant varieties as referred to by G-1/98 Transgenic plant/NOVARTIS II and 'essentially derived varieties' (T-475/01: para. 8). Hence, in the Board's view, if a claim passes the G-1/98 Transgenic plant/NOVARTIS II test, this is sufficient to demonstrate that it is not excluded, even if operation of the invention leads to essentially derived varieties.

According to the Board, Art. 4 (1)(a) and Art. 4(2) EBD, in conjunction with Art. 53(b) and Rule 27(b) EPC, implied that only plant varieties are not patentable. By contrast, inventions that concern plants were patentable if the performance of the invention was not limited to particular plant varieties. With the entry into force of the EBD, the Board stated, an EU-wide consensus was achieved, which was reflected in G-1/98 Transgenic plant/NOVARTIS II, that claims to plants that are not restricted to individual plant varieties are patentable when the use of the invention is not limited to a specific plant variety (T-475/01: para. 9).

In June 2004 the TBoA rejected Dr Then's Appeal.

7.12 Plants: T-179/01 Herbicide resistant plants/MONSANTO

Monsanto filed a patent application (Barry *et al.* 1992) in August 1991 concerning the genetic modification of plants in order to make them resistant to their herbicide glyphosate (Round-Up®). The claims related to methods for producing plants and for selectively controlling weeds in a field, as well as to DNA sequences, plant cells and plants per se. We will only focus on the latter. The main claim directed to plants, claim 24, read as follows: 'A glyphosate tolerant plant comprising plant cells [as specified in Claim 20].' The working examples provided in the patent application related to tobacco, canola, soybean and corn.

The patent (Barry *et al.* 1996) was granted in June 1996 and oppositions were filed by Greenpeace, Syngenta and two individuals (Dr Christoph Then and Thomas Schweiger, supported by the NGOs Global 2000, Kein Patent auf Leben and numerous other organisations and individuals from various European countries). Unlike Greenpeace and Then and Schweiger, Syngenta unsurprisingly did not oppose the grant of the patent on the basis of Art. 53(b) EPC.

Greenpeace referred to T-356/93 Plant cells/PLANT GENETIC SYSTEMS and noted that there was 'no material difference' between some of the claims that were refused in that decision and some of the claims of Monsanto's patent (Correspondence *Greenpeace* 1997: 2). The glyphosate-tolerant transgenic plants were said to be 'largely the same in their characteristics and remain the same within specific tolerances after every propagation or propagation cycle' and so should be considered to be 'plant varieties'. The second half-sentence of Art. 53(b) EPC offered no way out, according to Greenpeace, for the plants in question were the products of a multi-step process involving an initial microbiological process step of transforming plant cells, followed by regenerating and reproducing steps. Again, reference was made to T-356/93 Plant cells/PLANT GENETIC SYSTEMS, which had held that such processes could not be considered to be 'microbiological processes' and so neither could the resulting plants be regarded as 'products of microbiological processes' (Correspondence *Greenpeace* 1997: 3). Moreover, Greenpeace correctly added in this regard that the patent claims covered, for example, 'the 10th generation from the originally transformed plant', which could obviously not be regarded as the product of a microbiological process but was a product of ordinary plant reproduction (Correspondence *Greenpeace* 1997: 4).

Opponents Then and Schweiger argued that some of the claims encompassed plant varieties and that in accordance with T-356/93 Plant cells/PLANT GENETIC SYSTEMS this was not permitted. As Then and Schweiger correctly pointed out, T-356/93 Plant cells/PLANT GENETIC SYSTEMS was the relevant case law *at the time the Monsanto patent was accepted and granted.* Indeed, case G-1/98 Transgenic plant/NOVARTIS II had not even commenced. Moreover, the EPO president's referral of July 1995 (in which he sought to have T-356/93 Plant cells/PLANT GENETIC SYSTEMS overturned) had been rejected by the EBoA in G-3/95 Inadmissible referral in November 1995, that is well before the Monsanto patent was granted. Thus, the Examining Division had clearly ignored T-356/96 Plant cells/PLANT GENETIC SYSTEMS when granting the patent. However, the Opposition Division did not issue its summons to oral proceedings until November 1999, after the EPC Rules had been amended to conform to the EBD, and did not issue its decision until April 2000, after the EBoA had issued its decision G-1/98 Transgenic plant/NOVARTIS II in December 1999.

Monsanto responded to the opponents' arguments that the objections raised under Art. 53(b) EPC essentially corresponded to the issues raised in T-1054/96 (I) Transgenic plant/NOVARTIS (TBoA 3.3.04's referral of questions to the EBoA in G-1/98 Transgenic plant/NOVARTIS II discussed above) and that '[s]ince the decision of the Enlarged Board … will therefore affect the present proceedings, it does not seem useful to provide a detailed response to the rather generic arguments presented by the opponents at this stage'. As a 'preliminary indication' of its position, Monsanto merely referred to the observations submitted by epi (the Institute of Professional Representatives before the European Patent Office) in T-1054/96 (I) Transgenic plant/NOVARTIS in October 1997 and expressed general agreement with those observations (Correspondence *Monsanto* 1988: 6). According to Monsanto, the claims did not violate Art. 53(b) EPC or any other EPC provision and thus the patent had to be maintained as granted.

In a communication accompanying the summons to oral proceedings, the Opposition Division summarised its preliminary opinion. With regard inter alia to Art. 53(b) EPC, the Opposition Division referred to the publication, in September 1999, of the decision of the Administrative Council of the EPO to amend the Implementing Regulations to the EPC. It was then added that in view of this, 'and in particular of Rule [27(b)] EPC, the [Opposition Division] is of the preliminary (non-binding) opinion that none of the grounds for opposition … preclude the maintenance of the opposed patent' (Correspondence *EPO* 1999: 2). Not the slightest argumentation was provided, as if a mere reference to an EPC Rule would be sufficient.

In its decision, the Opposition Division argued that:

> [T]he teachings of the granted patent as soon as put into practice must be carried out in a 'plant variety' and … are only exemplified by plant varieties … However, there is no doubt that the [granted isolated DNA sequences] can be used in the transformation of many plants … It is true that the objected claims embrace plant varieties but they cannot be limited to any plant variety and they are much broader and general in scope. In agreement with … Rule [27(b)] EPC,

the overall technical feasibility of the opposed patent is not confined to any of these particular plant varieties but these teachings are feasible in all plants and varieties thereof. None of the granted claims identifies a specific plant variety (Rule [26(4)] EPC) and thus, even if the granted claims cover plant varieties, they cannot be seen as directed to a variety or varieties in the sense of decision G1/98 [Transgenic plant/NOVARTIS II]. (Correspondence *EPO* 2000: 6)

The Opposition Division concluded that the patent met all the requirements of Art. 53(b) EPC and decided to maintain the patent on the basis of Monsanto's first auxiliary request, submitted during oral proceedings.[15]

The decision was appealed by Monsanto itself, as well as by Greenpeace and Syngenta.[16] Monsanto disputed the findings of the Opposition Division regarding novelty and requested that the patent be maintained as granted (Correspondence *Monsanto* 2001: 1–5). At the oral proceedings in appeal in April 2005, Monsanto filed a set of claims that was identical to the claims as granted except for the deletion of a claim relating to a gene sequence.

Greenpeace maintained its objections under Art. 53(b) EPC (Correspondence *Greenpeace* 2001: 1). It argued that Rule 27(b) EPC,[17] which had entered into force in September 1999, represented such a significant change that it should have been made in the Articles of the EPC and not in the Implementing Regulations, that is following agreement by a Diplomatic Conference rather than simply as an Administrative Council decision. Moreover, Greenpeace argued, claim 24 clearly related to several essentially derived plant varieties and was consequently unacceptable in view of Art. 53(b) EPC (T-179/01: para. 8).

As to Greenpeace's point regarding the Rule, TBoA 3.3.08 (Chairman Galligano) referred to its earlier decision, T-315/03 Transgenic animals/HARVARD (p. 37), according to which the decision to legislate in the articles or in the rules of the EPC was entirely up to the legislator and that, as long as a Board perceives no conflict between a Rule and an Article, 'it has no power to prevent the operation of correctly enacted legislation' (T-179/01: para. 9). No such conflict was at

15 This auxiliary request was the same as the main request, except for the introduction of a disclaimer in two of the claims to nucleotide sequences, in order to overcome novelty objections.

16 As Syngenta did not invoke Art. 53(b) EPC, we will not go into their grounds for appeal.

17 'Biotechnological inventions shall also be patentable if they concern: ... (b) plants or animals if the technical feasibility of the invention is not confined to a particular plant or animal variety.'

issue here, according to the TBoA. However, the Board did not provide any arguments whatsoever to substantiate its finding that there was no conflict. As we will argue below, in section 7.17, the Board was wrong. There was (and continues to be) a conflict between the Article and the Rule, for the Rule contains a logically untenable interpretation of the Article.

As to the argument regarding 'essentially derived varieties', the Board referred to its decision T-475/01 Phosphinothricin resistant gene/BAYER, discussed in in section 7.11, where 'like here', 'a claim to plants comprising essentially derived plant varieties' was at issue and where the Board had 'made it abundantly clear that such a claim was not excluded from patentability under Article 53(b) EPC together with Rule 23c(b) EPC for the reasons already explained in the Enlarged Board decision G 1/98 [Transgenic plant/NOVARTIS II]' (T-179/01: para. 9).

The Board decided in April 2005 to remit the case to the Opposition Division with an order to maintain the patent on the basis of the main request filed during the oral proceedings in appeal. The patent was reissued in July 2006.

7.13 Animals: T-315/03 Transgenic animals/HARVARD

As mentioned in section 7.4, in May 1992 a patent (Leder and Stewart 1992) was granted to Harvard with claims directed to a 'transgenic nonhuman mammalian animal'. Inter alia on the basis of Art. 53(b) EPC, seventeen parties opposed this patent: Compassion in World Farming (UK); Bundesverband der Tierversuchsgegner *et al.* (Germany); Oekologische Demokratische Partei (Germany); R. Büchner *et al.* (Germany); A. Meinel *et al.* (Germany); U. Fuchs *et al.* (Germany); R. Paulig *et al.*, Faction of the 'Greens' in the Bavarian parliament (Germany); Evangelischer Stadtkirchenverband Köln (Germany); Bundesland Hessen, represented by the Ministry for Youth, Family and Health (Germany); F. Koechlin *et al.* (Belgium); J. Voggenhuber *et al.*, parliamentary faction of the 'Greens' (Austria); Keine Patente auf Leben (Switzerland); S. Hamberger *et al.* (Germany); Bundeszentrale der Tierversuchsgegner Österreichs (Austria); Wiener Tierschutzverein und Zentralverband der Tierschutzvereine Österreichs (Austria); H. Helletsberger (Germany); and Deutsches Tierhilfswerk (Germany). The opposition and subsequent appeal proceedings lasted no less than eleven years.

Oral proceedings took place in 1995 and 2001, and in January 2003 the Opposition Division rejected all the objections of the opponents, except for those under Art. 53(a) EPC (see Chapter 8). Thus, Art. 53(b) EPC was not seen as an impediment. The Opposition Division noted that, apart from T-19/90 Onco-mouse/HARVARD, no Board of Appeal had addressed the patentability of animals. Reference was made to G-1/98 Transgenic plant/NOVARTIS II as well as to Rule 27(b) EPC, which provides that there is no bar to patentability if the technical feasibility of the invention is not confined to a particular plant or animal variety. On this basis, the Opposition Division concluded:

Living matter and in particular plants and animals are accessible to patent protection. This has been laid down in Rule [27(b)] EPC and it is not only process protection but also product protection which is allowable when Recital 31 of Directive 98/44/EU is taken into account for interpretation. The latter points out that a plant grouping which is characterized by a specific gene (and not its whole genome) is not covered by the protection of new varieties and is therefore not excluded from patentability even if it comprises new varieties of plants. Thus, the recital clarifies Rule [27(b)] EPC which admittedly could be interpreted differently by virtue of its language 'if they concern plants or animals' in that product protection has been foreseen in the law. Although the recital refers to plants only since it mentions the specific protection scheme for plant varieties, Rule [27(b)] EPC could not be interpreted differently with regard to animals. (Correspondence *EPO* 2003a: 23)

According to the Opposition Division, the feasibility of the invention was not limited to a particular animal variety, so the argument of the opponents that the mouse strains mentioned in the patent were animal varieties, which were unpatentable under Art. 53(b) EPC, had to fail (Correspondence *EPO* 2003a: 23).

Further, the Opposition Division argued that the findings of G-1/98 Transgenic plant/NOVARTIS II could be transferred to the interpretation of the exclusion of animal varieties and made the following observations regarding the purpose of the exclusion of animal varieties:

As far as plant varieties are concerned the purpose of Article 53(b) EPC, in following the purpose of the SPC [Strasbourg Patent Convention], was the ban on dual protection with the UPOV Convention. The question arises then what the purpose of the SPC was in excluding animal varieties as well although no protection was visible at that time, nor at present, for animal varieties as products of animal breeding. The most obvious reason for this must have been the intention or at least the keeping open of the possibility to create such a law for the protection of animal varieties later on ... The equal linguistic treatment of plant and animal varieties in [the SPC and the EPC] is a clear indication that the purpose of the exclusions must have been the same for both. (Correspondence *EPO* 2003a: 23–4)

The Opposition Division also noted that, for the reasons pointed out in G-1/98 Transgenic plant/NOVARTIS II with regard to plants, there was no inconsistency between allowing claims encompassing animal varieties and not allowing claims directed to specific varieties (Correspondence *EPO* 2003a: 24). It was decided to maintain the patent in amended form, with claims directed to 'rodents' (instead of non-human mammals, as allowed by the Examining Division). Six of the seventeen opponents appealed.

In its written decision, TBoA 3.3.08 (Chairman Davison-Brunel) started by observing that 'in a case concerning animals, ascertaining the exact meaning of Article 53(b) EPC is not straightforward due in particular to differences of language' (T-315/03: 56). Indeed, as noted earlier, the German version of Art. 53(b) EPC provides that '*Tierarten*' (animal *species*) are excluded from patentability, whereas the French version uses the term '*races animales*' (animal *races*). Both terms differ from the one used in the English version, 'animal *varieties*'.

According to Harvard, the approach suggested for plants in EBoA decision G-1/98 Transgenic plant/NOVARTIS II should also be followed in the case of animals. The Board agreed with this and decided that a patent could not be obtained for a single animal variety (or species or race) but could be granted if varieties fell within the scope of its claims (T-315/03: 58). Thus the Board explicitly defended the *higher taxonomic level* approach in relation to animals.

The Board went on to note that, unlike the EBoA in G-1/98 Transgenic plant/NOVARTIS II, it did not have the benefit of earlier TBoA case law, and no clear definition of 'animal variety' (or 'animal race' or 'animal species') was available (T-315/03: 58). Yet it decided that 'a definition by reference to taxonomical rank would be both consistent with the position in relation to plant varieties and in the interest of legal certainty' (T-315/03: 58). After explaining that 'species' represents a higher taxonomic order than 'variety' and 'race' and that, therefore, in view of the provision in Art. 177(1) EPC that the three texts of the EPC are equally authentic, this 'would lead to the absurd result that the outcome of an Article 53(b) EPC objection would depend on the language of a case – with German ... being of the highest taxonomic order and thereby offering the widest objection' (T-315/03: 60). Such legal uncertainty was not only undesirable, according to the Board, it was also 'unnecessary ... to pursue this matter further in the present case' since the patent concerned 'a taxonomic category of animals higher than "species"' (T-315/03: 60).

In response to the argument of the Appellants that 'species' was an abstract concept and that the intention of the legislator had been to exclude animals belonging to any species from patentability, the Board argued that only 'a limited category of animals' was excluded by Art.

53(b) EPC and that, while the differences in the words used in the three languages of the EPC was unfortunate, 'it is at least clear beyond any doubt that the Article does not represent a general exclusion of all animal patents' (T-315/03: 78).

TBoA 3.3.08 decided in July 2004 that Art. 53(b) EPC did not preclude the patentability of Harvard's first auxiliary request (i.e. a set of amended claims submitted by Harvard), with claims limited to 'mice' (instead of 'rodents' as permitted by the Opposition Division).[18]

7.14 Plants: T-788/07 Brassica/PIONEER

Pioneer Hi-bred International applied for a patent in December 1997 relating to *Brassica* containing an improved fertility restorer gene. The application (Charne *et al.* 1998) was refused by the Examining Division in May 2002 for lack of novelty. Pioneer appealed and the decision of the Examining Division was overruled by TBoA 3.3.04 in March 2004 (T-1026/02 Oilseed brassica/PIONEER). The application was remitted to the Examining Division and, after Pioneer submitted another set of claims, a second oral hearing before the Examining Division took place in January 2006. The patent was rejected again and Pioneer appealed in January 2007.

Claim 1 of the set of claims under consideration at that stage read:

> A hybrid seed comprising an inheritable and stable fertility restorer gene ... or hybrid plant thereof, produced by a cross between a plant obtained from seed deposited as Brassica napus olifiera ... as a male parent and a second Brassica plant as a female parent, wherein the second Brassica plant has a glucosinolate level that is sufficiently low to ensure that the hybrid plant yields oilseeds having a total glucosinolate content of less than ... (T-788/07: para. XII)

TBoA 3.3.04 (Chairman Kinkeldey) made a comment on this claim that is relevant to the interpretation of Art. 53(b) EPC: 'Hybrid seed or plants thereof according to claims 1 to 5 are not considered as units with regard to their "suitability for being propagated unchanged" (Rule 26(4)(c) EPC)[19] and are therefore not regarded as plant varieties which are excluded from patentability (Article 53(b) EPC)' (T-788/07: para. 3).

[18] The reason why the claims were limited from 'rodents' to 'mice' had to do with Art. 53(a) and Rule 28(d) EPC, namely that the 'tests' to be passed under that Article and that Rule were not met since the 'likelihood of substantial medical benefit' was not satisfied for 'rodents', whereas for 'mice' it was, according to the Board (T-315/03: 62). We will return to this in Chapter 8.

[19] '"Plant variety" means any plant grouping within a single botanical taxon of the lowest known rank, which grouping, irrespective of whether the conditions for the grant of a plant variety right are fully met, can be: ... (c) considered as a unit with regard to its suitability for being propagated unchanged.'

In January 2008 the TBoA ordered the Examining Division to grant the patent. The patent (Charne *et al.* 2009) was granted in March 2009 and, since then, has been opposed by Syngenta, KWS Saat and Deutsche Saatveredelung together with four other companies including a daughter company of Limagrain. Unsurprisingly, Syngenta has not invoked Art. 53(b) EPC. KWS Saat has done so (Correspondence *KWS Saat* 2009: 8–10) as have Deutsche Saatveredelung *et al.* (Correspondence *Deutsche Saatveredelung* 2009: 11–17). The Patentee responded (Correspondence *Pioneer* 2010: 4–5). In December 2011, the Opposition Division revoked the patent on the grounds of Art. 53(b) EPC on the basis that the claims were directed to plant varieties. Pioneer has appealed and the appeal will proceed as T-1208/12 PIONEER.

7.15 Plants: T-1854/07 Oil from seeds/CONSEJO SUPERIOR

Consejo Superior de Investigaciones Cientificas (CSIC), the Spanish National Research Council, filed a patent application in June 2000 concerning sunflower seeds, obtainable by crossing and selection, with a modified fatty acid composition. The patent was granted in September 2004 (Martinez-Force *et al.* 2004).

The patent was opposed by Greenpeace on the basis of Art. 53(b) EPC, but the Opposition Division maintained the patent on the basis of a set of claims filed during the oral hearing. Claims 1 and 11, which were directed to seeds, read as follows:

1. Sunflower seeds that contain an oil having an oleic acid content of more than 5% and less than 65% ... a linoleic acid content of more than 1% and less than 65% ... a palmitic acid content of more than 20% and less than 40% ... a stearic acid content of more than 3% and less than 15% ... characterized in that the palmitoleic acid content is less than 4% ... and the asclepic acid content is less than 4% ... obtainable by crossing the high stearic line CAS-3 ... with a high palmitic line to introduce the stearoyl desaturase enzymatic activity of the high stearic line in the high palmitic line, and selecting seed of F2 generations in which the amount of palmitoleic and the amount of asclepic acid are decreased to less than 4% ...

11. Seeds according to any one of claims 1–10, obtainable by crossing sunflower seeds of the mutant sunflower line IG-1297M ... with the mutant sunflower line CAS-3. (Correspondence *EPO* 2007)

The other claims related inter alia to oil extracted from the claimed seeds, as well as to plants and progeny of the plants.

Greenpeace appealed the decision and at the oral hearing in appeal, in May 2010, they argued inter alia that it followed from Rule 26(4)(a)

EPC[20] and G-1/98 Transgenic plant/NOVARTIS II that plant inventions could only be patented if the single genetic components underlying the claimed characteristic could be identified and transferred between species. In CSIC's case, according to Greenpeace, the claimed characteristic (the fatty acid profile) resulted from the entire (combination of) genotype(s), together with epigenetic effects, hence the characteristic could only be stably transmitted as a whole and not as a single transferable technical feature or genetic component. G-1/98 Transgenic plant/NOVARTIS II only dealt with plant varieties as products of modern genetic modification, Greenpeace argued, whereas the CSIC case related to plants and seeds produced by traditional breeding methods involving crossing and selection. Thus these claims could not be granted in view of Art. 53(b) EPC. Moreover, according to Greenpeace, it was clear from Rule 26(4)(b) EPC[21] and G-1/98 Transgenic plant/NOVARTIS II that a single phenotypic trait was sufficient for a plant to fall under the definition of a plant variety if the trait allowed the plant to be distinguished from any other plant grouping and the trait was stably passed on to subsequent generations. Since this applied to the plants claimed in CSIC's patent, the patent had to be revoked in view of Art. 53(b) EPC. It was not necessary, Greenpeace noted, that the plant be homogeneous in all its traits. The acts described in claim 1, quoted above, of crossing the CAS-3 sunflower line with a high palmitic sunflower line and selecting seeds of plants of the F2 generation, inevitably resulted in a plant variety (T-1854/07: para. VII).

CSIC responded to these objections, arguing inter alia that, according to Rule 26(4)(b) EPC, a 'variety' was an entire plant grouping that had to be able to be propagated unchanged in every morphological, including biochemical, feature (for example same height, leaf and seed shape, flower colour, etc.). In the definition of 'variety', the entire genetic constitution or complete genotype had to be considered. Even if the claimed characteristic was the result of more than one genetic component, or an interaction between multiple genetic components, this did not imply that claim 1 related exclusively to a plant variety. It was

[20] '"Plant variety" means any plant grouping within a single botanical taxon of the lowest known rank, which grouping, irrespective of whether the conditions for the grant of a plant variety right are fully met, can be: … (a) defined by the expression of the characteristics that results [*sic*] from a given genotype or combination of genotypes.'

[21] '"Plant variety" means any plant grouping within a single botanical taxon of the lowest known rank, which grouping, irrespective of whether the conditions for the grant of a plant variety right are fully met, can be: … (b) distinguished from any other plant grouping by the expression of at least one of the said characteristics [i.e. those that result from a given genotype or combination of genotypes].'

not at all certain, CSIC asserted, that the parent lines recited in claim 1 met the requirements of Rule 26(4)(a) and (c) EPC. In the claimed plants and seeds, only a part of the genotype rather than a complete genetic constitution was responsible for the claimed technical feature (the change in the fatty acid profile). This feature could be conferred upon many different sunflower lines, and hence the claim was not limited to varieties and did not contravene Art. 53(b) EPC (T-1854/07: para. VIII).

In its decision, TBoA 3.3.04 (at that time no longer chaired by Kinkeldey but by Rennie-Smith) noted that 'although claims 1 and 11 are directed to sunflower seeds, the latter will be interchangeably considered as plants, given that plants may be grown from seeds, which represent one stage in the life cycle of the plant' (T-1854/07: para. 4).

The Board referred to G-1/98 Transgenic plant/NOVARTIS II, according to which the use of two different terms ('plant varieties' and 'plants') in the first half-sentence of Art. 53(b) EPC had to have some meaning and that meaning had to be that it had not been the intention of the legislator to exclude plants as a group embracing in general varieties as products, for otherwise the product exclusion would have used the more general term 'plants', as is the case for the process exclusion (the exclusion of essentially biological processes for the production of 'plants' and animals) (T-1854/07: para. 7).

Subsequently, the Board responded to what it labelled Greenpeace's 'major argument in this appeal', namely that G-1/98 Transgenic plant/NOVARTIS II was only concerned with plant varieties as products of recombinant gene technology and therefore did not apply to the CSIC case for this related to seeds and plants produced by classical plant breeding methods consisting of crossing and selection. It followed from G-1/98 Transgenic plant/NOVARTIS II, according to Greenpeace, that a patent was only allowed if the claimed plants could be defined by the introduction of a single identifiable trait (i.e. the claimed phenotype), but that patenting was prohibited if the claimed plants were the result of the interaction of several genetic components (including whole genomes), which was the case with methods based on crossing and selection (T-1854/07: para. 9).

The Board rejected this interpretation of G-1/98 Transgenic plant/NOVARTIS II and noted that the EBoA had observed, with regard to the definition of a 'plant variety' provided in UPOV 1991 and in CPVRR, as well as in in Rule 26(4(a) EPC, that the words 'expression of the characteristics that results from a given genotype or combination of genotypes' was a reference to 'the entire constitution of a plant or a set of genetic information' (T-1854/07: para. 10.2). Moreover, the EBoA had found that:

> In contrast, a plant defined by single recombinant DNA sequences is not an individual plant grouping to which an entire constitution can be attributed ... It is not a concrete living being or grouping of concrete living beings but an abstract and open definition embracing an indefinite number of individual entities defined by a part of its genotype or by a property bestowed on it by that part. (G-1/98: 125–6)

The TBoA went on to refer to another finding of G-1/98 Transgenic plant/NOVARTIS II, namely that 'The exception to patentability in Article 53(b), 1st half-sentence, EPC applies to plant varieties irrespective of the way in which they were produced. Therefore, plant varieties containing genes introduced into an ancestral plant by recombinant gene technology are excluded from patentability' (G-1/98: 141). Hence, according to the TBoA, Greenpeace's statement that G-1/98 Transgenic plant/NOVARTIS II only applied to genetically manipulated plants was incorrect (T-1854/07: para. 10.4). The contrary was said to be the case: 'On the contrary, decision G 1/98 [Transgenic plant/NOVARTIS II] makes clear beyond doubt that, whether or not a plant is considered to be a plant variety depends only on whether or not it meets the criteria set out in the definition in Rule 26(4) EPC ... The method for its production, be it by recombinant gene technology or by a classical plant breeding process, is not relevant for answering this question' (T-1854/07: para. 10.4).

As mentioned earlier, Greenpeace had argued that the claimed phenotypic trait (the fatty acid profile) did not result from a single transgene but from the interaction of multiple genetic components, or even of the entire genotype or combination of genotypes together with epigenetic effects, and that the trait could only be stably transmitted by these as a whole and not as a single (identifiable and transferable) technical feature or genetic component – and that therefore the seeds and plants obtained by the method described in claim 1 fulfilled all the criteria for being a 'plant variety' mentioned in Rule 26(4) EPC. The Board disagreed with this line of argument. It noted that the claimed trait was 'determined by a limited number of enzymes (and DNAs encoding them) rather than by a complete genetic constitution' and that the part of the genotype that was responsible for the claimed trait could be bestowed upon many different sunflower lines. According to the Board, the genetic equipment defining one specific trait of a plant or seed does not constitute its 'genotype', which defines its entire genetic makeup, and hence the claimed plants and seeds did not meet the requirement of Rule 26(4)(a) EPC of being 'defined by the expression of the characteristics that result from a given genotype or combination of genotypes' (T-1854/07: para. 13). Based on its view that the genetic equipment defining one specific trait of a plant or seed does not constitute its 'genotype', the Board also rejected Greenpeace's argument that, from a strict reading of Rule 26(4)(b) EPC, it had to be concluded that a single phenotypic trait was enough for the plant to fall within the definition of 'plant variety', provided that this trait allowed the plants to be distinguished from any other plant grouping and was stably passed on (T-1854/07: para. 14).

The last question that needed to be addressed, in the Board's view, was whether Greenpeace was right that applying the method described in claim 1 (crossing the CAS-3 sunflower line with a high palmitic sunflower line and subsequently selecting seeds of plants of the F2 generation) 'inevitably' resulted in a plant variety. The Board began by noting that the parent line was a 'breeding line' and that, according to CSIC, an application for plant variety protection had failed. Greenpeace, on the other hand, had expressed the view that 'a breeding line (in German "*Linie*") and a variety (in German "*Sorte*") defined the same entity with the only exception that a variety was registered and a breeding line not', but according to the Board Greenpeace had not provided evidence for this assumption. However, CSIC had provided expert declarations stating that the CAS-3 line was not 'uniform'. Thus, the Board argued, given the evidence, there was no reason to assume that the CAS-3 line was a plant variety (T-1854/07: para. 16). Moreover, according to the Board:

> The 'high palmitic' line [with which the CAS-3 line is to be crossed according to] claim 1 is not restricted to any particular deposited line or variety. Thus the claim allows the use of any sunflower provided it has a high palmitic acid content. There is also no requirement in the claim that the genetic background of the high palmitic lines be the same as that of the [CAS-3 line]. Therefore, the only possible way in which the claimed progeny could result in a variety or group of varieties is if the stabilisation of the desired phenotype through backcrossing led to phenotypic homogeneity. In the present case, the wording of the claim ('selecting seed of the F2 generation') only requires a single backcross. There is no evidence before the board that this single backcross would result in a plant variety. (T-1854/07: para. 16)

The Board consequently came to the conclusion that claims 1 and 11 did 'not individually claim a plant variety even though they may embrace plant varieties' and that therefore Art. 53(b) EPC did not constitute a bar to patentability[22] (T-1854/07: para. 18). The Board decided in May 2010 to remit the case to the Opposition Division, ordering it to maintain the patent on the basis of the claims filed at the oral hearing in appeal. The patent reissued in September 2011.

7.16 Plants: T-775/08 Glyphosate tolerant alfalfa/ MONSANTO

Monsanto filed a patent application (Beazley *et al.* 2004) in January 2004 concerning the genetic modification of alfalfa in order to make it tolerant to the herbicide glyphosate. In November 2007 the Examining Division refused the application for lack of novelty and inventive step as well as insufficient clarity and conciseness. Monsanto appealed and filed a new set of claims at the oral hearing, claim 1 of which read as follows:

> A glyphosate tolerant alfalfa plant, or a seed thereof, or a progeny thereof, the genome of said plant, seed or progeny comprises the transgene genetic elements [described in the application], the transgene genetic elements ... being present in the alfalfa event J-101 deposited with American Type Culture Collection (ATCC) with Accession No. PTA-4814. (T-775/08: para. VII)

In a communication annexed to the summons to oral proceedings, TBoA 3.3.08 (Chairman Heath) informed Monsanto of its preliminary opinion on some of the issues to be discussed and, with regard to 'possible issues regarding Article 53(b) EPC and Rule 26(5) EPC',[23] drew attention to the then pending referrals before the EBoA G-2/07 Broccoli/PLANT BIOSCIENCE and G-1/08 Tomatoes/STATE OF ISRAEL (T-775/08: para. IV).

In its decision, the Board referred to a deposit made by Monsanto in the American Type Culture Collection and observed that:

> It is acknowledged that the [deposited] alfalfa ... is a specific alfalfa variety which, as such, is excluded from patent protection by Article 53(b) EPC and Rule 27(b) EPC[24] (cf. G 1/98 [Transgenic plant/NOVARTIS II] ...).

[22] These claims are to plants (seeds) 'obtainable by' conventional crossing and selection breeding processes. In G-2/07 Broccoli/PLANT BIOSCIENCE such processes were found to be excluded from patentability under Art. 53(b) EPC. The question as to whether the products of such processes can be patented is, as discussed in Chapter 6, being put to the EBoA in T-1242/06 (12) Tomatoes II/STATE OF ISRAEL.

[23] 'A process for the production of plants or animals is essentially biological if it consists entirely of natural phenomena such as crossing or selection.' As explained in Chapter 6, this Rule was discredited by the Enlarged Board in G-2/07 Broccoli/PLANT BIOSCIENCE. However, it is not relevant to the present discussion.

[24] 'Biotechnological inventions shall also be patentable if they concern: ... (b) plants or animals if the technical feasibility of the invention is not confined to a particular plant or animal variety.'

However, the subject-matter of claim 1 is not limited to the specific deposited alfalfa variety but encompasses all possible alfalfa varieties having in their genome the transgene genetic elements [described in the application]. (T-775/08: para. 16)

The Board also admitted that 'the advantageous (physiological and morphological) characteristics described in the application ... have been demonstrated, only and exclusively, for the deposited glyphosate tolerant alfalfa plant'. However, the Board felt that, 'in the absence of any evidence to the contrary', it had no reason to question Monsanto's assertion that those advantageous characteristics were also obtained in other alfalfa varieties that would fulfil all the requirements mentioned in claim 1 (T-775/08: para. 17).

Therefore, the claimed subject-matter was said not to contravene Art. 53(b) EPC and Rule 27(b) EPC. In February 2011 the Board decided to remit the case to the Examining Division with an order to grant a patent on the basis of Monsanto's request filed during the oral proceedings. The Examining Division decided in October 2011 to grant the patent.

7.17 General comments

7.17.1 How necessary is product protection?

The earliest decision on the exclusion of varieties, T-49/83 Propagating material/CIBA-GEIGY, set the stage for many subsequent decisions. On the one hand, Ciba-Geigy as well as TBoA 3.3.01 were obviously right that the claimed innovation (the chemical treatment) did not cause genetic modification of the plants whose seeds had undergone the treatment, nor was the effect of the treatment transmissible to future generations. Indeed, no new plant varieties were created. However, the question arises as to *whether a product claim was necessary at all*. As pointed out by Ciba-Geigy itself, their invention concerned a non-biological process and its *direct* products and, according to Art. 64(2) EPC, if the subject-matter of a European patent is a process, the protection extends to the products directly obtained by that process. Referring to the writings of Rainer Schulte (Schulte 1981), Ciba-Geigy argued that a plant that cannot be patented as such under Art. 53(b) EPC could nonetheless get patent protection as a direct product of a patented non-biological process. The main conclusion we can draw from this is that the Board erred since a product claim (to the propagating material per se) was *totally unnecessary* and ought not to have been granted. As was later pointed out by TBoA 3.3.04 with regard to genetically modified plants, protection is possible via 'method claims leading to the preparation of the genetically engineered plants, product claims relating to the gene expressing the desired feature, and claims to the vector by which transformation of the plant cells is carried out', so it is 'plainly wrong to say that the inventors are deprived of all protection' (T-1054/96 (I): 530).

Moreover, in the earliest plant decision (T-49/83 Propagating material/CIBA-GEIGY), TBoA 3.3.01 made several problematic statements regarding both the purpose of the exclusion of plant varieties and the way it should be interpreted. The erroneous assumptions and arguments of this decision have had a huge impact on almost all the later decisions.

7.17.2 The purpose of the exclusion

In T-49/83 Propagating material/CIBA-GEIGY, TBoA 3.3.01 stated that plant varieties were excluded from patentability '*mainly* because' several parties to the EPC had developed plant breeders' rights protection. This was repeated by a different TBoA in T-320/87 Hybrid plants/ LUBRIZOL. Yet another TBoA noted, in T-1054/96 (I) Transgenic plant/NOVARTIS, that the existence of a separate protection system for plant varieties was an important, although *not the only*, reason for the exclusion of plant varieties in the EPC. Yet all these decisions remained silent as to the *other* reason(s) why the EPC legislator excluded plant varieties from patentability, and in later decisions '*mainly* because' would become '*only* because'.

As to animals, TBoA 3.3.02 stated in T-19/90 Onco-mouse/ HARVARD that 'the preparatory documents to [Art. 53(b) EPC] are completely silent as to the purpose of excluding "animal varieties" from patentability' (T-19/90: 487).

The argument in T-49/83 Propagating material/CIBA-GEIGY that Art. 53(b) EPC was intended to exclude *only* new individual plant varieties that could be protected under UPOV, became very popular, as shown by the discussion of TBoA case law in this chapter. In the first EBoA decision, too, it was explicitly stated that the purpose of the exclusion of varieties was only to exclude inventions that were eligible for protection by plant breeders' rights (G-1/98: 132–4). In this context, the EBoA referred to the observation of Klaus Pfanner – a civil servant involved in the UPOV, SPC and CEPL negotiations on behalf of the government of (West-)Germany – that the patent system was 'less suited' for 'biological developments' and that the legislator intended for these to be protected by the system of plant breeders' rights. However, the EBoA added that this *implied* that 'technical inventions related to plants' must be patentable, whereas of course it does not automatically follow that plants as such rather than technical processes for producing them should be patentable.

The EBoA's statement that there should be no gaps in protection in the field of plants, that is that everything should be protectable by either plant breeders' rights (for specific plant varieties) or by patents (for technical teachings which can be implemented in multiple plant varieties), which remains the EPO's position up to the present day, is quite simply unconvincing. First, it cannot be correct in view of the exclusion from patentability of *animal* varieties. The meaning of the term 'variety' must make sense for *both* plants and animals. As rightly noted by TBoA 3.3.04 in T-1054/96 (I) Transgenic plant/NOVARTIS: 'The purpose suggested for [Article 53(b) EPC] by [Novartis] was to achieve harmonisation with UPOV 1961. However, this answer ... leaves open the question of what purpose the provision in Article 53(b) EPC excluding animal varieties from the grant of a patent was to achieve. There was no provision for industrial property rights specifically for animal varieties' (T-1054/96 (I): 524). Thus, since there *is* a gap in protection as far as animal varieties are concerned, there can be no doubt that the legislator's intention was not 'to leave no gaps'.

Second, the *travaux préparatoires* simply do not support the EBoA's 'no gaps' view. The reference to Pfanner given by the EBoA in support of this view is misleading, since all Pfanner does in the article in question is to accurately report on the stage of the SPC negotiations as of November 1962. He discusses the exclusions from patentability in the then draft SPC and notes, in relation to the exclusion of types of plants and animals and essentially biological processes for the production of plants and animals, that:

> Der Ausschluß der Pflanzensorten oder Tierarten sowie der vorwiegend biologischen Verfahren zur Züchtung von Pflanzen oder Tieren ist darauf zurückzuführen, daß nach der überwiegenden Meinung der Sachverständigen für biologische Verfahren und Erzeugnisse die traditionellen Formen des Patentschutzes wenig geeignet sind ... Es handelt sich jedoch nur um eine Ausnahme von der Verpflichtung, den Patentschutz vorzusehen, nicht um ein Verbot der Patentierung mit Wirkung für alle Mitgliedstaaten. (Pfanner 1962: 547–8)

Thus Pfanner is saying that the reason for the exclusion of types of plants and animals and essentially biological processes for the production of plants and animals is that the predominant opinion amongst the framers of the SPC was that the traditional form of patent protection was little suited for covering *biological processes and products*. He goes on to confirm that the SPC exclusion simply absolved the Contracting States of any obligation to provide patent protection for types of plants and animals, rather than banning them from patenting such subject-matter under their *national* laws. Thus, Pfanner is *not* saying that protection *should* be available for all subject-matter either through plant variety protection or (European) patents.

The other 'evidence' from the *travaux préparatoires*, mentioned in G-1/98 Transgenic plant/NOVARTIS II in support of the 'no gaps' view, is also problematic for it refers to discussions on the patentability of (biological and technical) processes rather than products.[25]

In T-475/01 Phosphinothricin resistant gene/BAYER, and again in T-179/01 Herbicide resistant plants/MONSANTO, TBoA 3.3.08 held that if a claim passes the G-1/98 Transgenic plant/NOVARTIS II test, this was sufficient to demonstrate that patent protection can be obtained, *even if* operation of the invention leads to 'essentially derived varieties' that were clearly protectable under the CPVRR. TBoA 3.3.08's conclusion therefore clearly contradicts the view defended in G-1/98 Transgenic plant/NOVARTIS II that Art. 53(b) is only intended to exclude subject-matter that is protectable by plant breeders' rights.

In G-1/98 Transgenic plant/NOVARTIS II, the EBoA did give a coherent and accurate explanation as to the reason why the exclusion appears in Art. 53(b) EPC. Roughly summarised, given the existence of SPC and UPOV, it was simplest to exclude plant and animal varieties from patentability:

> When the legislator drafted the requirements for patentability in the EPC, the basis was the harmonisation already achieved by the SPC in the framework of the Council of Europe ... In the early nineteen sixties, the work on both Conventions proceeded in parallel. Whereas it was possible for most provisions of the SPC concerning patentability simply to be transferred to the EPC, this was not the case with Article 2(b) SPC since a choice had to be made whether or not to make use of the possible exclusion of patents in respect of plant varieties. It was not appropriate for the legislator to allow the grant of patents for plant varieties in general because some EPC Contracting States offered plant variety protection under the UPOV system and were prevented under the

[25] For example the reference to the Haertel draft of 1961 (see Chapter 2): 'The idea that the exclusion in the EPC should correspond to the availability of protection in UPOV was expressed in the early stages of the preparatory work on the EPC. In the remarks on Article 12 of the Haertel Draft 1961 proposing the exclusion of inventions relating to processes of breeding of plant or animal varieties, it was said that it remained to be considered whether the patentability of technical processes for breeding new plants (e.g. by radiation) had to be taken expressly into the Draft or whether this was self-evident from general principles' (G-1/98: 132).

ban on dual protection from granting patents. Nor was it possible under the EPC to exclude patent protection only in respect of those varieties for which a plant breeders' right was available (the approach taken by Belgium, Germany, France and Spain in their national legislation ...). Plant breeders' rights at a European level were not available and at the national level the availability of plant breeders' rights differed from country to country. To take account of the specific situation in each designated State for each individual application would have been contrary to the principle of uniform patent protection in all Contracting States (cf. Article 118 EPC). For these reasons, the most obvious choice was to make full use of the possibility in Article 2(b) SPC to exclude the grant of patents in respect of plant varieties entirely. (G-1/98: 131–2)

However, none of this implies that the intention of the framers was to leave no gaps.

7.17.3 The meaning of 'varieties'

As pointed out by TBoA 3.3.02 in T-320/87 Hybrid plants/ LUBRIZOL, the EPC does not contain any definition of varieties. It would have been very straightforward for the drafters of EPC to add that the term 'variety' had to be defined in accordance with UPOV if that was what they intended. Yet they did not. Thus, the frequent references to UPOV in the decisions described in this chapter come through as an unsubstantiated argument of authority.

Moreover, even though virtually all the decisions discussed earlier refer to UPOV when talking about the definition of 'plant variety', significant differences can be noted as regards the definitions that have been produced by different Boards. According to TBoA 3.3.01 in T-49/83 Propagating material/CIBA-GEIGY, '[p]lant varieties ... are all cultivated varieties, clones, lines, strains and *hybrids* which can be grown in such a way that they are clearly distinguishable from other varieties, *sufficiently* homogeneous, and stable in their *essential* characteristics' (T-49/83: 114, emphasis added). Shortly afterwards, TBoA 3.3.02 ruled in T-320/87 Hybrid plants/LUBRIZOL that hybrid plants *are* patentable.

Arguably the best definition of 'plant variety' suggested by the Boards so far is the one provided by TBoA 3.3.04 in T-356/93 Plant cells/PLANT GENETIC SYSTEMS, which added two elements to the definition proposed by the T-49/83 Propagating material/ CIBA-GEIGY Board, namely the reference to botanical taxon and the sufficiency of one distinguishing characteristic: '[Any] plant grouping within a single botanical taxon of the lowest known rank which, irrespective of whether it would be eligible for protection under the UPOV Convention, is characterised by at least one single transmissible characteristic distinguishing it from other plant groupings and which is sufficiently homogeneous and stable in its relevant characteristics' (T-356/93: 571). Even this definition is insufficient, though, as homogeneity and stability need only be sufficient for *any* feasible reproductive or propagation method, that is including cloning, using clippings, and growth from tubers.

Later on, the criteria came to be interpreted in an increasingly narrow sense, as shown for example by decisions T-788/07 Brassica/PIONEER and T-1854/07 Oil from seeds/CONSEJO SUPERIOR.

T-320/87 Hybrid plants/LUBRIZOL was the first time a TBoA considered a patent application for *a new type of* plant. The Lubrizol Board emphasised sufficient homogeneity and stability in the essential characteristics as preconditions for a variety. However, since the UPOV 1961 definition of 'plant variety' includes 'clones' as examples of plant varieties, stability on sexual reproduction must be irrelevant. The TBoA also overlooked this in T-356/93 Plant cells/PLANT GENETIC SYSTEMS. It argued that the transformed plants were varieties since they displayed normal fertility and the second-generation seedlings were homozygous for the herbicide resistance gene. Yet in view of the existence of cloning, homozygosity of the second generation is irrelevant.

Right from the very first plant decision, much emphasis has been put on the fact that the first half-sentence of Art. 53(b) EPC refers to 'plant varieties' whereas the second half-sentence simply refers to 'plants'. The result is that much effort has gone into attempts to define the word 'variety', using UPOV as the guideline. This has been one immense red herring. The *travaux préparatoires* clearly show that the second half-sentence was intended to exclude processes for the production of plants or animals of old and new species. There was no need for any qualification in this half-sentence. The first half-sentence, however, relates to new types of plant or animal, as old types could obviously not be patented since novelty is a fundamental requirement for patentability. Simply saying 'new animal' or 'new plant' would not be enough, since each new generation produces new animals and plants of the same type. The early drafts of the exclusion therefore referred to 'new varieties', 'new species', and so on. As explained in Chapter 2, the word 'variety' was finally settled upon, despite the fact that it had no clear taxonomic meaning, since it had been chosen as the appropriate word for 'type' or 'kind of' in the (then recently signed) UPOV 1961.

7.17.4 The second half-sentence

In T-19/90 Onco-mouse/HARVARD, TBoA 3.3.02 ruled that 'animals' were patentable if they were the product of a microbiological process and stated explicitly that the second half-sentence of Art. 53(b) could be interpreted in a way that sets aside the first half-sentence. TBoA 3.3.04 followed this line in T-356/93 Plant cells/PLANT GENETIC SYSTEMS and argued that herbicide-resistant plant varieties would be patentable if they could be regarded as the product of a microbiological process. Later, in G-1/98 Transgenic plant/ NOVARTIS II, the EBoA, correctly to our minds, decided against this view that the second half-sentence of Art. 53(b) EPC can set aside the first half-sentence.

According to TBoA 3.3.04, in T-1054/96 (I) Transgenic plant/ NOVARTIS, what the legislator meant by 'product of a microbiological process' (where the product is a living organism) were yeasts, bacteria and other micro-organisms, that is products that were already considered patentable at the time of the SPC. This indeed appears to be correct.

7.17.5 The approach to the exclusion

Like TBoA 3.3.01 in T-49/83 Propagating material/CIBA-GEIGY (T-49/83: 115), TBoA 3.3.02 in T-320/87 Hybrid plants/LUBRIZOL clearly rejected a *novelty* approach and decided that a claim that encompassed the excluded was not excluded, that is it opted for a *higher taxonomic level* approach:

> Even if the totality of the hybrid generation resulting from the crosses of the cloned selected parent plants were to *comprise* single individual plants which would be stable for a certain trait when further crossed and propagated, this fact does not in itself contradict the stated non-stability of the population *taken as a whole*. Furthermore, such single individual plants are not to be construed as embraced within the subject-matter of the product claim. (T-320/87: 79–80, emphasis added)

However, TBoA 3.3.04 convincingly argued in both T-356/93 Plant cells/PLANT GENETIC SYSTEMS and T-1054/96 (I) Transgenic plant/NOVARTIS that such an approach is contrary to the rules of logic. As we argue in Chapter 9, even if the *novelty* approach is unworkable, the *higher taxonomic level* approach is not sufficient. Notwithstanding this, the EBoA came up with a most remarkable piece of reasoning: the taxonomic category to which the claimed plants belong 'is not specified' by the applicant, hence the claimed invention 'neither expressly nor implicitly defines' a single variety, hence it does not 'define' a multiplicity of varieties that necessarily consists of several individual varieties, and hence the subject-matter of the invention 'is neither limited nor even directed to' a variety or varieties (G-1/98: 126–7). Clearly, this line of reasoning relies on logically impermissible 'jumps', starting with a question regarding excluded matter being 'specified' or 'defined' in the claims (or not) and ending with a conclusion regarding the invention being 'limited to' or 'directed to' excluded matter (or not). The EBoA further added that a patent must be refused if the subject-matter is 'directed to' plant varieties, but that such is not the case in 'the absence of the identification of a specific plant variety in a product claim'. Thus another category ('identifying') was added to the possible categories of 'specifying', 'defining', 'being limited to' and 'being directed to'. However, these terms are not equivalent and should not be used interchangeably. A claim may be 'directed to' a plant variety simply by encompassing one within its scope. A claim may 'define' or 'specify' a set of plant varieties simply by reciting a characteristic that can be transferred between propagation cycles, or 'specify' or 'define' a single plant variety by reciting the set of characteristics that together distinguish it from all other plant varieties. A claim is not 'limited to' a plant variety if it covers things that are not plant varieties. This disparity in language was picked up by the Kinkeldey 3.3.04 Board in T-1054/96 Anti-pathogenic compositions/NOVARTIS III.

The fact must not be overlooked that G-1/98 Transgenic plant/NOVARTIS II was handed down at a stage when to decide that Art. 53(b) EPC meant otherwise would have had two serious repercussions. First, the president and the Administrative Council of the EPO would have been shown to have acted beyond their powers in September 1999 by introducing Rules reflecting the terms of the EBD. Second, the EPC would have been shown to be non-compliant with the EBD, which would have required amendment either of the EBD or of the EPC to avoid the agrochemical industry abandoning the EPO in favour of filing national patent applications in EU countries where the national patent laws had been brought into line with the EBD. Moreover, G-1/98 Transgenic plant/NOVARTIS II was the first decision on substantive patentability of the EBoA under a new chairman (Peter Messerli) and the internal and external pressure to follow the line of the EBD would have been huge.

As rightly noted by TBoA 3.3.04 in T-1054/96 (I) Transgenic plant/NOVARTIS, treating the (then draft) EBD, which expressed the 'more than a single variety' (i.e. *higher taxonomic level*) approach, as evidence of any agreed subsequent practice under the EPC is problematical. Indeed, EBoA decision G-2/07 Broccoli/PLANT BIOSCIENCE, discussed in Chapter 6, has confirmed that the EBD is not binding, in the same way as TBoA 3.5.01 has pointed out in decision T-1173/97 Computer program product/IBM that the TRIPS Agreement is not binding (see Chapter 3). Likewise, the definition of 'plant variety' in UPOV is not binding on the EPO.

7.18 Conclusion

Art. 53 EPC contains in three paragraphs several different exclusions from patentability. The wording used to effect the exclusion is the same for all, namely: 'European patents shall not be granted in respect of ...' and, as a result, the exclusions need to be interpreted in the same way. A different approach to each of the exclusions is not supported by the presence of this common language. In practice, the Examining Division and the TBoAs of the EPO have chosen between three alternative approaches when addressing the exclusions of Art. 53 EPC, the ones we have referred to in Chapter 3 as the *contamination* approach, the *higher taxonomic level* approach, and the *novelty* approach.

The *contamination* and *higher taxonomic level* approaches result in claims being granted that would seem to be infringed by the very subject-matter expressly stated to be unpatentable in Art. 53 EPC. The *novelty* approach, the approach that was argued for most forcefully by the Kinkeldey Board in both T-356/93 Plant cells/PLANT GENETIC SYSTEMS and T-1054/96 (I) Transgenic plant/NOVARTIS, while attractive, is unworkable because of the manner in which patent claims are written and construed. We will return to this in Chapter 9. The EBoA in G-1/98 Transgenic plant/NOVARTIS II chose the politically more comfortable *higher taxonomic level* approach without apparently realising that this was inconsistent with earlier decisions relating to other Art. 53 EPC exclusions and indeed is inconsistent with later decisions by the EBoA in relation to the other Art. 53 EPC exclusions. This can be put into context by considering a claim directed to a method of surgery on a human being. Under the *higher taxonomic level* approach such a claim would be permissible if in place of human being the applicant wrote 'living organism'. Such a claim, being accepted under the *higher taxonomic level* approach, would be infringed by a surgeon operating on a living human patient. Similarly, claims to human embryonic stem cells (see the G-2/06 Use of embryos/WARF decision discussed in Chapter 8) could be granted simply by referring to 'stem cells' rather than 'human embryonic stem cells'. On its own, the *higher taxonomic level* approach makes a mockery of the public policy exclusions of Art. 53 EPC.

The case law of the EPO regarding the exclusion of plant and animal varieties clearly shows a major rift, initially, between TBoA 3.3.02

under the chairmanship of Pierre Lançon (responsible, inter alia, for T-320/87 Hybrid plants/LUBRIZOL) and TBoA 3.3.04 under the chairmanship of Ursula Kinkeldey (responsible, inter alia, for T-356/93 Plant cells/PLANT GENETIC SYSTEMS).

TBoA 3.3.04 (under the chairmanship of Kinkeldey) correctly observed that varieties should remain excluded from patentability until the *legislators* reconsider the matter. Indeed, the *travaux préparatoires* for the EPC repeatedly mention that changing exclusions from patentability requires a diplomatic conference of the EPC Member States. It should not and cannot (legitimately) be done by the EPO, yet, unfortunately, this is what we are witnessing in practice.

8 Morality and 'ordre public'

> The grant of patents by the EPO presupposes that there is a legal order in the Contracting States which allows granted patent rights to be enforced. Article 53(a) EPC can be considered as the expression that it would be incompatible with such legal order to grant patents for inventions whose exploitation would be contrary to 'ordre public' or morality. The provision of Article 53(a) might thus be considered as a legal norm of higher rank than the provisions of Article 52(1) EPC, which latter must yield in case of conflict.
>
> (Correspondence *EPO* 2008: para. 10)

8.1 Introduction

Art. 53(a) EPC provides that:

> European patents shall not be granted in respect of ... inventions the commercial exploitation of which would be contrary to 'ordre public' or morality; such exploitation shall not be deemed to be so contrary merely because it is prohibited by law or regulation in some or all of the Contracting States. (EPO 2010a: 107)

This Article was amended when the EPC was revised in 2000 and no longer excludes inventions the *publication* of which would be contrary to 'ordre public' or morality. The word 'commercial' was also inserted before 'exploitation'.

In this chapter we will discuss the development of the EPO's approach to questions of morality and explain how it has been affected by changes in the introduction of EPC Rules deriving from the EBD. The new Rules recently resulted in a decision from the EBoA in relation to human embryonic stem cells, G-2/06 Use of embryos/WARF, which showed a fundamental shift in the EPO's approach to morality – away from the consequentialist or 'balancing' approach, which had until then always been taken by the EPO, to a deontological or principle-based approach, according to which certain things may be morally impermissible, *even* if they would produce more benefits than disadvantages.

We will first give an overview of the important TBoA and EBoA decisions on the exclusion of inventions the (commercial) exploitation of which would be contrary to 'ordre public' or morality. Afterwards we will provide general comments and criticisms of the ways in which this exclusion has been interpreted and applied. Unlike Chapter 7, the discussion of cases will not be purely chronological. Rather, the decisions will be grouped according to the nature of the subject-matter, namely:

- animals;
- plants;
- controversial medical interventions (euthanasia compositions);
- human genes and genetic diagnostic tests; and
- stem cells and uses of human embryos.

8.2 Animals: T-19/90 Onco-mouse/HARVARD

As discussed in Chapter 7, Harvard filed a patent application relating inter alia to animals whose germ cells and somatic cells contained an activated oncogene sequence (Leder and Stewart 1986: 18).

Rejecting the application in 1989, the Examining Division commented on the relevance of Art. 53(a) EPC:

> The idea of the patenting of higher organisms has encountered severe criticism for ethical and economic reasons, particularly in the USA ... This example clearly shows that the ethical questions need to be considered under the given circumstances.
>
> At the Oral Proceedings specific questions were considered which related to
>
> (a) the desirability of applying non-animal models in the sort of cancer tests concerned,
> (b) the fact that the present invention is not aimed at improving any specific feature, but at producing tumours in the test animal,
> (c) the fact that animals are regarded as an object,
> (d) the danger that descendants of the transgenic animals might escape into nature and spread through mating the foreign malignant genes, and
> (e) the problem of drastically disrupting evolution.
>
> In considering [the Guidelines for Examination in the European Patent Office] and particularly also considering that the present invention might have a beneficial effect on mankind, the Examining Division concludes that the patent law is not the right legislative tool for regulating problems which may arise in view of the dangers mentioned [above]. Article 53(a) EPC is, consequently, not used to refuse the present application. (Correspondence *EPO* 1989: 10–11)

Harvard appealed and in T-19/90 Onco-mouse/HARVARD in October 1990, TBoA 3.3.02 (Chairman Lançon) noted that:

[T]he Examining Division argued that patent law is not the right legislative tool for regulating problems arising in connection with genetic manipulation of animals. The Board considers, however, that precisely in a case of this kind there are compelling reasons to consider the implications of Article 53(a) EPC in relation to the question of patentability. The genetic manipulation of mammalian animals is undeniably problematical in various respects, particularly where activated oncogenes are inserted to make an animal abnormally sensitive to carcinogenic substances and stimuli and consequently prone to develop tumours, which necessarily cause suffering. There is also a danger that genetically manipulated animals, if released into the environment, might entail unforeseeable and irreversible adverse effects ... Considerations of precisely this kind have also led a number of Contracting States to impose legislative control on genetic engineering. *The decision as to whether or not Article 53(a) EPC is a bar to patenting the present invention would seem to depend mainly on a careful weighing up of the suffering of animals and possible risks to the environment on the one hand, and the invention's usefulness to mankind on the other.* It is the task of the department of first instance to consider these matters.[1] (T-19/90: 490, emphasis added)

The patent was granted with claims directed to a 'transgenic non-human mammalian animal' and is discussed further in the next section.

8.3 Animals: T-315/03 Transgenic animals/HARVARD

Seventeen parties (see Chapter 7, section 7.13) opposed the 'Onco-mouse' patent (Leder and Stewart 1992). All the opponents invoked Art. 53(a) EPC. In January 2003 the Opposition Division rejected all the objections except for those under Art. 53(a) EPC, starting by arguing that 'Rule [27(b)] EPC in principle declares animals patentable subject-matter provided certain conditions are met. Consequently all arguments pointing out that patents on living matter or patents on animals are generally not allowable under Article 53(a) EPC must fail as a matter of principle' (Correspondence *EPO* 2003a: 25–6). The Opposition Division proceeded by commenting on the meaning of the concepts of 'morality' and 'ordre public', clearly ignoring the second half-sentence of Art. 53(b) EPC:

For the purposes of Article 53(a) EPC, 'ordre public' and morality have to be assessed primarily by looking at laws or regulations which are common to most of the European countries because these laws and regulations are the best indicator about what is considered right or wrong in European society. *In so far as such laws or regulations*

[1] This 'careful weighing up' we will refer to as the 'Harvard test'.

> *concerning the relevant issue exist, it appears neither necessary nor appropriate to rely on other possible means of assessment* ... [S]tatutory law regulating the use of [test animals] is highly indicative because it shows whether the exploitation of the invention is de facto prohibited or not. The use of animals for experimental or other scientific purposes is allowed under certain conditions in most if not all of the states being party to the EPC ... It is therefore concluded that *patenting of those animals ... complies with the principle requirement of morality because the exploitation of the invention is explicitly allowed.* (Correspondence *EPO* 2003a: 26, emphasis added)

On this basis, the Opposition Division concluded that:

> [C]laims to animals as such and to processes for making them are allowable under Article 53(a) EPC to the extent that at least representative categories of the animals claimed fulfil the criteria of being test animals in accordance with laws in the member states of the EPC. The claims ... which are directed to non-human mammalian animals do not fulfil this condition because many categories of animals are covered by these claims not falling under the provision of being test animals. These claims are therefore not allowable under Article 53(a) EPC. (Correspondence *EPO* 2003a: 28)

The Opposition Division decided to maintain the patent in amended form, with claims directed to 'rodents'. Six of the seventeen opponents appealed.

In T-315/03 Transgenic animals/HARVARD, from July 2004, TBoA 3.3.08 (Chairman Davison-Brunel) first explained that 'This case is ... not, as [four of the six appellants] asserted, concerned with the patentability of animals. This case is concerned with whether or not the EPC allows the patentability of the particular animal invention in question and, if so, how broadly that invention may be claimed' (T-315/03: 31).

With regard to the applicability of the 'package' of Rules 26 to 29 EPC, in particular Rule 27 and 28 EPC, the Board argued that there could be no doubt that these Rules applied as the patent unquestionably concerned a biotechnological invention (T-315/03: 34), although it was noted that:

> [Four of the six appellants] and [Harvard] formed an unholy alliance against applicability of the new Rules to this case, albeit their reasons were vastly different. [The appellants] saw the new Rules as a fundamental amendment to the EPC to provide, with both retrospective and prospective effect, for the patenting of animals. Those appellants argued that changes of such significance should be made in the EPC itself and not in the Implementing Regulations ... [Harvard's] position was more complex ... The principal argument [was that] Rule [28] EPC, by introducing the concept of 'substantial medical benefit', made a previously unpredictable change to the interpretation of Article 53(a) EPC. (T-315/03: 34–5)

In response to the argument that such significant changes had to be made in the *Articles* of the EPC, the Board disagreed:

> The Boards do have jurisdiction inter alia to interpret the EPC – whether Articles enacted by the Contracting States in conference or Rules enacted by the Administrative Council – and must have jurisdiction to refuse enforcement of, and to declare invalid, legislation which has been defectively enacted (for example, if passed by an insufficient number of States or Administrative Council delegations), since otherwise parties could be prejudiced by 'laws' which in fact do not exist. The Boards also have jurisdiction to give effect to Article 164(2) EPC – to refuse enforcement of a Rule of the Convention which conflicts with an Article. But none of these powers mean that the Boards have any power, express or necessarily implied, to prevent the operation of correctly enacted legislation and, as regards the passage of legislation, the choice between Articles and Implementing Regulations is one exclusively for the legislator. (T-315/03: 37)

The Board then commented on Rule 28(d) EPC,[2] noting that, in view of the use of the words 'in particular', the Rule was not intended to provide an exhaustive list of inventions excluded from patentability under Art. 53(a) EPC, and that, thus, '[a] case not falling within the Rule does not thereby "escape" Article 53(a) EPC'. However, the Board also argued, wrongly as we will explain in section 8.16, that 'a case falling within one of the four categories must ipso facto be denied a patent under Article 53(a) EPC and there is no need to consider that Article further' (T-315/03: 40). This led the Board to assert that if an invention failed the 'balancing test' prescribed by the Rule – the operation of which was said to be 'triggered' by a likelihood of animal suffering – a patent had to be denied, whereas if the invention passed the Rule test, it was subsequently to be assessed under the Article (T-315/03: 40–1).

Harvard had argued that the Rule was inconsistent with the 'Harvard test' (see section 8.2) as that was different from the one prescribed by the Rule (weighing up of the likelihood of animal suffering on the one hand and substantial medical benefit to man or animal on the other). It followed from this, according to Harvard, that the Rule had broadened the exclusion laid down in Art. 53(a) EPC, for 'usefulness to mankind' was broader than 'substantial medical benefit to man or animal'. Thus, inventions that might have passed the Harvard test could fail the Rule test. The Board disagreed, arguing that, since it was unimaginable

[2] 'Under Article 53(a) European patents shall not be granted in respect of biotechnological inventions which, in particular, concern the following: ... (d) processes for modifying the genetic identity of animals which are likely to cause them suffering without any substantial medical benefit to man or animal, and also animals resulting from such processes.'

that cases falling within any of the four categories listed in the Rule would not always have been considered under Article 53(a) EPC to be excluded, it was incorrect to say that the new Rule broadened the law (T-315/03: 43). According to the Board, 'the ... Rules are interpretative ... [and] the effect of this interpretation is to insert a test which, depending on the facts and thus on the outcome of the test, may be either additional or alternative to that previously established by the case law' (T-315/03: 45).

As to the standard of evidence required by the Rule, the Board expressed the view that:

> [The Rule] requires three matters to be evaluated, namely, whether animal suffering is likely; whether likely substantial medical benefit has been established; and whether the suffering and the medical benefit both exist in relation to the use of the same animals ... Rule [28(d)] EPC should be applied to ensure that any patent should only extend to those animals whose suffering is balanced by a medical benefit ... [I]t is important to resist seeing the two integers of the test as requiring different degrees of proof. The expression 'likely to cause suffering without any substantial medical benefit' may appear at first sight to contrast the words 'likely' and 'substantial' with the result that one seeks to balance mere likelihood of suffering by a medical benefit which, since it must be 'substantial', is therefore actual or real – with the result that one looks for proof of the existence of such a benefit at the relevant date. The Board considers this is not in fact the case. (T-315/03: 47)

The Board concluded on that basis that, since only a likelihood of animal suffering needed to be proved, the degree of suffering and the availability of non-animal alternatives did not need to be considered under the Rule. However, it was rightly added that 'This does not mean such matters should be ignored when considering the case under Article 53(a) EPC generally' (T-315/03: 48).

The appellants had argued that the evidence to be considered should not be limited to the evidence mentioned in the patent application, since patent applicants will always assert that their invention has substantial benefits. Harvard, on the other hand, had pointed out that any threshold that went beyond relying on the evidence mentioned in the application would represent a novel and unacceptable requirement that applicants must reduce their inventions to practice before filing a patent application. The Board expressed the following, somewhat unclear, position on this issue:

> The Board agrees with [Harvard] that it cannot be necessary to set a standard which requires reduction to practice before filing, but also agrees with the appellants that evidence cannot be confined to that in existence at the effective date: additional evidence, both for and against the patentee, may be considered

subsequently but this must be evidence which demonstrates the state of affairs at the effective date. Such evidence may be open to the objection of hindsight (which, if established, may tell against the party relying on it) but the alternative – to allow only evidence in existence at the effective date – is subject to the greater criticism that only a patentee is likely to have admissible evidence. It must be acknowledged that some information about certain inventions will only emerge after, and on occasions some considerable time after, patent applications have been filed ... The Board considers the position in this respect to be analogous to that regarding evidence of sufficiency of disclosure under Article 83 EPC. Just as it is considered necessary for an initial disclosure in a patent application ... to establish plausibly that the invention disclosed can be performed, so the Board considers a patent application must plausibly establish the likelihood of medical benefit to balance any animal suffering evident from the application. In practice, in Rule [28(d)] EPC cases it will of course be clear beyond doubt from a patent application that, in a case of genetic manipulation of animals, suffering is at least likely even if not expressly mentioned ... [J]ust as opponents may file evidence in which they attempt to demonstrate insufficiency (for example, by trying and failing to work examples in a patent), so opponents may file evidence seeking to demonstrate that ... medical benefit was not likely. (T-315/03: 49–50)

With regard to the assessment under the Article (which, in the Board's view, was only necessary if the invention passed the Rule test), reference was made to the definitions of morality and 'ordre public' in T-356/93 Plant cells/PLANT GENETIC SYSTEMS, discussed in section 8.5, and agreement was expressed with the dismissal of evidence based on opinion polls (T-315/03: 53).

According to the Board, the starting point for assessment under Art. 53(a) EPC had to be the Harvard test. Once again, the differences between the Harvard test and the Rule test were emphasised:

[W]hereas the Rule ... test only requires a likelihood of animal suffering (that is, any suffering, however minor) and a likelihood of substantial medical benefit, the T 19/90 [Onco-mouse/HARVARD] test requires a 'careful weighing up' of the matters to be balanced. That clearly allows the scope or extent of, on the one hand, the animal suffering and/or environmental risk and, on the other hand, the usefulness to mankind to be considered. Accordingly factors such as the degree of suffering and the possible use of non-animal alternatives can be taken into account. (T-315/03: 54)

Moreover, in view of the word 'mainly' in the Harvard test, the Board argued that it was permissible for other considerations to be taken into account when making the assessment under the Article:

[E]ither by way of adapting the test – if, for example, other issues than animal suffering or environmental risk were advanced as contrary to 'ordre public' or morality – or by way of considering other matters outside the framework of

> the test. For example, in the present case the arguments under Article 53(a) EPC included an alleged threat to evolution, alleged increased trade in genetically manipulated animals and alleged moral unacceptability of such manipulation ... There is no apparent reason why other such arguments could not be deployed as part of the T 19/90 [Onco-mouse/HARVARD] test ... Yet ... these arguments like all arguments must be substantiated. (T-315/03: 54–5)

With regard to Harvard's 'main request' (i.e. preferred set of claims), the Board first made a number of observations in relation to the Rule test.

> [It is] agreed by the parties – that the process is likely to cause [the] animals suffering. As the request embraces all animals within the taxonomic order Rodentia, suffering will – and must – be present in the case of every such animal – not just mice but also squirrels, beavers, porcupines and every other rodent. In any event, no other conclusion would be possible in respect of a request in which claim 1 causes ... an abnormal – benign or cancerous – tissue growth which results in the animals suffering and eventually in their death. Animal suffering is not just a likelihood but an inevitable consequence of the very purpose of the patent ... The two questions which thus arise are first, whether there is also a likelihood of a substantial medical benefit to man or animal and second, whether that benefit is obtained in the case of all the animals which are likely to suffer. (T-315/03: 62)

In the Board's view there was no evidence that any benefit was likely to be derived with any rodents apart from mice.

> [T]here is quite simply no evidence to show that all the various animals in the category of rodents are so different that each of them would provide a contribution to cancer studies, such as being specifically suited as a model for studying a specific type of cancer. Thus [Harvard's] argument appears to be no more than argument – it is purely hypothetical and unsubstantiated by any evidence. (T-315/03: 62–3)

The Board concluded that the broad claims could not pass the Rule test and therefore had to be rejected. It was added 'in passing' that 'Taking into account other matters, such as the degree of animal suffering and the availability of alternative non-animal methods, would ... merely tilt the balance further against acceptance of the request' (T-315/03: 63).

Next, the Board considered the 'first auxiliary request' submitted by Harvard, in which the claims related to 'mice' instead of 'rodents'. How did these claims fare under the Rule test? Concerning the likelihood of animal suffering, the Board noted that there was 'not just a likelihood but a certainty of animal suffering' (T-315/03: 64). The likelihood of substantial medical benefit, according to the Board, could 'at the very least be inferred from the patent itself', for 'the purpose of both the claimed method and the oncomice thereby produced and used for test purposes is to further cancer research. Additionally there is evidence on file ... demonstrating actual medical benefits achieved using mice such as those obtained by the claimed process' (T-315/03: 64–5).

Since the animals that would suffer as a result of the invention were of the same genus as those 'offering the prospect of a contribution to medical research', these claims were said to pass the Rule test and therefore also had to be assessed under the Article 'without reference to' the Rule (T-315/03: 66). The application of the Harvard test also led to the conclusion that the claims were acceptable, for while suffering of the mice was certain, actual medical benefit, useful to mankind, had been demonstrated in the Board's view (T-315/03: 67). As to 'other considerations' that could be taken into account when applying the Harvard test, in particular the issues, raised by the appellants, of the degree of suffering and the possibility of achieving the stated aims by using non-animal alternatives, the Board first noted that:

> To suggest that the degree of suffering could be material is to suggest the possibility of a distinction between 'acceptable suffering' and 'unacceptable suffering'. In the Board's opinion this is not a distinction which the parties in question really wished to evoke and it is certainly not a distinction which would assist in deciding this or similar cases ... [I]t would be not only distasteful but effectively impossible for the Board (or any other decision-making instance) to make findings as to degrees of suffering. (T-315/03: 67)

Further, on the use of non-animal alternatives, the Board observed that the appellants had not provided any evidence that using cell cultures would produce similar or better results as compared with using onco-mice. Reference was also made to an expert declaration that onco-mice produced better results than cell cultures. The Board concluded that 'if this alternative is added to the matters to be weighed up in the T 19/90 Onco-mouse/HARVARD test, the result will be, on the available evidence, to tilt the balance away from the appellants and in favour of [Harvard]' (T-315/03: 67).

As regards environmental risks, which also had to be balanced against usefulness to mankind under the Harvard test, the Board noted that what was at issue were 'possible threats to the environment if oncomice were to escape (or to be released, deliberately or accidentally) into the wild'. Since no evidence had been produced, the Board found that 'the environmental issues are at the utmost of neutral effect on the case' since the risks in question were 'minimally more than hypothetical' in view of the secure conditions in laboratories and the regulations in force in most countries (T-315/03: 68–9).

On this basis, the Board concluded that claims to mice passed the Harvard test. Finally, the Board considered some of the other arguments that had been put forward by the appellants, inter alia the argument that the Harvard patent would promote trade in animals and lead to an increase in the number of transgenic mice used in cancer research. In the Board's view this argument was quasi-irrelevant.

The Board's final conclusion with regard to Art. 53(a) EPC was that:

> [I]n current European culture ... animals are on the one hand respected as sentient beings which are not to be gratuitously abused or misused ... and, on the other hand, animals are accepted as being important in the testing of medicaments and curative methods prior to human application ... One result of this dichotomy is ... the 'unease' which may arise in relation to patents involving animals ... *However, there is nothing before the Board to suggest that such unease could be elevated to the status of moral disapproval in European culture of the use of animals for medical research, let alone moral disapproval of the use of mice in cancer research* – i.e. moral disapproval of the exploitation of the present invention. *Accordingly, Article 53(a) EPC does not constitute a bar to patentability of the subject-matter of the first auxiliary request.* (T-315/03: 77, emphasis added)

The case was remitted to the Opposition Division with an order to maintain the patent with claims to mice. Harvard failed to take the steps necessary to maintain the patent and the patent was revoked.

8.4 Animals: T-606/03 Gene trap/ARTEMIS

In October 2000 Artemis Pharmaceuticals and Frankgen Biotechnologie filed a patent application (Kühn *et al.* 2001) relating inter alia to a gene-trapping construct causing mutations in genes and to transgenic organisms incorporating the gene-trapping construct.

In its decision in January 2003, the Examining Division refused the application on the basis inter alia of Art. 53(a) EPC and Rule 28 EPC.[3] It was pointed out that some of the claims related to methods for modifying the germline of humans and to transgenic humans (Correspondence *EPO* 2003b: 6).

In May 2003 Artemis and Frankgen appealed and filed an amended set of claims in which the product claims to transgenic organisms were limited to non-human organisms. One of the process claims, to a 'process [for the generation of conditional mutations in all genes of an

[3] 'Under Article 53(a), European patents shall not be granted in respect of biotechnological inventions which, in particular, concern the following: ... (b) processes for modifying the germ line genetic identity of human beings.'

organism] being a process for preparing transgenic mammals, wherein ... the gene trapping construct is installed in an ES cell' (original claim 15, claim 16 in the amended claim set), was left unchanged.

In their Statement of Grounds of Appeal the appellants did not comment on Art. 53(a) EPC. In the summons to attend oral proceedings in January 2006, TBoA 3.3.08 (Chairman Galligani) drew attention to T-315/03 Transgenic animals/HARVARD and, accordingly, an amended set of claims was submitted, this time referring to 'mice' instead of 'mammals'.

The appellants argued that the claimed mice were potent tools for investigating the role of specific genes, which would allow the development of pharmaceuticals to relieve effects caused by malfunctioning of those genes. Since the mice were animal models reflecting what might happen in humans, it was argued, the mice and their use clearly represented a substantial medical benefit. Artemis and Frankgen did admit that, in mutated form, the mice would be likely to suffer. However, they argued that the mice were likely to suffer much less than already developed transgenic mice with a gene trap construct in their genome. Their gene trap construct, they noted, could be inserted in the genome in two different orientations, one of which would cause a mutation whereas the other would not. The mice would mostly remain in a non-mutated state and thus they would not suffer. Suffering might only occur when the mice were used for the purpose of substantial medical benefit. Thus, the claim to the *process* for preparing transgenic mice incorporating a gene-trapping construct (claim 16) was said not to contravene Art. 53(a) and Rule 28(d) EPC.[4] With regard to the *product* claim, which had been restricted to mice that carried the gene trap in the non-mutagenic orientation, the appellants argued that those mice would not suffer and that therefore Rule 28(d) EPC did not apply.

The Board began by referring to T-315/03 Transgenic animals/HARVARD, and noted that the first step in the assessment under Art. 53(a) EPC had to be an investigation as to whether Rule 28(d) EPC applied (T-606/03: para. 1). The Board noted that claim 16 extended to mice for which the genetic modification resulted in a mutated phenotype and that, as the appellants had admitted, in cases where the mutated gene was an essential one, the mice would suffer (T-606/03: para. 2).

[4] 'Under Article 53(a), European patents shall not be granted in respect of biotechnological inventions which, in particular, concern the following': ... (d) processes for modifying the genetic identity of animals which are likely to cause them suffering without any substantial medical benefit to man or animal, and also animals resulting from such processes.'

Moreover, the Board added, not all the claimed mice would be of any medical benefit since, as evidenced by the patent specification, 'the benefit to be expected, namely serving as models for the development of pharmaceutical drugs – will more often than not depend on previous research having established the role of the targeted gene in a given pathology' (T-606/03: para. 3). Thus, for those mice, the Board argued, the likely suffering was not outweighed by a likely substantial medical benefit to man or animal. Hence Art. 53(a) and Rule 28(d) EPC precluded patentability (T-606/03: para. 4).[5]

One amendment to the process claim, filed at the oral proceedings, required the mice to carry the gene trap construct in an intron in an antisense direction relative to the gene that was trapped. In these mice, according to the patent specification, the construct did not affect their metabolism and hence they did not suffer. Thus, according to the Board, producing these mice did not imply suffering and therefore the Harvard test did not apply (T-606/03: para. 12).

The Board then proceeded by admitting that:

> It is true that mice which can be 'derived' from these claimed mice by acquisition and expression of the recombinase gene will be mutated mice – the gene trap will have been flipped in the activated orientation – and that ... some of them at least are likely to suffer. *However, these 'subsequent' mice are not claimed and, therefore, do not fall within the invention and, thus, are outside the board's power of investigation*. (T-606/03: para. 13, emphasis added)

As we will explain below, this approach is inadequate as it presupposes that the assessment to be made under Art. 53(a) EPC is *only* of the subject-matter to which the claims are *specifically directed* and not of the *use* or *provenance* of that subject-matter. This restricted approach was found to be incorrect in G-2/06 Use of embryos/WARF as it ignores the totality of actions involved in the 'commercial exploitation' referred to in Art. 53(a) EPC.

Further, the Board again referred to T-315/03 Transgenic animals/ HARVARD and pointed out (T-606/03: para. 14) that, in addition to investigating whether Rule 28(d) EPC constituted a bar to patentability, the Harvard test had to be considered. The Harvard test was said to be relevant in cases where the genetically modified animals were

[5] By way of comparison, in T-385/09 LELY ENTERPRISES, TBoA 3.2.04 decided that a method of cooling animals, such as cows, by blowing air over them while wet, did not contravene Art. 53(a) EPC. To the argument that cooling might cause suffering, the Board responded that the requirement of the claim that 'the animals go to the milking stall spontaneously' would only be met if the treatment were pleasant.

likely to suffer. However, this was not the case for the mice that were the subject of the amended claim (T-606/03: para. 14).

Finally, the Board observed that:

> [In T-315/03 Transgenic animals/HARVARD] objections of economic, religious, moral or socio-cultural nature were presented against the patentability of animals in general as well as objections of an environmental nature such as that there might be a danger if the transgenic mice were to escape from the laboratory. These are issues which do not depend on whether or how the claimed animals have been manipulated and which, therefore, could equally arise in relation to the presently claimed transgenic mice. In the earlier decision, extensive reasons were given why they then had no bearing on patentability ... In the board's judgment, the present situation is no different in relation to these objections so that the same conclusion is warranted. (T-606/03: para. 15)

In January 2006 the Board remitted the case to the Examining Division with an order to grant a patent based on the amended claims filed during the oral proceedings. The patent was granted in August 2007.

8.5 Plants: T-356/93 Plant cells/PLANT GENETIC SYSTEMS

Plant Genetic Systems (PGS) applied for a patent relating to the genetic engineering of plants to make them herbicide-resistant. The patent was granted in October 1990 (Leemans *et al.* 1990) with claims to processes for producing plants and reproduction material of plants as well as to plant cells, seeds and plants per se.

Greenpeace opposed, inter alia on the basis of Art. 53(a) EPC, arguing that the Examining Division had not properly applied the Harvard test (Correspondence *Greenpeace* 1991: 2). According to Greenpeace, the Examining Division had overlooked the fact that 'The grant of a patent for plant life forms offends against the principle of morality that plant genetic resources are a common heritage of humankind which should be freely available to all and preserved intact for future generations'. Life forms ought not to be treated as (monopolisable) objects. The patenting of genes, plants and seeds would threaten the free availability of genes to farmers and plant breeders (Correspondence *Greenpeace* 1991: 2). Greenpeace also noted that the majority of the genetic diversity in the world was located in the less developed nations and that they would not benefit from the exploitation and patenting of those genetic resources by companies from industrialised countries (Correspondence *Greenpeace* 1991: 3).

Greenpeace also argued that the grant of patents for genetically engineered organisms 'facilitates and, in effect, acts as enabling legislation for the release of genetically engineered organisms to the environment' and that the EPO had the duty to weigh possible risks to the environment against the invention's usefulness to mankind (Correspondence *Greenpeace* 1991: 3). A number of environmental risks were mentioned that were said to outweigh the claimed usefulness: the creation of new pests (e.g. the transgenic plants becoming weeds); the spreading of the herbicide-resistant genes to weeds; the risk of selection pressure on indigenous flora to evolve herbicide resistance; the increase of genetic uniformity of crops, making them more vulnerable to disease; the likely reduction of biological diversity; and increased use of glutamine synthetase inhibitor herbicides resulting in environmental damage (Correspondence *Greenpeace* 1991: 4–8).

In its response from January 1992, PGS argued that exceptions to patentability had to be narrowly construed and that 'an invention can only be excluded from patentability by Art. 53(a) EPC if there exists virtually universal agreement that exploitation of the invention should be prohibited under any and all circumstances' (Correspondence *Plant Genetic Systems* 1992: 2). PGS noted that the exploitation of their invention was not prohibited per se in any of the EPC Contracting States but, on the contrary, was permissible, subject to government regulations, in every Contracting State. Referring to the Guidelines for Examination in the European Patent Office, it was also pointed out that the invention was not 'abhorrent' (Correspondence *Plant Genetic Systems* 1992: 3). A patent, according to PGS, did not grant its owner a positive right to exploit his invention, and exploitation of a patented invention was always subject to governmental regulation and control (Correspondence *Plant Genetic Systems* 1992: 3). It was observed that the public (including farmers and breeders) remained free to exploit exactly the same plants as they could before the patent application was filed (Correspondence *Plant Genetic Systems* 1992: 4). Moreover, PGS asserted, the invention, which made non-plant genes available in plants, could *increase* genetic diversity and aid developing countries (Correspondence *Plant Genetic Systems* 1992: 5). As to any risks associated with the release of genetically modified organisms into the environment, PGS referred to EU legislation aimed at avoiding the adverse effects of such release (Correspondence *Plant Genetic Systems* 1992: 6).

It was also stressed that 'The EPO has not been empowered or equipped to gather evidence of potential risks and benefits, let alone risks and benefits to the environment, from the exploitation of each and every patent claim. Nor has the EPO been empowered or equipped to evaluate such evidence' (Correspondence *Plant Genetic Systems* 1992: 7, footnote omitted).

As to T-19/90 Onco-mouse/HARVARD, PGS argued that the TBoA responsible 'did *not* establish general guidelines for the Examining Division to follow in deciding all cases or even all biotechnology cases under Article 53(a). Nor did the Board hold that a detailed factual evaluation had to be carried out in every case' (Correspondence *Plant Genetic Systems* 1992). PGS went on to claim that the benefits of the invention, including the environmental benefits, exceeded the risks:

> The GSI herbicides, against which [the] transformed plants of the PATENT are rendered resistant, generally last a much shorter time in the environment after use than do other, more persistent herbicides … [T]he GSI herbicides are … relatively easily degraded in the environment, normally leaving no residues under field conditions from year to year … However, the GSI herbicides do not distinguish between weeds and crops. Hence, for the GSI herbicides to be useful after the emergence of crops, the crops must be protected against the herbicides. Only the invention [underlying this patent] provides plants with resistance (rather than just tolerance) to such herbicides. (Correspondence *Plant Genetic Systems* 1992: 10–11)

The Opposition Division decided to maintain the patent as granted and, in its written decision of February 1993, argued that opposition proceedings were not an appropriate forum for discussing benefits and disadvantages of the genetic engineering of plants (Correspondence *EPO* 1993). The Opposition Division did not feel bound by T-19/90 Onco-mouse/HARVARD to carry out an analogous balancing exercise. Moreover, the Opposition Division noted that the invention would not be regarded as so abhorrent by the vast majority of the public that the grant of a patent would be inconceivable. The existence of risks had not been proved by Greenpeace and perceived risks could change during the life of a patent. More importantly, according to the Opposition Division, the assessment of risks and the regulation of the exploitation of the invention were a matter for bodies other than the EPO.

In April 1993 Greenpeace appealed and oral proceedings took place in December 1994. Greenpeace repeated most of the arguments it had raised during the opposition. It also responded to the Opposition Division's written arguments, inter alia by pointing out that the EPO *did* have a duty to carry out the balancing test required by T-19/90 Onco-mouse/HARVARD and that:

> [I]f it is the duty of the EPO to perform such a test, it cannot be a reason for refusal to do so that performing it would be difficult. The fact that there might be other areas where a similar investigation is called for cannot … justify a refusal to undertake an investigation in this case … [We] do not suggest

that the EPO will necessarily have information itself concerning the risks and benefits of inventions. However, when such evidence is presented to the EPO, it cannot refuse to assess such evidence because it might not be able to do so in other cases where no evidence is presented. Further, the possibility that the EPO will not be able to perform the balancing exercise in every case cannot be a reason for refusing to perform it in a case in which extensive submissions and evidence have been directed to that issue. (Correspondence *Greenpeace* 1993: 2–3)

In its decision TBoA 3.3.04 (Chairman Kinkeldey) referred to the statement in the *travaux préparatoires* (Document IV/2767/61-E: 7–8) that there was no 'European definition' of morality and 'ordre public'. According to the Board, for an assessment under Art. 53(a) EPC to be possible, the meaning of both concepts had to be determined (T-356/93: 557). 'Ordre public' was interpreted as follows:

It is generally accepted that the concept of 'ordre public' covers the protection of public security and the physical integrity of individuals as part of society. This concept encompasses also the protection of the environment. Accordingly, under Article 53(a) EPC, inventions the exploitation of which is likely to breach public peace or social order (for example, through acts of terrorism) or to seriously prejudice the environment are to be excluded from patentability as being contrary to 'ordre public'. (T-356/93: 557)

Next, the Board interpreted the concept of 'morality':

The concept of morality is related to the belief that some behaviour is right and acceptable whereas other behaviour is wrong, this belief being founded on the totality of the accepted norms which are deeply rooted in a particular culture. For the purposes of the EPC, the culture in question is the culture inherent in European society and civilisation. Accordingly, under Article 53(a) EPC, inventions the exploitation of which is not in conformity with the conventionally-accepted standards of conduct pertaining to this culture are to be excluded from patentability as being contrary to morality. (T-356/93: 557)

With regard to the second half-sentence of Art. 53(a) EPC, the Board rightly noted that this implied that '[A] particular subject-matter shall not automatically be regarded as complying with the requirements of Article 53(a) EPC merely because its exploitation is permitted in some or all of the contracting states. Thus, approval or disapproval of the exploitation by national law(s) or regulation(s) does not constitute per se a sufficient criterion for the purposes of examination under Article 53(a) EPC' (T-356/93: 558).

According to the Board, the *travaux préparatoires* as well as EPO case law showed that it was permissible to grant patents 'in respect of inventions concerning plants or animals (excluding plant or animal varieties) as well as inventions relating to processes of a technical nature for their production'. Thus, plants per se were not to be considered as excluded from patentability under Art. 53(a) EPC merely because they represented 'living' matter (T-356/93: 559).

With regard to the 'common heritage of mankind' principle invoked by Greenpeace, the Board noted that the patenting of 'wild-type plant resources' that could be used as starting material was not at issue and that therefore the 'common heritage of mankind' was not threatened (T-356/93: 559).

In this case, the assessment under Art. 53(a) EPC was said to involve an assessment as to whether the exploitation of the claimed subject-matter was 'either likely to seriously prejudice the environment or [be] contrary to the conventionally accepted standards of conduct of European culture' (T-356/93: 560).

Concerning the survey and opinion poll data submitted by Greenpeace, the Board argued that the results of surveys or opinion polls could not be considered decisive in the context of Art. 53(a) EPC, inter alia because such results could fluctuate significantly within short periods and could easily be biased by selecting particular questions, respondents, and so on (T-356/93: 561). More importantly, the Board noted that:

> Like national law(s) and regulation(s) approving or disapproving the exploitation of an invention … a survey or an opinion poll showing that a particular group of people or the majority of the population of some or all of the contracting states opposes the granting of a patent for a specified subject-matter, cannot serve as a sufficient criterion for establishing that the said subject-matter is contrary to 'ordre public' or morality. (T-356/93: 561)

According to the Board, plant biotechnology could not be regarded as more contrary to morality than selective breeding 'because both traditional breeders and molecular biologists are guided by the same motivation, namely to change the property of a plant by introducing novel genetic material into it in order to obtain a new and, possibly, improved plant'. The only difference was said to be that the use of genetic engineering allowed 'a more powerful and accurate control' of genetic modifications as well as a crossing of species barriers (T-356/93: 562).

With regard to 'morality', the Board concluded that none of the patent claims related to a misuse or destructive use of plant biotechnology, since the methods and products 'cannot be considered to be wrong as such in the light of conventionally accepted standards of conduct of European culture' (T-356/93: 564).

As far as 'ordre public' was concerned, the Board first provided some general comments regarding the rights conferred by a patent and the role of patent offices. Regarding the former, it was noted that:

A patent confers on its owner(s) for a specified time an exclusive right to exploit the subject-matter of the claims, i.e. to manufacture, use and market it, and to prevent others from doing the same … However, the right to exploit the invention is not unconditional. On the contrary, the invention claimed in a patent may only be exploited within the framework defined by national laws and regulations regarding the use of the said invention. (T-356/93: 564)

The role of patent offices was described as follows:

The function of a patent office is to grant patents … The board agrees with the appellants' submission that patent offices are placed at the crossroads between science and public policy. However, at this crossroads patent offices are not alone, but find themselves side-by-side with an increasing number of other authorities and bodies, in particular regulatory authorities and bodies, whose function is inter alia to ensure that the exploitation of a given technology, regardless of whether it is protected by a patent or not, takes place within the regulatory framework provided by laws, international treaties, administrative provisions, etc. (T-356/93: 564–5)

The Board proceeded to observe correctly that in most cases any potential risks of the exploitation of an invention 'cannot be anticipated merely on the basis of the disclosure of the invention in the patent specification' and that:

the actual approval (or disapproval) by the competent authorities of the exploitation of pharmaceutical products is often obtained only after the grant of the patent. This is because a realistic assessment of therapeutical operability requires a comprehensive and time-consuming programme of testing and evaluation of the products. The results of such tests are usually not available to patent offices during the prosecution of a case … when risk and safety assessment by the competent authorities or bodies has either not yet taken place or not yet been completed … Also transgenic plants normally require regulatory approval in the majority of the countries where biotechnological developments are taking place before even initial small-scale field testing can be performed. (T-356/93: 565–6)

In view of the 'requirement' that exceptions to patentability under Art. 53(a) EPC had to be narrowly construed, the revocation of a patent on 'ordre public' grounds, in the Board's view, presupposed 'that the threat to the environment be sufficiently substantiated at the time the decision to revoke the patent is taken by the EPO' (T-356/93: 566). According to the Board, this burden of proof had not been met by Greenpeace since most of their arguments relied on mere possibilities of undesired and destructive events:

[T]he quoted documents do not lead to the definite conclusion that the exploitation of any of the claimed subject-matter would seriously prejudice the environment and is, therefore, contrary to 'ordre public'. It would be unjustified to deny a patent under Article 53(a) EPC merely on the basis of possible, not yet conclusively-documented hazards ... Should the competent authorities and bodies, after having definitively assessed the risks involved, prohibit the exploitation of the invention, the patented subject-matter could not be exploited anyhow. If, however, regulatory approval is given based on the finding that no risks or minimal risks are involved, then patent protection should be available. (T-356/93: 568–9)

The Board concluded that the patent claims did not contravene Art. 53(a) EPC, after making the general comment that:

In the present case, since no sufficient evidence of actual disadvantages has been adduced, the assessment of patentability with regard to Article 53(a) EPC may not be based on the so-called 'balancing exercise' of benefits and disadvantages ... The board observes that such a 'balancing exercise' is not the only way of assessing patentability with regard to Article 53(a) EPC, but just one possible way, perhaps useful in situations in which an actual damage and/or disadvantage ... exists. (T-356/93: 569)

In February 1995 the Board remitted the case to the Opposition Division, which, in July 1996, decided to maintain the patent in an amended form.

8.6 Plants: T-475/01 Phosphinothricin resistant gene/ BAYER

As mentioned in Chapter 7, in January 1988 Bayer CropScience applied for a patent concerning the genetic modification of plants in order to make them resistant to the herbicide phosphinothricin. The patent (Strauch *et al.* 1993) was granted in March 1993 and was opposed by Dr Christoph Then, inter alia on the basis of Art. 53(a) EPC. In this regard, Then argued that the *grant* of this patent was contrary to morality and 'ordre public'. The opposition was rejected in a decision from March 2001. As concerns Art. 53(a) EPC, the Opposition Division referred to the EBD and to T-356/93 Plant cells/PLANT GENETIC SYSTEMS to find that the grant of the patent was permissible.

Dr Then appealed, maintaining his objections under Art. 53(a) EPC. Oral proceedings took place in June 2004. Dr Then argued that there was an ethical border between technical inventions and non-patentable discoveries from living nature, and that this ethical border had to be guarded in patent law so that living organisms should neither be considered inventions of man nor be made the subject of patent monopolies.

TBoA 3.3.08 (Chairman Galligani) observed that the question of Art. 53(a) EPC had been considered in relation to similar subject-matter in T-356/93 Plant cells/PLANT GENETIC SYSTEMS, where it was found that claims to plants did not contravene Art. 53(a) EPC (T-475/01: para. 9). Referring to the EBD, the Board noted that this represented an EU-wide consensus to the effect that claims to plants were not inherently objectionable. The Board also pointed out that the EU legislators had accepted that the exploitation of such inventions would not typically be contrary to 'ordre public' and morality (T-475/01: para. 11).

In June 2004 the Board rejected Dr Then's appeal.

8.7 Plants: T-179/01 Herbicide resistant plants/ MONSANTO

In August 1991 Monsanto filed a patent application (Barry *et al.* 1992) concerning the genetic modification of plants in order to make them resistant to the herbicide glyphosate (see Chapter 7). The claims related to methods for producing plants and for selectively controlling weeds in a field, as well as to DNA sequences, plant cells and plants per se. The main product claim directed to plants, claim 24, read as follows: 'A glyphosate tolerant plant comprising plant cells [as specified in Claim 20].'

The patent (Barry *et al.* 1996) was granted in June 1996. Oppositions were filed by Greenpeace, Syngenta and two individuals (Dr Christoph Then and Thomas Schweiger). Only Then and Schweiger opposed on the basis of Art. 53(a) EPC. As regards morality, they argued that the patenting of living organisms in general, and of plants in particular, was contrary to the cultural and ethical norms of Western society. Most of their arguments related to 'ordre public'. They asserted that, through the patenting of genetically modified seeds, a process had been set in motion that would severely distort the conventional plant breeding industry. Since for conventional plant varieties there is no protection available that is as strong as patents, economic interests would force breeders, on market strategy grounds, to seek patents and thereby adopt gene technology as the basis for their breeding work. Because patents give a form of protection that covers products that have not yet come into existence, and therefore can be applied for relatively quickly, whereas plant variety protection rights relate to already produced products, Then and Schweiger argued that there was a particular problem for the breeders, which they called the variety-hare and patent-hedgehog problem ('*Sorten-Hase*' and '*Patent-Igel*', referring to a German fairy story equivalent to Aesop's fable of the hare and the tortoise) (Correspondence *Then and Schweiger* 1997: 8). When the variety-hare eventually arrives at his goal, he finds the patent-hedgehog already in place and demanding licence fees. The problem, according to Then and Schweiger, was further exacerbated as, unlike with plant variety rights, a new variety might find itself covered by many patents. Granting patents for plants would thus negatively affect breeders and farmers.

Monsanto responded by referring to T-356/93 Plant cells/PLANT GENETIC SYSTEMS, according to which patents may be granted in respect of plants and animals (Correspondence *Monsanto* 1988: 3). It also noted that patents *always* potentially influence the position of competitors in the field (Correspondence *Monsanto* 1988: 5).

In November 1999 the Opposition Division issued a summons to oral proceedings referring to the new EPC Rules and adding that, in view of these, none of the grounds for opposition under Art. 53(a) EPC precluded the maintenance of the patent (Correspondence *EPO* 1999: 2).

Oral proceedings took place in April 2000 and in its written decision the Opposition Division argued with regard to Art. 53(a) EPC that the new Rules were introduced 'in order to bring into line the EPC with the [EBD] of the European Parliament, a democraticly [*sic*] elected Institution which can be assumed to represent the "European society" referred to by [the opponent] … [N]one of the exceptions to patentability laid out in Rule [28] EPC apply to the subject matter of the opposed claims' (Correspondence *EPO* 2000: 5).

It was also noted that T-356/93 Plant cells/PLANT GENETIC SYSTEMS had found that Art. 53(a) EPC did not constitute a bar to patentability, and that the conclusion reached there was applicable to Monsanto's case (Correspondence *EPO* 2000: 5). The Opposition Division concluded that Monsanto's patent met all the requirements of Art. 53(a) EPC and decided to maintain the patent on the basis of a set of claims slightly amended to overcome novelty objections.

The decision was appealed by Monsanto itself, as well as by Greenpeace and Syngenta. Monsanto disputed the findings of the Opposition Division regarding novelty and requested that the patent be maintained as granted (Correspondence *Monsanto* 2001: 1–5).

Oral proceedings took place in April 2005. As Greenpeace and Syngenta had not invoked Art. 53(a) EPC, we shall not go into their arguments here. The Board briefly referred to T-356/93 Plant cells/PLANT GENETIC SYSTEMS and noted that no evidence had been brought forward on appeal which would require a reconsideration of the Opposition Division's finding that the claimed subject-matter did not contravene Art. 53(a) EPC (T-179/01: para. 7).

TBoA 3.3.08 (Chairman Galligani) decided in April 2005 to remit the case to the Opposition Division with an order to maintain the patent on the basis of the claims filed during the oral proceedings in appeal. The patent was reissued in July 2006.

8.8 Controversial medical intervention: T-866/01 Euthanasia compositions/MICHIGAN STATE UNIVERSITY

In December 1991 Michigan State University (MSU) filed a patent application, the initial claim of which read:

> A method for providing euthanasia in a mammal which comprises introducing into the heart of the mammal an aqueous solution comprising ... a cardiotoxic compound ... and a ... gamma-hydroxybutramide ... wherein euthanasia occurs in the mammal. (Sawyer *et al.* 1992: 15)

Claims 2–14 also related to methods of euthanasia. Claims 15–23 were directed to compositions that could be used for providing euthanasia. When the patent application entered the European phase, a new claim set was submitted in which all of the claims were directed to the composition. In June 1994 a further claim set was submitted, this time including a non-therapeutic use claim (claim 14, which read: 'Use of the composition according to any of claims 1 to 13 for providing euthanasia in a lower mammal'). This was, in effect, a claim to a method of euthanising lower mammals. In November 1994 the use claim was changed into 'Swiss-type use' format (see Chapter 5). This amendment appears to have been carried out by the Examining Division and subsequently approved by the patent applicant. This is the form in which the claim was ultimately granted.

The patent was granted in April 1996 and contained the following claims:

1. A composition which comprises an aqueous solution comprising,
   (a) a cardiotoxic compound ...; and
   (b) embutramide in a lethally anesthetic amount ...
14. Use of the composition according to any of claims 1 to 13 for preparing a medicament for providing euthanasia in a lower mammal. (Sawyer *et al.* 1996: 9–10)

In January 1997 the patent was opposed by Dr Anita Knötgen *et al.*, Hubert Hüppe (a member of the German Parliament) and Intervet International, inter alia on the basis of Art. 53(a) EPC. The main argument under Art. 53(a) EPC was that the purpose of the invention was the provision of a composition for killing all kinds of living beings, including human beings.

MSU responded in October 1997, arguing that the use of the invention indicated in the patent was for mercy killing of *lower* animals and that therefore the intended use of the invention did not contravene 'ordre public' or morality, even though the invention *could* be exploited in a way that would possibly infringe some fundamental principle of morality or 'ordre public'.

Oral proceedings took place in May 2000 and the Opposition Division decided to maintain the patent in amended form. In three claims that mentioned specific dosages per kg weight of a mammal, the word 'lower' was inserted before the word 'mammal'. The specification was also amended to replace all references to 'mammal' or 'animal' with references to 'lower mammal'.

The Opposition Division noted that, in view of the disclosure of the invention in the description, it was at least doubtful whether the subject-matter of claims 1 to 13 as granted was limited to the use of the claimed compositions for producing humane death *solely* in lower animals. The claimed compositions 'could be used for producing death in all kind of mammals including human beings' (Correspondence *EPO* 2001: para. 2.11). The Opposition Division therefore concluded that claims 1–13 as granted included subject-matter the exploitation of which would be contrary to 'ordre public' and morality.

With regard to the amendments proposed during the oral proceedings, the Opposition Division stated that euthanasia or mercy killing of animals was neither immoral nor contrary to 'ordre public'. It found that the patent so amended no longer covered the use of the compositions on humans and, accordingly, did not contravene Art. 53(a) EPC (Correspondence *EPO* 2001: para. 3.1).

In July 2001 the first opponent (Dr Anita Knötgen *et al.*) appealed and in April 2005 TBoA 3.3.02 (Chairman Oswald) asked MSU to demonstrate that a generally accepted meaning existed for the expression 'lower mammal'. In May 2005 MSU responded that, in the pharmaceutical field, 'lower animal' always means 'less than human'.

Oral proceedings took place in May 2005. According to Dr Knötgen *et al.*, MSU's argument that a possible use of the claimed invention that was morally acceptable and thus allowable should prevail over another possible use that was immoral and thus unallowable, was untenable. The mere possibility of a use of the invention contrary to 'ordre public' or morality was argued to be sufficient evidence of the immorality of an invention. This is in effect the *novelty* approach to a patentability exclusion, referred to in Chapter 3.

Knötgen *et al.* argued that the Opposition Division had rightly relied on the advice provided in the Guidelines for Examination in the European Patent Office (for the current version, see EPO 2011), that

'A fair test to apply is to consider whether it is probable that the public in general would regard the invention as so abhorrent that the grant of patent rights would be inconceivable'. On the basis of that test, it was said, the Opposition Division had correctly found that the claimed subject-matter contravened Art. 53(a) EPC. However, they had then incorrectly decided to maintain the patent with amended claims, even though those claims still contravened Art. 53(a) EPC. The amendment of some of the claims whereby the word 'lower' had been inserted before 'mammal' did not change the fact that the compositions *could* be used for producing death in all kinds of mammals, including human beings, Knötgen *et al.* argued. Even after the amendments, the stated purpose of the invention remained the provision of 'euthanasia compositions' and the description did not contain any limitation of the use of these compositions to euthanasia in lower animals.

Moreover, Knötgen *et al.* argued, the animal tests underlying the patent were cruel. Weighing up of the suffering of animals against the possible benefits of the invention clearly demonstrated that some alleged but not demonstrated benefits did not outweigh the negative aspects, such as the suffering of animals. Thus, the requirements of Art. 53(a) EPC were not met.

The second opponent, Hubert Hüppe, referred to the European Convention on Human Rights (ECHR) as a relevant source for the interpretation of the term 'ordre public' in Art. 53(a) EPC. Art. 2 ECHR, according to which 'no one shall be deprived of his life intentionally', was said to guarantee the protection of everybody's right to life. Granting a European patent for euthanasia compositions created at least a real risk to the integrity and protection of life and hence was unacceptable under Art. 53(a) EPC. The claimed compositions, it was argued, could only be used for a single purpose, namely to terminate animal and human life.

Still according to Mr Hüppe, the Opposition Division had erred by allowing the product claims because the modification of the description had no limiting effect on the scope of protection of the composition claims. Case law of the Boards of Appeal was quoted in support of the assertion that the patent protection of products was not limited to the end-use suggested but was instead absolute.

MSU responded that only the use of the claimed composition for providing euthanasia in a lower mammal was described in the patent specification. According to conventionally accepted standards of European culture, mercy killing of animals in order to alleviate suffering was neither immoral nor contrary to 'ordre public'. It was said to be irrelevant for the purposes of patentability whether the invention could *also* be used in a manner that might be considered to be immoral or contrary to 'ordre public'. This was clear from the fact that *any* chemical composition could be misused, for example for killing someone, if only the dosage was high enough, yet the EPO generally granted patents for chemical compositions, without normally requiring any limitation in the claims to the use of such compositions in a specific dosage or for a specific purpose. In this context, T-356/93 Plant cells/PLANT GENETIC SYSTEMS and G-1/98 Transgenic plant/NOVARTIS II were referred to, which were said to demonstrate clearly that the *intended* use of an invention was decisive for establishing whether its exploitation would contravene 'ordre public' or morality. Since the claimed composition was to be used for mercy killing of animals to alleviate suffering, it served an acceptable purpose and was thus not excluded from patentability under Art. 53(a) EPC.

TBoA 3.3.02 issued its decision in May 2005. With regard to Art. 53(a) EPC, the Board began by stating that this provision 'is to be construed narrowly, given the EPC's underlying objective of establishing a comprehensive patent protection between the contracting states (see Preamble of the EPC, paragraph 2)' (T-866/01: para. 5.2). In this regard, however, we should point out that paragraph 2 of the Preamble to the EPC does not say anything about 'comprehensive' patent protection.

The Board went on to say that 'it appears to be generally accepted that Article 53(a) EPC is to be construed narrowly' (T-866/01: para. 5.4). In this context, references were made inter alia to Mellulis (2002: paras. 7–8), Bruchhausen (1988: para. 2) and Schatz (2003: 85), as well as to T-356/93 Plant cells/PLANT GENETIC SYSTEMS. According to the latter source:

> From the historical documentation relating to the EPC it appears that the view according to which 'the concept of patentability in the European patent law must be as wide as possible' predominated (see [D]ocument IV/2071/61-E, page 5, point 2, first paragraph). Accordingly, the exceptions to patentability have been narrowly construed. (T-356/93: 558)

However, with regard to Document IV/2071/61-E, it is worth pointing out that this document contained a first preliminary draft of the CEPL (see Chapter 2), prepared in advance of the first meeting of the EEC's Patents Working Party. The quoted comment comes from those responsible for preparing the first preliminary draft in advance of this meeting and does not represent the recommendations or conclusions of the PWP as a whole.

Schatz (2003), one of the other sources referred to by the TBoA in support of the claim that Art. 53(a) EPC must be construed narrowly, is also being referred to in an intellectually dishonest way. What Ulrich Schatz (former Principal Director International Affairs at the EPO) in fact mentions, with regard to the construction of the morality exclusion, is the following:

> Art. 53 is an exception to the general entitlement to patent in Art. 52(1) ... and is to be construed narrowly given the EPC's underlying objective of establishing a comprehensive patent protection between the Contracting States ... *However, this principle of construction only applies with restrictions to Art. 53(a), which gives priority to the principles of the general legal and moral order over the patent law competition order.* (Schatz 2003: 85, emphasis added)

Of course these comments by Schatz are inaccurate, since what is said about the Preamble is incorrect and since nothing can be derived from either the *travaux préparatoires* or the EPC itself that indicates that any of the provisions of Art. 53 EPC ought to be construed narrowly (as was pointed out by Brigitte Günzel, legal member of the EBoA, at the oral hearing before the EBoA in G-2/08 Dosage regime/ABBOTT RESPIRATORY). But the point we wish to make here is that Schatz's comments were misrepresented.

Following its argumentation regarding narrow construction of the exclusion, the Board proceeded to make some substantive comments on Art. 53(a) EPC:

> [T]he exclusion under Article 53(a) EPC is only applicable if either or both of the objective facts ... publication and/or exploitation of the invention would contribute causally to the infringement of the fundamental principles of 'ordre public' and morality. Accordingly, Article 53(a) EPC raises in the present case, for example, no question of
>
> (a) whether or not *the invention per se*, i.e. the claimed composition per se, or their preparation might be regarded as breach of the principles of 'ordre public' or morality ...
> (b) whether and under what conditions *the act of granting the patent* either for the claimed compositions per se or for their preparation or for their use might be regarded as an infringement of ethical principles and contrary to 'ordre public' within the meaning of Article 53(a) EPC ...
> (c) whether or not *the making of the present invention* as such or the inventor's activities during making or development of his invention or the development of the present invention as such might be regarded as breach of the principles of 'ordre public' or morality. (T-866/01: para. 5.6, emphasis added)

Next, the Board stated that 'exploitation of the invention' within the meaning of Art. 53(a) EPC was 'to be construed as the normal avowed use indicated in the patent ... of the invention's teaching' (T-866/01: para 5.7) and that patent protection was only to be denied if 'the intended exploitation, i.e. the avowed use indicated in the patent' of the invention, would contravene 'ordre public' or morality (T-866/01: para. 5.8). Thus, it was said that, if the *intended exploitation* does not infringe Art. 53(a) EPC, 'it is not sufficient that one out of several or more or even all other conceivable exploitations or uses of the invention's teaching would be or could be regarded as breach of the principles of "ordre public" or morality, even if that exploitation constituted a serious breach of the principles of "ordre public", for example a criminal offence' (T-866/01: para. 5.8).

On the basis of those general remarks, the Board commented on the acceptability of euthanasia compositions under Art. 53(a) EPC. It was noted that several of the arguments raised by the appellants related to issues that were not relevant to the case. The argument that the purpose of the invention was to provide a composition for killing all kinds of animals, including human beings, was said to be based on an incorrect interpretation of the teaching of the patent (T-866/01: para. 6.3). According to the Board:

> The avowed use or exploitation of the euthanasia compositions disclosed in the patent for any other conceivable purpose than for the sole intended purpose indicated in the patent in accordance with the present invention i.e. for producing humane death (mercy killing) in lower animals, has neither been indicated nor contemplated nor foreshadowed at all in the present patent. (T-866/01: para. 6.4)

On the basis of its earlier comments on the meaning of 'exploitation' in Art. 53(a) EPC, the Board concluded that the appellant's argument that the patent contravened Art. 53(a) EPC because the animal experiments reported in the patent were contrary to morality and 'ordre public', needed no further consideration since 'These experiments were carried out during the making or development of the invention and as such do not fulfil the condition of being part of the exploitation of the present invention' (T-866/01: para. 6.8). This point of view was later challenged in G-2/06 Use of embryos/WARF (see section 8.14).

Subsequently, the Board commented specifically on 'ordre public'. Reference was made to the following description of the meaning of 'ordre public' by Schatz:

> [I]n general 'Ordre public' is formed by the ethically based constitutional or other rules, usually backed up by penal provisions, that reflect the basic values prevailing in society and trade. These protected values can in particular include public safety, the integrity of the individual and nowadays, certainly also the protection of environment. (T-866/01: para. 6.9, referring to Schatz 2003: 88)

With respect to the patent in question, the Board argued that the evidence on file showed that:

> [T]he unequivocal, generally accepted and exclusive meaning and scope in the field of veterinary medicine and practice for the expression 'euthanasia' is the humane killing or mercy killing of animals by trained personnel ... In veterinary practice animals are generally euthanised to prevent their suffering from incurable or painful conditions ... [T]he killing of animals for any other reasons than those mentioned above does not fall within the meaning and scope of the term 'euthanasia'. (T-866/01: para. 6.10)

Thus, according to the Board, the exploitation of the invention, that is euthanising lower animals, 'would [not] breach or even jeopardise public peace or social order or seriously prejudice the environment. On the contrary ... veterinarians are generally authorised to euthanise animals to alleviate their suffering'. Thus, there was no conflict with 'ordre public' (T-866/01: para. 6.11).

The Board then made some observations regarding the concept of 'morality'. As a general remark, it was noted that:

> Morality ... was adopted in western legal systems from Roman law as 'boni mores'. Morality is one of the fundamentals of our legal system and at the same time forms the basis for the inclusion of extra-legal principles of ethics in the law ... Morality constitutes actual ethically-based norms of behaviour that have become socially binding through being generally accepted. The exploitation of an invention only infringes morality if it is regarded as reprehensible by society in general or at least by the trade concerned. (T-866/01: para. 6.12, referring to Schatz 2003: 89–90 and to T-356/93 Plant cells/PLANT GENETIC SYSTEMS: 557)

Then, reiterating its earlier remark on the meaning of the term 'euthanasia' in veterinary medicine, 'namely the humane killing or mercy killing of animals suffering from incurable or painful conditions by trained personnel for the sole purpose of preventing prolonged suffering of the animals', the Board observed that '[V]eterinarians consider [euthanasia] as their moral obligation based on generally accepted ethics and norms which the board accepts are deeply rooted in the culture inherent in European society and civilisation. Moreover ... no veterinarian is obliged to kill animals that are not suffering and may refuse to do so if the animals could be placed with other people'. Thus, it was concluded that there was no conflict with morality either (T-866/01: paras. 6.13–6.14).

The Board also commented on the appellant's objections to the acceptability of the product claims. Since the claimed composition met the requirements for patentability – including those of Art. 53(a) EPC, since 'the intended exploitation (the avowed use indicated in the patent) of the invention' did not contravene 'ordre public' or morality – the patent holder was said to be entitled 'to seek absolute substance protection for that particular composition' (T-866/01: para. 9.5). In this regard, it was also noted that:

> The patenting of an invention does not grant the patent holder a positive right to exploit the invention ... Conversely, the refusal of patent protection does not mean that the exploitation of the invention is forbidden. Accordingly, patent law is generally not a legal instrument for averting or preventing abuses or risks associated with the exploitation of an invention ... Article 53(a) EPC is merely intended to prevent an invention, the publication or exploitation of which would infringe the fundamental principles of 'ordre public' or morality *being given an appearance of approval through a patent issued by an international authority.* (T-866/01: para. 9.7, emphasis added)

The Board dismissed the appeal.

8.9 Human genes and genetic diagnostic tests: T-272/95 Relaxin/HOWARD FLOREY INSTITUTE

As described in Chapter 4, HFI filed a patent application relating inter alia to DNA fragments encoding the human protein H2-preprorelaxin, sub-units of such DNA, processes for isolating these DNA fragments, processes for synthesising human H2-preprorelaxin, synthetic human H2-preprorelaxin and human H2-preprorelaxin analogues. The contribution made by the patent applicants was said to be the production of recombinant human relaxin, to alleviate complications associated with labour induction and caesarean section.

The Examining Division raised no objections under Art. 53 EPC and the patent (Hudson *et al.* 1991) was granted in April 1991. In January 1992 an opposition was filed on behalf of the faction of the 'Greens' in the European Parliament and its president, Mr Paul Lannoye, inter alia on the basis of Art. 53(a) EPC.

The opponents argued that genes are part of the common heritage of mankind. Converting what belongs to the common heritage into private property violates human dignity, which is inviolable. Thus, the patent was said to contravene Art. 53(a) EPC (Correspondence *Aglietta et al.* 1992: 6–8).

HFI responded that 'the present invention clearly provides benefit to humankind without concomitant suffering or environmental damage. Accordingly [it] is patentable in the light of Article 53(a) EPC' (Correspondence *Howard Florey* 1993: 2). It was added that:

[T]he ovarian tissue obtained, for extraction of the mRNA therefrom, was obtained at the time of a [surgical intervention] for ectopic (tubal) pregnancy. Ectopic pregnancy is a life-threatening condition ... Thus, the (excised) ovarian tissue has to be removed from the patient in order to ensure that the patient lives ... The material was obtained with patient consent and appropriate Ethics Committee approval was obtained for the collection of this tissue. mRNA was also isolated from [material from an intervention] carried out during a cesarian section. ... The tissue from which the mRNA was obtained would otherwise have been discarded. There was nothing unethical in the obtaining of the mRNA. (Correspondence *Howard Florey* 1993: 4)

Oral proceedings took place in December 1994. In its decision the Opposition Division referred to the Guidelines for Examination in the European Patent Office, according to which objections under Art. 53(a) EPC should only be raised if it is probable that the public in general would regard the invention as so abhorrent that the grant of patent rights would be inconceivable. The Opposition Division observed that, according to HFI, the women whose tissue was used had consented. Further, it was noted that the use of human tissue as a source of useful products was accepted and even welcomed by the vast majority of the public. The Opposition Division also referred to Art. 13 of the (then) Draft Bioethics Convention of the Council of Europe, which was said to explicitly approve of 'the use for other purposes of parts of the human body removed during the course of an intervention ... provided there are appropriate information and consent procedures' (Correspondence *EPO* 1995: 13). As to the opponents' arguments regarding human dignity and self-determination, the Opposition Division responded that the patent did not affect any woman, since there was no need to use human beings as a source for the H2-relaxin: 'The only stage at which a woman was involved was at the beginning of the making of the invention, as a (voluntary) source for the relaxin mRNA' (Correspondence *EPO* 1995: 14).

The Opposition Division decided to maintain the patent as granted. In March 1995 the opponents appealed. Allowing a patent monopoly on reproduction of genetic material, according to the Greens, 'constitutes appropriation and exploitation of the donor's body over which as a matter of public policy those donors have and are entitled to have complete dominion ... [T]o permit the private appropriation of the genetic information embodied in a human being fundamentally violates a person's integrity' (Correspondence *Aglietta et al.* 1995: 5). In this regard the Greens referred to T-356/93 Plant cells/PLANT GENETIC SYSTEMS, the only decision that elaborated on the meaning of the concepts of morality and 'ordre public', according to which 'the protection of ... the physical integrity of individuals as part of society' fell under the concept of 'ordre public' (T-356/93: 557).

Since the importance of DNA lies in the *information* it embodies, rather than in the actual physical material itself, according to the Greens, the argument raised by the Opposition Division, that with this invention there was no need to use human beings as the source for the protein, was untenable. What was being used was the genetic information from a human being, and the essence of the patent was that such information was claimed (Correspondence *Aglietta et al.* 1995: 5). This was said to amount to exploitation of the human body, and to contravene fundamental principles of human rights, human dignity and integrity of the person. The Opposition Division, it was argued, had erred by only taking into account the use of physical *material* from the woman and not considering the fact that genetic *information* from the woman was being used:

> It is not suggested that individual women are repeatedly affected physically by the use of the subject matter of the patent in that physical material is repeatedly taken from them. What is objectionable in this case – and uniquely objectionable in the case of patents of this kind – is the use of human genetic material (and the information embodied in it) as a foundation for a claim to monopoly rights by another person. (Correspondence *Aglietta et al.* 1995: 6)

The Greens further repeated their argument that patents of this kind were of concern not only to the public at large but also to the research community: 'While very few oppose medical research as such, very many are against the assertion of claims of proprietary rights – such as patents – in discoveries about the nature of the human body – such as genetic material – and do not believe that granting such rights will promote medical and scientific research' (Correspondence *Aglietta et al.* 1995: 6). It was noted that substantial sections of the scientific research community, as well as groups concerned with the promotion of medical research, held the view that allowing this kind of patent was likely to hinder medical research (Correspondence *Aglietta et al.* 1995: 6).

HFI responded that, during the time the case had been pending, significant changes had taken place regarding the patentability of biotechnological inventions. Reference was made to the incorporation of provisions from the EBD into the EPC Rules in September 1999. With regard to Art. 53(a) EPC, HFI noted that Rule 28 EPC mentioned four categories of biotechnological inventions that were to be considered as exceptions to patentability under the morality clause, and that the claimed invention did not fall under any of these categories and consequently was patentable.

TBoA 3.3.04 (Chairman Kinkeldey) issued its decision in October 2002. The Board referred to the amendment of the EPC Rules in 1999, whereby Rules 26 to 29 EPC had been added:

> The Board concludes from the absence of transitional provisions that the Administrative Council must have been of the opinion that Rules [26 to 29] EPC only gave a more detailed interpretation of the meaning of Article 53 EPC as intended from its inception, and hence were also applicable to cases already pending before 1 September 1999 such as the present case. (T-272/95: para. 4)

The Board then noted that, in view of Art. 164(2) EPC, it had to examine 'whether or not the new rules insofar as they relate to Article 53(a) EPC are in conformity with this article' (T-272/95: para. 4). Reference was made to G-1/98 Transgenic plant/NOVARTIS II, which had found that there was no conflict between one Rule relevant to Art. 53(b) EPC and the Article itself and that the Rule was 'only interpretative'. It was then added that 'The present Board adopts this view, considers that the same holds true for the new rules as far as they relate to the interpretation of Article 53(a) EPC and, thus, will apply Rules [28 and 29]' (T-272/95: para. 5).

On that basis, *instead of addressing the arguments* raised by the appellant and investigating whether the patented subject-matter contravened morality or 'ordre public', the Board merely referred to the new Rules and suggested that no further assessment was needed.

> Rule [28] provides a list of processes and uses which are exceptions to patentability but does not mention any products. However, it is a non-exhaustive list, which implies that product claims relating to biological material may equally be found unallowable under Article 53(a) EPC. Rule [29(2)], however, defines which biological material originating from the human body may be patented. It states that:
>
> '(2) An element isolated from the human body or otherwise produced by means of a technical process including the sequence or partial sequence of a gene may constitute a patentable invention, even if the structure of that element is identical to that of a natural element'.
>
> It follows from the text itself that the [claimed subject-matter] is not to be considered as an exception to patentability under Article 53(a) EPC ... Thus, the Appellants' arguments under Articles 53(a) ... are answered by the new implementing Rules [28 and 29] EPC. (T-272/95: paras. 7–9)

The Board dismissed the appeal, leaving the patent maintained unamended.

8.10 Human genes and genetic diagnostic tests: T-1213/05 Breast and ovarian cancer/UNIVERSITY OF UTAH

As described in Chapter 4, Myriad Genetics, UURF and the United States of America filed a patent application relating inter alia to isolated DNA coding for BRCA1 (a 'breast cancer gene') or modified forms of it which are functionally equivalent or associated with a predisposition to breast or ovarian cancer, corresponding RNA, probes and primers for this DNA and corresponding RNA, methods of producing the DNA, genetic tests to diagnose a predisposition to breast or ovarian cancer, DNA substantially homologous and substantially similar in function to the 'wild-type' (i.e. naturally occurring) DNA for use in gene therapy, and methods for screening cancer drugs. After a long period of back-and-forth argument between the Examining Division and the patent applicants regarding inter alia novelty but not morality, the patent (Skolnick *et al.* 2001a) was granted in November 2001.

Eight parties (see section 4.7) opposed the patent, on the basis inter alia of Art. 53(a) EPC, and an oral hearing took place in January 2005. Three of the opponents – the Swiss Social-Democratic Party (SSP), Greenpeace and Dr Rolf Wilhelms – raised objections under Art. 53(a) EPC, inter alia regarding the lack of a valid consent of the tissue sample donors to the patenting, and the adverse effects of the patent (and the way it was enforced by Myriad) on research as well as on the provision of health care. With regard to the latter, it was argued that not only morality but also 'ordre public' was violated. The impediment of health care provision, it was argued, had to do with the fact that all samples to be tested had to be sent to a single laboratory in the USA or to one of the few licensed laboratories.

The Opposition Division rejected all these arguments. It referred to Rule 29 EPC and its 'source', Art. 5(2) EBD, according to which 'An element isolated from the human body or otherwise produced by means of a technical process, including the sequence or partial sequence of a gene, may constitute a patentable invention, even if the structure of that element is identical to that of a natural element'. In the view of the Opposition Division, this Rule 'not only concretizes the distinction between an invention and a discovery for the human body and its elements but is also to be regarded as an implementation of Article 53(a) EPC' (Correspondence *EPO* 2005b: 27). In this regard, reference was also made to T-272/95 Relaxin/HOWARD FLOREY INSTITUTE.

As to the opponents' other arguments, the Opposition Division responded that:

> Article 53(a) EPC does however not provide the EPO with the competence to refuse or revoke a patent by assessing certain alleged negative consequences which may result from the grant of an exclusive right in an individual case. The EPO has not been vested with the task of taking into account the economic effects of the grant of patents in specific areas and of restricting the field of patentable subject-matter accordingly. (Correspondence *EPO* 2005b: 27–8)

The Opposition Division decided to maintain the patent in amended form. The patentees as well as one of the opponents (the SSP) appealed. Oral proceedings in appeal took place in September 2007. UURF repeated that all the objections raised by the opponents under Article 53(a) EPC were unsubstantiated and thus had to be rejected.

The SSP repeated its argument that no proof had been provided by UURF that the donors of the cells that had been critical to identify the BRCA1 gene had given advanced informed consent to the use of the cells. For the informed consent to be valid, the SSP argued, it would have had to include explicit consent to the commercial exploitation of the research results by patents, as well as an agreement regarding benefit sharing. Since such proof was lacking, it had to be assumed that severe breaches of ethics had been involved in producing the research results, and thus that 'ordre public' or morality had been violated. The Board's response was that:

> [T]he EPC contains no provision establishing a requirement for applicants to submit evidence of a previous informed consent or a benefit sharing agreement. According to Rule [26(1)] EPC, [the EBD] … shall be used as a supplementary means of interpretation of the relevant provisions of the Convention and of … the Implementing Regulations. (T-1213/05: para. 48)

In this context, TBoA 3.3.04 (Chairman Kinkeldey) quoted Recital 26 EBD, which provides that 'if an invention is based on biological material of human origin or if it uses such material, where a patent application is filed, the person from whose body the material is taken must have had an opportunity of expressing free and informed consent thereto, in accordance with national law'. From the wording of this Recital, the Board concluded that the 'legislator [had] thus not provided for a procedure of verifying the informed consent in the framework of the grant of biotechnological patents under the EPC' (T-1213/05: para. 49). The SSP's argument regarding the necessity for and requirements of valid informed consent was rejected.

The morality-related arguments submitted by Greenpeace in the appeal proceedings were both, like those of the SSP, principle-based or duty-based (in ethics jargon, 'deontological') arguments and utilitarian arguments (ones focusing on the consequences of granting patents like the current one).

From a principle-based perspective, Greenpeace observed that patients suspected of having a predisposition to breast cancer would suffer severe disadvantages as a result of this patent and would become dependent on the patent proprietor, an outcome that violated human dignity.

Greenpeace's main utilitarian arguments against the patent were that it would result in increased costs for patients and affect the way in which diagnosis and research would be carried out in Europe. In sum, according to Greenpeace the patent was clearly detrimental to patients and doctors and thus violated Art. 53(a) EPC.

The Board did not respond to the 'human dignity' objection. As to the arguments regarding the detrimental effects of the patent, the Board pointed out that Art. 53(a) EPC excluded from patentability 'inventions the ... exploitation of which would be contrary to "ordre public" or morality'. Thus, what was at issue was the 'exploitation of the invention' and not the 'exploitation of the patent' (T-1213/05: para. 53). According to the Board, Greenpeace's objections related to the latter and hence fell outside the scope of Art. 53(a) EPC and had to be rejected. It was added that:

> In the Board's opinion the possible consequences of exploitation of the patent identified by [Greenpeace] are the result of the exclusionary nature of the rights granted by a patent, that is the right to stop competitors from using the invention.
>
> The objection of [Greenpeace], reduced to its essence, is that the inevitable consequences of the exploitation of the patent in suit are contrary to 'ordre public' or morality. Logically, such an objection applies to the exploitation of any patent, as the nature of the consequences of the exploitation of a patent (which derive from the exclusionary nature of private property rights), are the same for all patents. (T-1213/05: para. 53)

The Board also noted that the claimed subject-matter did not contravene Rule 29(2) EPC (T-1213/05: para. 56) and concluded that Art. 53(a) EPC did not constitute a barrier to patentability (T-1213/05: para. 57).

In September 2007 the Board dismissed the appeal, and in August 2008 the patent was reissued in amended form.

8.11 Human genes and genetic diagnostic tests: T-666/05 Mutation/UNIVERSITY OF UTAH

As described in Chapter 4, Myriad Genetics, the Centre de Recherche du Chul (Canada) and the Cancer Institute (Tokyo) filed a patent application with claims directed inter alia to isolated DNA coding for BRCA1 mutations and polymorphisms, probes, methods of producing the DNA, and methods for diagnosing a predisposition for breast and ovarian cancer in humans by determining whether a BRCA1 mutation indicative of it was present.

The patent (Shattuck-Eidens *et al.* 2001) was granted in May 2001 and opposed by six opponents (see section 4.8). Multiple grounds were invoked (inter alia novelty, inventive step and sufficiency of disclosure). Greenpeace additionally invoked Art. 53(a) EPC, referring to the non-patentable status of human genes as the common heritage of humanity, the patent's inhibitive effects on research and the fact that the patent made patients dependent, against their will, on one company, which would also impede the development and use of improved diagnostic methods (Correspondence *Greenpeace* 2002: 2).

Opponent VVSKG also invoked Art. 53(a) EPC. They referred to the right to health care and the sovereignty that states should have to ensure this right, which would be jeopardised by the patent, thus constituting a violation of 'ordre public'. They also argued that the fact that the patent allowed Myriad to force persons to send their tissue samples to a foreign country was unethical, especially since the country in question might not maintain a strict separation between forensic and clinical genetic databases. The patent, it was argued, forced people to choose between losing control of their genetic information and not obtaining a diagnosis as to cancer susceptibility. Another morality-related objection of VVSKG was that genetic information has a very unique and personal character and that therefore each person should have the freedom to have their genetic information analysed and interpreted by the organisation of her choice. Such a choice was rendered impossible by the patent, which was thus contrary to morality (Correspondence *VVSKG et al.* 2002: 7).

Oral proceedings took place in January 2005. The patentees argued that there was no problem of access to health care, since any doctor could order a test via Myriad's website. Moreover, they argued, without patent monopolies there would be fewer diagnostics (Correspondence *EPO* 2005c: 9).

The Opposition Division rejected all the arguments submitted under Art. 53(a) EPC. The Opposition Division also argued that Rule 29(2) EPC 'clearly defines which biological material originating from the human body may be patented … It follows from the text of the Rule itself that the matter of the patent in suit is not to be considered as an exception to patentability under Article 53(a) EPC' (Correspondence *EPO* 2005d: 16). The patent was maintained in amended form. The patentees appealed and submitted a new set of claims with its Statement of Grounds of Appeal. The Institut Curie, the Assistance Publique – Hôpitaux de Paris and the Institut Gustave Roussy also (jointly) appealed.

Oral proceedings in appeal took place in November 2008. With regard to Art. 53(a) EPC, TBoA 3.3.04 (Chairman Kinkeldey) referred to its earlier decision in T-1213/05 Breast and ovarian cancer/ UNIVERSITY OF UTAH, observing that in that decision it had already 'dealt with the socio-economic and ethical consequences of the patenting of diagnostic methods involving the use of human genetic material' (T-666/05: para. 82).

In its decision, the Board rejected all the objections under Art. 53(a) EPC, the case was remitted to the Opposition Division, and the patent was maintained with amended claims.

8.12 Human genes and genetic diagnostic tests: T-80/05 Method of diagnosis/UNIVERSITY OF UTAH

As described in Chapter 4, Myriad Genetics, UURF and the United States of America filed a patent application with the initial claim relating to 'A method for diagnosing a predisposition for breast and ovarian cancer in a human subject which comprises determining whether there is a germline alteration in the sequence of the BRCA1 gene or a BRCA1 gene regulatory sequence in a tissue sample of said subject, said alteration being indicative of a predisposition to said cancer'.

The patent was granted in January 2001 (Skolnick *et al.* 2001b), with some amendments to the claims in response to comments from the Examining Division regarding lack of novelty and inventive step, as well as lack of clarity and support of the patent claims. Oppositions were filed by the Institut Curie, Assistance Publique – Hôpitaux de Paris, the Institut Gustave Roussy, the Belgian Society of Human Genetics, and an Italian cancer research organisation (Associazione Angelaserra per la ricerca sul cancro).

The Belgian Society of Human Genetics and the Associazione Angelaserra per la ricerca sul cancro invoked Art. 53(a) EPC as one of the grounds for opposition. The Belgian Society raised the same morality-based objections as those raised by VVSKG in the case discussed in section 8.11 above.

An oral hearing took place and the Opposition Division decided, in November 2004, to revoke the patent inter alia on the basis of lack of inventive step and lack of clarity of the claims. The morality-related objections were not addressed. This decision was appealed by the patentees in January 2005 and they submitted amended sets of claims. Essentially, the claims were restricted to a method wherein a specific preferred class of mutations (frameshift mutations) were determined.

The patentees argued that the morality-related objections were unsubstantiated (Correspondence *Myriad et al.* 2005: 2–3). In June 2005 the case was transferred from TBoA 3.3.08 to TBoA 3.3.04, in view of certain technical aspects of the appeal. Oral proceedings in appeal took place in November 2008.

According to the Board (Chairman Kinkeldey), the amended claims did not pose any of the problems raised by the Opposition Division. With regard to Art. 53(a) EPC, the Board referred to its decision T-1213/05 Breast and ovarian cancer/UNIVERSITY OF UTAH (discussed in section 8.11) and noted that, in that decision, it had already 'dealt with the socio-economic and ethical consequences of the patenting of diagnostic methods involving the use of human genetic material'. On the basis of that decision, the morality-related objections were rejected (T-80/05: para. 65).

In November 2008 the Board decided to remit the case to the Opposition Division, ordering it to maintain the patent in amended form, which was done.

8.13 Stem cells/embryos: T-1374/04 (I) Stem cells/WARF

The Wisconsin Alumni Research Foundation (WARF) filed an international patent application in January 1996 (Thomson 1996). The application related to primate embryonic stem cells (i.e. including human embryonic stem cells or hES cells) and processes for preparing them.

Following oral proceedings in June 2004, in a decision from July 2004 the Examining Division rejected the application under Art. 53(a) EPC and Rule 28(c) EPC.[6] At issue was the question as to whether the exclusions from patentability under Art. 53(a) and Rule 28(c) EPC had to be construed narrowly or broadly. In its decision, despite claiming that it was not doing so, the Examining Division came down in favour of a broad construction of morality-based exceptions to patentability. This went against previous EPO practice and case law in terms of construing exclusions.[7]

[6] 'Under Article 53(a), European patents shall not be granted in respect of biotechnological inventions which, in particular, concern the following: ... (c) uses of human embryos for industrial or commercial purposes.

[7] In G-1/04 Diagnostic methods of December 2005, the EBoA noted that narrow construction of exclusions need not always be correct: 'It is also true that the frequently cited principle, according to which exclusion clauses from patentability laid down in

More specifically, the Examining Division stated:

The application ... discloses the generation of the claimed cell cultures exclusively by carrying out methods which require the dissociation of the component tissues of a preimplantation embryo ... The use of an embryo as starting material for the generation of a product of industrial application, is considered to equal industrial use of this embryo. In the case of generation of a cell culture of human ES cells, the method disclosed implies the use of a human embryo for this purpose and thus, the provisions of Rule [28(c)] EPC are relevant. Considering that the claimed subject-matter is directed to cell cultures rather than to a method for the generation of these cultures, the relation of the product to the generating method was examined ... Since no alternative starting material is given but preimplantation embryos, the ... cultures of embryonic stem cells are inseparable from the methods that generate them and from the use of the embryo as starting material. (Correspondence *EPO* 2004a: 3–4)

The Examining Division explicitly confirmed that the morality provisions of the EPC 'are not directed exclusively to the claimed subject-matter but they rather concern inventions, thus, including all aspects that make the claimed subject-matter available to the public' (Correspondence *EPO* 2004a: 5). The Examining Division denied that it had taken the approach 'of a broad interpretation of Rule [28(c)] EPC wherein the exclusion from patentability of human embryos is extended to exclude from patentability human embryonic stem cells', but claimed instead that the 'relevance of Rule [28(c)] EPC in assessing the patentability of the claimed subject-matter is found to stem not from a broad interpretation of said Rule but rather from the significance of the teachings of the entire application (use of a human embryo ...) which are indispensable for the generation of the claimed subject-matter' (Correspondence *EPO* 2004a: 7). This appeared to leave open the possibility that hES cells might be considered to be patentable by the EPO as long as they were produced by a procedure that did not involve 'use' of a human embryo.

Having established that the use of an embryo was an indispensable part of the WARF application, the Examining Division considered whether there might be any exceptions to the exclusion of such

the EPC are to be construed in a restrictive manner, does not apply without exception' (G-1/04: 20). A similar point of view was later taken in G-2/06 Uses of embryos/WARF. At the oral hearing before the EBoA in G-2/08 Dosage regime/ABBOTT RESPIRATORY, which was attended by one of the present authors, when Abbott referred to 'the principle of narrow interpretation of exclusions from patentability' one of the legal members of the EBoA, Brigitte Günzel, asked where in the EPC Abbott's representative had found such a principle. Abbott's representative then admitted that such a principle was not present in the EPC.

commercial use of human embryos from patentability, but decided that the only potential exception did not apply.[8]

The Examining Division's decision explicitly took notice of WARF's warning that, should the interpretation of Rule 28(c) EPC sketched above be correct, 'all downstream products, for example, growth factors or other important medicinal products, isolated from embryonic tissues or [which could] in any way be traced back to be derived from embryonic tissues would be excluded from patentability and such an exclusion from patentability would affect gravely biotechnological inventions' (Correspondence *EPO* 2004a: 5).

WARF appealed[9] and in its Statement of Grounds of Appeal, submitted in November 2004, argued, first, that hES cells were pluripotent and that:

> The principal source of human embryos used to create hES cells are supernumerary embryos created for infertility treatment to enhance the success rate of IVF, which are ultimately not used for this purpose and are donated for research by the couples concerned. If these embryos were not used in this way they would otherwise be discarded. (Correspondence *WARF* 2004: 3–4)

The appeal was based largely on arguments regarding the appropriate scope of Rule 28(c) EPC. According to WARF:

> The purpose and effect of Rule [28] is to exclude from patentability *the specific activities and products listed* [in that Rule] … Whether or not a patent application contravenes Rule [28] is to be judged solely by reference to the matter for which protection is sought i.e. as set out in the claims … Although the Application discloses that hES cells cultures may be derived from preimplantation embryos (and to that extent discloses the use of human embryos) the claimed subject matter is confined to cultures of embryonic stem cells … It can be seen that the principal issue on this appeal involves a question of construction. That is to say whether Rule [28(c)] EPC should be construed narrowly (thereby excluding from patentability only applications whose claims are directed to the use

[8] The Examining Division referred to the exception, sanctioned by Recital 42 EBD, of inventions 'which are applied to the human embryo and are useful to it'. It rightly concluded that 'the present case does not appear to fall under this one exception because the generated ES cell cultures may hardly be considered to serve any … purpose that is useful to the embryo that gave rise to said cultures since said embryo does not exist any more as such' (Correspondence *EPO* 2004a: 5).

[9] The WARF appeal 'leapfrogged' another stem cell case, the so-called 'Edinburgh patent' (Smith *et al.* 1999), granted to the University of Edinburgh in December 1999. This patent raised issues that were very similar to those raised in the WARF case. The 'Edinburgh patent' was opposed and the Opposition Division agreed in October 2008 that it could be maintained with both the product and process claims limited to exclude embryonic stem cells. Edinburgh appealed, but at the oral proceedings in appeal in November 2007 the appeal was withdrawn. The patent reissued in amended form in October 2008.

of human embryos) or broadly (thereby extending the exclusion to products whose isolation necessitates the direct and unavoidable use of human embryos). (Correspondence *WARF* 2004: 6, emphasis added)

WARF pointed out that various EU bodies had made encouraging comments about human stem cell research, and that the European Commission, for example, had stated that European companies needed to be encouraged to work in this field and that granting patents could play an important role in this regard.[10] According to WARF: 'The EPO should therefore be very cautious in applying the exclusion under Article 53(a) in this area. This would inevitably involve the EPO acting as a moral censor which should be avoided' (Correspondence *WARF* 2004: 7).

WARF also drew attention to three TBoA decisions – T-320/87 Hybrid plants/LUBRIZOL, T-19/90 Onco-mouse/HARVARD and T-356/93 Plant cells/PLANT GENETIC SYSTEMS – in which the Board had stated that exclusions from patentability were to be construed narrowly (Correspondence *WARF* 2004: 20–1).

WARF further contended that a broad construction of Rule 28(c) EPC was 'ethically artificial' since it failed to distinguish between existing hES cell lines and 'hES cells obtained by other means'. More specifically, WARF noted that 'hES cells in practice can now be obtained readily without handling or disposition of an embryo. The ethical issues relating to such cell lines are clearly not the same as those relating to hES cell cultures established de novo from an embryo' (Correspondence *WARF* 2004: 15). According to this line of reasoning, hES cells would be patentable as long as they were derived from a deposited cell line. However, such a cell line could of course itself have only been established by a procedure involving the use of an embryo. We will come back to this below, when commenting on the relevance of moral complicity for addressing patentability under Art. 53(a) EPC.

In WARF's view, the EPO 'should be particularly vigilant not to adopt a broad interpretation of Article 53(a)' EPC in two circumstances: (1) where there was no consensus among the Member States of the EPC as to the ethical (un)acceptability of an invention; and (2) where there was an on-going moral debate in relation to the ethics of the invention, particularly where it was apparent that moral attitudes were changing. WARF argued that '[i]n such circumstances, it would be presumptuous

[10] WARF referred to Document COM(2002) 545 final. However, one should bear in mind that the EPO is not an EU institution and that not all Member States of the EPC belong to the EU.

for the EPO to interfere in the public debate or in any way pre-empt its outcome' (Correspondence *WARF* 2004: 21–2).

WARF's key argument as to why they were entitled to the patent was that 'Rule [28(c)] relates to the *direct use of human embryos*. It does *not* prohibit patents in respect of *products* which are derived from human embryos' (Correspondence *WARF* 2004: 26, emphasis added).

WARF suggested four questions for referral to the EBoA. Oral Proceedings took place in November 2005 and WARF presented some additional arguments. Referring to T-315/03 Transgenic animals/HARVARD, WARF argued that two questions had to be asked: first, whether the claimed subject-matter contravened the Rule, and, if this was not the case, whether the claimed subject-matter complied with Art. 53(a) EPC (Correspondence *EPO* 2005a).

TBoA 3.3.08 (Chairman Galligani) noted that all the techniques described in the patent application necessarily implied the destruction of embryos (T-1374/04 (I): 328). As to a narrow versus broad interpretation of the Rule, the Board correctly observed that only one EBoA decision existed that addressed the issue of whether exceptions to patentability had to be interpreted narrowly: G-1/04 Diagnostic methods of December 2005, where the EBoA had said that the frequently cited principle according to which exclusion clauses from patentability laid down in the EPC were to be construed in a restrictive manner did not apply without exception (G-1/04: 350). As rightly noted by the TBoA, the 'breadth' of an exclusion clause should be determined on the basis of an intensive analysis of the clause in question, an analysis which involves 'all the usual methods of legal interpretation', that is considering 'the wording, the object and purpose of the provision, the interests involved, the consequences of a narrow or broad interpretation, respectively, and the aspect of legal certainty' (T-1374/04 (I): 333).

As to WARF's argument that, since its application did not claim processes or methods, it could not be excluded by the Rule that mentioned *uses*, the Board noted: 'the category of a claim appears to the Board not to be something relevant per se where the law enshrines, in the prohibition of patenting, ethical objections against the exploitation of the technology involved in the claimed subject-matter' (T-1374/04 (I): 335). What mattered according to the Board was the essence of exclusion clauses, rather than claim categories.

In response to WARF's claim that the assessment under Art. 53(a) EPC involved the Harvard test, the following comment was made:

The Board has doubts whether, when it comes to human life, it would be ethically acceptable to make a decision by weighing the interests of human beings who could potentially benefit from the exploitation of the technology against a right, if any, of human embryos (whether or not they can already be qualified as human beings), to get to life and of not being destroyed for the benefit of others. (T-1374/04 (I): 338)

This indicated a totally new approach to the morality exclusion, as we will explain below.

In April 2006 TBoA 3.3.08 referred the following four questions to the EBoA:

(1) Does Rule [28(c)] EPC apply to an application filed before the entry into force of the rule?
(2) If the answer to question 1 is yes, does Rule [28(c)] EPC forbid the patenting of claims directed to products (here: human embryonic stem cell cultures) which – as described in the application – at the filing date could be prepared exclusively by a method which necessarily involved the destruction of the human embryos from which the said products are derived, if the said method is not part of the claims?
(3) If the answer to question 1 or 2 is no, does Article 53(a) EPC forbid patenting such claims?
(4) In the context of questions 2 and 3, is it of relevance that after the filing date the same products could be obtained without having to recur to a method necessarily involving the destruction of human embryos (here: e.g. derivation from available human embryonic cell lines)?[11]

8.14 Stem cells/embryos: G-2/06 Use of embryos/WARF

Following the referral mentioned in section 8.13, the EBoA invited submissions (*amicus curiae* briefs) from interested parties and, in March 2008, after receiving hundreds of such submissions, it issued a summons to WARF to attend an oral hearing in June 2008 (Correspondence *EPO* 2008).

In the summons the EBoA interestingly commented on how the assessment of the application under the morality clause ought to be made. Until then, the EPO had consistently taken a 'balancing' approach to ethical questions – an approach which ethicists label 'consequentialist' or 'utilitarian', which involves investigating whether or not the benefits of the invention outweigh its disadvantages. Clearly

[11] We will not go into the arguments raised by WARF and the EBoA regarding Question 1. For the purposes of this chapter it is sufficient to note that the EBoA concluded that the Rule applied to WARF's patent application.

aware of this trend, the EBoA suggested that such an approach may not be appropriate where human dignity is concerned. According to the EBoA, human dignity was indeed the core issue at stake in the WARF case. As stated in the summons:

> [T]he legislator['s] intended purpose [of enacting Rules 26 to 29 EPC is] preserving human dignity. An argument that there should be a balancing of human dignity against benefits to be achieved, concedes that some benefits outweigh human dignity. What basis is there for this view? If there is a basis for this view for some benefits, does it require there to be immediate concrete benefits, or is a vague hope for hypothetical benefits sufficient? (Correspondence *EPO* 2008: para. 12)

In November 2008 the EBoA decided that Rule 28(c) EPC precluded the patentability of WARF's claims. After providing some comments on the *travaux préparatoires* for Art. 6(2)(c) EBD, the 'counterpart' of Rule 28(c) EPC, the EBoA concluded that:

> On its face, the provision of Article 6(2)(c) of the Directive and thus also of Rule 28(c) ... EPC is straightforward and prohibits the patenting if a human embryo is used for industrial or commercial purposes. Such a reading is also in line with the concern of the legislator to prevent a misuse in the sense of a commodification of human embryos ... and with one of the essential objectives of the whole Directive to protect human dignity. (G-2/06: 324)[12]

As to WARF's argument that Rule 28(c) EPC would only preclude patentability of a use of human embryos that had been *claimed*, which was not the case with their patent application, the EBoA rightly commented that:

> What needs to be looked at is not just the explicit wording of the claims but the technical teaching of the application as a whole as to how the invention is to be performed. Before human embryonic stem cell cultures can be used they have to be made. Since in [this] case ... the only teaching of how to perform the invention to make human embryonic stem cell cultures is the use (involving their destruction) of human embryos, this invention falls under the prohibition of Rule 28(c) ... To restrict the application of Rule 28(c) ... EPC to what an applicant chooses explicitly to put in his claim would have the undesirable consequence of making avoidance of the patenting prohibition merely a matter of clever and skilful drafting of such claim. (G-2/06: 326)

Thus it was no surprise that the EBoA found that the Rule indeed excluded the WARF claims:

[12] However, the 'legislator' referred to here is of course the legislator responsible for the EBD, rather than the legislators responsible for Art. 53(a) EPC. Any effect that Rule 28(c) EPC or any of the other Rules may have on *the scope of the subject-matter* that may legitimately be patented under the EPC Articles is unenforceable.

> A claimed new and inventive product must first be made before it can be used. Such making is the ordinary way commercially to exploit the claimed invention and falls within the monopoly granted, as someone having a patent application with a claim directed to this product has on the grant of the patent the right to exclude others from making or using such product. Making the claimed product remains commercial or industrial exploitation of the invention even where there is an intention to use that product for further research. On the facts ... making the claimed product involves the destruction of human embryos. This use involving destruction is thus an integral and essential part of the industrial or commercial exploitation of the claimed invention, and thus violates the prohibition of Rule 28(c) ... EPC. (G-2/06: 327)

Subsequently, the Board argued that, since the prohibition of Rule 28(c) EPC remained within the scope of Art. 53(a) EPC, it was unnecessary and inappropriate to consider the arguments put forward by WARF, the EPO president and the *amici* regarding the (non-)acceptability of the WARF claims under the Article (G-2/06: 329–30). Thus, with regard to Question 3 (if the answer to question 1 or 2 is no, does the Article preclude patentability), the Board merely noted: 'Question 3 does not need answering', for the answer to question (1 and) 2 was 'yes' (G-2/06: 330).[13]

As we will explain below in section 8.16, the fact that Question 3 was ignored is the most problematic aspect of decision G-2/06 Use of embryos/WARF. Another problem with this decision is that the way in which it interprets the Rule created a loophole for patent applicants. To quote the Board: '[In this case the] use involving destruction [of human embryos is] an integral and essential part of the industrial or commercial exploitation of the claimed invention, and thus violates the prohibition of Rule 28(c) ... EPC' (G-2/06: 327). This wording implies that, if a product (e.g. an hES cell culture) is produced by a production method which *initially* involves the destruction of a human embryo, then if *further* production (e.g. by incubation of the cell culture) does not require further destruction of human embryos after the patent application filing date, patentability would not be precluded. This scenario can easily be created by depositing a sample of the cell culture at a recognised depository no later than the date the patent application is filed, that is G-2/06 Use of embryos/WARF has left a 'deposit loophole'

[13] Following the EBoA decision, in January 2009, TBoA 3.3.08 advised WARF that the claims as they stood would not be acceptable and invited them to respond. No response was made and the appeal and application were deemed withdrawn in May 2009.

(see also Sterckx and Cockbain 2010b: 92–5). This interpretation has meanwhile been confirmed by the EPO.[14]

8.15 Stem cells/embryos: T-522/04 Stem cells/CALIFORNIA

In July 1993 the California Institute of Technology (CIT) filed an international patent application (Anderson and Stemple 1994) designating Europe and entitled 'Mammalian multipotent neural stem cells'. The EPO Examining Division rejected the resulting European patent application in October 2003, inter alia on the grounds of Rule 28(c) EPC and Art. 53(a) EPC. CIT appealed in February 2004 and, with its Statement of Grounds of Appeal, submitted amended sets of claims. These were also regarded as unacceptable by the Examining Division, which referred the appeal to TBoA 3.3.08. In October 2006 the Board informed the applicant that it would be appropriate to stay the appeal proceedings until the WARF referral (G-2/06 Use of embryos/WARF) was dealt with by the EBoA. The proceedings were resumed in January 2009.

In its Statement of Grounds of Appeal, CIT argued that claim 1 of the main request (i.e. their preferred set of claims), which related to 'A method of proliferating in vitro a clonal population of mammalian neural crest stem cells', was not directed to cells from an embryo nor to a method of proliferating cells taken from an embryo as such. Moreover, they argued, the cells could be obtained not only from embryos, but also from the adult peripheral and central nervous systems, thus the use of a human embryo was not inevitable (T-522/04: para. XII).

In May 2009 the TBoA (Chairman Galligani) decided that CIT's contention, that the cells could also be obtained from adult nervous systems, was unsupported, and observed that the patent application only mentioned a method of producing human neural crest stem cells via a use (involving their destruction) of human embryos. Therefore, the Board concluded, Art. 53(a) and Rule 28(c) EPC were violated (T-522/04: paras. 5–7). The Board dismissed the appeal.

[14] As European patent attorney Philip Webber explains: '[Subsequent to G-2/06 Use of embryos/WARF] it has been the practice of the EPO to allow patents on stem cell inventions under circumstances where the inventions can be put into practice at the filing date without requiring the destruction of human embryos, for example if the inventions are based on human stem cells which have been grown in the laboratory (i.e. established cell lines). In particular, the EPO has established that human embryonic stem cell lines were readily available at least by May 2003; patent applications based on such material and filed after this date have generally not been deemed to be immoral' (Webber 2011).

Thus, according to this decision, a *mere allegation* that a non-excluded route to a product is available, when the application only describes the excluded route, is insufficient to support a claim to the product. This same point has arisen in the T-1242/06 (12) Tomatoes II/STATE OF ISRAEL case discussed in Chapter 6.

8.16 General comments

8.16.1 The EPO as a 'moral censor'

In its Statement of Grounds of Appeal in T-1374/04 (I) Stem cells/ WARF, WARF argued that the EPO 'is not and should not act as a moral censor of controversial technologies' and stressed that this had 'been expressed in the clearest possible terms both by the legislators involved in the drafting of the [EBD] and also by the EPO itself' (Correspondence *WARF* 2004: 15). However, the reference to 'the legislators' is spurious – the requirement to consider morality derives from Art. 53(a) EPC, which was not drafted or ratified by the same legislative bodies as were responsible for the EBD. The reference to the 'EPO itself' is equally spurious – the passages quoted by WARF in its Statement of Grounds of Appeal are comments by the president of the EPO and by an EPO Opposition Division, neither of which has any authority to produce a binding interpretation of the terms of the EPC, a task entrusted only to TBoAs and the EBoA.

The fundamental point to emphasise in this regard is that the EPC *requires* the EPO to act as a moral censor. As we have shown in Chapter 2, setting out the *travaux préparatoires* for the EPC, right from the very first report on applicable national laws (Document EXP/Brev (53) 18 rev), the 'ordre public' and morality exclusion has never seriously been questioned. Moreover, it is clearly so fundamental to the EPC that it was even incorporated into Art. 27(2) TRIPS and Art. 6(1) EBD.

Of course this is not to suggest that there are no limits to the extent to which the EPO should fulfil this task of 'moral censor' or 'moral assessor'. In case T-1213/05 Breast and ovarian cancer/UNIVERSITY OF UTAH, the Opposition Division argued that:

> Article 53(a) EPC does ... not provide the EPO with the competence to refuse or revoke a patent by assessing certain alleged negative consequences which may result from the grant of an exclusive right in an individual case. The EPO has not been vested with the task of taking into account the economic effects of the grant of patents in specific areas and of restricting the field of patentable subject-matter accordingly. (Correspondence *EPO* 2005b: 27–8)

Obviously, it would be unreasonable to expect the EPO to assess, for each application it receives, all the possible consequences of granting a patent. However, in some cases, particularly at the stage of appeal after grant of a patent, that is when some of the consequences of the grant of the patent may already be visible, ignoring clearly negative consequences could be argued to amount to failing to take the assessment under Art. 53(a) EPC seriously.[15] In the UURF cases mentioned above, the negative effects of the patent on access to health care were so clear, even at the opposition stage (see Gold and Carbone 2008 and US-AMP 2010), that it seems quite surreal to argue that taking these into account does not fall under the remit of Art. 53(a) EPC.

Again, the 'bounds' of Art. 53(a) EPC and the responsibilities this Article implies for the EPO should not be interpreted in an excessive way. As various commentators and Boards of Appeal have repeatedly noted, since granting a patent does not necessarily imply that the invention in question *will* be exploited and since refusing a patent does not imply that exploitation of the invention is prohibited, patent law should *not* be seen as the area of law that bears the *sole* burden of avoiding or preventing abuses or risks associated with the exploitation of inventions.[16] However, patent law *is* to be seen as a legal instrument

[15] Another blatant example of an incorrect application of Art. 53(a) EPC can be found in the Opposition Division decision in the 'onco-mouse' case, which argued that the assessment of animal suffering and medical benefit had to be made at the date of the patent application and that 'later evidence as to the actual outcome of the exploitation' had to be ignored (Correspondence *EPO* 2003a: 27). In T-315/03 Transgenic animals/HARVARD, the TBoA defended the same view: 'The ... date of assessment should, as with all criteria for the assessment of patentability, be the effective date ... of the patent or patent application. Any later date ... would be inconsistent with other areas of patent law and would lead to unjustified differences between otherwise similar cases ... [A]ssessment at the date of final decision in any proceedings would encourage parties to delay opposition or appeal proceedings in the hope of evidence for or against arising, would encourage late filing of evidence, and could make the outcome of cases dependent on the length of proceedings' (T-315/03: 46). However, even though it is logical to assess the patentability requirements of novelty, inventive step, susceptibility of industrial application and sufficiency of disclosure at the date of application, for the purposes of answering the question as to whether subject-matter falls under any of the exclusions of Art. 53 EPC it is perfectly logical to take later evidence into account, since the Art. 53 EPC exclusions are based on ethical and public policy grounds and thus might be subject to 'fluctuation'. The view that the date at which the Art. 53 EPC assessment must be made should be the latest possible in active proceedings was also supported by Rainer Moufang in his contribution to the authoritative *Münchner Gemeinschaftskommentar* (Moufang 1991: 29).

[16] In this context, however, we should note that several commentators argue that, since a patent merely confers the *negative* right to exclude others from exploiting the invention, rather than the *positive* right to exploit the invention, there is no need for a 'morality provision' in patent law. However, this argument is unconvincing. It is indeed true that a patent does not give its proprietor the right to exploit the invention. Some kinds of inventions may only be exploited after approval has been obtained from

for encouraging/discouraging inventions of which the state, on whose behalf patents are granted, approves/disapproves. This is one of the main reasons why the presence of Art. 53(a) EPC is of such crucial importance. As rightly noted by TBoA 3.3.02 in T-866/01 Euthanasia compositions/MICHIGAN STATE UNIVERSITY: 'Article 53(a) EPC is ... intended to prevent an invention, the publication or exploitation of which would infringe the fundamental principles of "ordre public" or morality being given an appearance of approval through a patent issued by an international authority' (T-866/01: para. 9.7). In a similar vein, UK patent barrister Daniel Alexander has noted that the grant of a patent implies 'a public body ... putting its imprimatur on [the invention]' (Alexander 2000: 310).

8.16.2 The relevance of the EBD-derived EPC Rules

Art. 53(a) EPC qualifies its exclusion from patentability by stating that 'the exploitation shall not be deemed to be so contrary merely because it is prohibited by law or regulation in some or all of the Contracting States'. By incorporating provisions of the EBD into the EPC Rules – that is by seeking to force certain subject-matter to be found to be contrary to the morality provisions of Art. 53(a) EPC because it is EU law that such subject-matter *shall* be unpatentable – the Administrative Council of the EPO appears to have acted against this qualification of Art. 53(a) EPC. Thus the Administrative Council seems to have acted *ultra vires*.

regulatory bodies and, obviously, if a law is in place that prohibits the exploitation of the invention, owning a patent will not allow the patentee to ignore that law. However, in most cases there will not be any such law in place and the grant of a patent may act as a *facilitator* of exploitation of the invention. Therefore, the argument that patents confer a negative right cannot support the conclusion that there is no need for a 'morality provision' in patent law. Moreover, as noted by Drahos, the claim that a patent does not give its owner the right to exploit, although factually correct, is misleading: 'The right of liberty, most would agree, is a fundamental right. Can one exercise the right by walking down the street? The answer is yes, unless there happens to have been an accident and the police have temporarily blocked off the street. Like a patent right it is a negative right – a right not to be interfered with. Negative rights create zones of non-interference. They correlate with negative duties. The holder of the right can, as a result of this zone, exercise the right, unless for some contingent reason a restriction is placed on the exercise of the right. The claim that the holder of the patent right does not have the right to exploit it is misleading. The effect of the patent right is to create a zone of non-interference in which the patent holder may exercise the right by undertaking activities of commercial exploitation. Rights carry with them the right to exercise the right. There would be very little point in having them otherwise. Just as the right to liberty allows one to walk down the street, so a patent right allows one to exploit the patent commercially unless for some contingent reason one cannot exercise the right' (Drahos 1999: 443).

It should be noted that, in accordance with Art. 35(1) EPC, the decision of the Administrative Council to make a rule change requires only a majority of the votes of the Council members, whereas an amendment of Art. 53(a) EPC itself would have required ratification by *all* the EPC Member States. The latter procedure would obviously have taken much longer and it is very likely that not all Member States would have agreed.[17]

Perhaps the provisions of the EBD should more properly have been introduced into the Guidelines for Examination in the European Patent Office, so as to require Examining and Opposition Divisions to treat the subject-matter in question as *prima facie* unpatentable, while leaving it open for the Boards of Appeal to rule otherwise.

The question as to whether Rule 28 EPC is *ultra vires* has been considered by TBoA 3.3.08 in T-315/03 Transgenic animals/HARVARD. This Board commented:

> [S]uch use of the term ultra vires appears incorrect. An administrative action or rule of subsidiary legislation is ultra vires if it falls outside the scope of a law which precludes or limits the legal power of the person or body doing the act or making the rule which is consequently invalid – the term ultra vires denotes an 'excès de pouvoir'. That is quite clearly not the case here. The law in question, Article 53(a) EPC, contains nothing which precludes or limits its own subsequent interpretation whether by case law … or by legislation (as in Rule [28] EPC) … Ultra vires requires an inconsistency but there is none … [The Article] remains unaffected by [the Rule] save that … the Rule deems four limited categories of inventions to fall within Article 53(a) EPC. That has been achieved in a perfectly valid – i.e. intra vires – manner. (T-315/03: 42–3)

However, Art. 53(a) EPC obviously *does* contain something that limits its interpretation, namely the statement that exploitation shall not be deemed contrary to 'ordre public' or morality merely because it is prohibited by law or regulation.

Moreover, Rule 28 EPC provides a list of examples of inventions that are contrary to Art. 53(a) EPC. However, when this Rule was introduced, Art. 53(a) EPC excluded inventions 'the exploitation [i.e. not merely the "commercial exploitation"] of which would be contrary to "ordre public" or morality'. It is possible that, at the time the Rule was implemented, an invention whose *commercial* exploitation was contrary to morality might *not* have been excluded by the Article if it had *non-commercial* applications which were *not* contrary to morality. If that were

[17] The fact that not even all EU Member States who are parties to the EPC would have been enthusiastic is evident, for example, from the attempt by the Netherlands to challenge the validity of the EBD (see *Netherlands* v. *European Parliament* (EU-Netherlands 2001)).

the case, then the Rule would have excluded more from patentability than the Article and would thus have limited the scope of inventions patentable under the EPC without the approval of all EPC Member States.

In view of the problems mentioned above, it would appear that the EBD-derived EPC Rules relating to morality should only be seen to serve as a recommended, rather than binding, interpretation of the scope of Art. 53(a) EPC.

8.16.3 The necessity to consider the Article, rather than (merely) the Rules

In G-2/06 Use of embryos/WARF, it was crystal clear that the Rule indeed forbade the patenting of some of the claimed subject-matter. Since embryos had to be destroyed in order to obtain the claimed hES cell cultures in the first place, and since *destroying* embryos obviously is an example of *using* embryos, the subject-matter of the patent application indeed concerned a *use* of human embryos – regardless of the wording of the claims. In view of the wording of the Rule, the question at issue was whether or not the use of human embryos was for *industrial* or *commercial purposes*. The answer to that question was also straightforward: what was at issue was a patent application and, as rightly noted by Board of Appeal member Rainer Moufang when writing as an academic expert on patents, 'the intention of commercialization ... is necessarily linked to a patent application' (Moufang 1994: 504), so the use of human embryos was indeed for commercial purposes.

However, the conclusion that the invention was excluded by the Rule could not be sufficient to conclude that the application had to be rejected. In view of the provision in Art. 164(2) EPC that, where Rules and Articles conflict, the Articles prevail, the question had to be answered as to whether Rule 28(c) EPC conflicted with Art. 53(a) EPC by excluding more than the Article. Answering that question obviously required an assessment of the patent application under the Article. Thus, demonstrating that the subject-matter of the patent application indeed concerned a 'use of human embryos for industrial or commercial purposes', although certainly important, was not enough. It was also necessary to demonstrate that the commercial exploitation of the invention was contrary to 'ordre public' or morality.

Unfortunately, still in G-2/06 Use of embryos/WARF, in view of the wording of Question 3 by TBoA 3.3.08, the question whether the subject-matter was excluded by the Article had to be answered *only* if the answer to Question 2 was that the Rule did *not* exclude the invention.

The EBoA rightly concluded that the Rule *did* exclude the invention, but then proceeded to ignore the question whether the Article excluded the invention. Again, based on the wording of the questions, the EBoA could get away with this, but it is highly unfortunate for this was the most important question. As noted by the rapporteur for the EBoA in the WARF case: 'The provisions of Article 53(a) EPC might thus be considered as a legal norm of higher rank than the provisions of Article 52(1) EPC [the requirements of novelty, inventive step and susceptibility of industrial application], which latter must yield in case of conflict' (Correspondence *EPO* 2008: para. 15). Thus, the moral assessment prescribed by Art. 53(a) EPC must be made and cannot be escaped by referring to the Rules.

8.16.4 The meaning of the Article

8.16.4.1 The 2000 amendment of the Article As noted in the introduction to this chapter, in its original form (i.e. from 1973 to 2007) Art. 53(a) EPC excluded both more and less from patentability than it does today. Inventions the *publication* of which would be contrary to 'ordre public' or morality were *also* excluded under the previous version, whereas inventions whose *non*-commercial exploitation was not contrary to morality or 'ordre public' might not have been excluded. As the EPO clearly could not prevent a patent applicant from publishing details of her invention elsewhere, the 'publication exclusion' had no real effect. As to the absence, in EPC 1973, of the word 'commercial' to qualify exploitation, in our view this omission was improper since, absent an 'implicit disclaimer' (as discussed in Chapter 9) it might have allowed patentees to invoke the 'enforcement machinery' of patent law to prevent others from doing things which, while contrary to morality in a commercial context, might be morally permissible when performed in a non-commercial context.[18]

However, what can be said regarding the *meaning* of Art. 53(a) EPC? We will address, in turn, the meaning of 'morality', the meaning of 'ordre public' and the meaning of (commercial) 'exploitation'.

8.16.4.2 The concept of 'morality' Only T-356/93 Plant cells/PLANT GENETIC SYSTEMS has provided a definition of morality:

[18] The difference can be illustrated with the example of organ selling versus organ donation or the example of using human embryos that are left-over from in vitro fertilisation cycles for research on fertility treatments versus using such embryos for manufacturing and selling a cosmetic product.

The concept of *morality* is related to the belief that some behaviour is right and acceptable whereas other behaviour is wrong, this belief being founded on the totality of the accepted norms which are deeply rooted in a particular culture. For the purposes of the EPC, the culture in question is the culture inherent in European society and civilisation. Accordingly, under Article 53(a) EPC, inventions the exploitation of which is not in conformity with the conventionally accepted standards of conduct pertaining to this culture are to be excluded from patentability as being contrary to morality. (T-356/93: 557)

One of the problems with this definition, of course, is that, given its emphasis on *accepted* norms and standards, it is a 'procedural' definition of morality.[19] Various decisions have followed this procedural approach. In T-866/01 Euthanasia compositions/MICHIGAN STATE UNIVERSITY, for example, TBoA 3.3.02 asserted that 'Morality constitutes actual ethically-based norms of behaviour that have become socially binding through being generally accepted. The exploitation of an invention only infringes morality if it is regarded as reprehensible by society in general or at least by the trade concerned' (T-866/01: para. 6.12).

However, definitions such as this and the one provided in the Guidelines for Examination in the European Patent Office reduce ethics (the discipline which studies morality) to 'sociology', as well as reducing moral judgements to 'counting noses' as in a vote or public opinion poll.[20] A norm may have become *socially binding* through being accepted by the majority or the totality of society. However, that is neither necessary nor sufficient to make that norm *morally binding*. What people happen to *regard* as contrary to morality may be relevant to sociology or to politics, and it may be interesting for ethicists to look at, but it certainly does not and cannot determine what *is* contrary to morality. The simple reason for this is that one of the primary rules of logic tells us that, in order for an argument to be valid, first, the premises must be true and, second, the conclusion must follow from the premises. With regard to the question we are considering here, a conclusion regarding *what is the case* can never logically follow from a premise regarding *what people believe to be the case*. So, even if the premise is true – (an overwhelming majority of) the public thinks X about invention Y – the

[19] Another problem is that this definition is an example of cultural relativism, according to which what is morally (im)permissible depends *entirely* on the cultural context. We cannot go into this here, but for some interesting criticisms of cultural relativism, see Rachels and Rachels (2007: 16–34).

[20] Even though, in T-315/03 Transgenic animals/HARVARD, evidence based on opinion polls was dismissed, rightly in our view, for regarding such evidence as decisive would reduce morality to an entirely *procedural* issue.

conclusion – invention Y is (not) contrary to morality – never follows from the premise.

In practice, since T-19/90 Onco-mouse/HARVARD, Boards of Appeal have generally advocated a *substantive* rather than a *procedural* approach to assessing morality. As explained at the beginning of this chapter, T-19/90 Onco-mouse/HARVARD prescribed a 'balancing' (or 'consequentialist' or 'utilitarian') approach, which determines whether something is contrary to morality by balancing positive and negative consequences. From T-19/90 Onco-mouse/HARVARD until the recent past, this was repeatedly referred to in Board of Appeal decisions as *the* 'recipe' for assessing inventions under the morality provision. The outcome of this type of assessment obviously does not depend on what the majority of the public thinks about the invention, and this approach is thus much more sound than a procedural approach. However, as we have seen in the discussion of T-19/90 Onco-mouse/HARVARD, TBoA 3.3.02 unfortunately did not apply the 'balancing exercise' in a serious fashion. Rather, it merely accepted Harvard's promise that significant benefits to humanity would flow from the invention. In T-315/03 Transgenic animals/HARVARD, TBoA 3.3.08 showed a much more serious application of the consequentialist test.

Nonetheless, apart from the fact that a consequentialist approach clearly represents an improvement over a 'hollow' procedural approach if the balancing test is done properly, the problem remains that consequentialism, although a very important and influential approach to ethics, is far too limited to 'capture' what matters with regard to morality (see, for example, Scheffler 1988). Therefore, it is to be applauded that, in its referral decision in the WARF case, in response to WARF's claim that the assessment to be made under Art. 53(a) EPC consisted of a 'balancing test', TBoA 3.3.08 commented as follows:

> The Board has doubts whether, when it comes to human life, it would be ethically acceptable to make a decision by weighing the interests of human beings who could potentially benefit from the exploitation of the technology against a right, if any, of human embryos (whether or not they can already be qualified as human beings), to get to life and of not being destroyed for the benefit of others. (T-1374/04 (I): 338)

After the TBoA had referred questions to the Enlarged Board, in March 2008 the EBoA issued a summons to WARF to attend an oral hearing (Correspondence *EPO* 2008). In the summons the EBoA commented on how the patent application had to be assessed under the morality clause. The EBoA suggested that such a balancing approach may not be appropriate where human life (and thus human dignity) are concerned:

An argument that there should be a balancing of human dignity against benefits to be achieved, concedes that some benefits outweigh human dignity. What basis is there for this view? If there is a basis for this view for some benefits, does it require there to be immediate concrete benefits, or is a vague hope for hypothetical benefits sufficient? (Correspondence *EPO* 2008: 6)

G-2/06 Use of embryos/WARF, even though it had some serious shortcomings as explained earlier, showed a fundamental but welcome shift in the EPO's approach to morality – away from the consequentialist approach to a principle-based or 'deontological' approach to morality (in this case, focusing on the principles of human dignity and non-commodification) according to which certain things may be contrary to morality *even* if they would produce more benefits than disadvantages. As one of the present authors has argued and illustrated elsewhere (Sterckx 2008: 487–91), the moral assessment prescribed by Art. 53(a) EPC must be made by applying *both a consequentialist and a deontological approach.*[21]

8.16.4.3 The concept of 'ordre public' As mentioned earlier, the concept of 'ordre public' was defined as follows in T-356/93 Plant cells/PLANT GENETIC SYSTEMS:

It is generally accepted that the concept of '*ordre public*' covers the protection of public security and the physical integrity of individuals as part of society. This concept encompasses also the protection of the environment. Accordingly, under Article 53(a) EPC, inventions the exploitation of which is likely to breach public peace or social order (for example, through acts of terrorism) or to seriously prejudice the environment are to be excluded from patentability as being contrary to 'ordre public'. (T-356/93: 557)

Another frequently quoted definition of 'ordre public' is provided by Ulrich Schatz (former Principal Director International Affairs at the EPO):

[I]n general 'Ordre public' is formed by the ethically based constitutional or other rules, usually backed up by penal provisions, that reflect the basic values prevailing in society and trade. These protected values can in particular include public safety, the integrity of the individual and nowadays, certainly also the protection of environment. (Schatz 2003: 88)

Elsewhere, Schatz has provided further comments on this topic:

I wish to underline that [in the context of national patent law], as a consequence of the concept of 'ordre public' being a body of certain laws, the exploitation

[21] In Sterckx (2008) and Sterckx and Cockbain (2010b) we have explained why, in the case of the WARF patent application, both a utilitarian and a deontological analysis indicate that this application contravened Art. 53(a) EPC.

of an invention can *only* offend 'ordre public' if it is *prohibited by law*. That law could be general criminal law, which would apply to the case of the letter bomb ... That law could also be constitutional law or special laws protecting human life and dignity and other basic values of society. I fully agree that this 'ordre public' legislation also now comprises provisions concerning the protection of the natural environment. (Schatz 2000: 219)

It thus becomes clear that the concept of 'ordre public' is usually explained in a way that suggests that it is very closely linked to (il)legality. However, this cannot be the whole story. In view of the second half-sentence of Art. 53(a) EPC, 'contrary to ordre public' cannot mean the same as 'illegal'. Something that is contrary to 'ordre public' may *also* be illegal, but illegality is neither a necessary nor a sufficient condition for something to be contrary to 'ordre public'. As noted by Schatz: 'Since [for the EPO] the concepts of "ordre public" and "morality" are [not] references to a body of positive legal and positive ethical norms ... the EPO has to define *by itself* the normative contents of these concepts and apply them' (Schatz 2000: 220).

Another question that arises is whether the concept of 'ordre public' is redundant in view of the reference to morality – in other words, whether inventions are conceivable that would *only* contravene 'ordre public' and not morality. Some of the 'usual suspects' that are mentioned in relation to 'ordre public', in particular the protection of the environment and the protection of physical integrity of the individual, clearly *also* fall under the 'umbrella' of the concept of morality. The other frequently mentioned 'candidates' (disruptions of the social order and disruptions of public peace or public safety) seem to be the ones that are 'captured' by the concept of 'ordre public'. Inventions that would only contravene 'ordre public' but not morality might include, for example: 'boom boxes' (portable noise machines that could be designed explicitly for carrying around in operation in public spaces, thereby seriously disturbing other members of the public); clothing that reveals the wearer's genitalia (although in many places wearing such clothing would be contrary to law, this is not necessarily the case and there would be a significant likelihood of disturbing the smooth functioning of society); and speed trap detectors (although these could be legitimately marketed to careful drivers who wish to be extra certain that they would not be breaking the speed limit, there is a significant likelihood that the majority of customers would use such devices to enable them to ignore speed limits, thereby neutralising attempts by the state to ensure public safety).

8.16.4.4 The concept of 'exploitation' As to the meaning of the other key term in Art. 53(a) EPC, 'commercial exploitation', this question was addressed by TBoA 3.3.02 in T-866/01 Euthanasia compositions/MICHIGAN STATE UNIVERSITY, according to which 'exploitation of the invention' within the meaning of Art. 53(a) EPC was 'to be construed as the normal avowed use indicated in the patent ... of the invention's teaching' (T-866/01: para. 5.7). It follows from such a construction of the term 'exploitation' that patent protection should *only* be denied if 'the intended exploitation, i.e. the avowed use indicated in the patent' of the invention, would contravene 'ordre public' or morality (T-866/01: para. 5.8).

However, this interpretation of 'exploitation' is problematic, for various reasons. First, what is 'avowed' by a patent applicant may be very different from what is 'intended' by that patent applicant, by its licensees or by their customers. Second, patent attorneys will of course only ever 'avow' an acceptable use of the invention. A third and more important reason why the construction of 'exploitation' suggested by the TBoA (and which seems to have been the general approach taken by the EPO until November 2008, when G-2/06 Use of embryos/WARF issued) is problematic, is that it is too narrow since it fails to take account of the ways in which Art. 53(a) EPC must have effect in order for this exclusion to achieve its intended purpose.

As we will explain below, Art. 53(a) EPC must 'operate' in *three ways* in order to achieve its intended goal. The construction of 'exploitation' mentioned above limits the 'operation' of the Article solely to the first of those three ways.

The fundamental principle underlying the grant of patents is that they *incentivise* invention/innovation/investment, by protecting ideas in a way that reduces potentially significant barriers to commercial exploitation (most importantly, by making 'free riders' punishable for infringement – see Chapter 1). Thus the grant of patents – which typically takes place *after* the invention has been made to work but *before* the stage of commercial exploitation – may act as a *facilitator*, in the sense that the grant of a patent *makes it more likely* (although not certain) that commercial exploitation of the invention will occur. The reason for having a morality provision in patent law is that the state, by which or on behalf of which patents are granted, obviously does not wish to encourage (through the grant of patents) the commercial exploitation of inventions that are contrary to morality or 'ordre public'.

Obviously, the state may use multiple methods to refrain from encouraging 'wrongful' inventions. Sometimes laws are enacted that prohibit or regulate particular applications of science and technology. Commentators who claim that patent laws should not contain a morality provision frequently argue that, if the state wishes to discourage particular inventions, it should do so via laws or regulations *outside* the domain of patents. However, this argument is unconvincing for the patent system is the only legal arena where technologies are investigated on a 'case-by-case' basis. As noted by UK patent barrister Daniel Alexander:

> [I]t is only in [patent offices] that these issues may be addressed on a sufficiently case-by-case basis, because a lot of these questions that one has to address are very particular questions, involving very particular facts and, for instance, if one is to go into environmental risks, very detailed evidence as to what those risks and benefits are. That is one reason why one might say that an institution such as the EPO is in fact not unsuited, but might be particularly suited to making decisions of this kind and ought to do so. (Alexander 2000: 255–6)

Thus, although other legal instruments can and should be brought into play by the state in the fulfilment of its role as a guardian of the social order and of fundamental moral principles, the patent system is and should remain an important legal instrument in this context. As noted by Schatz: 'the EPO … finds itself side-by-side with the increasing number of other regulatory authorities and bodies having the duty to assess the hazards stemming from the exploitation of certain technologies, in the field of biotechnology as much as in any other field of technology' (Schatz 2000: 221).

The morality and 'ordre public' exclusion – aimed at ensuring that the state does not encourage the commercial exploitation of inventions if this would imply violations of 'ordre public' and/or morality – must therefore 'operate' or 'have effect' in *three ways*.

First, in cases where *commercial performance*[22] *of the invention would be contrary to morality or 'ordre public'* (e.g. because human dignity would be violated), by not granting a patent the state reduces the likelihood of such performance and so Art. 53(a) EPC must be invoked. In this context it should be noted that, obviously (although non-industry parties opposing patents frequently do not seem to realise it), the possibility of there being uses of the invention that are contrary to 'ordre public' or morality *cannot* be sufficient to revoke (or refuse) a patent (application) if one or more use(s) of the invention are possible which

[22] We are using the word 'performance' here to refer to the actual *operation* of the invention in an overtly commercial context – i.e. 'performance' does not refer to the research or development phase of the invention.

do *not* contravene 'ordre public' or morality. Otherwise, it would be virtually impossible to grant patents. Almost any object *can* be used for an immoral purpose, even though it may not have been intended by its designer to be so used.

There may be cases in which, even though commercial performance of the invention would contravene 'ordre public' and/or morality, *non-commercial performance might not contravene.* An act may not be contrary to morality when performed outside a commercial context, but contrary to morality when performed for financial gain. For example, organ *donation* (i.e. not involving financial exchange) is deemed to be morally acceptable, whereas organ *sale* (i.e. when organ transfer takes place for financial gain) is deemed morally unacceptable. In these cases Art. 53(a) EPC must *still* be invoked, in view of the presence of the word 'commercial' in the Article.

The *second* way in which Art. 53(a) EPC must have effect has been explained by Rainer Moufang:

> [T]he term 'exploitation' employed by the legislature is sufficiently broad so as to exclude from patentability also such inventions, the use of which does not of its own accord generate a conflict with the *ordre public* ... [I]t is conceivable that the elementary conflict with the legal system derives from the intention of commercialization that is necessarily linked to a patent application. In such a case the legal system would disapprove not of the innovation itself or of its working in practice, but specifically of the *economic exclusionary position afforded by the patent* with regard to the particular innovation at issue. (Moufang 1994: 504, emphasis added)

> As already explained, a broad interpretation of the term 'exploitation' in Art. 53(a) EPC must be applied: Even if the concrete use of the invention may possibly be justified from an ethical point of view, the sole circumstance that an *exclusive right* will be granted for it for the purpose of commercialization may violate fundamental ethical principles. (Moufang 1994: 507, footnotes omitted, emphasis added)

So in these cases, *performance* of the invention (both commercially and non-commercially) may be acceptable, but *monopolisation* of the invention would be contrary to 'ordre public' and/or morality. Of course this 'dimension' of Art. 53(a) EPC will only be at issue in specific areas, for example if the invention concerns parts of the human body (see section 8.16.6 below). We should also point out in this context that cases where this effect of Art. 53(a) EPC operates must be distinguished from cases whereby moral problems are at issue because of the inappropriate limitation of access to primary goods, for example medicines. In the latter cases the problem should not be solved via Art. 53(a) EPC (or via 'morality exclusions' in national patent laws), but rather by the enactment or enforcement of particular exemptions from patent infringement, as well as by applying compulsory licensing provisions. In other words, this kind of moral problem arising from the effects of patents should be addressed at the level of national patent laws rather than by the EPO, for the problems we are referring to here are problems of patent *abuse* rather than patent *grant*.

The *third way in which Art. 53(a) EPC must have effect*, in order to achieve its purpose, is relevant to cases where a step *preceding* the patent application occurred that was contrary to morality or 'ordre public'. This is the topic of the following section.

8.16.5 Taking into account how an invention has been developed

According to TBoA 3.3.02 in T-866/01 Euthanasia compositions/ MICHIGAN STATE UNIVERSITY, the opponent's observation that the animal experiments reported in the patent were contrary to Art. 53(a) EPC needed no further consideration since 'These experiments were carried out during the making or development of the invention and as such do not fulfil the condition of being part of the exploitation of the present invention' (T-866/01: para. 6.8).

However, Schatz has noted that 'The question to be answered [for the purposes of Art. 53(a) EPC] is whether *the making or the use* of the invented product or process "would be" contrary to public order or morality' (Schatz 2000: 218, emphasis added). Thus, as Moufang has convincingly argued:

> [Article 53(a) EPC] may also apply with respect to inventions, *the development of which* was decisively characterized by an ethically dubious procedure … [T]he invention should be examined as regards its possibly unethical content according to its dynamics, *i.e. in its different stages*. Despite the far-reaching consequences of such an argumentation, there are indeed good reasons to take into account the development of an invention. (Moufang 1994: 504, footnote omitted, emphasis added)

Indeed, in some cases assessing a patent application under Art. 53(a) EPC will necessitate a consideration of the issue of *moral complicity*: is the patent applicant complicit in acts that are contrary to morality (but that might have been performed by others, possibly others with whom the patent applicant has no connection)?

In T-272/95 Relaxin/HOWARD FLOREY INSTITUTE, for example, the opponents rightly argued that, since the women whose ovarian tissue had been used as the basis for the patent application had not been asked whether they consented to *such use* of their body material, their fundamental right to autonomy had been violated.[23] This raises issues of moral complicity. The patent applicant may not be the person who removed the tissue from the women, that is the patent applicant may not be the one committing the wrongdoing but still *the patent applicant is complicit in the wrongdoing for he stands to benefit from it.*[24] In view of the meaning of the word 'exploitation' in Art. 53(a) EPC, as mentioned above, a violation of morality (here: a violation of the fundamental right to autonomy) occurring at a stage before the patent application is filed, implies that the application must be rejected under Art. 53(a) EPC.

The issue of complicity was also highly relevant in the WARF case. G-2/06 Use of embryos/WARF implies that, if the successful performance of the ethically dubious step means that that step need not be repeated, patentability would not be precluded. This is clearly a 'perverse' outcome of that decision, since it implies that patent applicants who have already performed the ethically dubious step (and, in the case of hES cells, deposited a cell culture) before filing their patent application, would be rewarded since they would be able to obtain a patent, whereas those who have not yet performed the ethically dubious step at the time of filing would be penalised. Since in both cases the *overall set of actions* required for the commercial exploitation of the invention would be the same, we would argue that the decision on patentability should also be the same. As we have already argued elsewhere:

[23] For some arguments supporting the view that consent can only be valid if it is informed, that the information provided to research participants should *include* information on the possibility of patenting of the research results, and that the consent forms should indicate whether or not the participant agreed to *this particular* aspect, see, for example, Sterckx and Van Assche (2011). See also Hofmann (2009).

[24] Ronald Green has made an interesting analysis of different forms of complicity or 'moral encouragement', as he calls it, which he discusses in general terms as well as with regard to the specific context of human embryonic stem cell research. Green distinguishes between three forms of moral encouragement, the first and the second of which are relevant to our discussion. The *first form* concerns 'direct encouragement through agency', where one person asks someone else to commit a wrongful deed and benefits from her agent's wrongdoing, although she is not directly involved in the performance of the wrongdoing. In these cases moral responsibility obviously cannot be escaped by the first person. The *second form* is 'direct encouragement through the acceptance of benefit', where one person performs a wrongful deed and, for some reason, another (unconnected) person experiences a benefit as a result of that deed, and decides to enjoy the benefit rather than to forego it. Such toleration of the wrongdoing then encourages the first person to repeat the wrongful act. As Green notes, 'this kind of benefiting from others' wrongful deeds is morally objectionable and inadmissible. Although less pernicious than wrongdoing through agency, it provides a powerful incentive for misconduct' (Green 2002: 549–50).

> [Since] the grant of a patent may be seen as official encouragement (i.e. by or on behalf of the state) to exploit an invention and thereby derive benefit, then the prospect of a grant of patent in the absence of any consideration of complicity [between the performer of a morally dubious act and the patent applicant] may serve as official encouragement of morally dubious behaviour which might be hoped to lead to patentable and profitable inventions. (Sterckx and Cockbain 2010b: 95)

Obviously the question arises *how far 'upstream'* (in the development process of an invention) a morally dubious act may 'taint' the downstream product or process, that is the invention for which a patent application is filed.[25] If we consider two acts, the first of which is (at least in some context) contrary to morality, whereas the second act (viewed in isolation) is morally acceptable, it would appear that if the performance of the second act is made possible by the performance of the first act, and if the performer of the second act might derive benefits from performing that act, then *the performer of the second act (who in the context of this discussion is the patent applicant) is morally complicit in the wrongdoing implied in the first act*. Such complicity is not avoided by a disjunct in timing or location between the acts and exists even if the performers of the acts do not know each other at all.

The 'connection' between the different acts may be *material* (e.g. there is some common identity between the objects of the acts) or *informational* (e.g. information derived from the first act is used to determine parameters for the second act). A *material* connection would appear to be sufficient to establish moral complicity (e.g. between the person using an hES cell line and the person who derived the hES cell line from a human embryo). If the connection between the different acts is merely *informational*, the extent of moral complicity may not be sufficient to cause the second act to be also contrary to morality. As we have explained elsewhere:

> If a researcher, reading a publication describing an immoral experiment, can recognise that that information can be deployed to the benefit of humanity, then an invention he makes on the basis of that information should perhaps not be excluded from patentability under Article 53(a) EPC. Consider the example of a researcher designing life jackets for air crew, taking into account

[25] In this regard, the following question was raised by European patent attorney Philip Webber: 'Does the use of slave labour to mine metals such as tin, tantalum, tungsten and gold for the mobile phone industry mean that mobile phone patents are immoral?' (Webber 2011). The answer to that question would seem to be: not necessarily, for the mining of those metals need not necessarily involve slave labour but may well be done through 'normal', morally acceptable labour. The case of hES cell lines, however, is different, since hES cell lines are always a product of the destruction of human embryos (see also EU-Brüstle 2011).

> the survival times of humans in cold water determined by experimentation on concentration camp inmates. It can be argued that allowing the researcher to use this information sends the signal to other researchers that even information generated by atrocities will be used as long as it can generate a benefit to society. This could lead future researchers to ignore ethical rules in order to promote their research, which would clearly be undesirable. Yet [in some cases] such undesirable effects may be outweighed by some degrees of benefit to society. (Sterckx and Cockbain 2010b: 103)

Clearly, in order for Art. 53(a) EPC to be applied properly, further reflection is required, not only on the interpretation of the concepts of 'morality' and 'ordre public', but also on the meaning of 'commercial exploitation' as well as on questions of moral complicity of patent applicants.

In a recent decision by the Court of Justice of the European Union (CJEU), *Brüstle* v. *Greenpeace* (EU-Brüstle 2011), the issue of complicity was addressed head on. Greenpeace sought the revocation of a German patent held by Professor Oliver Brüstle relating to neural precursor cells and processes for their production from embryonic stem cells and uses of the cells for therapeutic purposes.[26]

The CJEU held that, even if embryo destruction to yield hES cells is performed in a purely research context, should there be any attempt to patent the resulting cells or *anything* derived from them, the invention would be considered to involve the use of human embryos for commercial or industrial purposes and would consequently be excluded from patentability. In doing so, the CJEU effectively and rightly closed the 'deposit loophole' left by G-2/06 Uses of embryos/WARF, which

[26] It is worth mentioning that, in February 2006, the EPO granted a patent to Brüstle (Brüstle 2006). In January 2003 the EPO Examining Division had raised objections to Brüstle's application, on the grounds of Art. 53(a) EPC and Rule 28(c) EPC. During oral proceedings Brüstle submitted alternative sets of claims and the Examining Division accepted a set of claims, the first of which read: 'A ... cell composition obtained from mammalian embryonic stem cells, containing ... no more than 15% primitive embryonic cells ... obtainable by the steps of ... with the proviso that the method [*sic*] does not include destruction of human embryos.' However, this wording did not have the effect that the EPO intended. For many products it is only feasible to define the product by referring to the manner in which it is made. Product claims using such a definition are referred to as 'product-by-process' claims. The EPO has a preferred format for such claims in which the product is defined as being 'obtainable by' the particular process. With this 'obtainable by' language, the claim covers the product irrespective of the process by which it is made (i.e. also if made by a process involving the destruction of human embryos, even though this is what the Examining Division was trying to preclude). Brüstle's European patent was opposed by Geron (the licensee of WARF's stem cell patents). The Opposition proceedings were stayed, pending the outcome of the EBoA's decision in the WARF case. As of June 2012 the proceedings still appear to be on hold.

would have allowed patenting if performance of the invention would not require any *further* destruction of embryos.

The most notable aspect of this CJEU decision is that it makes the link between the use of embryos and the commercialisation of a downstream product unbreakable – that is moral complicity exists between the commercial actor and the embryo user. The CJEU decision clearly implies that the chain of moral complicity cannot be broken in respect of *materials* derived directly or ultimately from embryos, but *also* suggests that the chain might very well not be broken where *only information* deriving from embryo research is used in the making of an invention for which patent protection is sought. Thus, this decision appears to go beyond the interpretation of complicity we suggested above.

8.16.6 Special considerations in cases relating to the human body and its parts

In cases relating to the patentability of the human body and its parts, the relevance of human dignity should be considered. This is important for both legal and ethical reasons.[27] The concept of human dignity is frequently defined as the intrinsic value of human beings, which entitles them to respect. This concept, which is firmly established in the laws of various countries as well as in various international legal instruments,[28] is frequently criticised for being 'difficult to define'. However, this should not be a reason to regard the concept as unimportant – consider, for example, the crucial role of the concept of 'invention' in the EPC, whereas no definition at all is provided – and, more importantly, the concept is certainly not as vague as some of its critics claim it to be. Nor is it as narrow as is sometimes claimed.

[27] As to legal reasons, the example can be mentioned of the Charter of Fundamental Rights of the European Union (CFREU). Art. 1 CFREU provides that 'Human dignity is inviolable. It must be respected and protected.' Another example can be found in the EBD, Recital 16 of which provides that 'patent law must be applied so as to respect the fundamental principles safeguarding the dignity and integrity of the person'. However, since Art. 53(a) EPC rightly mentions that whether something is contrary to morality cannot merely depend on its legal (im)permissibility, we will not go into legal reasons here but rather focus on the ethical reasons for taking into account human dignity.

[28] See the previous footnote. See also, for example, the Universal Declaration of Human Rights (UDHR) and the Council of Europe's Convention for the Protection of Human Rights and Dignity of the Human Being with Regard to the Application of Biology and Medicine: Convention on Human Rights and Biomedicine (the Oviedo Convention – OC).

The concept of human dignity has several dimensions and can be translated into various concrete ethical principles.[29] Perhaps its most well-known dimension – human dignity as represented in some religious contexts – implies the ethical principle of the 'sanctity' or 'intrinsic value' of human life at all stages.[30] This principle is frequently criticised for being tenable only from a religious perspective. Yet the concept of human dignity also has other dimensions that are wholly independent of religion: the principle of non-instrumentalisation (sometimes also called non-commodification) of human beings; the principle of non-commercialisation of the human body; and the principle of respect for human rights. The principle of non-commodification prohibits using human beings as 'objects' or 'means'[31] – this principle was explicitly referred to by TBoA 3.3.08 in T-1374/04 (I) Stem cells/WARF. The second, the principle of non-commercialisation, forms the foundation of, inter alia, the legal prohibition of organ sales and organ trafficking in the laws of all countries except Iran. With regard to this principle of non-commercialisation, it is important to bear in mind that this not only prohibits the selling of human bodies and their parts themselves, but also prohibits making the human body or its parts a source of financial gain.[32] Obviously, something can be made a source of financial gain even if it is not itself being sold. The third religion-independent dimension of the concept of human dignity is, as noted above, the well-known human rights dimension.[33] From this perspective, human dignity is seen as the basis for human rights (in the 'moral' sense of the concept of 'rights', i.e. regardless of whether those rights are legally codified). Actions that violate basic human rights are thus also regarded as contrary to human dignity.[34]

As to the related issue of *informed consent* in cases relating to parts of the human body, this was raised in T-272/95 Relaxin/HOWARD

[29] For a recent highly interesting and compelling analysis of the concept of 'human dignity', see Foster (2011).

[30] For a critical perspective on this principle, see, for example, Singer (1995).

[31] See, for example, Immanuel Kant's (1724–1804) highly influential treatment of human dignity in his *Foundations of the Metaphysics of Morals* (Kant 1969) and of property in (parts of) the body in his *Lectures on Ethics* (Kant 1963). See also Green (2001).

[32] See, for example, Art. 3 CFREU and Art. 21 OC. See also Holland (2001).

[33] See, for example, Beyleveld and Brownsword (2001).

[34] For comments on the applicability of these dimensions of human dignity to the question of the patentability of hES cells, see Sterckx (2008: 490–1), arguing that exploitation of an invention concerning a use of human embryos for commercial purposes would violate human dignity since it implies a violation of the principle of non-instrumentalisation and, more importantly, of the principle of non-commercialisation of the human body and its parts.

FLOREY INSTITUTE. The opponents rightly pointed out that, in order for consent to be valid, the person in question must have been properly informed about the ways in which those asking for consent intend to use the body material in question. In the Relaxin case, unfortunately, the patentee's argument that valid consent had been obtained was uncritically accepted by the Opposition Division and Board of Appeal. As noted by the opponents:

> The Opposition Division recorded that the women who donated tissue ... consented to do so within the context of necessary gynaecological operations. However ... this misses the crucial point ... It was not suggested that any of the sources of the material consented to their material being used as the basis of a claim to this patent. There is no evidence that any of the donors were even asked for that consent let alone gave it ... The [patent holder] wishes to reap a commercial reward from using a person's [tissue] without the consent of that person to any such commercial exploitation.
>
> Where ... no prior informed consent has been sought or obtained by [the] donor for that exploitation, the exploitation of the invention is plainly contrary to EPC Article 53(a) as constituting a fundamental violation of the person's rights. (Correspondence *Aglietta et al.* 1995: 7)

Indeed, in this case Art. 53(a) EPC should have been invoked as a ground for refusing the patent, in view of the third 'operating effect' of the Article, as discussed above in section 8.16.4.

To conclude this chapter on Art. 53(a) EPC, we wish to highlight once more the enormous importance of this exclusion and its proper application, as explained by Moufang:

> Ethical considerations permeate the entire normative structure of the patent system and play a decisive role in its appropriate development by means of legalisation and case law. Patent law also provides adequate space to take into account specific bio-ethical arguments. The provision of Art. 53(a) EPC constitutes an important gate of entry for overarching moral concepts. (Moufang 1994: 514)

9 Towards a coherent interpretation of the exclusions

> A treaty shall be interpreted in good faith with the ordinary meaning to be given to the terms of the treaty in their context and in the light of its object and purpose.
>
> (Art. 31(1) Vienna Convention)

9.1 Introduction

Right from the earliest days of the preparation of the EPC and its precursors, it has been clear that the legislators felt that certain objects and actions should not be the subject of European patents. The legislators considered that these fell into two categories: (1) those which might be inventions but should not have patents granted in respect of them; and (2) those which, although they might be new, susceptible of industrial application and not obvious to the person of normal skill in the art having regard to what was already known, nonetheless were not 'inventions' in the sense that the word invention must be understood within patent law. Those two categories, with two different reasons for being excluded from patentability, have been placed in two separate Articles of the EPC, Articles 52(2) and 53 EPC.

Articles 52(2) and 53 EPC use different words to enact the exclusions. However, within Art. 52 EPC the operative wording for effecting all of the exclusions is the same, and within Art. 53 EPC, although different wording is used, it is the same for all the Art. 53 EPC exclusions.

Since the operative wording is the same, then, unless the wording is so obscure as to require resort to the *travaux préparatoires* to determine what the legislator intended, it is reasonable to expect that all exclusions within Art. 52(2) EPC must be interpreted in one and the same manner, and that the same should be true of the exclusions of Art. 53 EPC, although the manner of interpretation may differ between Art. 52(2) and Art. 53 EPC.

9.2 Approaches to the exclusions

In earlier chapters we have encountered various approaches to the interpretation of exclusions from patentability: *novelty*; *contamination*; *higher taxonomic level*; *technical character*; *anything added*; *technical contribution*; *COMVIK*; *further technical effect*; and *synergy*. The last four of these, *technical contribution*, *COMVIK*, *further technical effect* and *synergy*, are not actually ways of interpreting the exclusions but instead are additional tests to be applied in the examination for novelty and inventive step that must be undertaken if subject-matter is found not to be excluded by Art. 52(2) and (3) EPC. We must therefore test the first five approaches to see whether they can be applied coherently to subject-matter to arrive at a result that is in accordance with the clear and straightforward meaning of the words used, or alternatively in accordance with the intentions of the framers of the EPC.

The first five approaches operate as follows:

- *Novelty*. If a claim can encompass within its scope anything that is excluded subject-matter, then the claim must be rejected. This is the *substantive* approach proposed in T-1054/96 (I) Transgenic plant/NOVARTIS, but is also the approach adopted when examining a claim for novelty under Art. 54 EPC.
- *Contamination*. If a feature specifically recited in a claim is excluded subject-matter, then the claim must be rejected. This is the approach that has generally been adopted in relation to methods of therapy, surgery and diagnosis.
- *Higher taxonomic level*. If a claim encompasses excluded subject-matter that is not referred to specifically but instead is referred to in more general terms which *might* also cover non-excluded subject-matter, the claim can be accepted. This is the approach that the Boards of Appeal have favoured for 'plant and animal varieties', for example in T-49/83 Propagating material/CIBA-GEIGY, T-320/87 Hybrid plants/LUBRIZOL, and G-1/98 Transgenic plant/NOVARTIS II.
- *Technical character*. If the subject-matter of a claim has technical character, then the claim can be accepted. This is one of the approaches developed by TBoA 3.5.01.
- *Anything added*. If a claim is directed to a combination of excluded and non-excluded subject-matter, the claim can be accepted. This approach, also referred to as the *any hardware* approach, was proposed by TBoA 3.5.01 in T-258/03 Auction method/HITACHI.

The *further tests* that may be applied if a claim passes the approach applied are as follows:

- *Technical contribution.* In the case of a 'mixed' claim, for determination of inventive step, the contribution of the excluded subject-matter should be ignored. This was an approach applied for many years by TBoA 3.5.01 until rejected in T-1173/97 Computer program product/IBM.
- *COMVIK.* When examining for inventive step, only the features in a claim that have technical character can be considered. This approach was originally proposed by TBoA 3.5.01 in T-641/00 Two identities/ COMVIK.
- *Further technical effect.* When examining a 'mixed' claim for inventive step, a further technical effect for the excluded component, beyond that inherent to its very nature, must be found (unless the non-excluded component is itself novel and inventive).
- *Synergy.* When examining a 'mixed' claim for inventive step, a technical effect must arise from the synergistic interaction, in use, of the excluded and non-excluded components (unless the non-excluded component is itself novel and inventive).

It should be noted that, for a 'mixed' claim where the non-excluded component is itself novel and inventive, the claim will pass all four of these additional tests. We shall now consider how these approaches and additional tests fare when applied to the exclusions of Art. 52(2) and Art. 53 EPC.

9.3 Art. 52(2) EPC

In relevant part, Art. 52 EPC states that:

> European patents shall be granted for any *inventions*, in all fields of technology ... [But that t]he following *in particular* shall not be regarded as inventions [examples listed of subject-matter and activities] ... [This] shall exclude the patentability of the subject-matter or activities referred to ... only to the extent to which a European patent application or European patent *relates to* such subject-matter or activities *as such*. (EPO 2010a: 106, emphasis added)

Thus Art. 52(2) EPC excludes subject-matter that is not an 'invention' and provides a non-exhaustive list of such subject-matter, while Art. 52(3) EPC relaxes this by permitting claims incorporating features that are not themselves inventions.

It is worth bearing in mind that the words used in Art. 52(1) and (3) EPC in relation to the subject-matter of the European patent, that is 'for' and 'relates to', are not the same. Thus a European patent 'for' X need not provide exactly the same patent coverage as a European patent 'relating to' X. As explained below, we suggest that a patent 'for X' means a patent that would be infringed by X whereas a patent 'relating to X' means a patent with *claims* that encompass X.

In the case of the *novelty* approach, a claim must be rejected if it *could encompass* as a feature subject-matter that is excluded, for example a claim to 'a motor vehicle' (as such a vehicle could be decorated with an aesthetic creation). For the *contamination* approach, a claim must be rejected where it *explicitly recites* subject-matter that is mentioned as excluded, for example a claim to 'a computer under the operational control of a computer program'. Both of these approaches clearly far exceed the intention of the legislators as demonstrated by the 'as such' clause in Art. 52(3) EPC – a computer does not become a computer program by virtue of operating under its control and a motor vehicle does not become an aesthetic creation by virtue of having something painted onto it. In rejecting these approaches to the Art. 52(2) EPC exclusions, we do not require the words 'as such' to have anything other than their normal meaning.

Let us turn now to consider a *higher taxonomic level* description of subject-matter excluded by Art. 52(2) EPC. Where a plant of species *Lycopersicon esculentum* (tomato) is discovered that generates a new and health-giving chemical X in its fruit, or a new form of granite is found containing crystals of a new and useful compound Y, could they be claimed as 'a plant that generates X in its fruit' or 'a mineral containing Y'? Such a claim would encompass and be infringed by the plant or rock as discovered – in other words it *relates to* the excluded subject-matter as such and would be infringed by that subject-matter. Since Art. 52 EPC does not carry the 'disclaimer' of Art. 53 EPC that 'European patents *shall not be granted in respect of …*', and since the further tests of novelty, inventive step and susceptibility of industrial application would not necessarily catch a claim that escaped the Art. 52(2) EPC exclusion by virtue simply of having been drafted at a higher taxonomic level, it seems clear that this approach to the Art. 52(2) EPC exclusions cannot be correct either. Once again, no strained interpretation has to be given to the words 'as such' in order to arrive at this rejection of the *higher taxonomic level* approach to Art. 52(2) EPC.

The fourth approach to interpretation mentioned above, the *technical character* approach, was developed by TBoA 3.5.01 to try to satisfy the computer industry. It relies on the following syllogism: all patent-eligible inventions have technical character; anything with technical character is a patent-eligible invention; thus any example of subject-matter recited in Art. 52(2) EPC which has technical character must not be that subject-matter 'as such'. (All members of set X belong to set Y, all members of set Y belong to set X, Z belongs to set Y therefore Z must belong to set X.) This means that a computer program with technical character is not a computer program as such, but also that the plant and granite referred to in the previous paragraph are not discoveries as such.

However, there is nothing in the *travaux préparatoires* to support the suggestion that the framers did not intend to exclude computer programs, discoveries, and so on, if they could be put to technical use. Far from it; it is clear that excluded subject-matter *could* be claimed but *only* as *part* of an invention made using the excluded subject-matter. This was clear as far back as the Gajac Report:

> As a general rule, a patent can only protect an invention (a creation) and not a discovery, i.e. the mere becoming aware of a pre-existing reality. A natural product or a natural phenomenon could no more be the object of patent protection than the revelation of a law of nature, even though a patentable technical indication may be based on a discovery, and the scientific expression of an empirically known causality may, for example, provide an industrial activity with a precise and constant character and therefore yield a patentable application, if it takes the form of a concrete technical instruction addressed at industry. (Document EXP/Brev (53) 18 rev: 4, authors' translation from French)

The *technical character* approach is based on flawed logic, since it relies, without any justification, on the second premise, that anything with technical character must be patentable, being correct. It ignores the intentions of the framers of the EPC, and it requires the words 'as such' in Art. 52(3) EPC to be given a wholly bizarre interpretation that is quite at odds with the requirements of Art. 31 Vienna Convention. The *technical character* approach is clearly wrong, even if currently beloved by the EPO.

The fifth approach to the interpretation of exclusions to patentability, the *anything added* approach, seems at first glance to be equally outlandish. According to this approach *all* 'mixed' claims – that is claims that are directed to a *combination* of something that is listed as excluded in Art. 52(2) EPC with something else that is not listed as excluded – escape the Art. 52(2) EPC exclusion, on the basis that they do not relate to the excluded subject-matter as such. Thus, claims to 'a motor vehicle with a painting on the side' or to 'a computer loaded with a computer program' would not seem to relate to an aesthetic creation or to a computer program 'as such'. This indeed happens to be true: they are not claims to an aesthetic creation or to a computer program; they are claims to a motor vehicle and a computer, that is subject-matter that is *not* among the specific examples listed in Art. 52(2) EPC. The *anything added* approach therefore seems to work and requires the words 'as such' in Art. 52(3) EPC to have no more or less than their normal meaning.

However, the *anything added* approach is necessary but not sufficient. On its own, it would allow excluded subject-matter to be patented simply by combining it with anything that is not excluded, including things with which the excluded subject-matter, through its very nature, would normally have to be associated. Examples would include: a painting on a canvas; a novel on the pages of a book; and a computer program on a disc. Nonetheless, claims to combinations are routinely encountered in patent law, for example 'a machine comprising four wheels and a windscreen' (a motor vehicle). For a combination of independently unpatentable components to be found to be patentable, it is required that the combination of components (or a subset of that combination) *must interact in operation* so as to achieve a new and inventive technical effect in order that the presence of an inventive step can be recognised. In other words, as a combination they must have a further technical effect that goes beyond that implicit in the individual components. This is sometimes referred to as *synergy*. If this conventional requirement in the examination for inventive step is applied to the 'mixed' claims that escape the exclusions of Art. 52(2) EPC under the *anything added* approach, then the exclusions are found to have a full and meaningful effect. This, we suggest, is how Art. 52(2) EPC should be approached.

The *further technical effect* and *COMVIK* additional tests are flawed since they allow the relevant technical effect to be *of the excluded component alone*, thereby emasculating the exclusions and clearly going against the legislators' intentions (e.g. as illustrated by the quote from the Gajac report above). Likewise, the *technical contribution* test is flawed since it ignores any technical effect that arises from synergy between the excluded and non-excluded components, again going against the legislators' intentions as illustrated by the quote from the Gajac report.

9.4 The implications of the 'anything added plus a requirement for synergy' approach to Art. 52(2) EPC

For most if not all of the Art. 52(2) EPC exclusions, if our suggestion were to be followed, there would be little or no change to the claim types that would be accepted. The exceptions are computer programs, data carriers loaded with computer programs and elements isolated from the human body.

Claims to computer programs would be rejected as being to computer programs as such, and claims to data carriers loaded with computer programs would pass the *anything added* test but be rejected as lacking inventive step in view of the absence of *synergy* when in operation (the program simply functioning as a program and the carrier as a carrier).

However, such rejection is not unreasonable. As we have argued elsewhere (Sterckx and Cockbain 2010a), all inventions reside in methods or processes – a computer program may be a part of an invention but that invention will actually be a method of operating a computer to produce a new and useful technical effect. The program *itself* is no more than a set of instructions, subject-matter in the same category as rules for playing games, presentations of information and literary (aesthetic) creations.

Moreover, Art. 27(1) TRIPS would not be violated by the approach that we suggest since it only provides that 'patents shall be available for any inventions' and since, under this interpretation, and as clearly specified in Art. 52(2) EPC, computer programs are simply *not* 'inventions' for the purposes of patent law. TRIPS does not categorise computer programs as falling within the scope of the term 'inventions', and indeed it could not, as it could not then have been agreed to by the EPC Member States. Thus the EPC seems to be TRIPS-compliant when interpreted in line with our suggestion.

Regarding the other type of subject-matter that would be affected by the approach we suggest, elements isolated from the human body, we would point out that any approach must apply equally to the other subject-matter excluded by Art. 52(2) EPC. If we consider the case of a work of art, a painting perhaps, if such a painting is removed (isolated) from its packaging, or from a collection of paintings, it remains a painting, an aesthetic creation. An isolated mental act is also still a mental act. A plant found in nature remains a discovery even when uprooted. The act of isolation does not change the identity of the thing or act that is isolated.

The question therefore arises as to whether an '*anything added* plus a requirement for *synergy*' approach would make the EPC non-compliant with the EBD, and more particularly with Art. 5(2) EBD:

> An element isolated from the human body ... including the sequence or partial sequence of a gene, may constitute a patentable invention, even if the structure of that element is identical to that of a natural element.

This provision might suggest that a claim to 'an isolated human DNA molecule coding for protein X' would not be excluded by the provisions of Art. 52(2) EPC as a discovery. However, the wording of Art. 5(2) EBD is not so absolute. The Article only states that the isolated element *may* constitute a patentable invention. Read in conjunction with Art. 52(2) EPC, *this would allow an isolated element to be claimed in a 'mixed' claim*. Moreover, as has been pointed out by the EBoA in G-2/07 Broccoli/PLANT BIOSCIENCE, the EPC is not an EU instrument and is not guaranteed to be EBD-compliant. The EBoA in that case found that Art. 2(2) EBD did *not* override Art. 53(b) EPC.

9.5 The Art. 53 EPC exclusions

Art. 53 EPC, in focused form, provides that:

> European patents shall not be granted *in respect of*: (a) [any objects or methods] *the commercial exploitation of* which would be contrary to 'ordre public' or morality ... (b) [particular objects or methods] ... (c) [other particular methods].

Thus, for the objects or methods mentioned in paragraphs (a) and (b), the Art. 53 EPC ban is relatively simple – European patents cannot be granted 'in respect of' them – the ban is not concerned with their provenance or their use. For the Art. 53(a) EPC exclusion, however, not just the objects and methods themselves, but also their provenance and use must be considered (see G-2/06 Use of embryos/WARF).

Turning to the five approaches to interpreting the exclusions set out in section 9.2, we will first address the *anything added* and *technical character* approaches. If we add the initial method step of giving the subject a cup of tea to a claim defining a technical method of surgery, or to a claim defining a method of paid assassination using a technical method, we can see that the resulting method as defined will still be a method of surgery or will still be contrary to morality, and thus must still be excluded. Clearly, neither of these approaches can be the correct way of interpreting Art. 53 EPC.

Adding the requirement for a technical effect (whether additional, synergistic or whatever) to supplement these approaches would not render them acceptable – a claimed method of surgery or immoral act would remain a method of surgery or an immoral act.

The *novelty* approach would involve the rejection of any claim that included excluded subject-matter within its scope. Thus a claim to 'a method of imaging involving administering a contrast agent to the patient' (see T-992/03 MEDI-PHYSICS referred to in Chapter 5) would have to be rejected because the method of administration (e.g. by injection into the heart) might qualify as a 'method of surgery' in view of the risk to the patient. The patent applicant might respond to a rejection on this basis by adding a disclaimer. However, since virtually *any* invention *could* be commercially exploited in a way that contravenes morality or 'ordre public', such a disclaimer would have to be of *all* subject-matter excluded by Art. 53 EPC. This would apply to virtually all claims and would go against the requirement of Art. 84 EPC[1] that the claims be concise. The *novelty* approach therefore seems totally inappropriate.

The *contamination* approach would involve the rejection of a claim where the entire claim scope or an optional feature of the claim is an object or method as defined in Art. 53(a), (b) or (c), for example a claim to 'a method of amputating a limb from a living human'. In practice, the *contamination* approach is a more general version of the *higher taxonomic level* approach. Both result in claims that encompass the excluded although they do not mention it in specific terms. However, these approaches in effect ignore the wishes of the framers of Art. 53 EPC, since they allow the exclusions to be avoided simply by the patent attorney's choice of words when the claim is drafted, resulting in a claim that covers the excluded subject-matter, which may possibly be the major or only intended purpose of the invention. The patentee would therefore be free to collect licence fees or damages in respect of inventions that are unpatentable according to Art. 53 EPC, including the immoral. This would clearly ignore the intentions of the framers of the EPC. The potential solution of requiring an *explicit* disclaimer in each claim would be inappropriate as explained earlier.

The correct solution, we believe, lies in the words 'in respect of' in the opening part of Art. 53 EPC. These words can and should be read as an *implicit disclaimer*, implying that the claims of a granted European patent *cannot be construed to cover anything excluded by Art. 53 EPC*. Thus, to take the example of the imaging method mentioned above that requires administration of a contrast agent: where administration is by inhalation, the imaging method is covered by the claim, but where it is by injection into the heart (i.e. surgery) it is not.

This interpretation of the operative wording of Art. 53 EPC, 'European patents shall not be granted in respect of', allows the words 'shall not' the straightforward meaning that *European patents that have been granted are not 'in respect of' the excluded subject-matter, irrespective of the wording of the claims*. In other words, the EPO cannot err by granting a European patent which covers excluded subject-matter. This interpretation is also consistent with, and indeed is strongly supported by, the equivalent wording in the French and German versions of the EPC: 'Les brevets euopéens ne sont pas délivrés pour' and 'Europäische

[1] Art. 84 EPC provides that: 'The claims shall define the matter for which protection is sought. They shall be clear and concise and be supported by the description' (EPO 2010a: 140).

Patente werden nicht erteilt für'. Moreover, it is also consistent with the parallel wording of Art. 27 TRIPS, 'Members may exclude from patentability', that is the EPC is TRIPS-compliant if our interpretation is followed.

Finally, the suggested interpretation is also in accordance with Art. 31(1) Vienna Convention: 'A treaty shall be interpreted in good faith with the ordinary meaning to be given to the terms of the treaty in their context and in the light of its object and purpose.'

To avoid giving the public the impression that the EPO is granting patents that clearly cover subject-matter excluded by Art. 53 EPC, the EPO would of course have to ensure that claims are not accepted that explicitly recite excluded subject-matter, that is the *contamination* approach would still have to be followed by EPO examiners.

9.6 The implications of the *implicit disclaimer* approach to Art. 53 EPC

To judge the implications of this approach, it is instructive to see what result it would have achieved if applied to the cases discussed in Chapters 5, 6, 7 and 8. For *methods of medical treatment and diagnosis* we can see no change in the type of claim wording that would be acceptable. Moreover, the desire of the EPC framers that physicians and veterinarians should be free to carry out their unplanned work in their patient's best interests would be met. For inventions the commercial exploitation of which would be *contrary to morality*, there would be no change in the type of claim that would be permissible, but patentees would not be in a position to use their patents to benefit from acts contrary to 'ordre public' or morality.

The major change resulting from the approach, we suggest, would come in relation to *plant and animal varieties* and *essentially biological processes for the production of plants and animals*. A plant or an animal, which was a member of a 'variety', for example on the lowest taxonomic level, could not infringe a European patent and nor could dealings with it that left it unchanged. The simple growing of plants and animals, an essentially biological process practised by a farmer, could not be alleged to be or to contribute to an infringement of a European patent. Conventional breeding processes likewise could not infringe.

Technical processes for treating plants and animals, for example the seed treatment of T-49/83 Propagating material/CIBA-GEIGY, would be patentable. However, the higher normative ranking of Art. 53 EPC would ensure that the treated plant or animal, as well as dealings with it that leave it unchanged, could not infringe despite the provisions of Art. 64(2) EPC.[2]

As the EBoA stated in the Summons to Oral Proceedings in G-2/06 Use of embryos/WARF:

> The grant of patents by the EPO presupposes that there is a legal order in the Contracting States which allows granted patent rights to be enforced. Article 53(a) EPC can be considered as the expression that it would be incompatible with such legal order to grant patents for inventions whose exploitation would be contrary to 'ordre public' or morality. The provision of Article 53(a) might thus be considered as a legal norm of higher rank than the provisions of Article 52(1) EPC, which latter must yield in case of conflict. (Correspondence *EPO* 2008: para. 10)

Moreover, since Art. 83 EPC[3] requires an enabling disclosure, a claim that passes the *contamination* test, where *the only enabling disclosure* is for subject-matter that would be excluded if claimed specifically, must be rejected under Art. 83 EPC. This, in effect, was commented on in T-522/04 Stem cells/CALIFORNIA and is the point at issue in T-1242/06 (12) Tomatoes II/STATE OF ISRAEL.

That the exclusions of Art. 53 EPC as a whole are a higher ranking legal norm is made clearer by the comments made by the Enlarged Board in relation to Art. 53(c) EPC:

> [T]he exclusion from patentability of [medical] methods under Article [53(c)] EPC seems actually to be based on socio-ethical and public health considerations. Medical and veterinary practitioners should be free to take the actions they consider suited to diagnose illnesses by means of investigative methods. Consequently, the policy ... appears to be aimed at ensuring that those who carry out diagnostic methods as part of the medical treatment of humans or veterinary treatment of animals are not inhibited by patents. (G-1/04: 348)

2 Art. 64(2) EPC provides that: 'If the subject-matter of the European patent is a process, the protection conferred by the patent shall extend to the products directly obtained by such process' (EPO 2010a: 120).

3 Art. 83 EPC provides that: 'The European patent application shall disclose the invention in a manner sufficiently clear and complete for it to be carried out by a person skilled in the art' (EPO 2010a: 140).

10 Conclusion

With this book we set out to describe the history of the exclusions from patentability that are found in Art. 52(2) and Art. 53 EPC, how they came to be drafted and how they have been interpreted by the EPO since the law came into force in 1978. Our intention was to determine whether a coherent approach to the interpretation of the exclusions could be identified.

We do not seek to challenge the importance and social value of the patent system, indeed rather the reverse. As mentioned in Chapter 1, the economic driving force of the IP system has become clear to all, and over the last few decades IP has become the 'New Wealth of Nations'. We do consider, however, that, as privileges granted by or on behalf of the state for the ultimate benefit of its citizens, privileges that are exceptions to the usual controls on monopolies, it is logical and perfectly reasonable that the granting and enforcement of patents should be subject to constraints. Safeguards that are in place include requirements for novelty, inventiveness, usefulness and disclosure. However, the most fundamental of the constraints is the one that is the subject of this book, the exclusions from patent-eligibility of certain subject-matter, for if this operates correctly then there can be no abuse of the privilege in the fields in question. This constraint, as the book has made clear, is based on social, ethical and political reasons, as well as the understanding that patent law is not always the proper vehicle for protecting new products and processes – other laws, such as plant variety protection and copyright laws, may be more appropriate. Moreover, as Hettinger noted: 'Property rights in the created object are not the only possible reward. Alternatives include fees, awards, acknowledgements, gratitude, praise, security, power, status, and public financial support' (Hettinger 1989: 41).

As Chapters 2 to 8 have shown, inventors, their assignees, industrial and professional associations, and even patent office officials and government representatives, have long pushed against the boundaries of the patent-eligible, implicitly or explicitly arguing that such boundaries are unnecessary and discriminatory (in their fields) and should be rolled back or removed. The wording of Art. 27(1) TRIPS has been a weapon in this campaign: 'patents shall be available for any inventions ... in all fields of technology.' However, this campaign has carefully glossed over one of the realities of patent law: inventions generally have several aspects that can be claimed *separately*. A new drug compound, for example, might give rise to claims to: the compound per se; compositions containing the compound; the compound 'for use in medicine'; processes for preparing the compound; and, in the USA, methods of medical treatment using the compound. The fact that *one* of these claim formats is not available under the EPC does not mean that the invention cannot be patented or that the EPC is thereby non-compliant with TRIPS. For computer programs, for example, the fact that the program itself should not be patented according to Art. 52(2) EPC does not mean that the underlying invention, the process that is carried out when the program is run, cannot be patented.

There is no need and no justification to grant applicants patents with claims to *every* aspect of their inventions, when, after many decades of deliberation, the legislators had decided that some aspects should not be patentable. To quote from the eminent British judge Sir Robin Jacob: '[I]t by no means follows that because of pressure from applicants, the grant of patents for excluded categories should be allowed or that the excluded categories ... should be construed narrowly. Just as with arms, merely because people want them is not sufficient reason for giving them' (UK-Aerotel 2006: para. 19). The founding father of utilitarianism, Jeremy Bentham, of course had a point when he observed that 'he who has no hope that he shall reap will not take the trouble to sow' (Bentham 1785: 71). However, we would argue that, even if the exclusions to patent-eligibility are properly applied, sufficient prospects of obtaining IP coverage remain that the incentive to invent and innovate will not be dulled.

As Chapters 3 to 8 have shown, the pressures exerted from the various circles mentioned above did result in an erosion of the boundaries of the patent-eligible in the EPO. David Lange has correctly noted that 'the field of intellectual property [has begun] to resemble a game of conceptual Pac Man in which everything in sight is being gobbled up' (Lange 1981: 147, 156). Reassuringly though, in the last decade the EPO's Enlarged Board of Appeal has shown a willingness to halt the erosion and rebuild the boundaries. This is shown in many decisions from the Enlarged Board under the chairmanship of the recently retired Peter Messerli, but is particularly evident in G-2/06 Use of embryos/WARF, G-2/07 Broccoli/PLANT BIOSCIENCE and G-2/08 Dosage regime/ABBOTT RESPIRATORY.

In this book we have identified and discussed the possible approaches to interpreting the exclusions and we have reached the conclusion that the same approach cannot be used for the exclusions of both Art. 52(2) and Art. 53 EPC, primarily because of the 'as such' qualification to the Art. 52(2) EPC exclusions (expressed in Art. 52(3) EPC) and because of the factual statement with which Art. 53 EPC opens: 'European patents shall not be granted for ...'.

Having examined the repercussions of applying each of the approaches to Art. 52(2) and Art. 53 EPC, we defend the view that the correct approaches are the, at first sight somewhat unsatisfactory, *anything added* and *contamination* approaches respectively. Both, however, are inadequate on their own and require further qualification. In the case of the *anything added* approach to Art. 52(2) EPC, before acknowledging the presence of an inventive step as required by Art. 56 EPC, it seems necessary to insist upon there being a *synergy* between the excluded and non-excluded components that results in a technical effect which neither component on its own achieves. In the case of Art. 53 EPC, it seems necessary to acknowledge that the words 'European patents shall not be granted' means that anything that is excluded by Art. 53 EPC cannot fall within the scope of that which can be found to be patent infringement.

For most industries, our suggested interpretations will have little effect on the current status quo. The exceptions are the computer industry (which would be denied patent cover for computer programs and programs on carriers, but not computers running those programs) and agribusiness (which would be denied patents on seeds and would not be able to enforce its patents against farmers and breeders carrying out conventional biological processes such as growing or breeding plants and animals). The biomedical industry would be unable to obtain patent cover for products materially derived from human embryos or for products isolated from nature. However, for those seeking a private property right in something already existing in nature, we feel that the law is clear – isolation is not enough: 'something more is necessary' (US-Morton 1862).

We hope that, with this book, we have made a meaningful contribution to the task of finding approaches to the interpretation of Art. 52(2) and Art. 53 EPC that are coherent, that are not in contradiction to the wishes of the legislators as expressed in the *travaux préparatoires*, and that also do not require a tortured (mis)interpretation of the wording of the law.

Correspondence from EPO files

These documents can be accessed from the EPO files by following the link at the end of this paragraph, using the European patent, or patent application, number for the case, e.g. EP891130. Letters *to* the EPO may be indexed a day or so after the date they bear as the indexed date is the date of receipt at the EPO. See https://register.epo.org/espacenet/regviewer (last accessed 9 April 2012).

Aglietta et al. (1992), Notice of opposition to European Patent No. 112149, 10 January 1992.

(1995), Statement of Grounds of Appeal in T-272/95, 26 May 1995.

Belgian Society of Human Genetics (2001), Notice of opposition to European Patent No. 699754, 10 October 2001.

Brimelow, Alison (2008), G-3/08 referral letter, 22 October 2008.

Ciba-Geigy (1982), Letter to the EPO in relation to European patent application no. 79103164, 19 August 1982.

(1983), Statement of Grounds of Appeal in T-49/83, 17 February 1983.

Deutsche Saatveredelung et al. (2009), Notice of opposition to European Patent No. 891130, 18 December 2009.

EPO (1988), Decision of the Examining Division re European patent application no. 83307553, 4 November 1988.

(1989), Decision of Examining Division re European patent application no. 85304490, 14 July 1989.

(1991), Summons to oral proceedings in relation to European patent application no. 88300090, 19 September 1991.

(1993), Decision of the Opposition Division in European Patent No. 242236, 15 February 1993.

(1995), Decision of the Opposition Division in European Patent No. 112149, 18 January 1995.

(1997a), Decision of the Opposition Division in relation to European Patent No. 408403, 17 November 1997.

(1997b), Summons to oral proceedings in case T-869/95, 16 January 1997.

(1999), Summons to oral proceedings in the opposition to European Patent No. 546090, 10 November 1999.

(2000), Decision of the Opposition Division in relation to European Patent No. 546090, 11 April 2000.

(2001), Decision of the Opposition Division in relation to European Patent No. 516811, 22 May 2001.
(2003a), Decision of the Opposition Division in relation to European Patent No. 169672, 16 January 2003.
(2003b), Decision of the Examining Division in relation to European patent application no. 00974397, 7 January 2003.
(2004a), Decision of the Examining Division in relation to European Patent Application No. 96903521, 13 July 2004.
(2004b), Summons to oral proceedings in relation to European Patent No. 705903, 26 April 2004.
(2005a), Minutes of Oral Proceedings relating to European Patent Application No. 96903521, 18 November 2005.
(2005b), Decision of the Opposition Division in relation to European Patent No. 705902, 19 September 2005.
(2005c), Minutes of the Opposition Division oral proceedings in relation to European Patent No. 705903, 9 June 2005.
(2005d), Decision of the Opposition Division in relation to European Patent No. 705903, 25 January 2005.
(2005e), Minutes of Opposition Division oral proceedings in relation to European Patent No. 705902, 21 January 2005.
(2007), Decision of the Opposition Division in relation to European Patent No. 1185161, 17 September 2007.
(2008), Summons to Oral Proceedings in case G-2/06, 20 March 2008.
Greenpeace (1991), Notice of opposition to European Patent No. 242236, 9 July 1991.
(1993), Statement of Grounds of Appeal in T-356/93 Plant cells/PLANT GENETIC SYSTEMS, 11 June 1993.
(1997), Notice of opposition to European Patent No. 546090, 27 February 1997.
(2001), Statement of Grounds of Appeal in T-179/01, 28 May 2001.
(2002), Notice of opposition to European Patent No. 705903, 22 February 2002.
Harvard (1991), Letter to the EPO in relation to European patent application no. 85304490, 16 April 1991.
Howard Florey (1993), Response to notices of opposition to European Patent No. 112149, 10 November 1993.
KWS Saat (2009), Notice of opposition to European Patent No. 891130, 18 December 2009.
Monsanto (1998), Response to notice of opposition to European Patent No. 546090, 28 April 1998.
(2001), Statement of Grounds of Appeal in T-179/01, 22 May 2001.
Myriad et al. (2005), Statement of Grounds of Appeal in T-80/05, 21 March 2005.
Pioneer (2010), Response to notices of opposition to European Patent No. 891130, 25 August 2010.
Plant Genetic Systems (1992), Response to notice of opposition to European Patent No. 242236, 29 January 1992.

Sterckx, Sigrid (2011), Letter to the EPO in case T-1242/06, 1 November 2011.
Then, Christoph and *Schweiger, Thomas* (1997), Notice of Opposition to European Patent No. 546090, 17 March 1997.
VVSKG et al. (2002), Notice of opposition to European Patent No. 705903, 25 February 2002.
WARF (2004), Statement of Grounds of Appeal in relation to European Patent Application No. 96903521, 18 November 2004.

References

Alexander, Daniel (2000), 'The Case For and Against the Patenting of Biotechnological Inventions', in Sigrid Sterckx (ed.), *Biotechnology, Patents and Morality*, 2nd reworked edn, Aldershot: Ashgate, pp. 254–8.

Anderson, David J. and Stemple, Derek L. (1994), *Mammalian multipotent neural stem cells*, International Patent Application Publication No. WO94/02593, Geneva: WIPO.

Arrow, Kenneth Joseph (1962), 'Economic Welfare and the Allocation of Resources for Invention', in National Bureau of Economic Research, *The Rate and Direction of Inventive Activity: Economic and Social Factors*, Princeton University Press, pp. 609–25.

Atkins, Beryl T., Duval, Alain, Milne, Rosemary C., Cousin, Pierre-Henri, Lewis, Hélène M. A., Sinclair, Lorna A., Birks, Renée O. and Lamy, Marie-Noëlle (eds.) (1987), *Collins–Robert French–English Dictionary*, 2nd edn, London: Collins.

Baird, Douglas (1983), 'Common Law Intellectual Property and the Legacy of International News Service v. Associated Press', *University of Chicago Law Review* 50, 411–29.

Barry, Gerard Francis, Kishore, Ganesh Murthy and Padgette, Stephen Rogers (1992), *Glyphosate tolerant 5-enolpyruvylshikimate-3-phosphate synthases*, International Patent Application Publication No. WO92/04449, Geneva: WIPO.

(1996), *Glyphosate tolerant 5-enolpyruvylshikimate-3-phosphate synthases*, European Patent No. 546090, Munich: EPO.

Beazley, Kim, Ferreira, Kenneth L., Fitzpatrick, Sharie N., McCaslin, Mark H. and Reyes, Carlos C. (2004), *Glyphosate tolerant alfalfa events and methods for detection thereof*, International Patent Application Publication No. WO2004/070020, Geneva: WIPO.

Bentham, Jeremy (1785), *A Manual of Political Economy*, Works of Jeremy Bentham, Bowring, John (ed.), Vol. III, Edinburgh: William Tate.

Beyleveld, Derek and Brownsword, Roger (2001), *Human Dignity in Bioethics and Bio-Law*, Oxford University Press.

Bodenhausen, Georg. H. C. (1969), *Guide to the Application of the Paris Convention for the Protection of Industrial Property as Revised at Stockholm in 1967*, Geneva: United International Bureaux for the Protection of Intellectual Property (BIRPI).

Boyle, James (2003), 'The Second Enclosure Movement and the Construction of the Public Domain', *Law and Contemporary Problems* 66: 33–74.

Brockhaus, Friedrich Arnold (1987), *Brockhaus Enzyklopädie in vierundzwanzig Bänden*, 19th edn, Vol. IV, Mannheim: F. A. Brockhaus von Selbstverlag.

Brownawell, Darrell William, Norris, Donald James and Shaub, Harold (1988), *Removal of carcinogenic hydrocarbons from used lubricating oil*, European Patent Application Publication No. 275148, Munich: EPO.

Bruchhausen, Karl (1988), in Georg Benkard and Karl Bruchhausen (eds.), *Beck'sche Kurz Kommentare: Georg Benkard Patentgesetz: Gebrauchsmustergesetz*, 8th edn, Munich: C. H. Beck.

Brüstle, Oliver (2006), *Neural precursor cells, method for the production and use thereof in neural defect therapy*, European Patent No. 1040185, Munich: EPO.

Charne, David G., Grant, Ian, Kraling, Konrad, Patel, Jayantilal D., Pruvot, Jean-Claude M. and Tulsieram, Lomas K (1998), *Oilseed Brassica containing an improved fertility restorer gene for ogura cytoplasmic male sterility*, International Patent Application Publication No. WO98/27806, Geneva: WIPO.

(2009), *Oilseed Brassica containing an improved fertility restorer gene for ogura cytoplasmic male sterility*, European Patent No. 891130, Munich: EPO.

Cockbain, Julian and Sterckx, Sigrid (2011a), 'A Sun-Tanned or 3D Smurf? Patentability of Computer Programs in Europe', *Journal of Intellectual Property Law & Practice* 6(4), 254–61.

(2011b), 'Is the Enlarged Board of Appeal of the European Patent Office Authorized to Extend the Bounds of the Patentable?', *International Review of Intellectual Property and Competition Law* 42(3), 257–71.

(2012), 'Are products of essentially biological processes patentable in Europe? The purple radish sprouts case in The Netherlands', *European Intellectual Property Review* 34(6), 422–444.

Cohen, Wesley, Nelson, Richard and Walsh, John (2000), *Protecting their Intellectual Assets: Appropriability Conditions and Why US Manufacturing Firms Patent or Not*, Working paper 7552, Cambridge: National Bureau of Economic Research.

Conley, John M. and Makowski, Roberte (2004), 'Rethinking the Product of Nature Doctrine as a Barrier to Biotechnology Patents in the United States – and Perhaps Europe as Well', *Information & Communications Technology Law* 13(1): 3–40.

Crespi, R. Stephen (1992), 'Patents and Plant Variety Rights: Is There an Interface Problem?', *International Review of Intellectual Property and Competition Law* 23(2), 168–84.

David, Paul A. (1993), 'Intellectual Property Institutions and the Panda's Thumb: Patents, Copyrights, and Trade Secrets in Economic Theory and History', in Mitchel B. Wallerstein, Mary Ellen Mogee and Roberta A. Schoen (eds.) (1993), *Global Dimensions of Intellectual Property Rights in Science and Technology*, Washington DC: National Academy Press, pp. 19–61.

Drahos, Peter (1999), 'Biotechnology Patents, Markets and Morality', *European Intellectual Property Review* 21(9), 441–9.

(ed.) (2005), *Death of Patents*, Oxford: Law Text Publishers.

Drahos, Peter with Braithwaite, John (2002), *Information Feudalism: Who Owns the Knowledge Economy?*, London: Earthscan Publications.

Dutfield, Graham (2009), *Intellectual Property Rights and the Life Science Industries: Past, Present and Future*, 2nd edn, Singapore: World Scientific.

Dutton, Harry I. (1984), *The Patent System and Inventive Activity During the Industrial Revolution, 1750–1852*, Manchester University Press.

EPO (2006), *Convention on the Grant of European Patents (European Patent Convention) of 5 October 1973*, 12th edn, Munich: EPO.

(2010a), *Convention on the Grant of European Patents (European Patent Convention) of 5 October 1973 as revised by the Act revising Article 63 EPC of 17 December 1991 and the Act revising the EPC of 29 November 2000*, 14th edn, Munich: EPO.

(2010b), *Case Law of the Boards of Appeal of the European Patent Office*, 6th edn, Munich: EPO.

(2011), *Guidelines for Examination in the European Patent Office*, Munich: EPO.

Evans, Ronald M., Kliewer, Stephen A. and Umesono, Kazuhiko (1993), *Multimeric forms of members of the steroid/thyroid superfamily of receptors*, International patent application publication no. WO93/11235, Geneva: WIPO.

Foster, Charles (2011), *Human Dignity in Bioethics and Law*, Oxford: Hart.

Gold, Richard and Carbone, Julia (2008), *Myriad Genetics in the Eye of the Policy Storm*, Montreal: McGill Centre for Intellectual Property Policy.

Government of the Federal Republic of Germany (1972), *Munich Diplomatic Conference for the Setting Up of a European System for the Grant of Patents, 1973 (Munich, 10 September to 6 October 1973)*, Munich: Wila Verlag für Wirtschaftswerbung.

(1973), *Minutes of the Munich Diplomatic Conference for the Setting Up of a European System for the Grant of Patents (Munich, 10 September to 5 October 1973)*, Berlin: Bundesdruckerei Berlin.

Green, Ronald Michael (2001), 'What Does it Mean to Use Someone as "a Means Only": Rereading Kant', *Kennedy Institute of Ethics Journal* 11(3), 247–61.

(2002), 'Benefiting from "Evil": An Incipient Moral Problem in Human Stem Cell Research', *Bioethics* 16, 544–56.

Grubb, Philip W. (2004), *Patents for Chemicals, Pharmaceuticals, and Biotechnology: Fundamentals of Global Law, Practice, and Strategy*, 4th edn, Oxford University Press.

Haddon, R. Lee (2008), 'The Heringen Collection of the US Geological Survey Library, Reston, Virginia', *Earth Sciences History* 27(2), 242–65.

Hettinger, Edwin C. (1989), 'Justifying Intellectual Property', *Philosophy & Public Affairs* 18(1), 31–52.

Hofmann, Bjørn (2009), 'Broadening Consent and Diluting Ethics?', *Journal of Medical Ethics* 35, 125–9.

Holland, Susan (2001), 'Contested Commodities at Both Ends of Life: Buying and Selling Gametes, Embryos and Body Tissues', *Kennedy Institute of Ethics Journal* 11(3), 263–84.

Hudson, Peter John, Niall, Hugh David and Tregear, Geoffrey William (1991), *Molecular cloning and characterization of a further gene sequence coding for human relaxin*, European Patent No. 112149, Munich: EPO.

Hughes, Justin (1988), 'The Philosophy of Intellectual Property', *Georgetown Law Journal* 77, 287–366.

Jeffreys, Diarmuid (2008), *Hell's Cartel: IG Farben and the Making of Hitler's War Machine*, London: Bloomsbury Publishing.

Johnson, Samuel (1755), *A Dictionary of the English Language*, Vol. I, London: Richard Bentley.

Kant, Immanuel (1963), *Lectures on Ethics*, Infield, Louis (trans.), New York: Harper & Row.

(1969), *Foundations of the Metaphysics of Morals*, Beck, Lewis White (trans.), Indianapolis: Bobbs-Merrill.

Kolle, Gert (1974), 'The Patentable Invention in the European Patent Convention', *International Review of Intellectual Property and Competition Law* 5(2), 140–56.

Kühn, Ralf, Von Melchener, Harald and Altschmied, Joachim (2001), *Conditional gene trapping construct for the disruption of genes*, International patent application publication no. WO01/29208, Geneva: WIPO.

Landau, Sidney I., Becker, E. Lovell, and Manuile, Alexandre (eds.) (1986), *International Dictionary of Medicine and Biology*, Vol. III, New York: John Wiley & Sons.

Lange, David (1981), 'Recognizing the Public Domain', *Law and Contemporary Problems* 44(4), 147–78.

Lawrence, Robert Howard Jr and Hill, Phillip Eugene (1982), *A process for the rapid development of hybrid plants and commercial production of hybrid seed*, European Patent Application Publication No. 44723, Munich: EPO.

Leder, Philip and Stewart, Timothy A. (1986), *Method for producing transgenic animals*, European Patent Application Publication No. 169672, Munich: EPO.

(1992), *Method for producing transgenic animals*, European Patent No. 169672, Munich: EPO.

Leemans, Jan, Botterman, Johan, de Block, Marc, Thompson, Charles and Maoura, Rao (1990), *Plant cells resistant to glutamine synthetase inhibitors, made by genetic engineering*, European Patent No. 242236, Munich: EPO.

Levin, Richard, Klevorick, Alvin, Nelson, Richard and Winter, Sidney (1987), 'Appropriating the Returns from Industrial Research and Development', *Brookings Papers on Economic Activity* 3, 783–820.

Llewelyn, Margaret and Adcock, Mike (2006), *European Plant Intellectual Property*, Oxford: Hart Publishing.

Locke, John (1988/1690), *Two Treatises of Government*, Laslett, Peter (ed.), Cambridge University Press.

Machlup, Fritz (1958), *An Economic Review of the Patent System*, Study No. 15 of the Subcommittee on Patents, Trademarks, and Copyrights of the

Committee on the Judiciary, United States Senate, 85th Congress, 2nd Session. Washington DC: United States Government Printing Office.

MacLeod, Christine (1988), *Inventing the Industrial Revolution. The English Patent System, 1660–1800*, Cambridge University Press.

Mandich, Giulio (1948), 'Venetian Patents (1450–1550)', Prager, Frank D. (trans.), *J. Pat. Off. Soc'y* 30(3), 166–224.

Mansfield, Edwin (1986), 'Patents and Innovation: An Empirical Study', *Management Science* 32(2), 173–81.

Martinez-Force, Enrique, Perz-Vich, Begona, Fernandez-Martinez, José Maria and Garces, Rafael (2004), *Oil from seeds with a modified fatty acid composition*, European Patent No.1185161, Munich: EPO.

Maskus, Keith E. (2000), *Intellectual Property Rights in the Global Economy*, Washington DC: Institute for International Economics.

Maskus, Keith E. and Reichman, Jerome (eds.) (2005a), *International Public Goods and Transfer of Technology Under a Globalized Intellectual Property Regime*, Cambridge University Press.

Maskus, Keith E. and Reichman, Jerome (2005b), 'The Globalization of Private Knowledge Goods and the Privatization of Global Public Goods', in Maskus and Reichman (2005a), pp. 3–45.

Matthews, Duncan (2002), *Globalising Intellectual Property Rights: The TRIPs Agreement*, London: Routledge.

Meek, Ronald Lindley, Raphael, David Daiches and Stein, Peter G. (eds.) (1978), *Adam Smith: Lectures on Jurisprudence*, Oxford University Press.

Mellulis, Klaus-Jürgen (2002), 'Ausnahmen von der Patentierbarkeit', in Barbara Dobrucki *et al.* (eds.), *Benkard: Europäisches Patentübereinkommen: Kommentar*, Munich: Verlag C. H. Beck.

Moufang, Rainer (1991), *Kommentierung des Europäischen Patentübereinkommens: Artikel 53: Ausnahmen von der Patentierbarkeit*, in Friedrich-Karl Beier, Kurt Haertel and Gerhard Schricker (eds.), *Europäisches Patentübereinkommen: Münchner Gemeinschaftskommentar*, Vol. XV, Munich: Carl Heymanns Verlag.

(1994), 'Patenting of Human Genes, Cells and Parts of the Body – the Ethical Dimensions of Patent Law', *International Review of Intellectual Property and Competition Law* 25, 487–515.

Nozick, Robert (1974), *Anarchy, State, and Utopia*, Oxford: Basil Blackwell.

Penrose, Edith Tilton (1951), *The Economics of the International Patent System*, Baltimore: Johns Hopkins Press.

Pfanner, Klaus (1962), 'Vereinheitlichung des materiellen Patentrechts im Rahmen des Europarats', *Gewerblicher Rechtsschutz und Urheberrecht, Internationaler Teil*, 545–54.

Pila, Justine (2005a), 'Dispute over the Meaning of "Invention" in Art. 52(2) EPC: The Patentability of Computer-Implemented Inventions in Europe', *International Review of Intellectual Property and Competition Law* 36(2), 173–91.

(2005b), 'Article 52(2) of the Convention on the Grant of European Patents: What Did the Framers Intend? A Study of the *Travaux Preparatoires*', *International Review of Intellectual Property and Competition Law* 36(7), 755–87.

(2009), 'Article 53(b) EPC: A Challenge to the Novartis Theory of European Patent History', *Modern Law Review* 72(3), 436–62.

(2010), *The Requirement for an Invention in Patent Law*, Oxford University Press.

Pompidou, Alain (2007), letter to Lord Justice Jacob, available at: www.ipo.gov.uk/pro-types/pro-patent/p-law/p-pn/p-pn-subjectmatter/p-pn-subjectmatter-letter.htm (last accessed 6 December 2011).

Prager, Frank D. (1944), 'A History of Intellectual Property from 1545 to 1787', *J. Pat. Off. Soc'y* 26(11), 711–60.

Rachels, James and Rachels, Stuart (2007), *The Elements of Moral Philosophy*, 5th edn, New York: McGraw-Hill.

Reifferscheid Martin and Weller, Siegfried (1989), *Chirurgie*, 8th edn, Stuttgart: Georg Thieme Verlag.

Rey, Alain (ed.) (1985), *Le Grand Robert de la Langue Française*, Vol. II, Paris: Le Robert.

Rogers, Rev. J. E. T. (1863), 'On the Rationale and Working of the Patent Laws', *Journal of the Statistical Society of London* 26, 121–42.

Ryals, John A., Gay, Philippe Bernard, Ahl Goy, Patricia A. and Garcia-Olmedo, Francisco (1991), *Anti-pathogenically effective compositions comprising lytic peptides and hydrolytic enzymes*, European Patent Application Publication No. 448511, Munich: EPO.

Sawyer, Donald C., Brody, Theodore M. and Langham, Marlee A. (1992), *Euthanasia compositions*, International Patent Application Publication No. WO92/11009, Geneva: WIPO.

(1996), *Euthanasia compositions*, European Patent No. 516811, Munich: EPO.

Schatz, Ulrich (2000), 'Patents and Morality', in Sigrid Sterckx (ed.), *Biotechnology, Patents and Morality*, 2nd reworked edn, Aldershot: Ashgate, pp. 217–28.

(2003), 'Article 53 Exceptions to Patentability', in Margarete Singer and Dieter Stauder (eds.), *The European Patent Convention: A Commentary*, Vol. I, Cologne: Carl Heymanns Verlag, pp. 84–102.

Scheffler, Samuel (ed.) (1988), *Consequentialism and its Critics*, Oxford University Press.

Scherer, Frederick M., Herzstein, Sigmund, Dreyfoos, Alex, Whitney, William, Bachmann, Otto, Pesek, Paul, Scott, Charles, Kelly, Thomas and Galvin, James J. (1959), *Patents and the Corporation: A Report on Industrial Technology under Changing Public Policy*, 2nd edn, Boston: Harvard University, Graduate School of Business Administration.

Schiff, Eric (1971), *Industrialization without National Patents: The Netherlands, 1869–1912: Switzerland, 1850–1907*, Princeton University Press.

Schmookler, Jacob (1965), 'Technological Change and Economic Theory', *American Economic Review* May, 333–41.

Schulte, Rainer (1981), *Patentgesetz*, 3rd edn, Cologne: Carl Heymanns Verlag.

Schwalm, Georg (1980), 'Chirurgie und Recht', in Rudolf Zenker, Franz Deucher and Wilhelm Schink (eds.), *Chirurgie der Gegenwart*, Vol. I, 'Allgemeine Chirurgie', Munich: Urban & Schwarzenberg.

Sell, Susan K. (1998), *Power and Ideas: North–South Politics of Intellectual Property and Antitrust*, Albany: State University of New York Press.

(2003), *Private Power, Public Law: The Globalization of Intellectual Property Rights*, Cambridge University Press.

Shattuck-Eidens, Donna M., Simard, Jacques, Emi, Mitsuru, Nakamura, Yusuke and Durocher, Francine (2001), *Mutations in the 17q-linked breast and ovarian cancer susceptibility gene*, European Patent No. 705903, Munich: EPO.

Shulman, Seth (1999), *Owning the Future*, Boston: Houghton Mifflin.

Singer, Peter (1995), *Rethinking Life and Death: The Collapse of our Traditional Ethics*, Oxford University Press.

Skolnick, Mark H., Goldgar, David E., Miki, Yoshio, Swensen, Jeff, Kamb, Alexande, Harshman, Keith D., Shattuck-Eidens, Donna M., Tavtigian, Sean V., Wiseman, Roger W. and Futreal, P. Andrew (2001a), *17q-linked breast and ovarian cancer susceptibility gene*, European Patent No. 705902, Munich: EPO.

(2001b), *Method for diagnosing a predisposition for breast and ovarian cancer*, European Patent No. 699754, Munich: EPO.

Smith, Austin Gerard and Mountford, Peter Scott (1999), *Isolation, Selection and Propagation of Animal Transgenic Stem Cells*, European Patent No. 695351, Munich: EPO.

Spector, Horacio M. (1989), 'An Outline of a Theory Justifying Intellectual and Industrial Property Rights', *European Intellectual Property Review* 11(8), 271–4.

Sterckx, Sigrid (2005), 'The Ethics of Patenting – Uneasy Justifications', in Peter Drahos (ed.), *Death of Patents*, Oxford: Law Text Publishers, pp. 175–211.

(2008), 'The European Patent Convention and the (Non-)Patentability of Human Embryonic Stem Cells – the WARF Case', *Intellectual Property Quarterly* 12(4), 478–95.

(2009), 'Is the Non-Patentability of "Essentially Biological Processes" Under Threat?', *Journal of World Intellectual Property* 13(1), 1–23.

Sterckx, Sigrid and Cockbain, Julian (2010a), 'The Patentability of Computer Programs in Europe: An Improved Interpretation of Articles 52(2) and (3) of the European Patent Convention', *Journal of World Intellectual Property* 13(3), 366–402.

(2010b), 'Assessing the Morality of the Commercial Exploitation of Inventions Concerning Uses of Human Embryos and the Relevance of Moral Complicity', *SCRIPTed – A Journal of Law, Technology & Society* 7(1), 83–103.

(2010c), 'Purpose-limited Pharmaceutical Product Claims under the Revised European Patent Convention: A Camouflaged Attack on Generic Substitution?', *Intellectual Property Quarterly* 14(1), 88–107.

Sterckx, Sigrid and Van Assche, Kristof (2011), 'The New Belgian Law on Biobanks: Some Ethical Reflections', *Health Care Analysis* 19(3), 247–58.

Strauch, Eckhard, Arnold, Walter, Alijah, Renate, Wohlleben, Wolfgang, Pühler, Alfred and Eckes, Peter (1993), *In Pflanzen wirksames Resistenzgen gegen Phosphinothricin und sene Verwendung*, European Patent No. 275957, Munich: EPO.

Straus, Joseph (1987) 'The Relationship between Plant Variety Protection and Patent Protection for Biotechnological Inventions from an International Viewpoint', *International Review of Intellectual Property and Competition Law* 18(6), 723–37.

Sturm, Elmar, Schempp, Heinrich and Martin, Henry (1980), *Schwefelhaltige Oxim-Verbindungen, Verwendung solcher und anderer schwefelhaltiger Oxim-Verbindungen zum Schutz von Kulturpflanzen*, European Patent Application Publication No. 10588, Munich: EPO.

(1985), *Schwefelhaltige Oxim-Verbindungen, Verwendung solcher und anderer schwefelhaltiger Oxim-Verbindungen zum Schutz von Kulturpflanzen*, European Patent No. 10588, Munich: EPO.

Taylor, Charles T. and Silberston, Z. Aubrey (1973), *The Economic Impact of the Patent System. A Study of the British Experience*, Cambridge University Press.

Thomson, James A. (1996), *Primate Embryonic Stem Cells*, International Patent Application Publication No. WO96/22362, Geneva: WIPO.

Tully, James (1980), *A Discourse on Property. John Locke and his Adversaries*, Cambridge University Press.

UPOV (1974), *Actes des Conférences internationals pour la protection des obtentions végétales: 1957–1961: 1972*, Geneva: UPOV.

USA (2010), *Amicus curiae* brief by the United States of America, dated 29 October 2010, available at: www.pubpat.org/assets/files/brca/CAFC/United%20States%20Amicus%20Brief.pdf (last accessed 28 December 2011).

van Benthem, Johannes Bob (1993), 'The European Patent System and European Integration', *International Review of Intellectual Property and Competition Law* 24(4), 435–45.

van den Berg, Paul (1996), 'Patentability of Computer-software-related Inventions', in Members of the Enlarged Board of Appeal of the EPO, *The Law and Practice of the Enlarged Board of Appeal of the European Patent Office During Its First Ten Years*, Cologne: Carl Heymanns Verlag, pp. 29–47.

van Empel, Martijn (1975), *The Granting of European Patents: Introduction to the Convention on the Grant of European Patents, Munich, October 5, 1973*, Leyden: A. W. Sijthoff.

Van Meilaert, Herman, Botterman Johan, Van Rie, Jeroen and Joos, Henk (1991), *Prevention of Bt resistance development*, European Patent Application Publication No. 408403, Munich: EPO

(1994), *Prevention of resistance development against Bacillus thuringiensis insecticidal crystal protein*, European Patent No. 408403, Munich: EPO.

Wadlow, Christopher (2008), 'Utility and Industrial Applicability', in Toshiko Taneka (ed.), *Patent Law and Theory: A Handbook of Contemporary Research*, Cheltenham: Edward Elgar, pp. 355–82.

(2010), 'The Great Pharmaceutical Patent Robbery, and the Curious Case of the Chemical Foundation', *Intellectual Property Quarterly* 14, 256–92.

Walker, C. Lester (1946), 'Secrets by the Thousands', *Harper's Magazine*, October 1946, 329–36.

Warshofsky, Fred (1994), *The Patent Wars: The Battle to Own the World's Technology*, New York: Wiley.

Webber, Philip (2011), 'Brüstle: What Will Happen Next?', Posting on the website of 'The IPKat', 29 October 2011, available at http://ipkitten.blogspot.com/search?q=webber (last accessed 8 April 2012).

WIPO (1970), *Records of the Washington Diplomatic Conference on the Patent Cooperation Treaty*, Geneva: World Intellectual Property Organization (WIPO).

Yamagishi, Hirofumi, Shigemura, Kouji, Yoneyama, Hirokazu, Segoshi, Tooru, Nakata, Yutaka and Yamashita, Motosogu (1993), *Projector-type head lamp for vehicles*, European Patent No. 295705, Munich: EPO.

Zagyansky, Yuly (2000), *Einstein-Bohr end: new atomic scale physics, electric field: neutinos and electrons in conversions, perpetual motion. Development: seisms, extinguished volcans, created islands, big bang energy*, International patent application publication no. WO00/52989, Geneva: WIPO.

Zipse, Erich (1973), 'Wird das künftige europäische Patenterteilungsverfahren den modernen, zukunftsintensiven Technologien gerecht?', *Gewerblicher Rechtsschutz und Urheberrecht, Internationaler Teil*, 182–9.

Index

Cambridge Intellectual Property and Information Law

Titles in the series (formerly known as *Cambridge Studies in Intellectual Property Rights*)

Brad Sherman and Lionel Bently
The Making of Modern Intellectual Property Law
978 0 521 56363 5

Irini A. Stamatoudi
Copyright and Multimedia Products: A Comparative Analysis
978 0 521 80819 4

Pascal Kamina
Film Copyright in the European Union
978 0 521 77053 8

Huw Beverly-Smith
The Commercial Appropriation of Personality
978 0 521 80014 3

Mark J. Davison
The Legal Protection of Databases
978 0 521 80257 4

Robert Burrell and Allison Coleman
Copyright Exceptions: The Digital Impact
978 0 521 84726 1

Huw Beverly-Smith, Ansgar Ohly and Agnès Lucas-Schloetter
Privacy, Property and Personality: Civil Law Perspectives on Commercial Appropriation
978 0 521 82080 6

Philip Leith
Software and Patents in Europe
978 0 521 86839 6

Lionel Bently, Jennifer Davis and Jane C. Ginsburg
Trade Marks and Brands: An Interdisciplinary Critique
978 0 521 88965 0

Geertrui Van Overwalle
Gene Patents and Clearing Models
978 0 521 89673 3

Jonathan Curci
The Protection of Biodiversity and Traditional Knowledge in International Law of Intellectual Property
978 0 521 19944 5

Lionel Bently, Jennifer Davis and Jane C. Ginsburg
Copyright and Piracy: An Interdisciplinary Critique
978 0 521 19343 6

Megan Richardson and Julian Thomas
Framing Intellectual Property: Legal Constructions of Creativity and Appropriation 1840–1940
978 0 521 76756 9

Dev Gangjee
Relocating the Law of Geographical Indications
978 0 521 19202 6

Andrew Kenyon, Megan Richardson and Ng-Loy Wee-Loon
The Law of Reputation and Brands in the Asia Pacific Region
978 1 107 01772 6

Annabelle Lever
New Frontiers in the Philosophy of Intellectual Property
978 1 107 00931 8

Sigrid Sterckx and Julian Cockbain
Exclusions from Patentability: How Far Has the European Patent Office Eroded Boundaries?
978 1 107 00694 2

Lightning Source UK Ltd.
Milton Keynes UK
UKOW06f0043091015

260119UK00008B/323/P

9 781107 542624